AF327430

Digital Photo 1

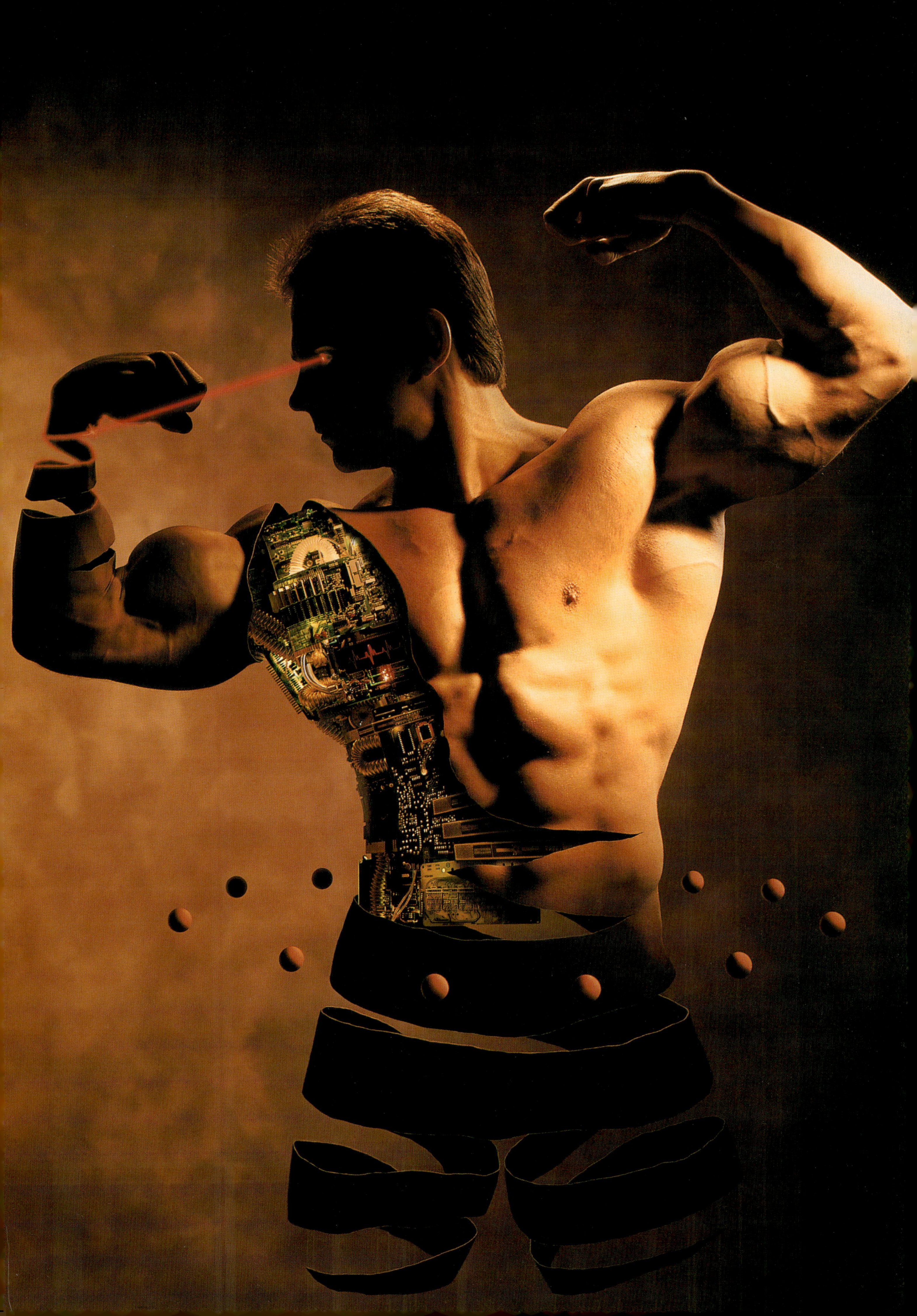

Digital Photo 1

An International Collection of Photography
Photographie im internationalen Überblick
Une compilation internationale de la photographie

Publisher and Creative Director: B. Martin Pedersen

Editor: Hildy Mesnik
Assistant Editors: April Heck, Vivian Babuts

Art Director: Massimo Acanfora
Graphic Designers: Ryuichi Minikawa, Delfin Chavez

Published by Graphis Inc.

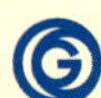

(opposite) Nick Vedros

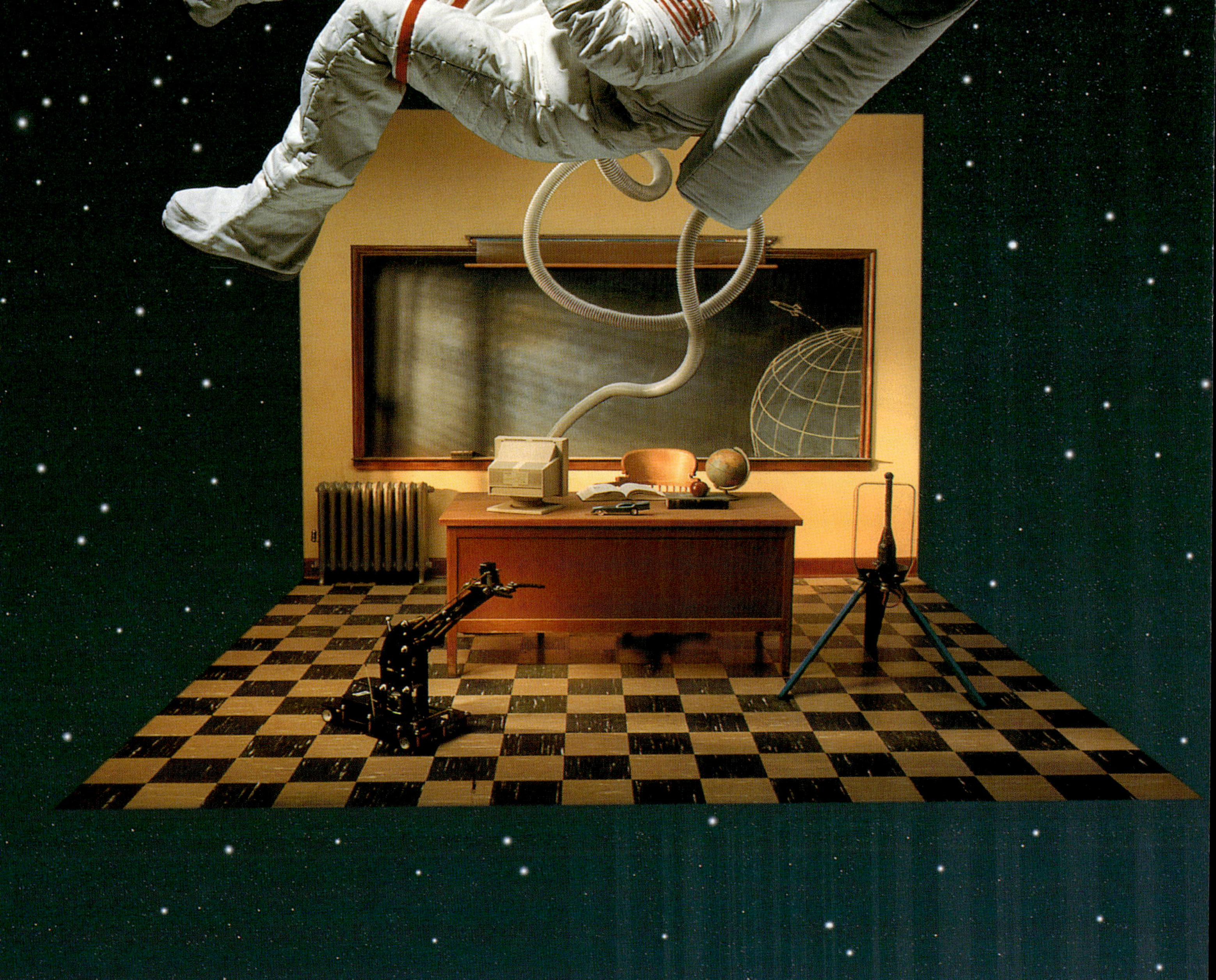

Contents Inhalt Sommaire

Remarks: We extend our heartfelt thanks to contributors throughout the world who have made it possible to publish a wide and international spectrum of the best work in the field of photography. Entry instructions for all Graphis Books may be requested from: **Graphis Inc.**, 141 Lexington Avenue, New York, NY 10016-8193 or visit our Website: www.graphis.com.

Anmerkungen: Unser Dank gilt den Einsendern aus aller Welt, die es uns durch ihre Beiträäge ermøglicht haben, ein breites, internationales Specktrum der besten arbeiten zu veröfentlichen. Teilnahmebedingungen für die Graphis-Bücher sind erhältlich bei: **Graphis Inc.**, 141 Lexington Avenue, New York, NY 10016-8193. Besuchen Sie uns im World Wide Web: www.graphis.com .

Remerciements: Nous remercions les participants du monde entier qui ont rendu possible la publication de cet ouvrage offrant un panorama complet des meilleurs travaux. Les modalités d'inscription peuvent être obtenues auprès de: **Graphis Inc.**, 141 Lexington Avenue, New York, NY 10016-8193. Rendez-nous visites sur notre site web: www.graphis.com.

ISBN: 1-888001-59-3 © Copyright under universal copyright convention copyright © 1998 by Graphis Inc., New York, NY 10016. Jacket and book design copyright © 1998 by Pedersen Design, 141 Lexington Avenue, New York, NY 10016, USA. No part of this book may be reproduced in any form without written permission of the publisher. Printed by DNP.

(opposite) Craig Andrews, Tom Balla *(following page)* Craig Van der Lende

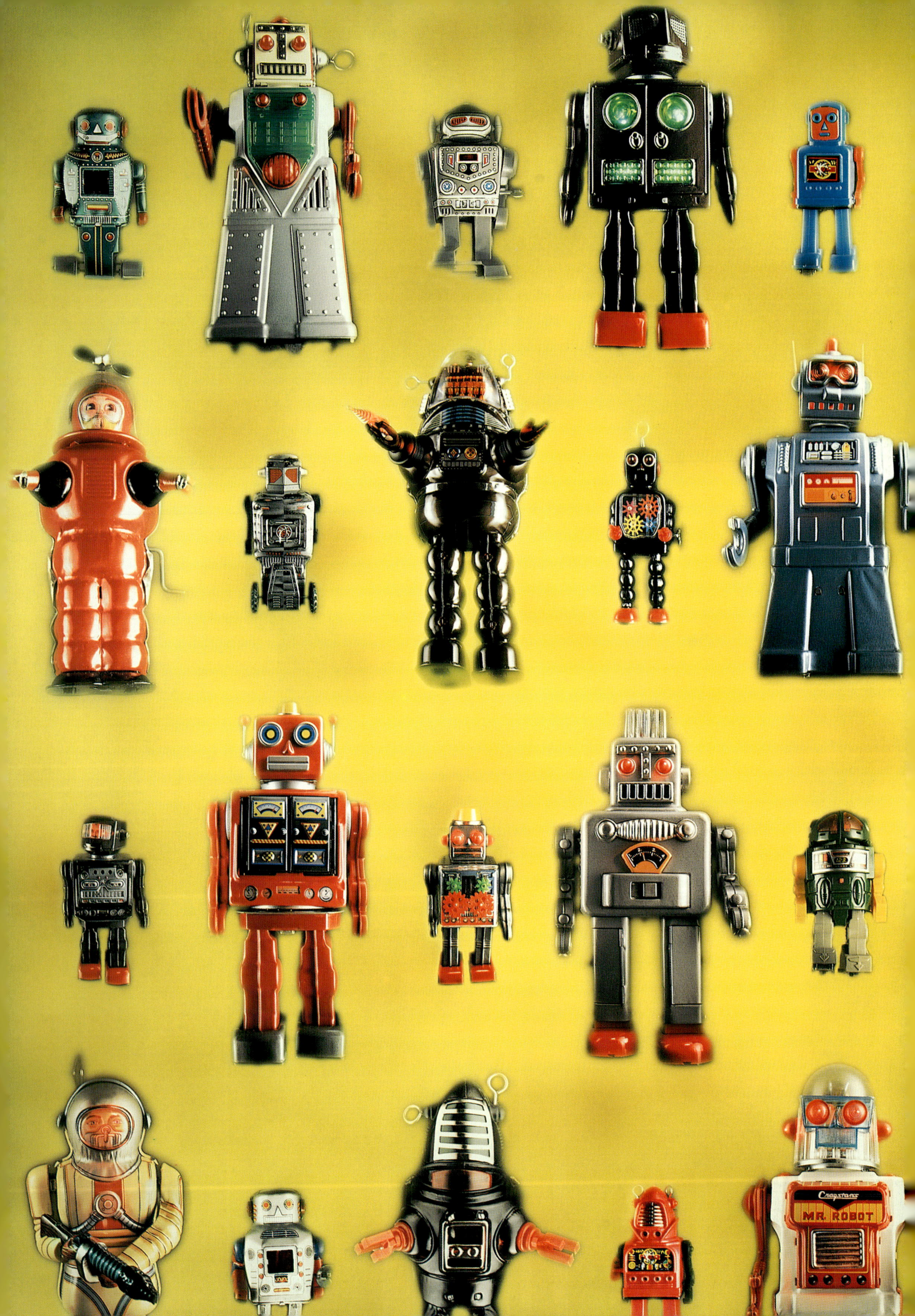

Commentary Kommentar Commentaire

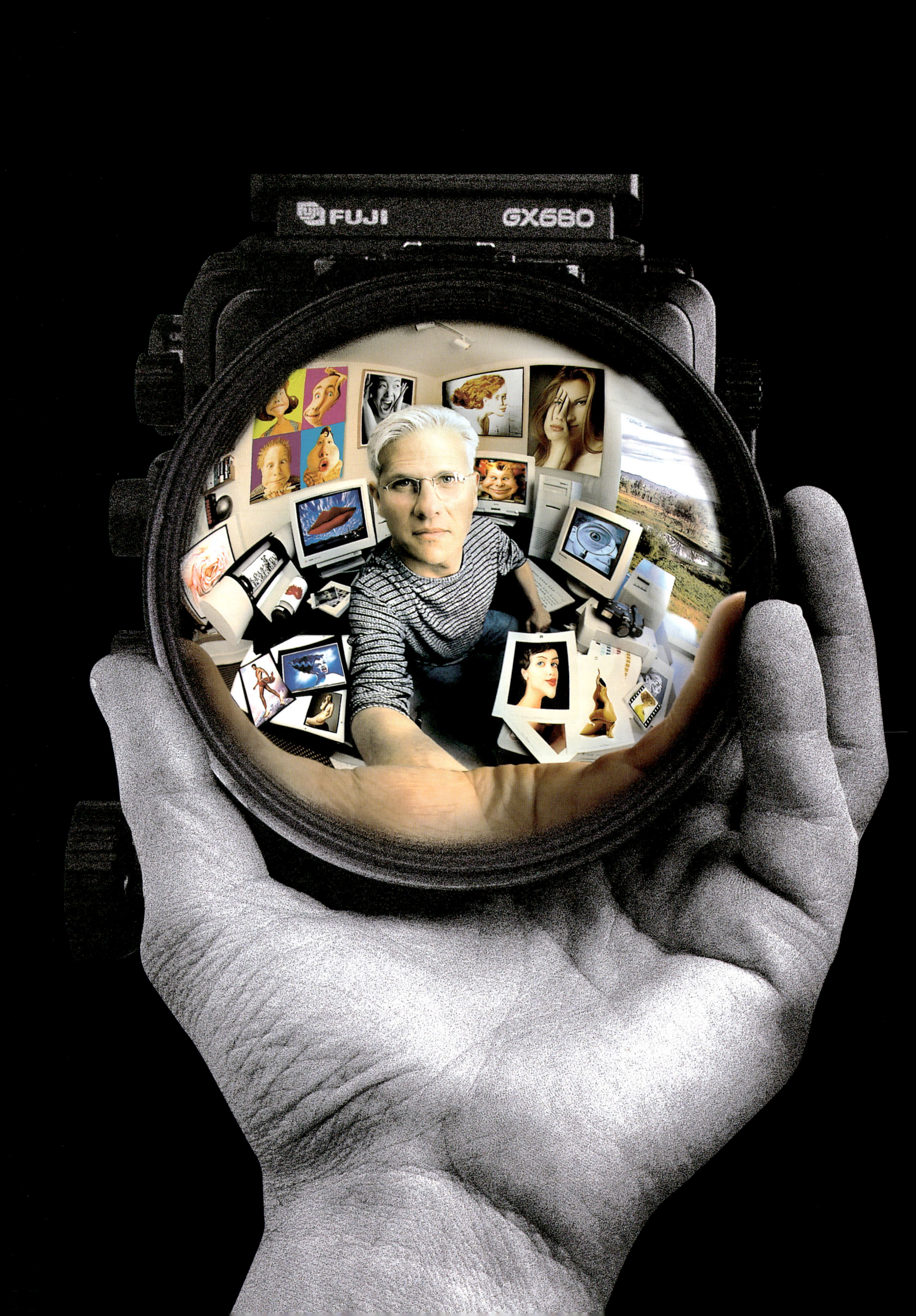

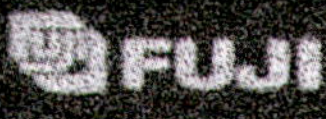

FUJI
GX680

Digital Stitchery: Gerald Bybee

I have always been captivated by images and light and craft. My grandmother's house was filled with dark wood and large rectangular windows that imbued every object inside with directional sidelight and large, soft, sculptural highlights. I would stand by the Singer sewing machine as my grandmother stitched simple fabrics into elegant garments. She was an example to me of the importance of hard work, fine craftsmanship, and self-reliance. Sometimes I think I should rename my Macintosh "Singer." As a youth, I devoured the photos in my mother's LIFE, LOOK, NATIONAL GEOGRAPHIC, TIME and NEWSWEEK magazines. Like most teenage boys, I especially loved looking at the feminine forms depicted in her VOGUE and BAZAAR magazines.

But I was equally fascinated by the light, line and style of photographers such as Penn and Avedon—names I wasn't aware of then but who I would come to revere throughout my career in photography.

Our father's Polaroid Land Camera enthralled my older brothers and me. A trap door opened in the back where we peeled out a curly, monochrome print that had to be slathered with wet, pungent goo. A few years later, Dad's "jack-in-the-box" SX70 camera beguiled us. The color images ejected and processed right before your eyes—and no coating to sting your nose! When my brothers each traveled to France years later, they used machines called "Pentax"s and "Canon"s to capture images of the enchanted French countryside. I envied their skill and ability to record such beauty and wonder.

In school I studied electronics and spent many hours in my basement workshop constructing crystal radio kits, crude electronic games, speakers for my garage band, and psychedelic strobes and black lights. I attempted to build a darkroom before I even owned my first camera, although I left for college before finishing it.

Not surprisingly, my electrical engineering goals were quickly abandoned for a major in communications and photography. I felt I could be more successful creating images with lenses and light than with paint and brush, pencil and paper, clay or bronze. The scanners, computers, and silicon chips I use today provide me with a sense of creative liberation just as the camera and darkroom did some 25 years ago. What I might have done with chemistry only five years ago I now do digitally, electronically.

The ongoing discussion and debate about digital imagery is rather frustrating. Photography is not necessarily reality; imagery should be evaluated as merely one perspective of reality. Photographs by the process itself are manipulated images. Every photographer uses unique tools to craft ideas and points of view into images. Each alters reality through lens selection, cropping, editing, exposure and even choice of film and chemistry. The process and craft are really no different than that of a painter, sculptor, or even a writer, editor or director.

I shoot a wide variety of subject matter on location and in the studio. About 95% of it is funneled through a digital process that allows me one more opportunity for creative control. The process is cleaner, hopefully more environmentally-friendly and affords immediate feedback by means of the computer screen. While the process seems speedier, the main advantage to me is the opportunity to experiment and explore many more variations and options in a given period of time. But in the end, the finished product is still the same; an image transmitting or reflecting light into the eyes and soul of a viewer. Hopefully the image tantalizes the eye and in some way touches the viewer.

I first became interested in digital imaging in the mid-1980s as a photographer directing Scitex operators who were working with my images. I prided myself on the ability to shoot images that would cut together quickly and seamlessly on these expensive computer systems that filled entire rooms. Becoming more involved, I longed for the opportunity to control the machines. As soon as the technology came to the desktop, I began to experiment. In the middle of a large campaign for Intel, a service bureau was unable to meet a major deadline. With no other option at hand, I took the files home, loaded them on my Macintosh and worked on them for 72 nonstop hours. On Monday, when I sent the file to be imaged it looked as good or better than the film from the million-dollar system. The only difference was the amount of sleep the operator got! From then on, I decided I would sacrifice my nights in order to do my own retouching and control my own projects from start to finish. I suppose you could say I learned digital imaging in my sleep.

I try to keep a photographic integrity to my images. I shoot traditionally and scan my own film. The difference now is that the film is not the finished product and generally contains only the essence of the subject matter. Many frames may be combined to capture one expression or body position or background. Elements are subtly or extremely distorted, molded, altered and/or layered until they feel right. Sometimes the image builds itself before my eyes. Other times I revisit the image time and time again, reworking the elements like a painter adding layers of pigment to an oil painting.

My imaging odyssey began on a Mac IICI and I suffered through all the beta software imaginable. I remember spending days applying distortion effects in Photoshop I.D. without previews, waiting literally hours for one variation to be rendered, only to drag it to the trash and try again. Today, the same process takes only moments to calculate. I can only imagine what the next decade will bring to the desktop.

The scanning process is similar to printing my own negatives. I use a Scanview drum scanner to extract, add, or alter the film to provide the broadest spectrum of information for the computer to address. One needs to understand that the 24-bit color space addressed by a central processing unit (CPU) is much less than the 36- or 48-bit space seen by a scanner photo multiplier tube (PMT), charged coupling device (CCD), or digital camera imaging chip. There is much subjective interpretation that is best manipulated in a higher bit depth while the scanner or digital camera is accessing the original information of the subject itself or scanning the original transparency.

I use a variety of software — Color Quartet from Scanview for scanning, Photoshop, and Live Picture, along with a collection of filters and specialized image-editing tools for compositing. Photoshop is by far the unifying industry standard. Almost a common language, its vast array of tools, plug-ins and controls can handle almost any image-editing task at hand. Live Picture is an amazing piece of software that works with large brushes on high resolution images in near-real time. While sometimes criticized for its interface, which was patterned after a paintbox rather than standard Adobe or Mac UIs, once mastered it allows for fast layer implementation, masking, and most importantly, the use of large, soft edge brushes on high resolution images in real time for applying effects, painting and distorting images. For me, it allows for much more intuitive hand-worked edges, painting, and localized application of effects, distortions and color correction.

While we enjoy the speed of the current generation of desktop computers, and fifth and sixth generation imaging software, digital cameras are just now entering their second generation. I've been evaluating and testing a variety of cameras and am now implementing them into my everyday toolbox. New interpolation technologies, like fractal compression software, may pave the way for the use of much smaller files from digital cameras to be manipulated faster, compressed and transmitted on the Internet, and then later decompressed and even enlarged for high-resolution output without degradation. New chip and capture technologies promise better image resolution and lower prices for digital cameras.

I still cast and shoot professional talent and work with clients in my San Francisco production studio, but my "digital" studio is in my home and barn on 80 acres of flood plain in the California wine country of western Sonoma County. Along with the John Deere tractor, I have a network of Macintosh computers, Fuji printers and a variety of cameras and scanners. Digital cameras and printers allow independence from city labs and help us fit into the local organic community. Our Website and the Internet allow us to market ourselves and communicate with clients globally. I have recently taken to creating image distortions in a style I've dubbed "photo cubist" and am embarking on the path to fine art prints, books such as the one you are holding, and a solo published work.

My four-year-old daughter wanders into my studio and critiques my images on the screen while she paints with watercolors on paper or on the Wacom tablet in Photoshop. In the spare moments between advertising deadlines, e-mail, phones and faxes, she and I marvel at rainbows and sunsets and watch the geese on the pond, have tea parties with Mom, or go on boat rides. Late night is still my most prolific and creative production time. I sit at my "Singer" and stitch together images for clients and for my own simple enjoyment of the craft and art of photography.

All images shown from pages 8 through 15 were photographed by Gerald Bybee.

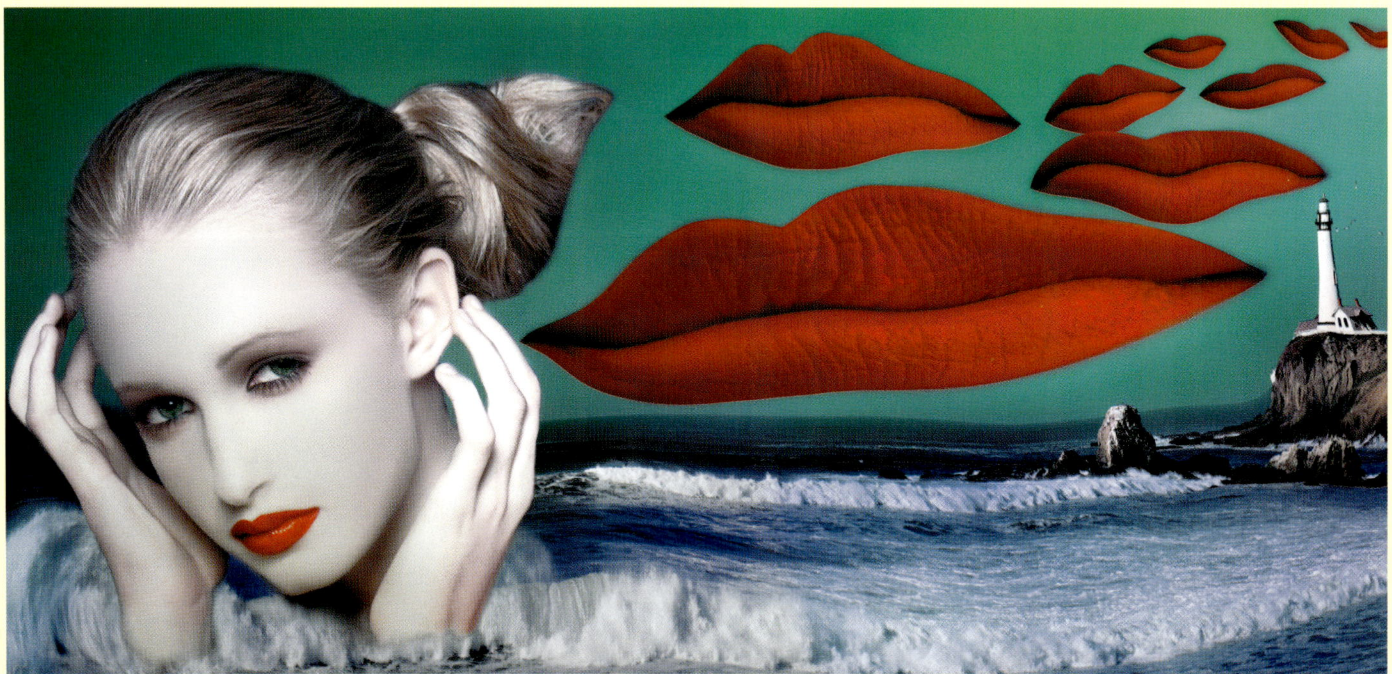

Gerald Bybee *was one of the first photographers to incorporate digital imaging into a successful advertising photography business. Bybee's early fascination with photography began with the instant pictures he and his brothers shot with their father's Polaroid. The allure held through adolescence, where he dabbled with electronics and "Rat Fink" model kits; through college where he shot weddings and ads for the university newspaper; to the establishment of his own photography studio in San Francisco and digital studio in Sonoma County, California. Bybee personally shoots, scans and manipulates his images from pre-production through delivery, with clients ranging from Adobe and AT&T to Wacom Technologies, Xerox Corporation and Young & Rubicam. (He is currently looking for a "Z" client.)*

Digitales Nähwerk: Gerald Bybee

Bilder, Licht und Handwerk haben mich seit jeher fasziniert. Im Haus meiner Grossmutter gab es viel dunkles Holz, und das weiche Licht, das durch die grossen Fenster fiel, beleuchtete jeden Gegenstand wie eine Skulptur. Ich sah meiner Grossmutter oft zu, wie sie mit ihrer Singer einfache Stoffstücke zusammennähte, aus denen elegante Kleider wurden. Von ihr lernte ich, wie wichtig Fleiss, handwerkliches Können und Selbständigkeit sind. Manchmal denke ich, ich sollte meinen Macintosh in «Singer» umtaufen. Als Jugendlicher verschlang ich die Photos in den Magazinen meiner Mutter: LIFE, LOOK, NATIONAL GEOGRAPHIC, TIME und NEWSWEEK, und, wie alle Jungen in meinem Alter, bewuderte ich vor allem die weiblichen Formen, die in VOGUE und HARPER'S BAZAAR zu sehen waren.

Aber ich war ebenso von dem Licht, den Formen und dem Stil von Penn und Avedon fasziniert, Photographen, die mir damals noch völlig unbekannt waren.

Meine älteren Brüder und ich waren begeistert von der Polaroid Land Camera unseres Vaters. Sie hatte hinten eine Klappe, aus der man den gewellten, einfarbigen Abzug herauszog, der dann mit einem nassen, klebrigen Zeug bedeckt werden musste. Ein paar Jahre später betörte uns Vaters neues SX 70 Modell, die sogenannte Jack in the Box Camera. Sie spuckte Farbbilder aus, die sie direkt vor unseren Augen entwickelte –, und die beissende Beschichtung war nicht mehr nötig.

Einige Jahre später reisten meine beiden Brüder nach Frankreich, und um die Schönheit der Landschaft einzufangen, benutzten sie Apparate, die Pentax und Canon hiessen. Ich beneidete sie um ihr Können und um die Möglichkeit, so etwas Schönes und Wunderbares im Bild festhalten zu können.

In der Schule konzentrierte ich mich auf naturwissenschaftliche Fächer und verbrachte Stunden in meinem Labor im Keller, wo ich piezoelektrische Radios zusammensetzte und einfache Computerspiele, Lautsprecher für meine Garagen-Band und psychedelische Beleuchtungen fabrizierte. Bevor ich selbst je eine Kamera besass, machte ich mich daran, in unserem Keller eine Dunkelkammer einzurichten. Sie wurde allerdings nie fertig, weil ich aufs College musste.

Ziemlich schnell beschloss ich, nicht, wie ursprünglich beabsichtigt, Elektrotechnik zu studieren, sondern Kommunikation und Photographie. Ich wollte Bilder herstellten, und ich wusste, dass mir das mit Hilfe von Objektiven und Licht besser gelingen würde als mit Farbe, Pinsel und Papier oder mit Ton oder Bronze. Die Scanner, Computer und Silizium-Chips, die ich heute einsetze, geben mir das gleiche Gefühl kreativer Befreiung, das ich vor 25 Jahren beim Gebrauch von Kamera und Dunkelkammer empfand. Was ich noch vor fünf Jahren mit chemischen Mitteln gemacht hätte, erreiche ich jetzt auf digitalem Wege.

Die gegenwärtige Diskussion über die Problematik digitaler Bilder ist für mich eher unverständlich, denn Photographie zeigt nicht unbedingt die Realität; Photos sollten lediglich als eine Perspektive der Realität betrachtet werden. Alle Photographien sind durch den photographischen Prozess schon von Natur aus manipulierte Bilder. Jeder Photograph benutzt seine speziellen Hilfsmittel, um seine Ideen und Standpunkte in Bildern auszudrücken. Jeder verändert die Realität durch die Wahl des Objektivs, Beschnitt, Belichtung und selbst des Films und der Chemikalien. Der Prozess und das Handwerk als solches unterscheiden sich nicht wirklich von der Arbeitsweise eines Malers, Bildhauers oder gar eines Autors oder Regisseurs.

Mein Themenspektrum ist breit, und ich photographiere in der Natur wie auch im Studio. 95% meiner Aufnahmen bearbeite ich digital –, und damit habe ich eine zusätzliche Möglichkeit, ein Bild nach meinen Vorstellungen zu gestalten. Dieser Prozess ist sauberer und hoffentlich umweltfreundlicher als die Behandlung mit Chemikalien, und ausserdem sieht man das Ergebnis sofort auf dem Bildschirm. Diese Art der Bearbeitung ist nicht nur schneller, ihr grösster Vorteil ist in meinen Augen die Möglichkeit zu experimentieren und viele Variationen innert kurzer Zeit auszuprobieren. Am Schluss ist das fertige Produkt auch nichts anderes als ein Bild, das Licht in die Augen und die Seele des Betrachters bringt.

Ich bin Mitte der achtziger Jahre zum ersten Mal mit der digitalen Bildverarbeitung in Berührung gekommen, als ich Scitex-Technikern, die mit meinen Bildern arbeiteten, Anweisungen gab. Ich war stolz auf meine Fähigkeit, Photos zu machen, die sich schnell und nahtlos auf diesen teuren Computer-Systemen, die ganze Räume füllten, zusammenschneiden liessen. Je mehr ich damit zu tun hatte, desto grösser wurde der Wunsch, selbst mit den Maschinen umgehen zu können. Sobald die Technologie auch für Desktop-Geräte verfügbar wurde, begann ich zu experimentieren. Eines Tages, mitten bei der Arbeit an einer grossen Kampagne für Intel, erklärte sich ein Service-Büro ausserstande, einen wichtigen Termin einzuhalten. Ich hatte keine andere Wahl, als die Dateien mit nach Hause zu nehmen, in meinen Macintosh einzuspeisen und dann 72 Stunden nonstop daran zu arbeiten. Das Resultat war ebenso gut, wenn nicht besser als der Film von einem Millionen-Dollar-System – nur dass ich im Gegensatz zu dem Techniker keinen Schlaf bekommen hatte. Damals beschloss ich, fortan einen Grossteil meiner Nächte zu opfern, um meine Bilder von Anfang bis Ende selbst zu bearbeiten. Man könnte sagen, dass ich die digitale Bildbearbeitung «im Schlaf» gelernt habe.

Ich bemühe mich, bei meinen Bildern eine gewisse photographische Integrität zu wahren. Ich benutze eine herkömmliche Kamera und scanne meinen eigenen Film ein. Der Unterschied zur herkömmlichen Methode liegt darin, dass der Film niemals das fertige Produkt ist, sondern meistens nur das Wesentliche des Themas enthält. Um einen bestimmten Ausdruck, eine bestimmte Körperhaltung oder einen bestimmten Hintergrund zu bekommen, werden unter Umständen viele Einzelaufnahmen kombiniert. Einzelne Elemente werden leicht oder auch extrem verzerrt, verformt, verändert und/oder überlagert, bis alles meinen Vorstellungen entspricht. Es kommt vor, dass sich das Bild wie von selbst vor meinen Augen ergibt. Dann wieder schaue ich ein Bild immer wieder an und verändere die einzelnen Elemente wie ein Maler, der Farbschicht um Farbschicht auf seine Leinwand aufträgt.

Meine Imaging-Odyssee begann mit einem Mac IIci, und ich quälte mich durch alle möglichen Softwareprogramme. Ich habe tagelang versucht, im Photoshop I.D. Verzerrungen hinzubekommen, und zwar ohne Preview; dabei dauerte es Stunden, bis eine Variation fertig war – nur um wieder im Papierkorb zu landen. Heute dauert der gleiche Prozess nur wenige Augenblicke. Ich kann mir vorstellen, was in den nächsten zehn Jahren alles im Desktop möglich sein wird.

Der Scanning-Prozess ähnelt dem Entwickeln von Negativen. Ich benutze einen Scanview-Trommel-Scanner, um weg-zunehmen, hinzuzufügen oder den Film zu verändern, um dem Computer soviele Bildinformationen wie möglich zu geben. Man muss sich klar darüber sein, dass der 24 bit Color Space, der von einem Central Processing Unit (CPU) verarbeitet wird, sehr viel geringer ist als der 36 oder 48 bit Space, den ein PMT (Scanner Photo Multiplier Tube), ein CCD (Charged Coupling Device) oder ein Imaging Chip einer digitalen Kamera verarbeitet.

Ich verwende verschiedene Software-Programme – Color Quartet von Scanview zum Einscannen, Photoshop und Live Picture sowie verschiedene Filter und spezielle Bildbearbeitungs-Tools für die Montage. Photoshop ist zweifellos das bei weitem populärste Programm. Es ist fast eine gemeinsame Sprache; sein grosses Spektrum von Tools, Plug-ins und Controls wird mit so ziemlich allen Bildbearbeitungsaufgaben fertig. Live Picture ist eine erstaunliche Software, bei der mit riesigen Pinseln auf hochauflösenden Bildern fast in Realtime gearbeitet wird. Manchmal wird die Benutzeroberfläche kritisiert, weil sie eher wie eine Paintbox als der Standard-Adobe oder MacUIs aufgebaut ist. Wenn man das Programm aber einmal beherrscht, lassen sich in kürzester Zeit Schichten auftragen, Abmaskierungen vornehmen und vor allem grosse, weiche Pinsel auf hochauflösenden Bildern in Realtime einsetzen, um punktuelle Effekte zu erreichen, Bilder zu malen oder zu verzerren. Mir gibt es vor allem die Möglichkeit, die Ränder intuitiv von Hand zu gestalten, zu malen und an bestimmten Stellen Effekte, Verzerrungen oder Farbkorrekturen anzubringen.

Während wir von der Schnelligkeit der gegenwärtigen Generation von Desktop-Computern und von der Imaging-Software der fünften oder sechsten Generation profitieren, gibt es von den digitalen Kameras gerade einmal die zweite Generation. Ich habe verschiedene Kameras geprüft und ausprobiert, und inzwischen gehören sie auch zu meiner Ausrüstung. Neue Interpolationstechnologien wie z.B. neue Kompressions-Software könnten zu kleineren Dateien von digitalen Kameras führen, die sich dann schneller manipulieren, komprimieren und ins Internet einspeichern liessen, um später wieder einer Dekompression unterzogen und sogar für hochauflösende Bilder ohne Verlust vergrössert werden zu können. Neue Chip- und Aufnahmetechnologien lassen auf bessere Bildauflösung und niedrigere Preise für digitale Kamerashoffen.

Ich arbeite nach wie vor auch mit professionellen Modellen und mit Kunden in meinem Produktionsatelier in San Francisco, aber mein digitales Studio befindet sich auf meinem 32 Hektar grossen Hof auf einer Ebene im kalifornischen Weingebiet im westlichen Sonoma County. Ich besitze einen Jim-Deer-Trecker und eine Reihe von Macs, Fuji-Druckern sowie verschiedene Kameras und Scanner. Digitale Kameras und Drucker machen mich unabhängig von Labors in der Stadt, und das hilft uns, uns hier auf dem Lande in die organisch gewachsene Gemeinschaft zu integrieren. Dank unserer Website und des Internets können wir auf uns aufmerksam machen und mit Auftraggebern in aller Welt kommunizieren. Ich habe vor kurzem begonnen, mit Verzerrungen zu arbeiten, und zwar in einem Stil, den ich «photo-kubistisch» nenne. Ich habe mich also in den Bereich der künstlerischen Photographie vor-gewagt, meine Arbeiten werden in Büchern wie diesem gezeigt, und bald wird auch eine Monographie erscheinen.

Meine vierjährige Tochter ist oft bei mir im Studio; sie kritisiert meine Bilder auf dem Bildschirm und malt selbst mit Aquarellfarben auf Papier oder auf der Wacom-Tafel im Photoshop. In der freien Zeit zwischen Terminen von Werbeaufträgen, E-mails, Anrufen und Faxen bestaunen wir Regenbogen und Sonnenuntergänge, beobachten die Gänse am Teich, trinken Tee mit ihrer Mutter oder fahren Boot. Ich bin nachts am produktivsten. Dann sitze ich an meiner «Singer» und nähe Bilder für Kunden zusammen oder für mich selbst, aus Freude am Handwerk und der Kunst der Photographie.

Gerald Bybee gehörte zu den ersten, denen es gelang, digitale Photographie erfolgreich für Werbeaufträge einzusetzen. Seine Begeisterung für die Photographie begann schon in jungen Jahren mit der Polaroid-Kamera des Vaters. Als Heranwachsender kam das Interesse an Elektronik hinzu; als College-Student photographierte er nebenbei Hochzeiten und gestaltete Anzeigen für die Studentenzeitung. Später eröffnete er ein eigenes Photostudio in San Francisco und ein digitales Studio in Sonoma County, Kalifornien. Bybee bearbeitet seine Aufnahmen von Anfang bis Ende selbst. Die Liste seiner Kunden reicht von Adobe bis zu Xerox und Young & Rubicam - es fehlt eigentlich nur noch ein Auftraggeber, dessen Name mit Z beginnt.

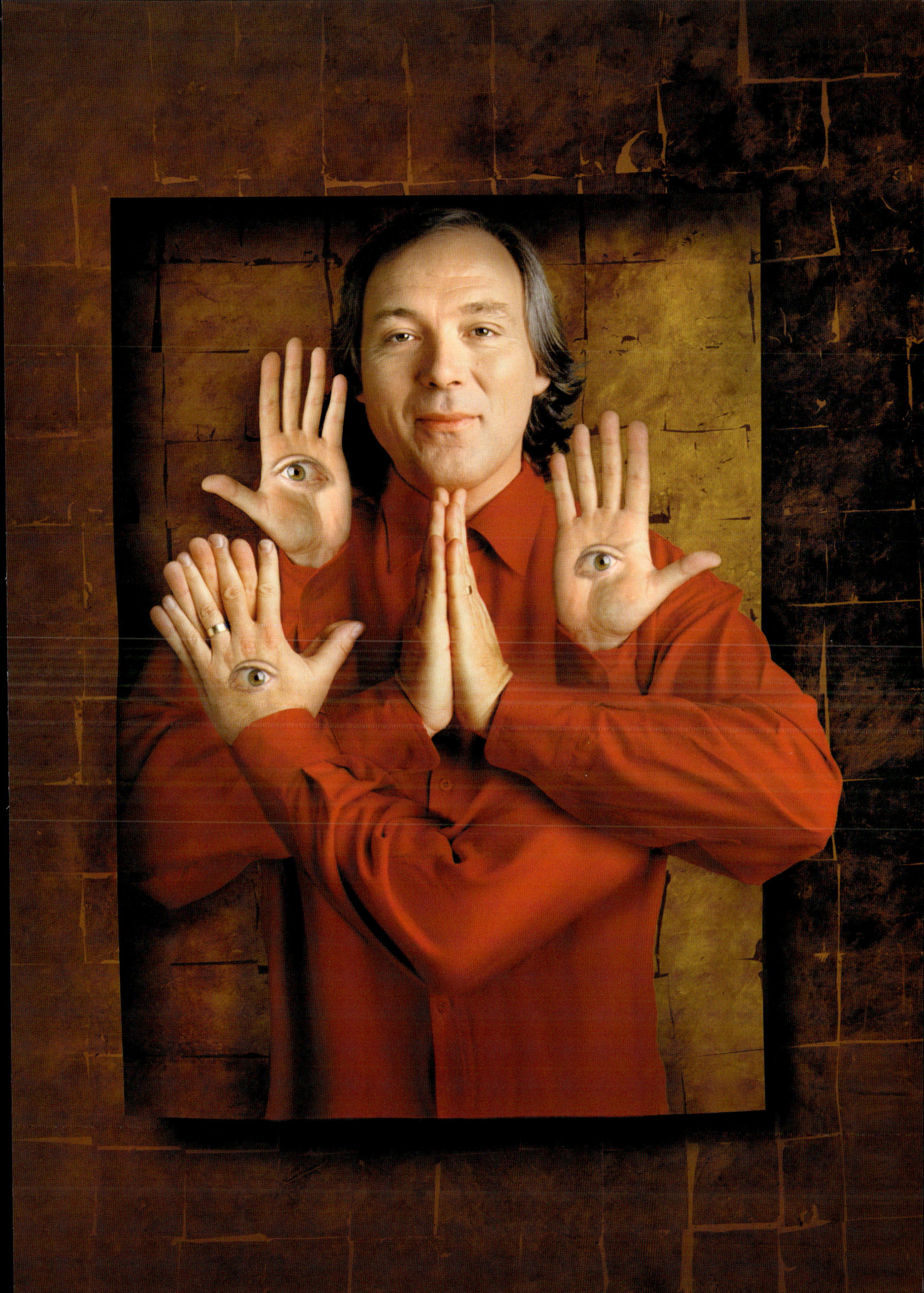

Raccommodage numérique: Gerald Bybee

J'ai toujours été fasciné par les images, la lumière et l'artisanat. La maison de ma grand-mère possédait de larges embrasures de fenêtre en bois sombre. La lumière pénétrant de l'extérieur nimbait chaque objet d'un éclairage doux, lui conférant une apparence sculpturale. Je restais debout près de la machine à coudre Singer tandis que ma grand-mère réalisait d'élégants vêtements à partir de simples bouts de tissu. Pour moi, elle incarnait l'assiduité, l'amour du travail bien fait et l'autonomie. Je pense parfois que je devrais rebaptiser mon ordinateur «Singer». Petit garçon, je dévorais les magazines de ma mère: LIFE, LOOK, NATIONAL GEOGRAPHIC, TIME et NEWSWEEK. Comme beaucoup d'adolescents, j'aimais par-dessus tout regarder les silhouettes féminines de VOGUE et de BAZAAR.

A l'époque, j'ignorais tout de la renommée de grands photographes comme Penn et Avedon, mais j'étais fasciné par la lumière, le style et les lignes de leurs images.

Mes frères aînés et moi-même étions enthousiasmés par l'appareil photo Polaroid Land de papa. Quand on ouvrait la petite trappe située au dos de l'appareil, on en tirait une photographie monochrome toute gondolée qu'il fallait ensuite enduire d'une sorte de colle humide. Quelques années plus tard, nous avons été séduits par le modèle SY70 (dit «Jack in the Box»). L'appareil photo crachait des images en couleur qui se développpaient lentement devant nous, sans cette affreuse colle qui nous piquait les yeux! Lorsque mes frères sont allés en France des années plus tard, ils ont utilisé des appareils Pentax et Canon pour prendre des photos des mag-

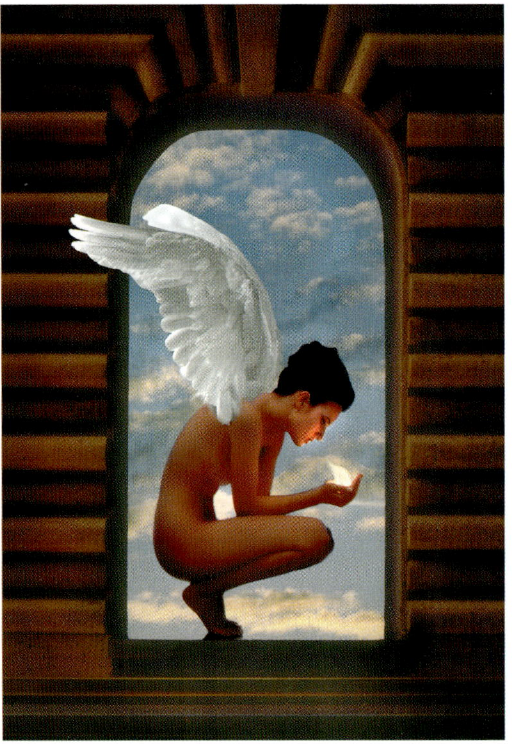

nifiques paysages de la campagne française. J'admirais leur habileté à capturer tant de beauté sur une image.

A l'école, j'ai étudié l'électronique et je passais beaucoup de temps dans la cave à construire des radios piézoélectriques, des jeux électro-niques, des enceintes acoustiques pour mon groupe de musique ainsi que des éclairages psychédéliques. J'ai créé ma première chambre noire dans la cave, avant même de posséder un appareil photo, mais j'ai dû quitter la maison pour aller à l'université avant d'avoir pu terminer mon œuvre.

Rapidement, mon intention première de devenir ingénieur électricien s'est transformée en une vocation pour les études de communication et de photographie. Je pensais que j'aurais de meilleures chances de réussir en créant des images à l'aide d'un objectif plutôt qu'avec des pinceaux, des crayons, du papier, de la terre cuite ou du bronze. J'utilise aujourd'hui des scanners, des ordinateurs et des puces en silicone parce qu'ils me donnent un sentiment de liberté tout comme l'appareil photo et la chambre noire il y a 25 ans. Ce que je réa-lisais il y a cinq ans grâce à un processus chimique, je le réalise aujourd'hui numériquement grâce à des logiciels.

Le débat actuel sur l'imagerie numérique me semble aussi vain que frustrant. La photographie ne représente pas la réa-lité pure, mais bien plus une perspective de la réalité. Le photographe manipule la réalité par le fait même qu'il la photographie, et chacun applique ses propres procédés afin de faire dire à l'image ce qu'il veut. Il peut s'agir du choix de l'angle, de l'objectif, de l'exposition, du découpage et même du choix du film et du développement. Cet art ne se différencie en somme guère de celui d'un peintre, d'un sculpteur, d'un écrivain ou d'un metteur en scène.

J'ai photographié toutes sortes de sujets en extérieur ou en studio, et 95% de mes images sont ensuite retravaillées grâce à la technologie numérique, ce qui me donne plus de contrôle sur le résultat final. Cette méthode est finalement plus propre et probablement plus écologique que le développement chimique et me permet de voir tout de suite le résultat apparaître sur mon écran d'ordinateur. Elle peut sembler plus rapide, mais le principal bénéfice que j'en tire est de pouvoir explorer et expérimenter quantité de variations et d'options dans un intervalle de temps très bref. Mais au bout du compte, le produit fini est toujours le même: une image qui transmet une impression laquelle se reflète dans les yeux et dans l'âme du spectateur.

Je me suis intéressé pour la première fois à la manipulation numérique des images au milieu des années 80, alors que je devais donner des instructions à des techniciens Scitex qui travaillaient avec mes photos. J'étais fier d'être capable de prendre des photographies qui surpassaient en rapidité et en précision tout ce que l'on pouvait réaliser à l'aide de systèmes informatiques qui remplissaient l'équivalent de toute une pièce. Mais plus je me frottais à cette technologie, plus j'avais envie de contrôler ces machines. Dès que les logiciels ont été proposés pour les ordinateurs de bureau, j'ai commencé à expérimenter. Au beau milieu d'une grosse campagne pour Intel, un sous-traitant n'étant pas en mesure de respecter les délais, j'ai ramené toutes les données chez moi, je les ai chargées sur mon Ma-cintosh et j'y ai travaillé 79 heures d'affilée. Le lundi, j'ai envoyé le travail pour qu'il soit flashé et le résultat était aussi bon, voire meilleur que s'il avait été réalisé sur un système d'un million de dollars! La seule différence résidait dans le fait qu'il me manquait des heures de sommeil. A partir de ce moment-là, j'ai décidé de sacrifier mes nuits afin de réaliser mes propres retouches et de contrôler mes projets du début à la fin. On pourrait dire que j'ai appris à utiliser la technologie numérique «dans mon sommeil».

J'essaie de conserver une sorte d'intégrité photographique à mes images. Je prends des photos de façon traditionnelle et je scanne mon propre film, la différence étant simplement que le film n'est plus le produit fini, mais ne contient que l'essence du sujet. Plusieurs angles différents peuvent être utilisés pour obtenir une expression, une pose ou un arrière-plan particulier. Les éléments sont distordus, parfois très légèrement, parfois jusqu'à l'extrême, ils sont façonnés, modifiés ou superposés jusqu'à ce qu'ils correspondent à ma représentation. Il arrive que l'image se crée d'elle-même sous mes yeux. Dans d'autres cas, je reviens un grand nombre de fois sur la même image, retravaillant différents éléments comme un peintre qui ajouterait quelques couches de pigments à une peinture à l'huile.

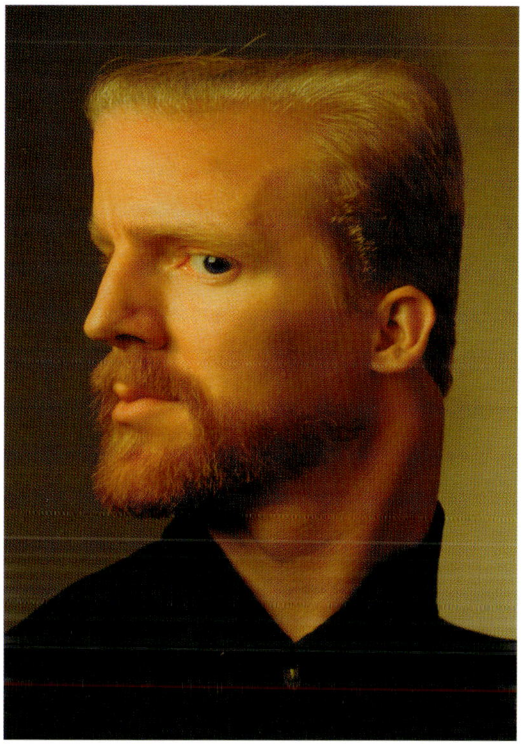

Mon odyssée numérique a commencé sur un Mac IIci et j'ai peiné avec tous les logiciels imaginables. Je me souviens avoir passé des jours entiers à essayer d'obtenir un effet de distorsion avec Photoshop I.D. et d'avoir patienté des heures pour obtenir une seule variante que je finissais par jeter à la poubelle. Aujourd'hui, ce même processus ne prend que quelques instants. J'essaie de m'imaginer tout ce qu'il sera possible de réaliser à l'écran dans une dizaine d'années.

Le processus de scannage est similaire au développement de mes propres négatifs. J'utilise un scanner à tambour Scanview pour découper les images, les transformer ou modifer le film et pour fournir à l'ordinateur le plus d'informations possibles. Il faut comprendre que l'espace de couleurs de 24 bits que peut traiter une unité centrale de traitement est bien plus faible que l'espace de 36 ou 48 bits que peut capter un PMT (scanner photo multiplier tube), un composant à couplage de charge ou la puce d'un appareil photo numérique.

J'utilise un grand nombre de logiciels: Color Quartet de Scanview pour le scannage, Photoshop et Live Picture, de même qu'une série de filtres et d'outils d'édition d'images. Photoshop est sans aucun doute le programme le plus populaire, presque une langue commune à tous les utilisateurs. Son large éventail d'outils, Plug-ins et Controls, permet de s'attaquer à presque n'importe quelle tâche. Live Picture est un logiciel étonnant, qui travaille par larges coups de pinceau sur des images à haute résolution en temps réel. On a critiqué son interface, basée plutôt sur Paintbox que sur le standard Adobe ou Mac. Mais l'outil, une fois maîtrisé, permet très rapidement de masquer ou de superposer des couches de couleur et surtout de retravailler des images à haute résolution en temps réel à l'aide de pinceaux très larges, de créer des effets, de corriger la couleur ou d'obtenir des distorsions. Pour moi, ce programme à l'avantage de me permettre de travailler de manière très intuitive et «artisanale».

Alors que nous profitons de la rapidité des ordinateurs actuels et de la cinquième et sixième générations de logiciels, les appareils photo numériques n'en sont qu'à leur deuxième génération. J'ai testé un grand nombre d'appareils photo et ils font dorénavant aussi partie de mon équipement. Les nouvelles technologies d'interpolation permettront bientôt de manipuler, de compresser et de transmettre via l'Internet des images prises avec un appareil photo numérique, puis de les décompresser et de les agrandir à l'autre bout sans que la qualité n'en souffre. L'amélioration de la technologie numérique promet des images à résolution encore plus fine et une baisse du prix des appareils photo numériques.

Je continue comme avant de travailler avec des modèles professionnels et avec mes clients dans mon atelier de production à San Francisco, mais mon studio numérique se trouve à mon domicile, dans le domaine de 32 hectares que je possède dans la région viticole de Sonoma County. Outre le tracteur qui me sert à parcourir l'exploitation, on y trouve une série d'ordinateurs Macintosh, d'imprimantes Fuji et une large gamme d'appareils photo et de scanners. Les appareils photo numériques et les imprimantes Fuji me permettent d'être indépendant des laboratoires situés en ville et de mieux m'intégrer dans la communauté locale. Le site Internet de mon entreprise me permet d'être en contact avec mes clients et de communiquer dans le monde entier. J'ai récemment commencé à créer un style d'images que je qualifierais de «photos cubistes». Je me suis lancé dans la photographie d'art et mes travaux sont publiés dans des livres tels que celui que vous tenez entre vos mains. J'ai également l'intention de publier une monographie.

Ma fille de quatre ans se balade dans mon studio et critique mes images à l'écran tandis qu'elle fait de l'aquarelle sur pa-pier ou sur la tablette Wacom de Photoshop. A mes moments perdus entre les délais publicitaires, le courrier électronique, les téléphones et les fax, ma fille et moi-même nous admirons les arcs-en-ciel et les couchers de soleil, les oies près de l'étang, nous prenons le thé avec sa mère ou allons faire un tour en bateau. Mes périodes d'inspiration et de créativité les plus fertiles sont les fins de soirée. Je suis assis devant ma «machine à coudre Singer» et je réalise des collages d'images pour des clients et parfois même pour le simple plaisir que me procure l'art de la photographie.

Gerald Bybee est l'un des premiers photographes à avoir appliqué avec succès la technologie numérique à la photographie publicitaire. Sa fascination pour la photographie remonte à son enfance, époque où lui et ses frères prenaient des instantanés avec le Polaroid de leur père. Adolescent, il s'intéresse à l'électronique et bricole des postes de radio. Etudiant, il prend des photos de mariage et fait publier ses prises de vues publicitaires dans le journal universitaire. Plus tard, il ouvre un studio de photographie à San Francisco et un autre, doté des derniers équipements numériques, à Sonoma County, Californie. Gerald Bybee travaille sans aucune aide extérieure: il prend des photographies, les scanne et les manipule. Il s'occupe de chaque détail, de la préproduction à la remise de ses clichés. Parmi ses clients figurent entre autres quelques noms prestigieux dont Adobe, Xerox Corporation et Young & Rubicam.

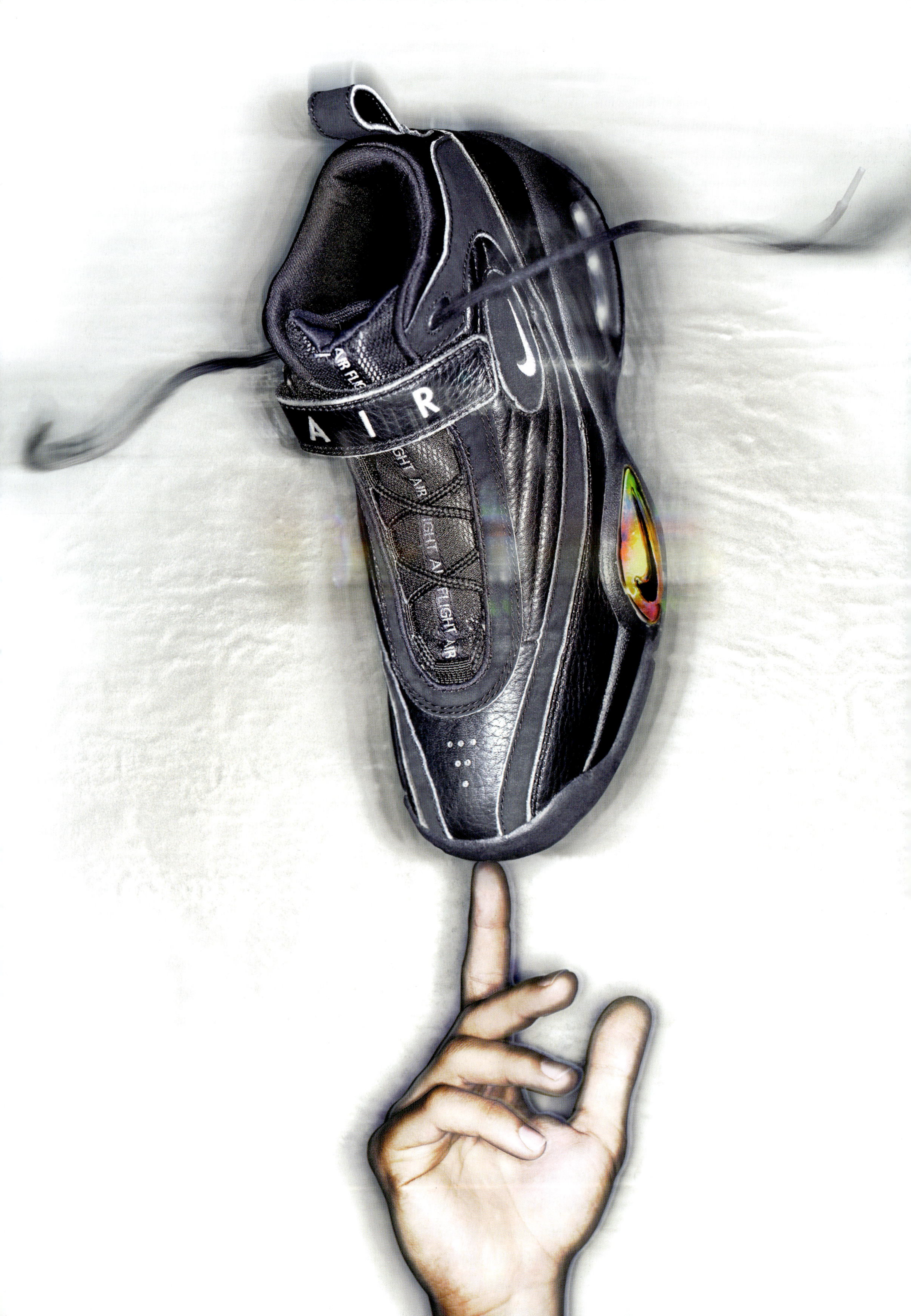

AIR
AIR FL
GHT AIR
IGHT AI
FLIGHT AIR

Digital Photo 1

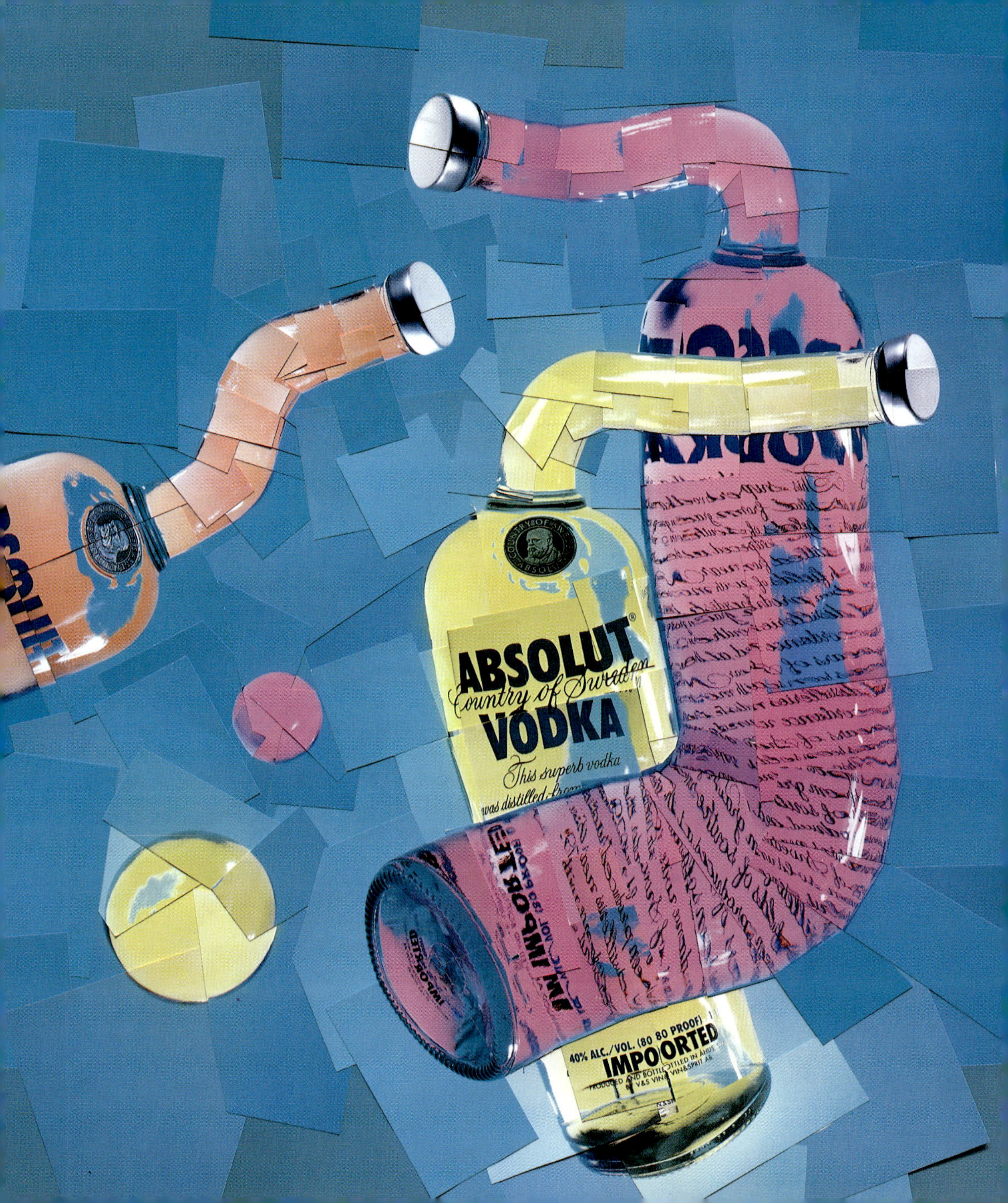

ABSOLUT VODKA
COUNTRY OF SWEDEN
This superb vodka
was distilled from
40% ALC./VOL. (80 80 PROOF)
IMPORTED

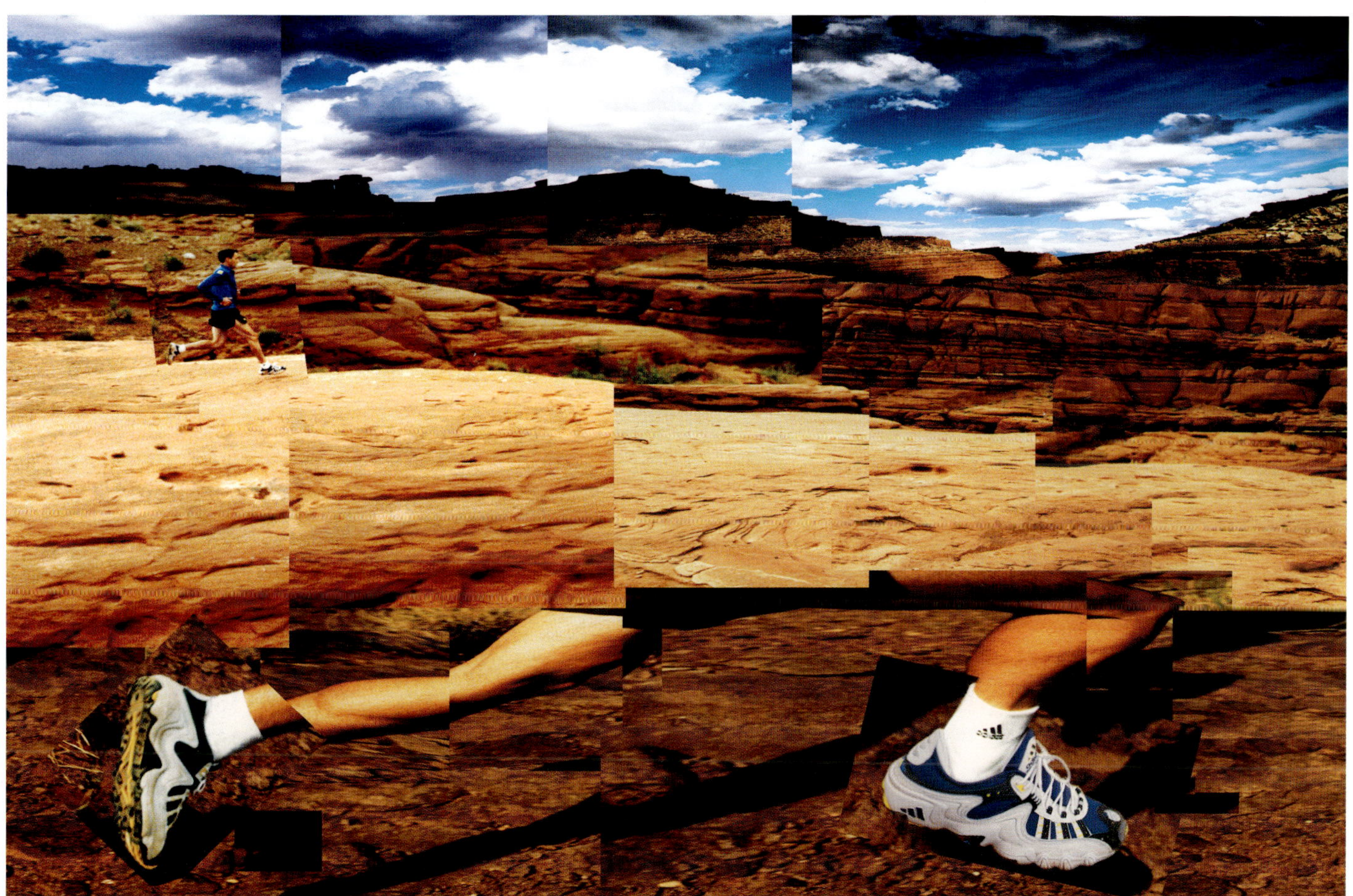

Mark **H**anauer

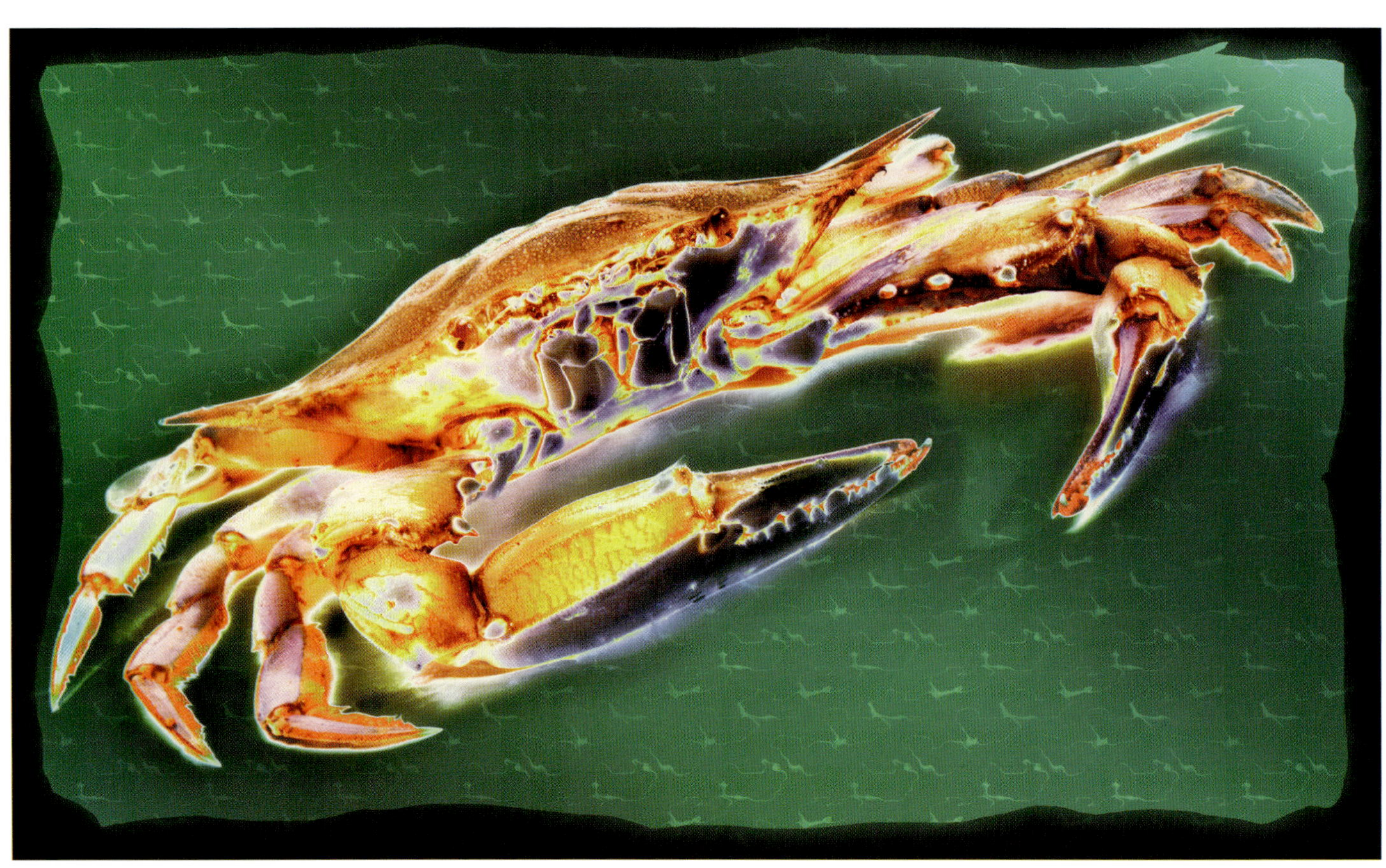

Judy Hermann, Michael Starke

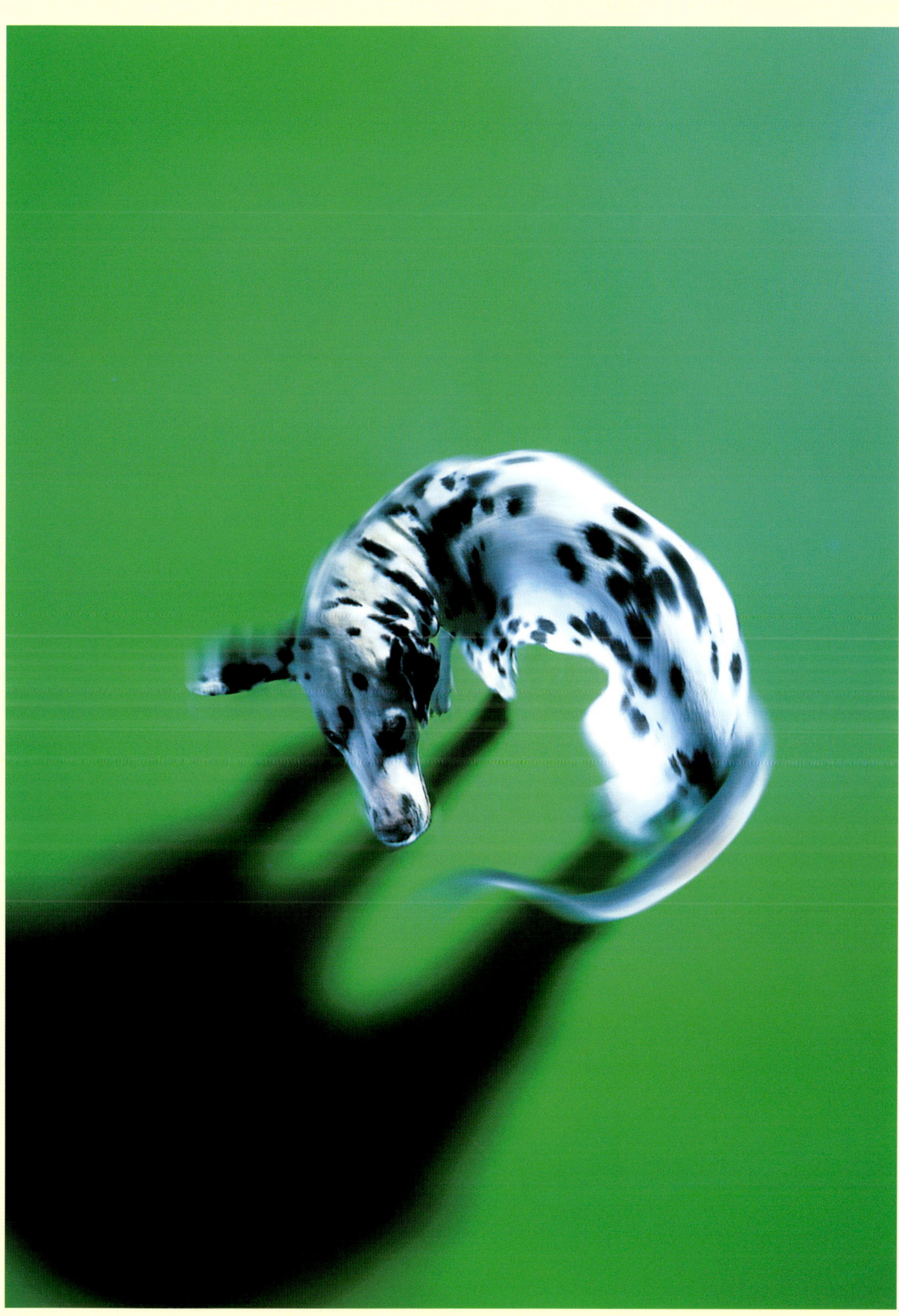

Frank Herholdt

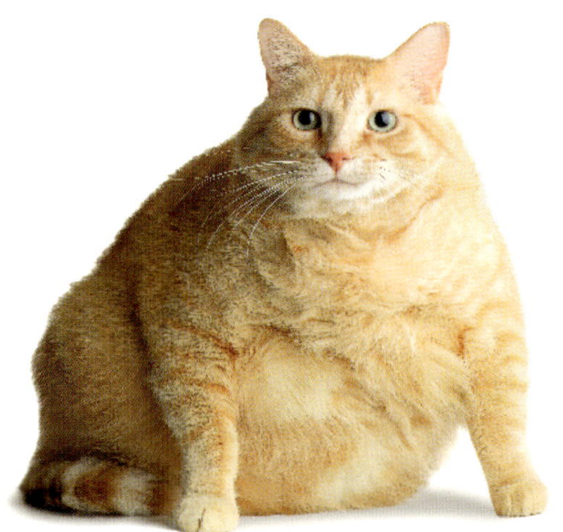

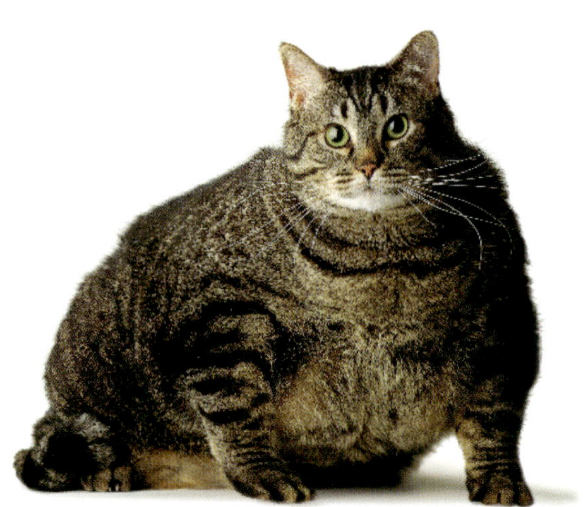

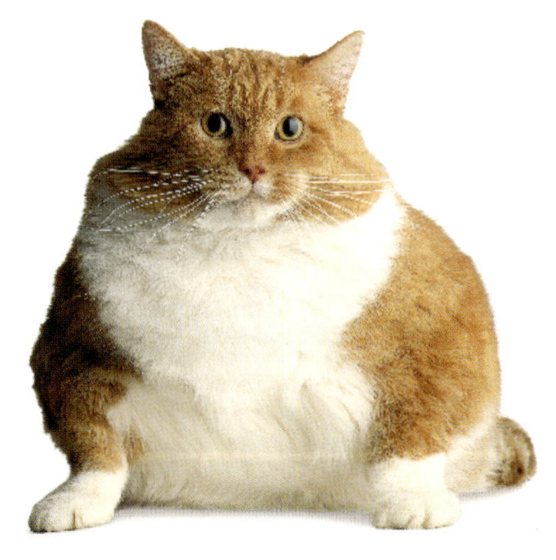

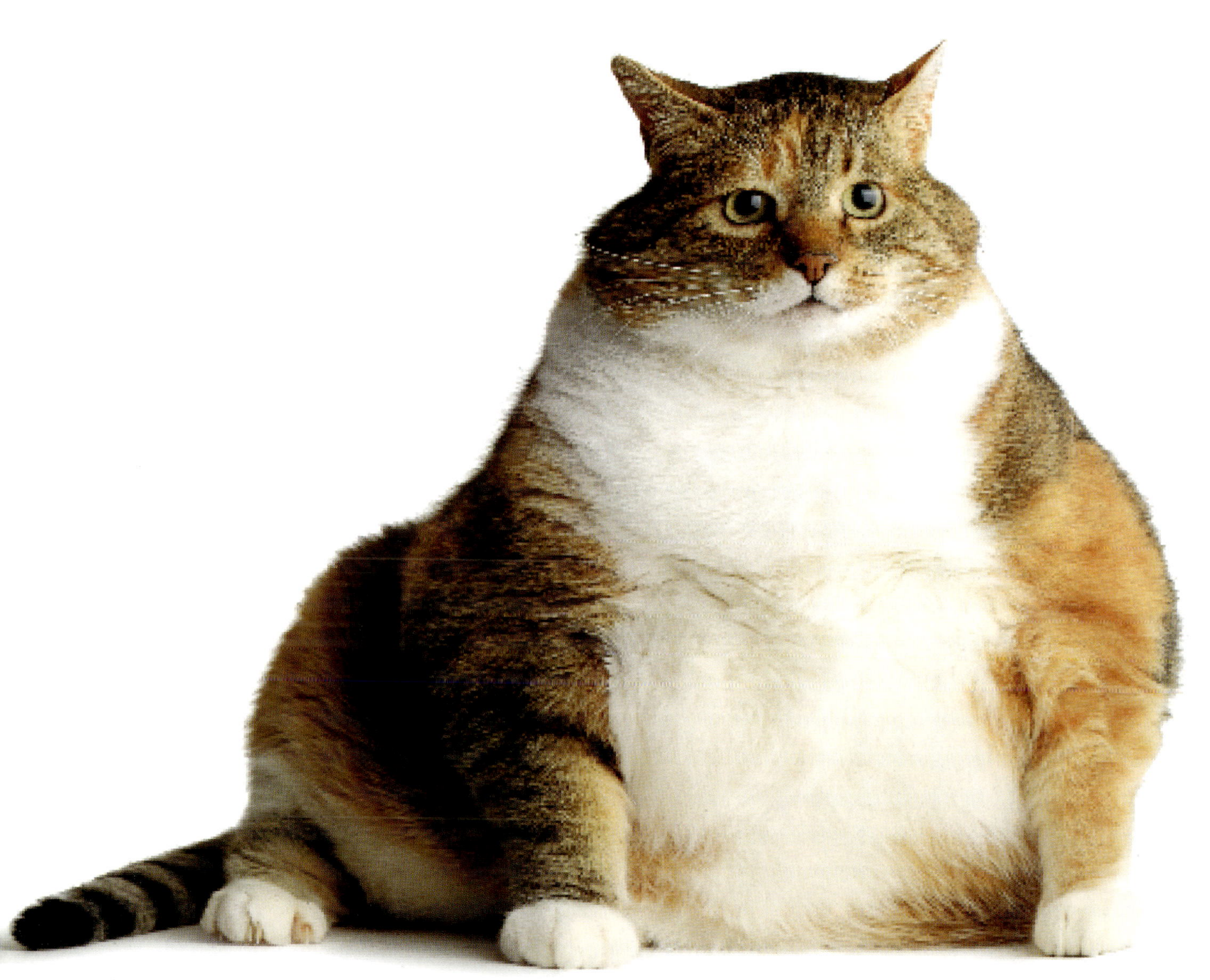

this spread: **R**ick **D**ublin

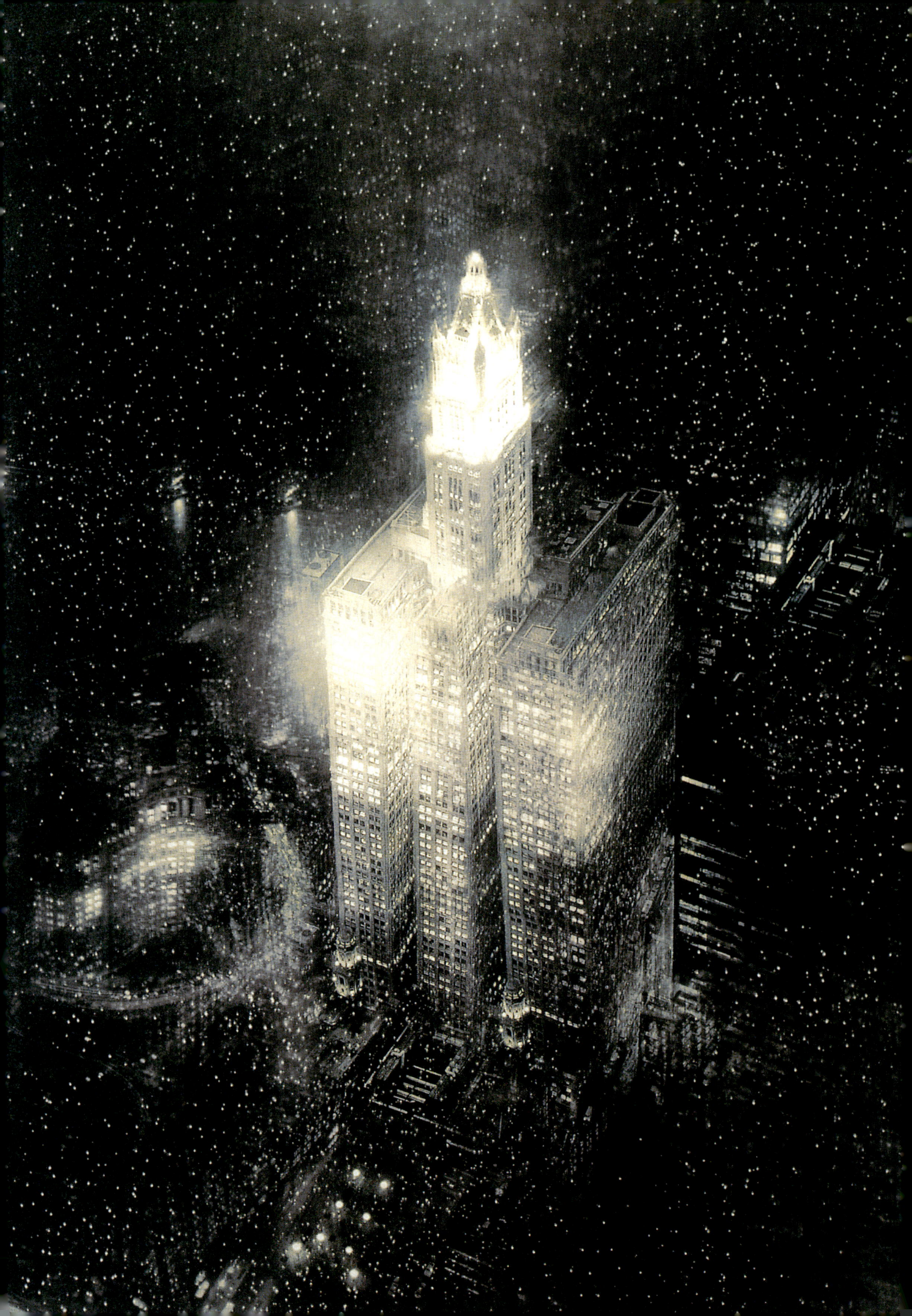

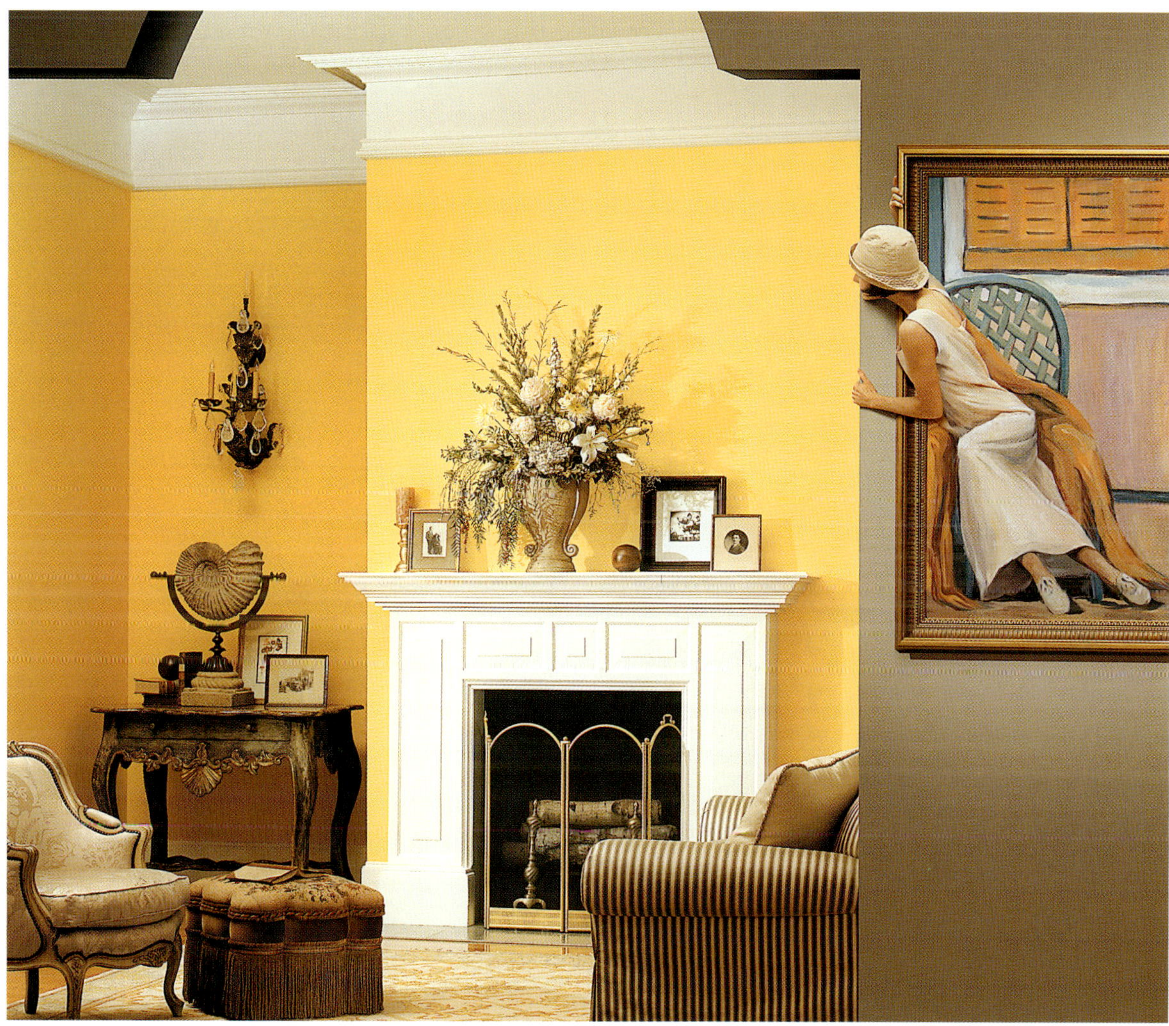

opposite: **S**anjay **K**othari this page: **L**ynn **S**ugarman

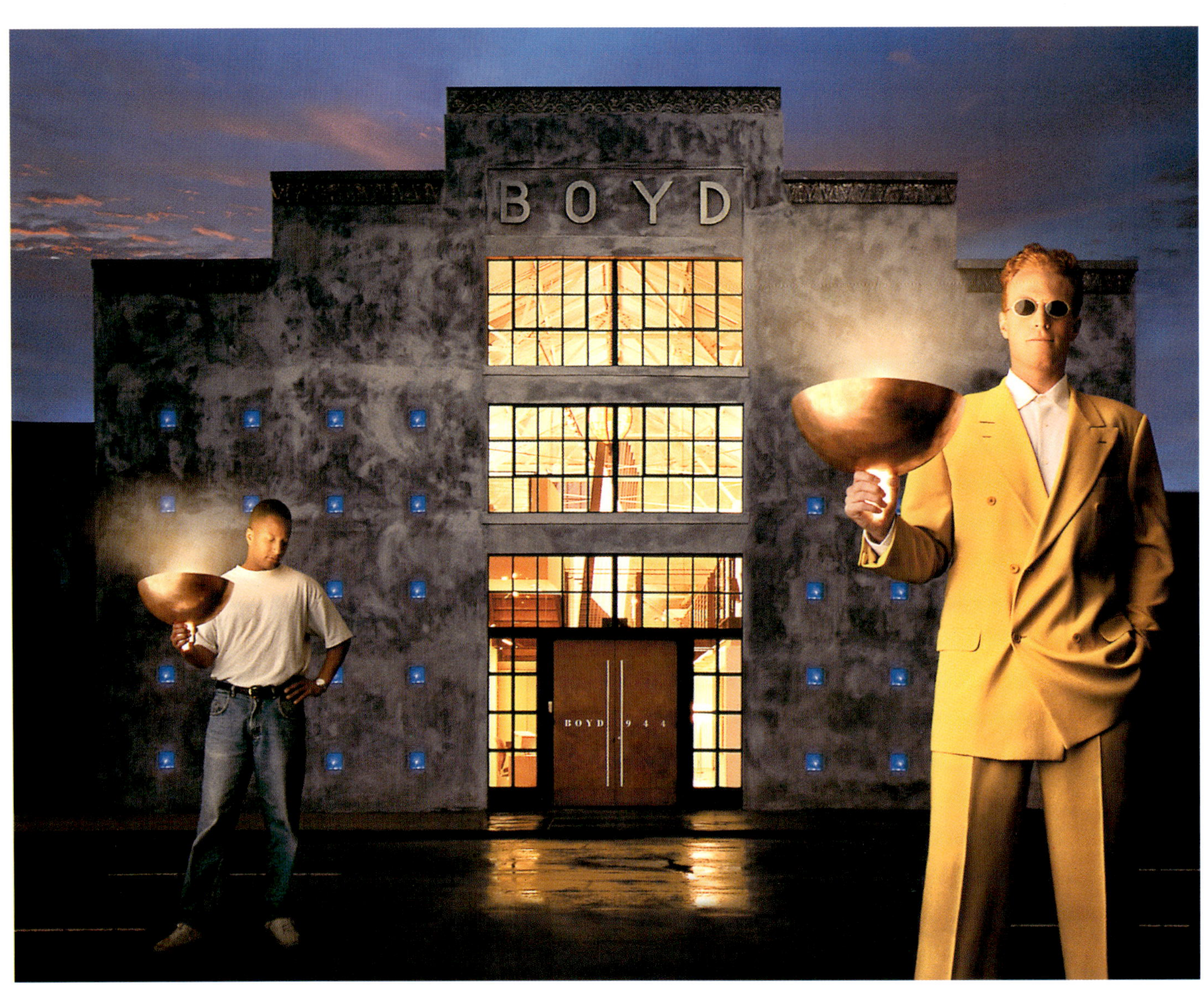

Jim Erickson

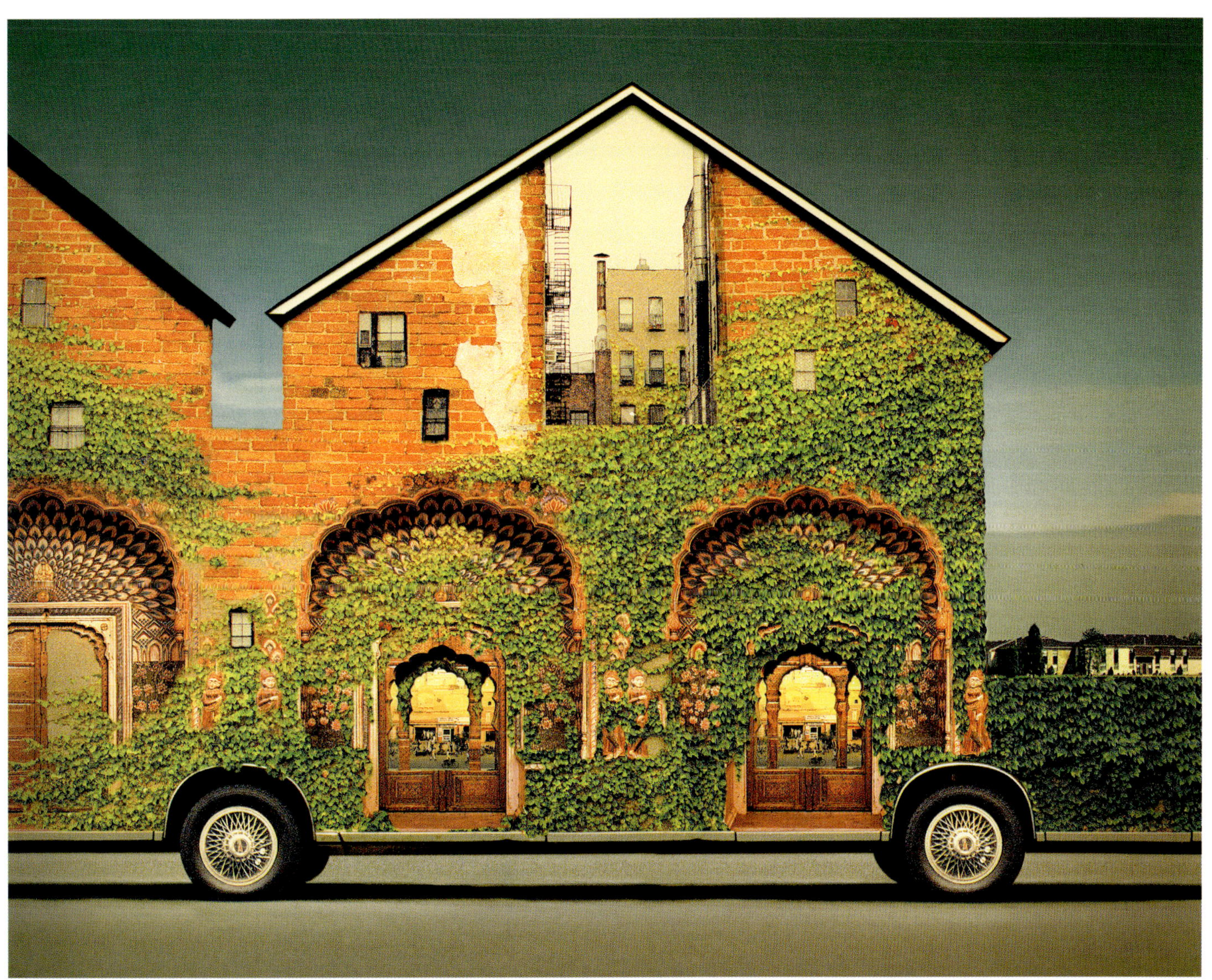

Sanjay Kothari

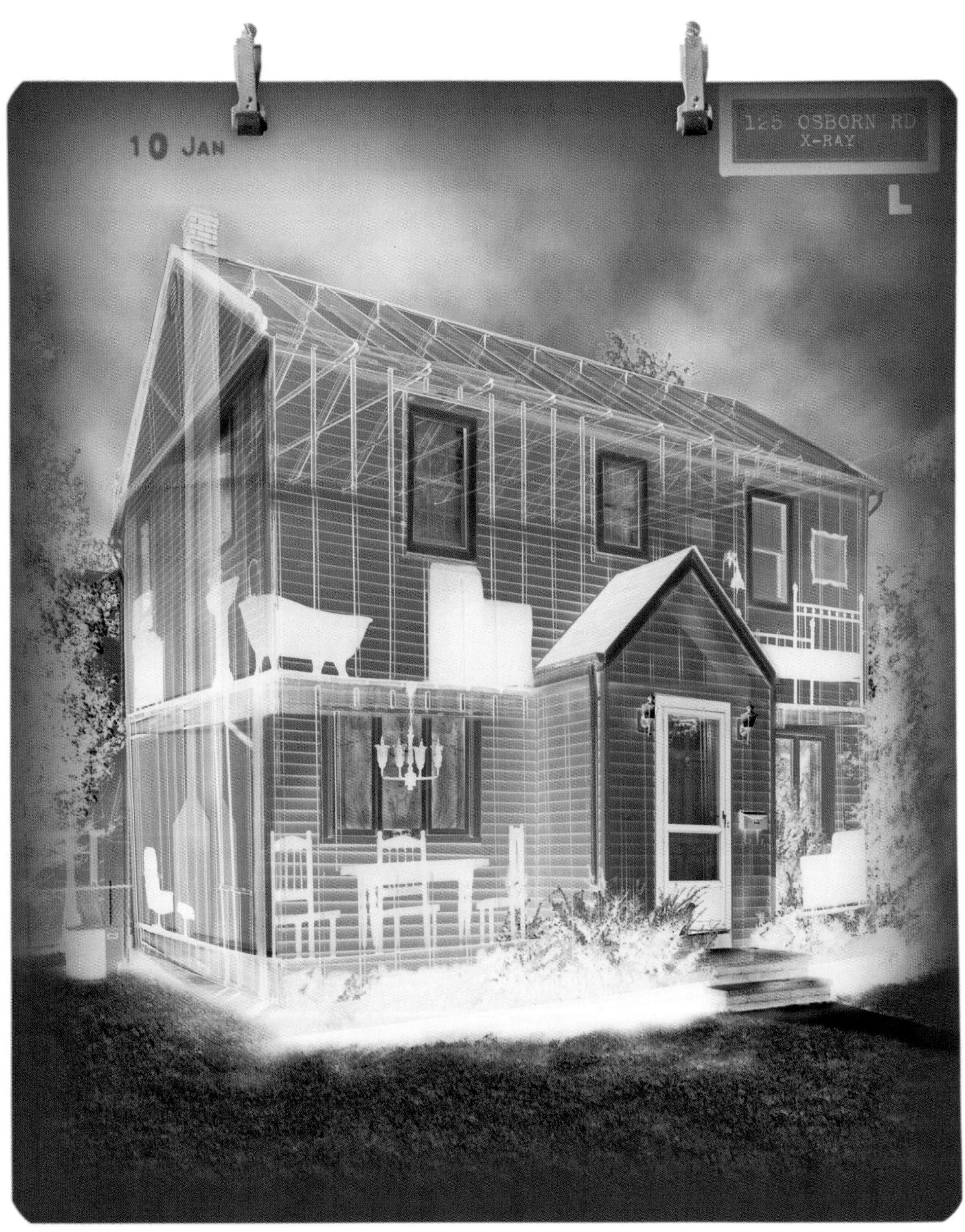

this page: **N**ick **K**oudis opposite: **T**im **G**riffith

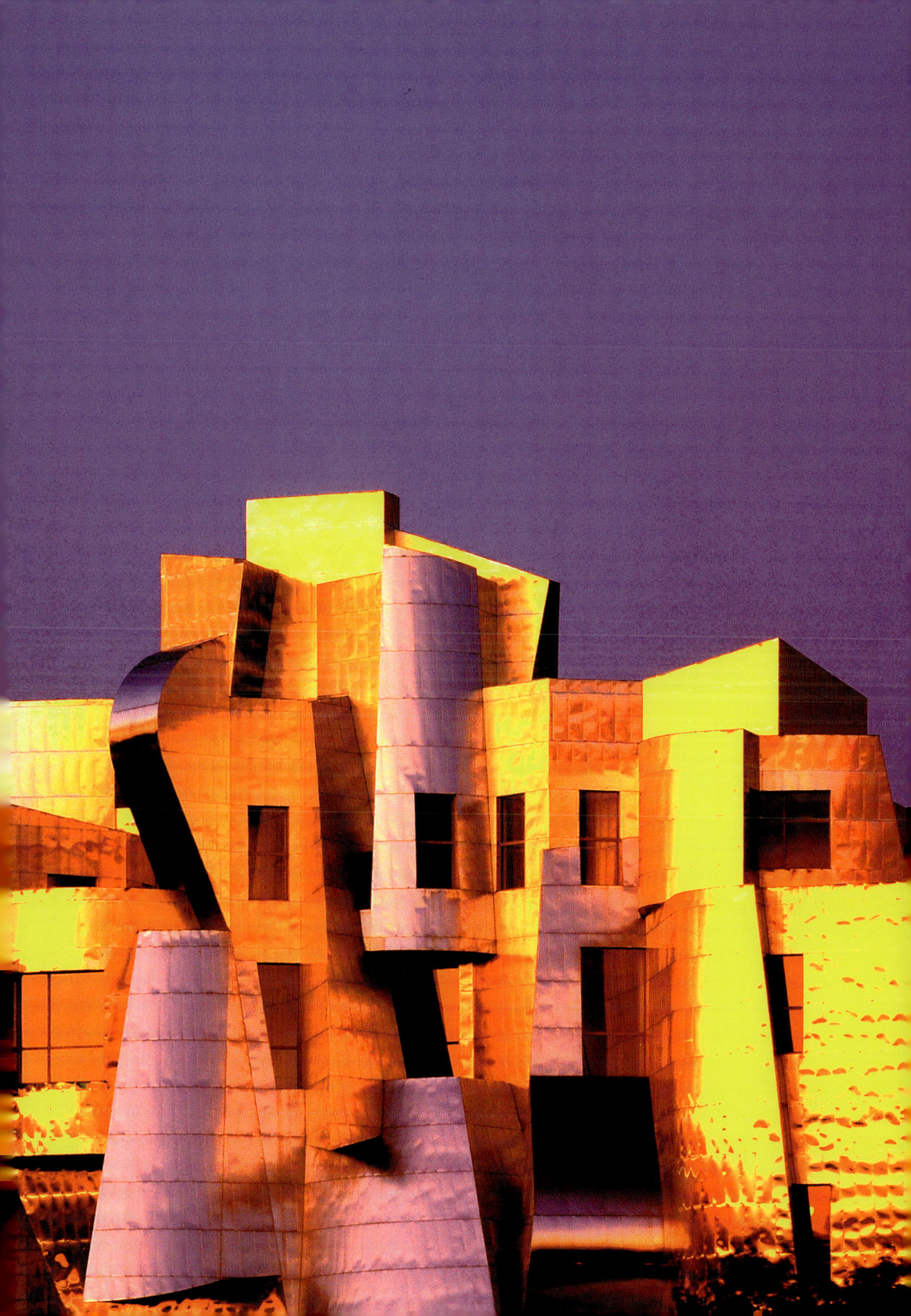

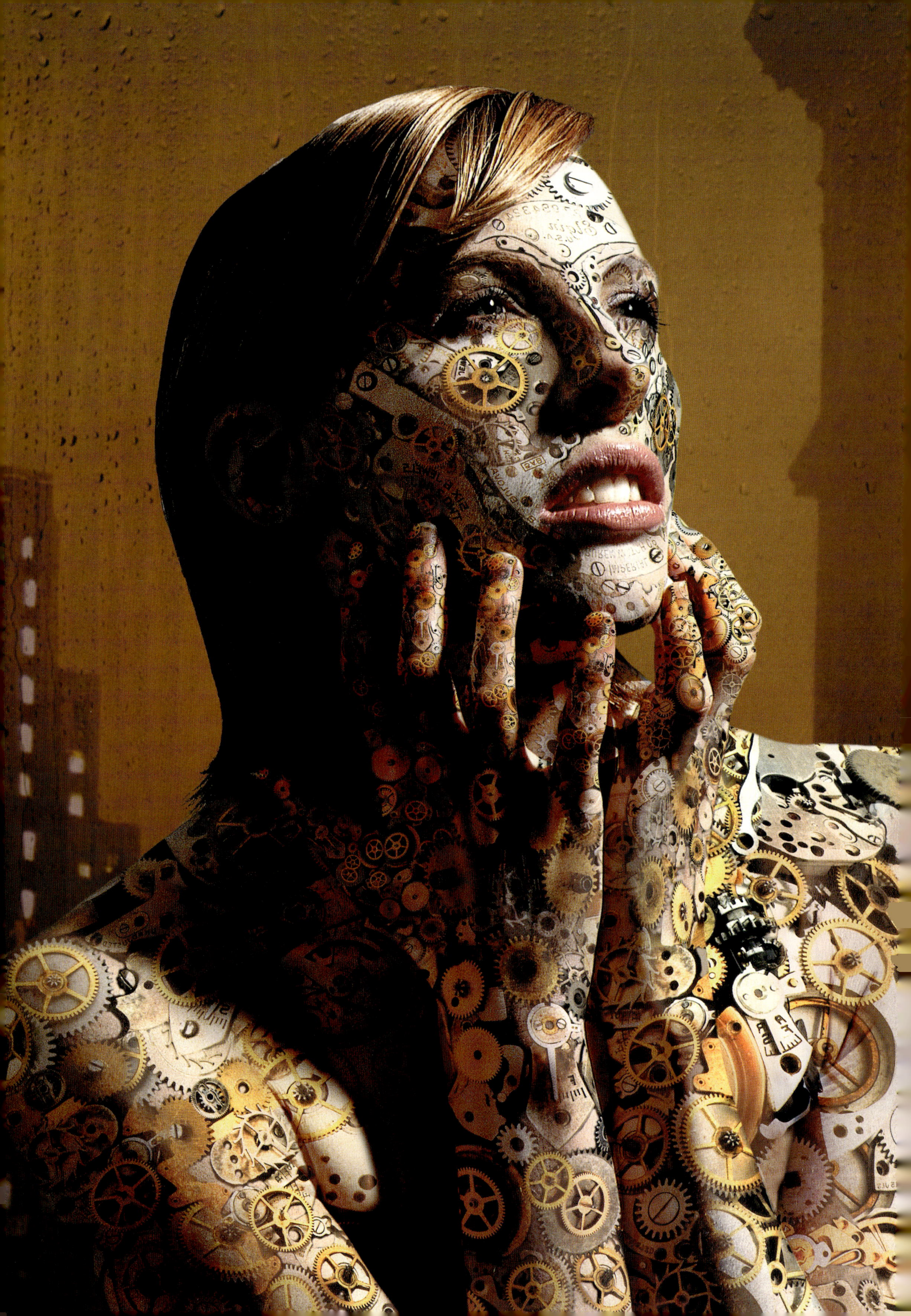

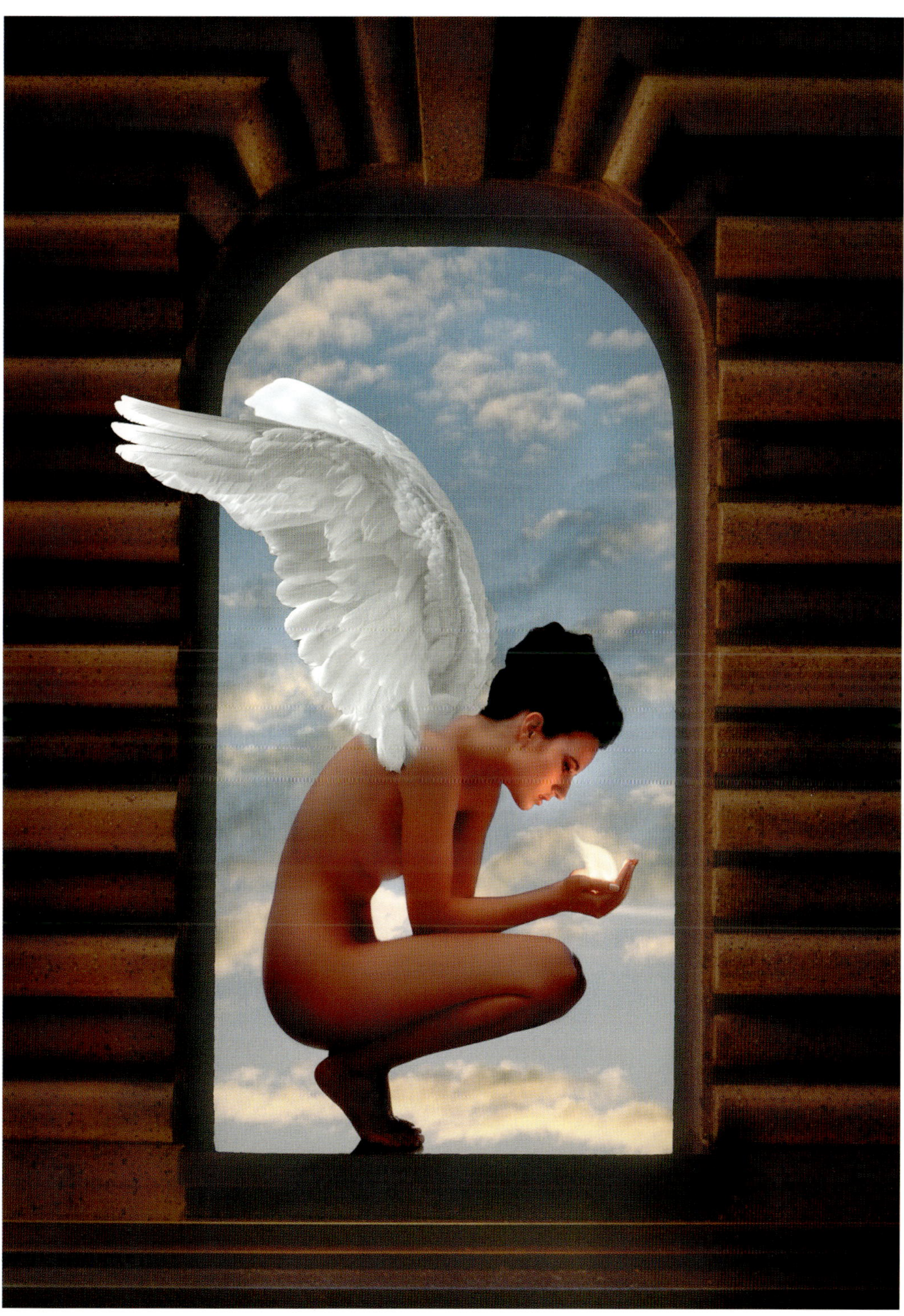

opposite: **J**ames **P**orto this page: **G**erald **B**ybee

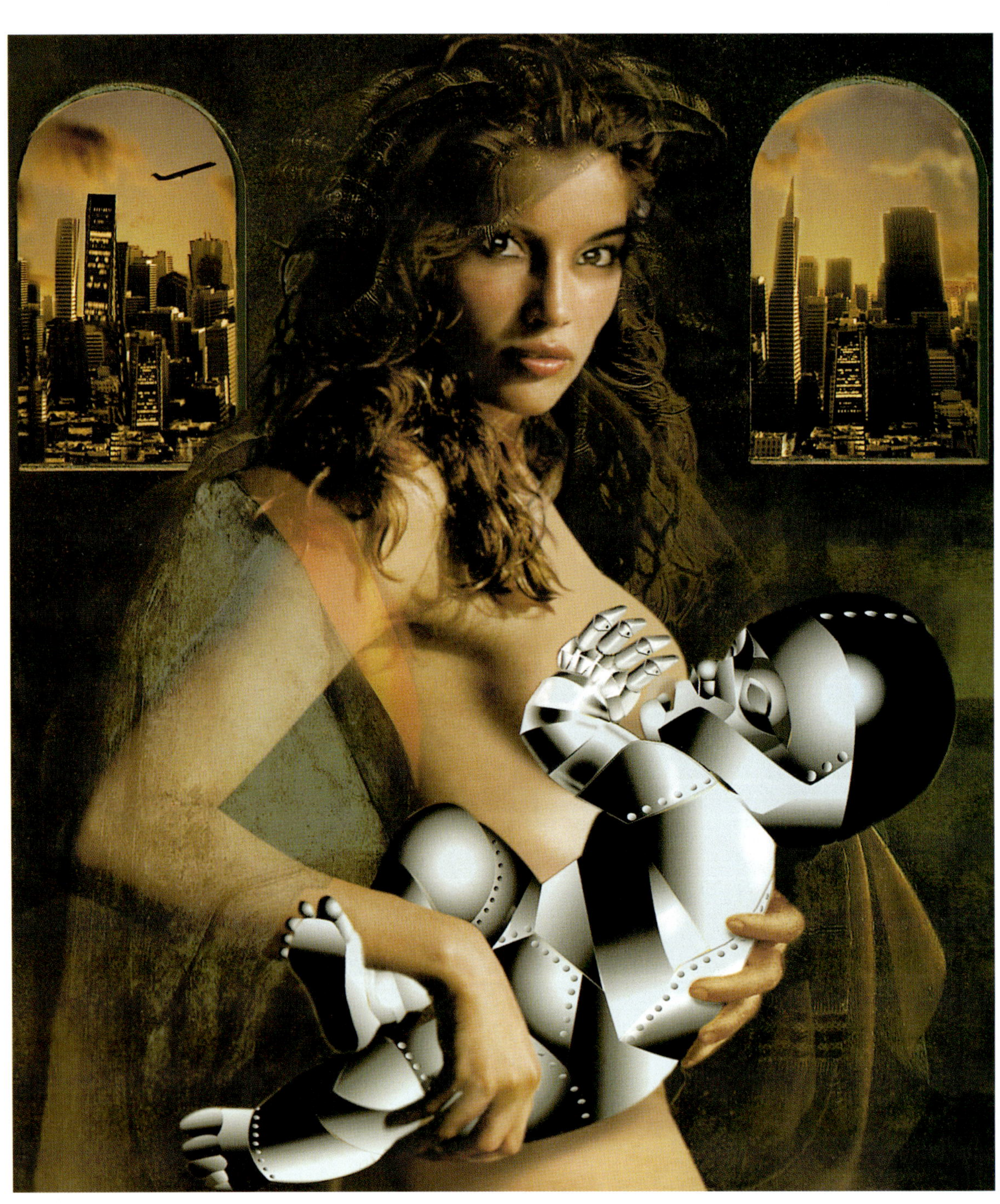

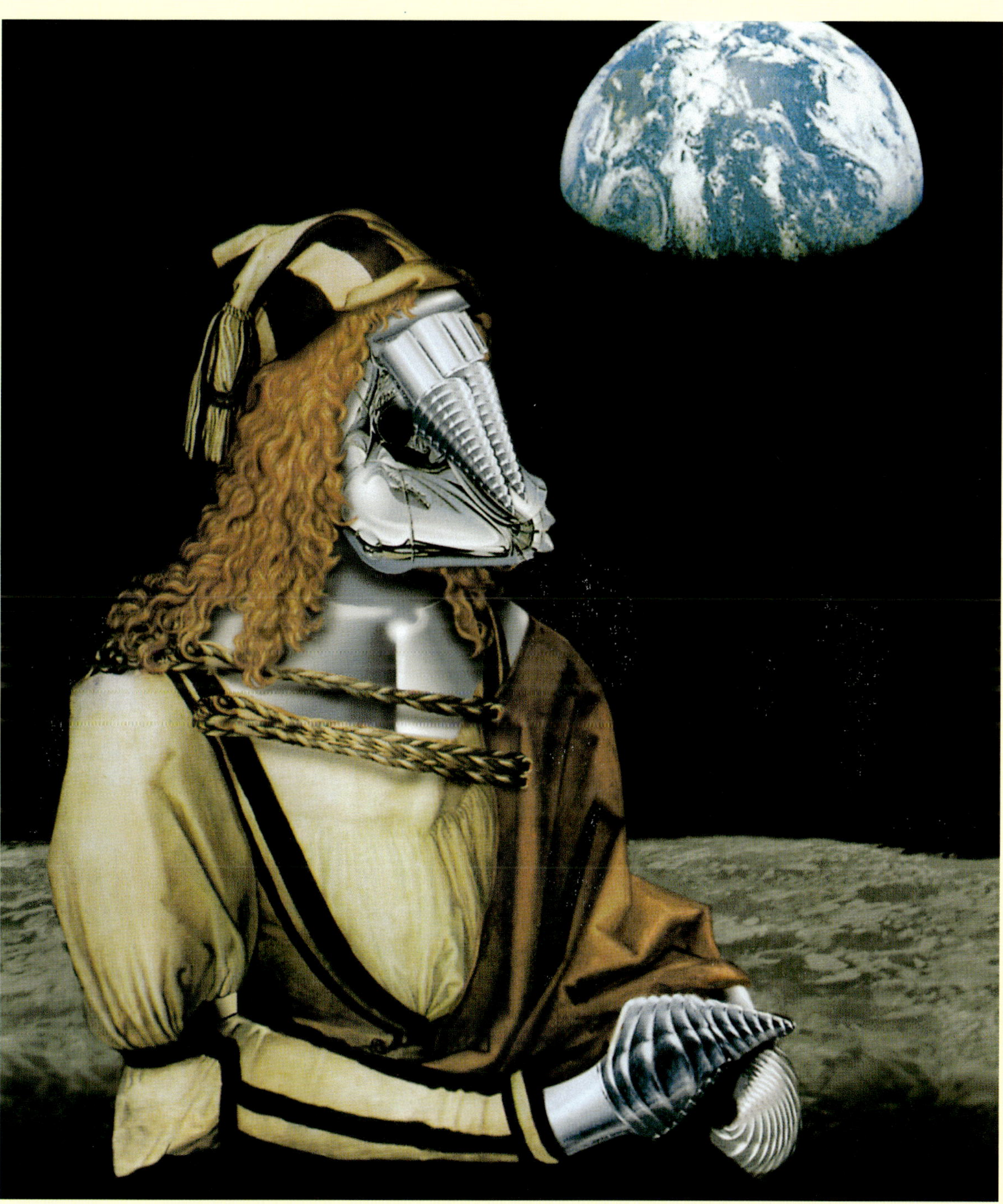

this spread: **E**va **S**wider

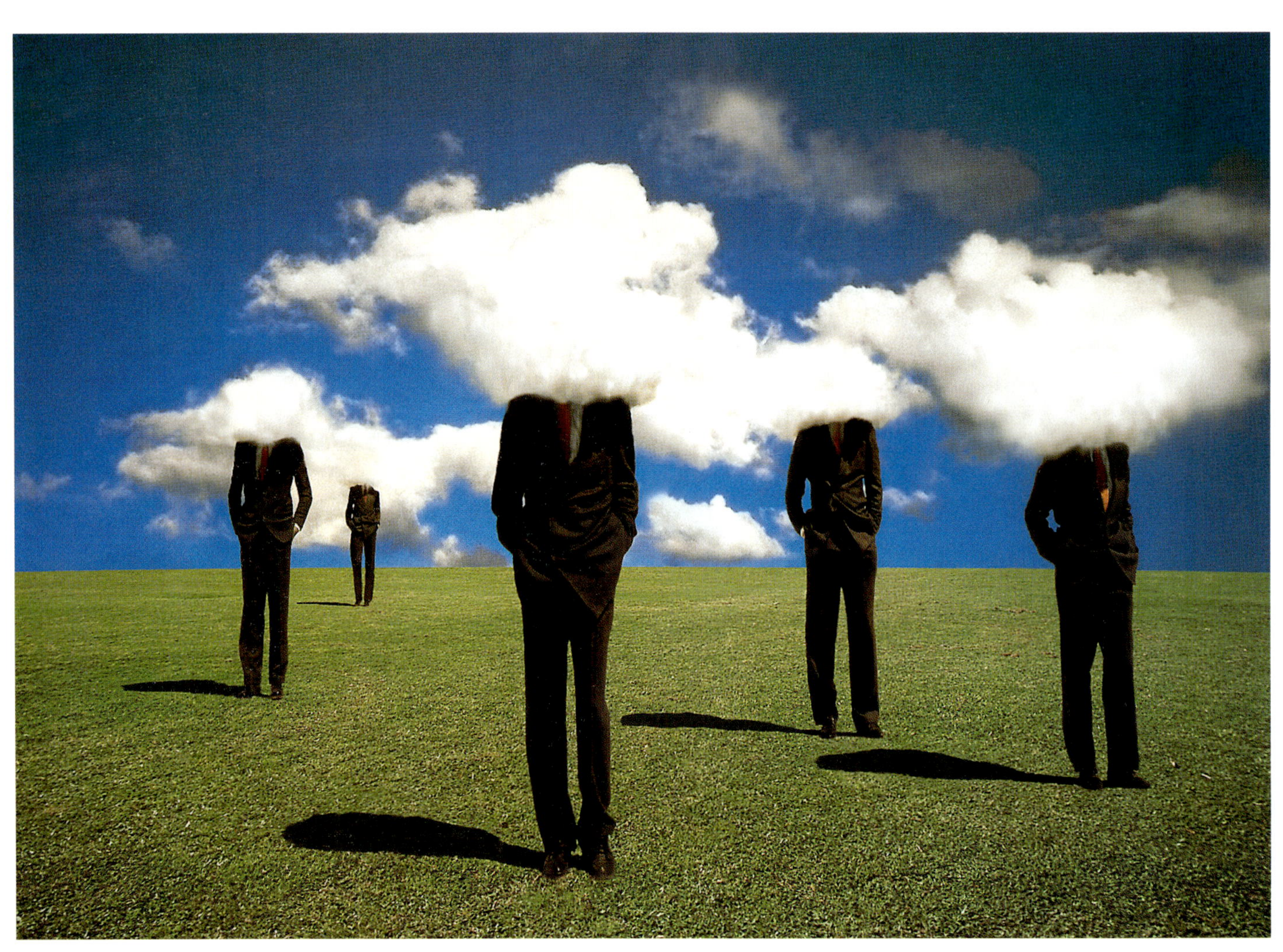

Paul **M**axon

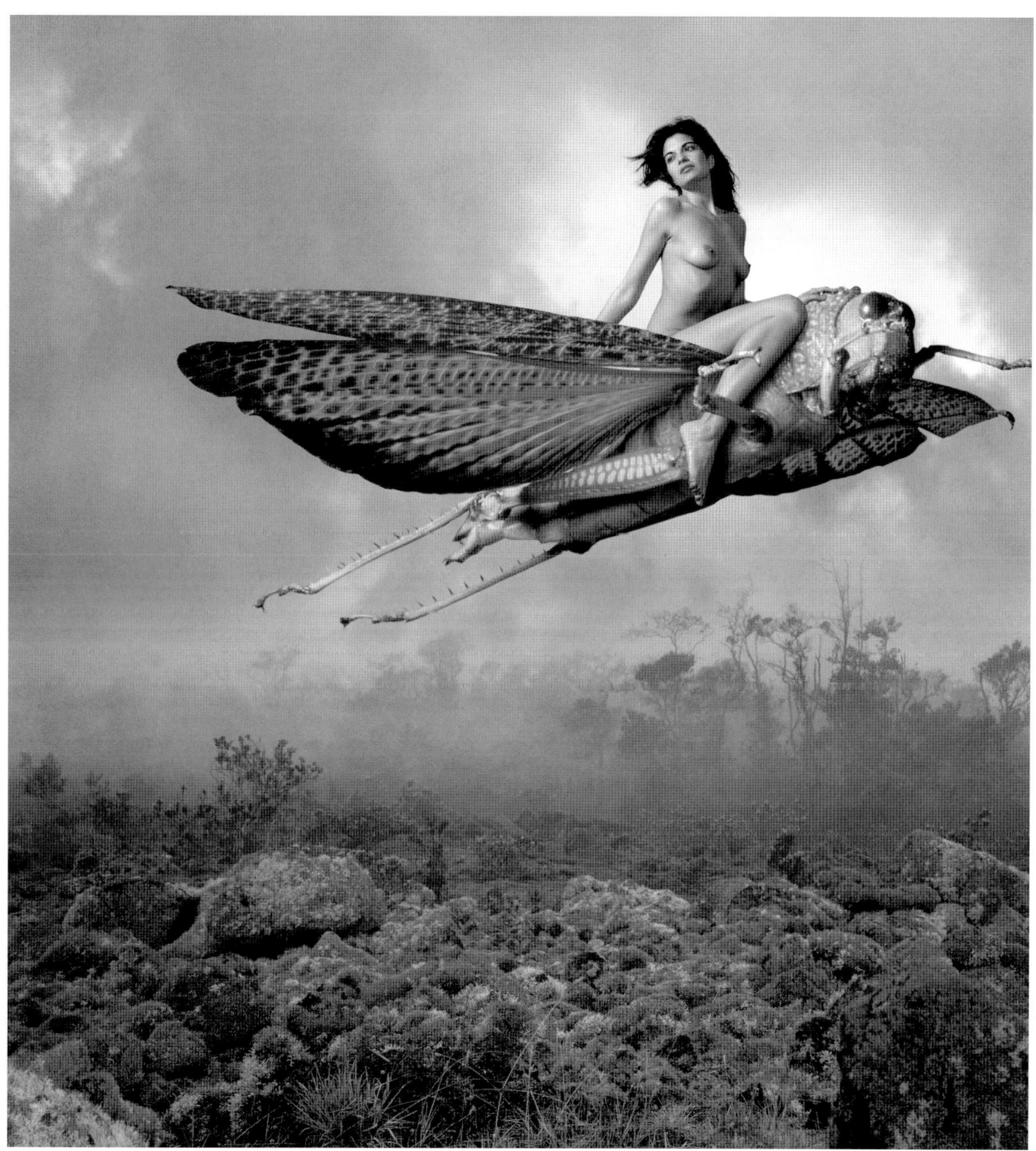

this page: **J**ames **P**orto following spread: **D**on **M**oravick

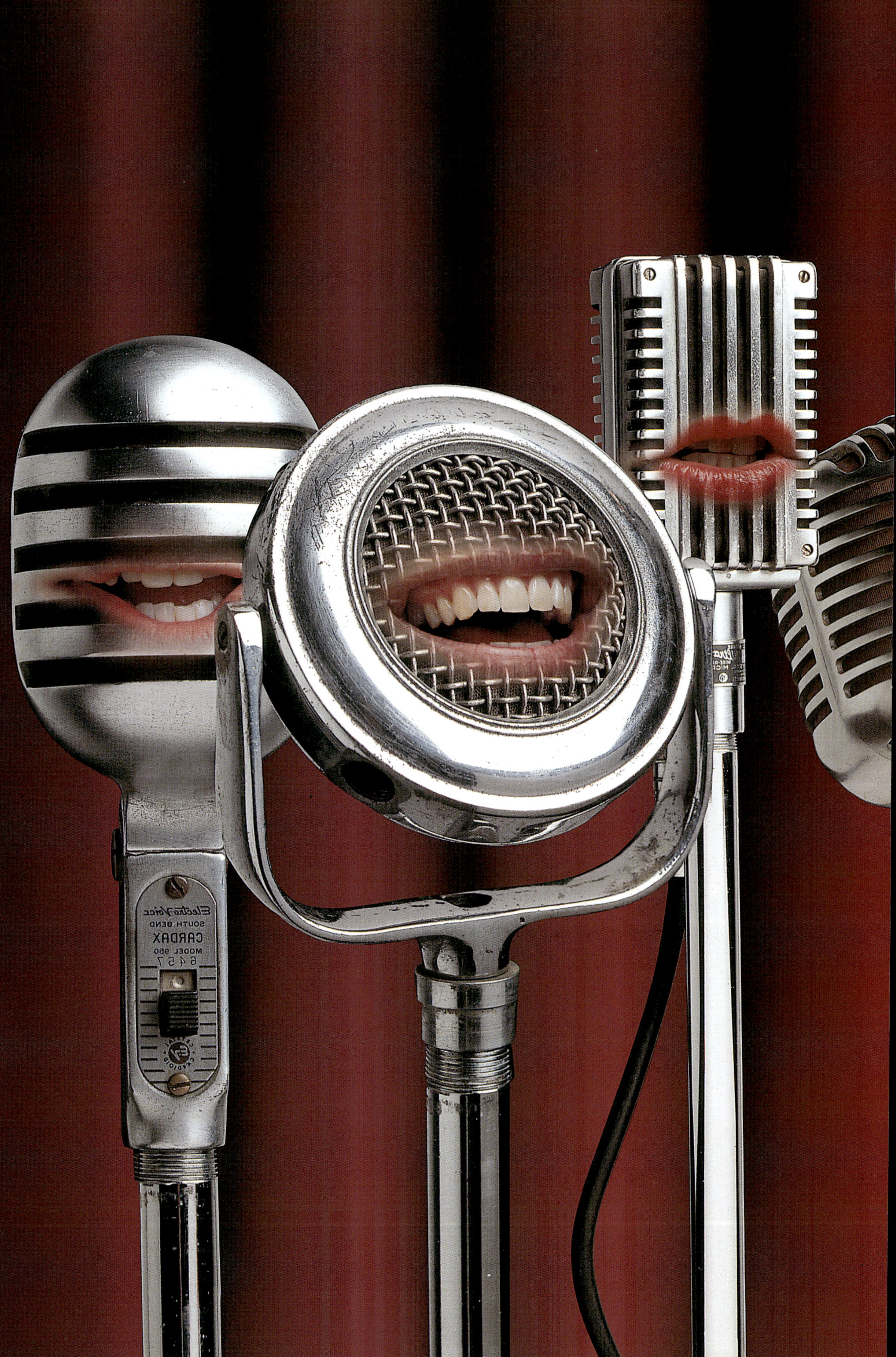
Electro Voice
SOUTH BEND
CARDAX
MODEL 950
8457

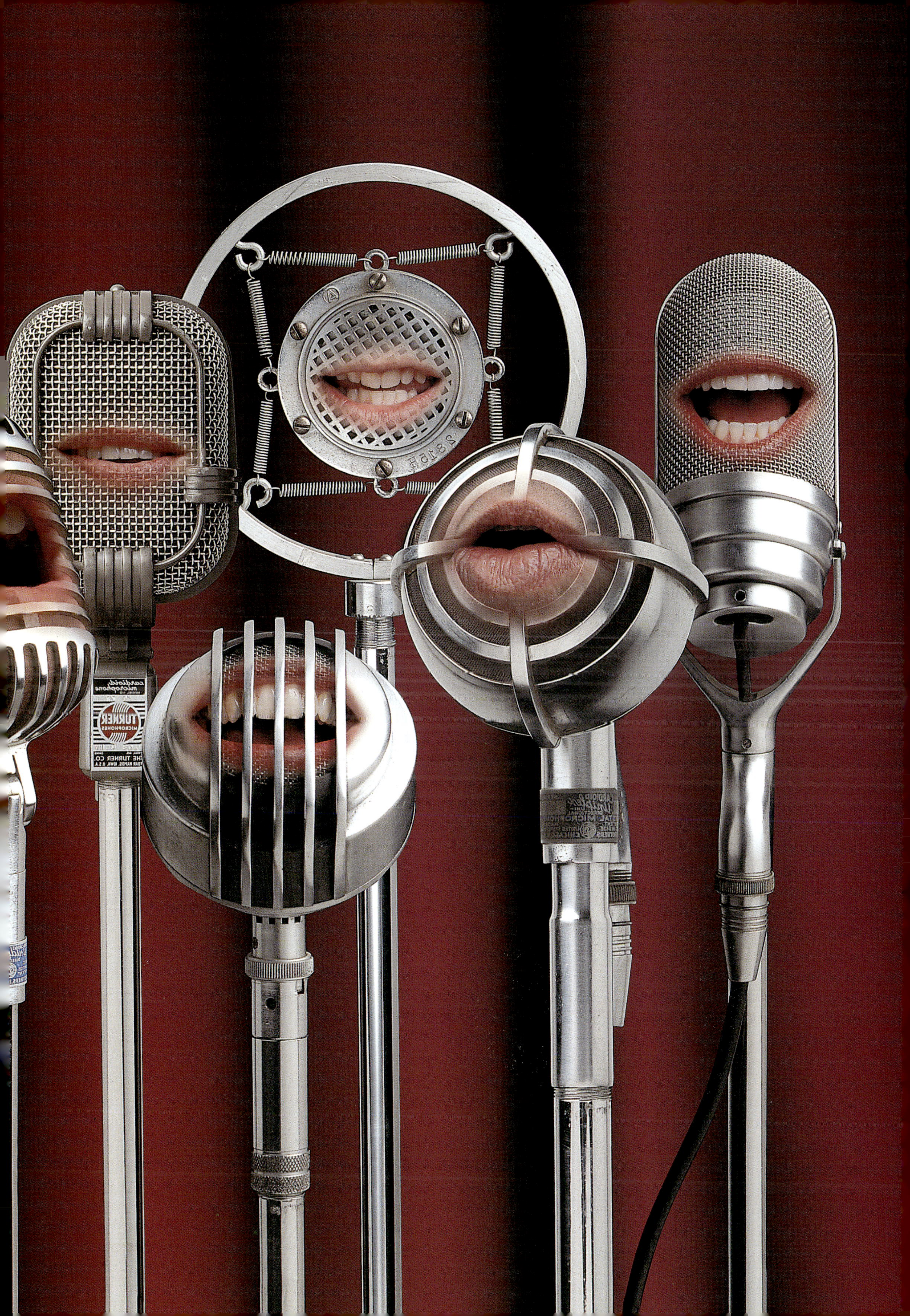

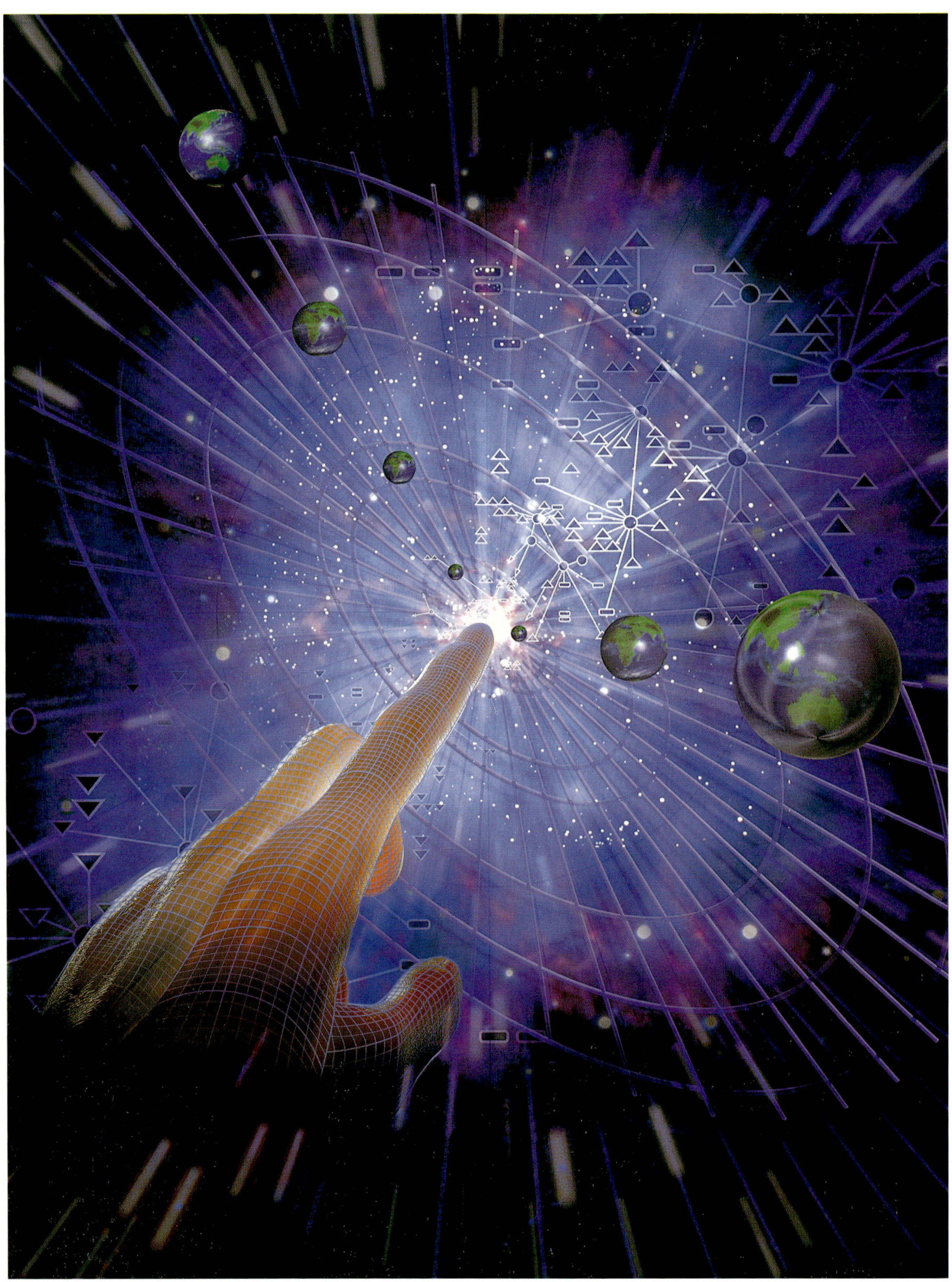

this spread: **H**ans **N**eleman

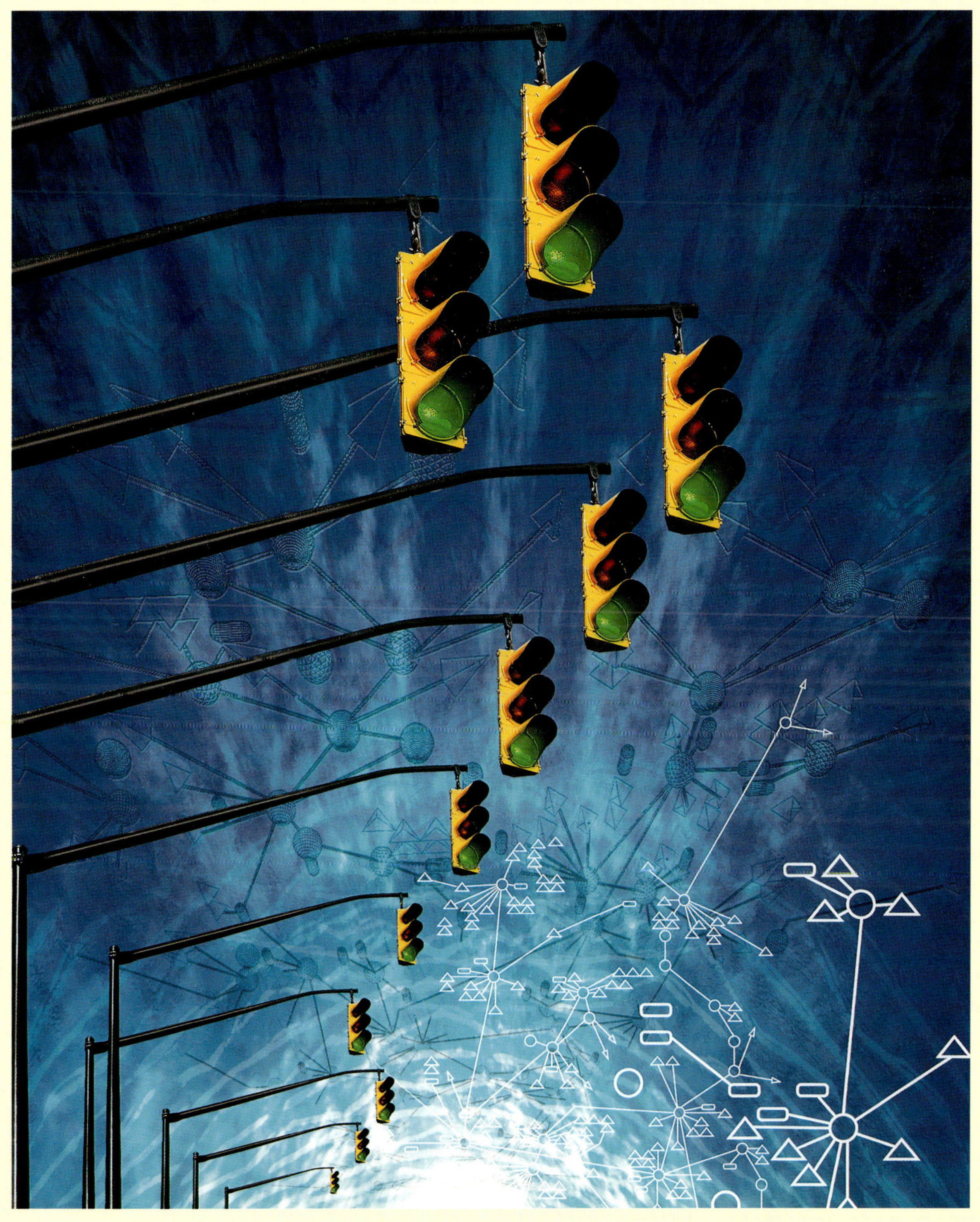

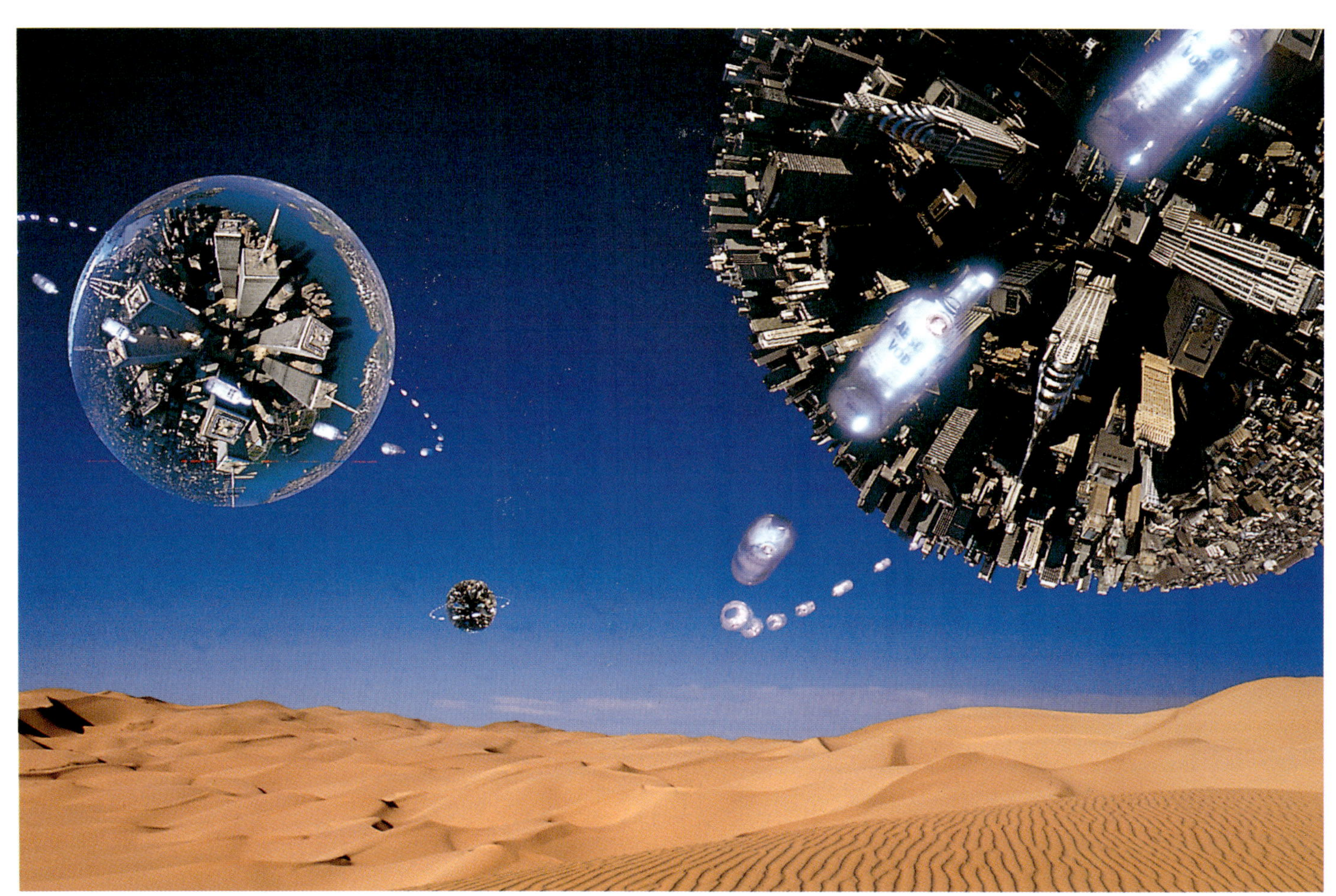

this page: **J**ames **P**orto opposite: **R**obert **S**ilvers

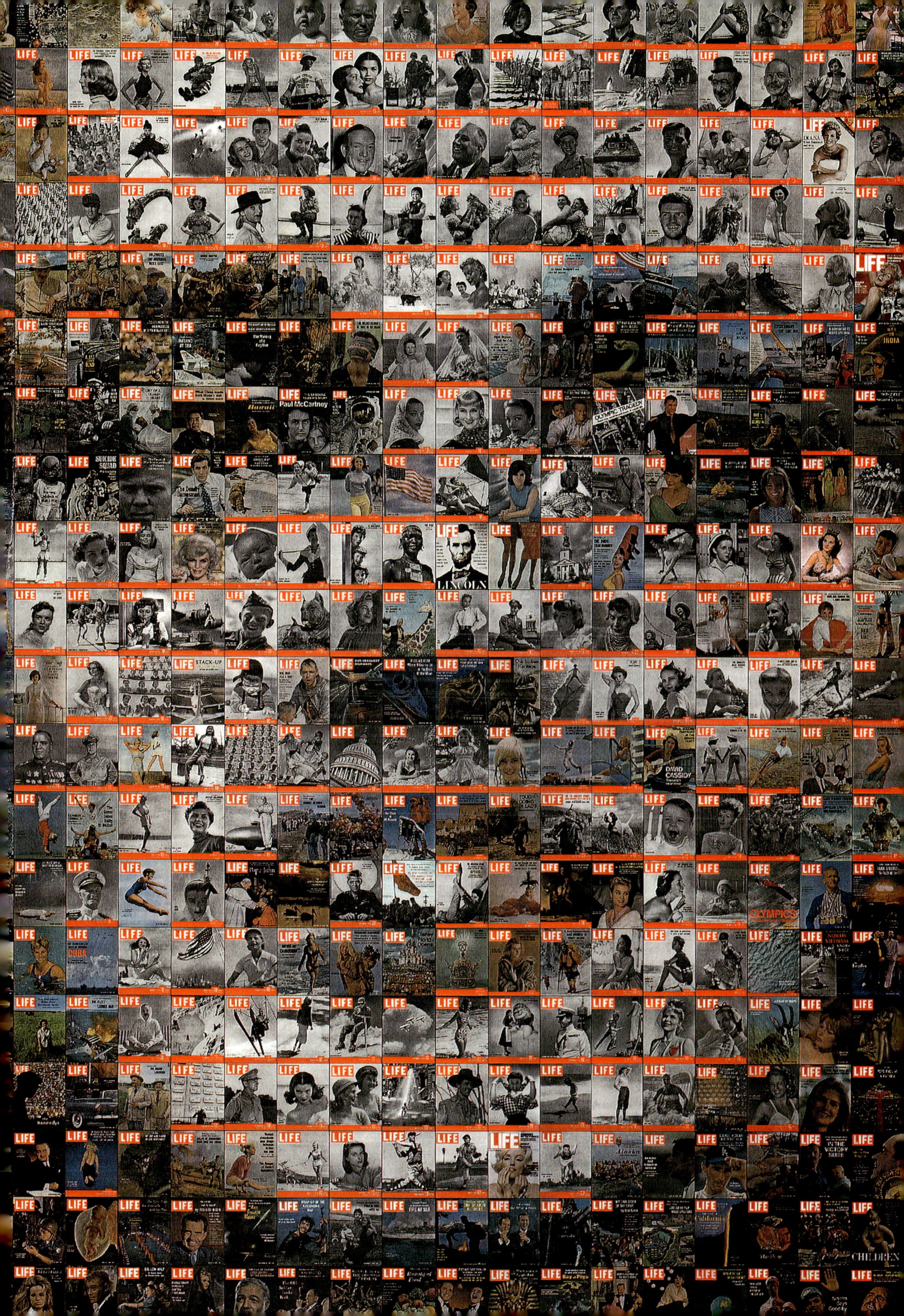

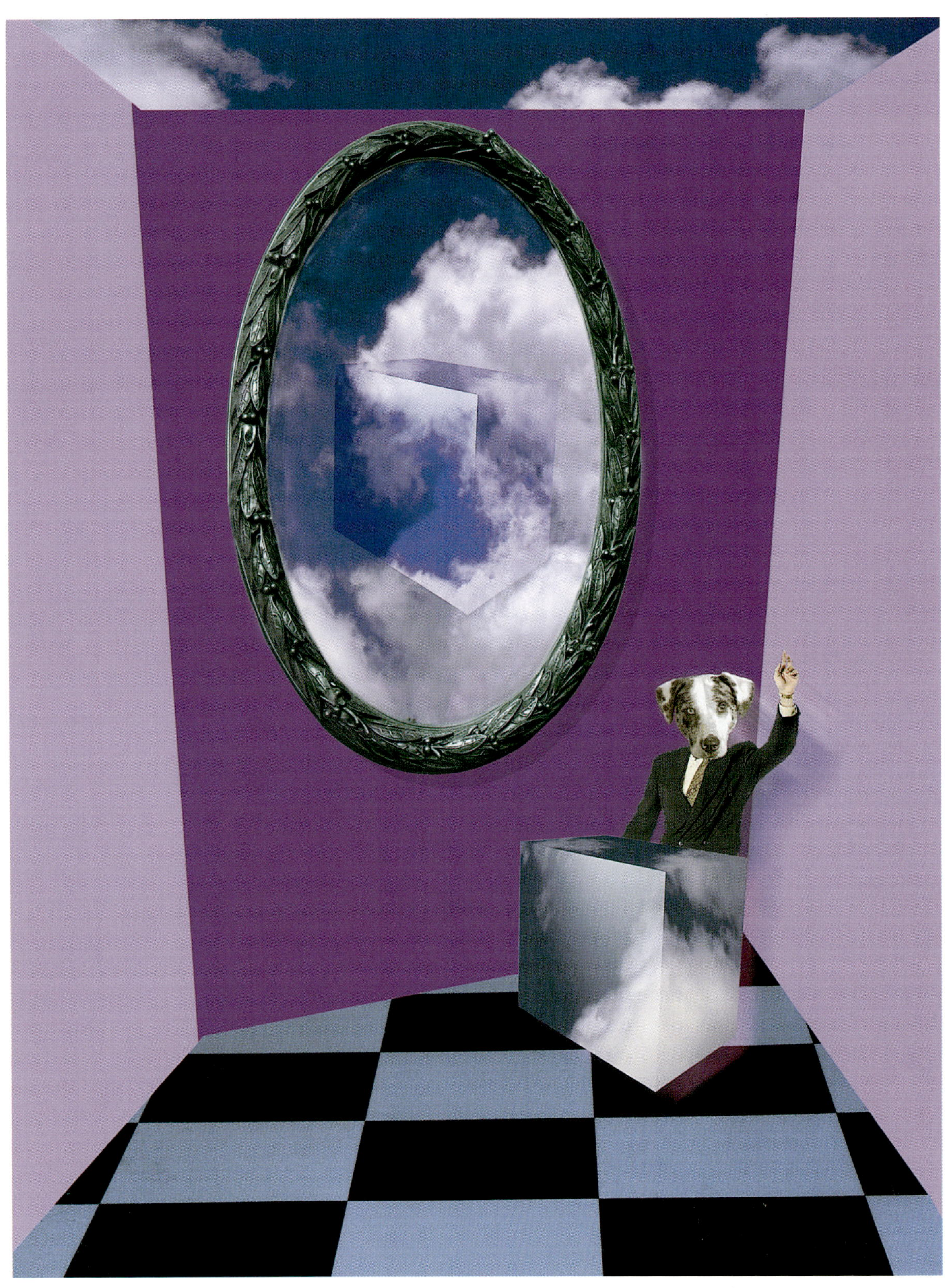

John Swain

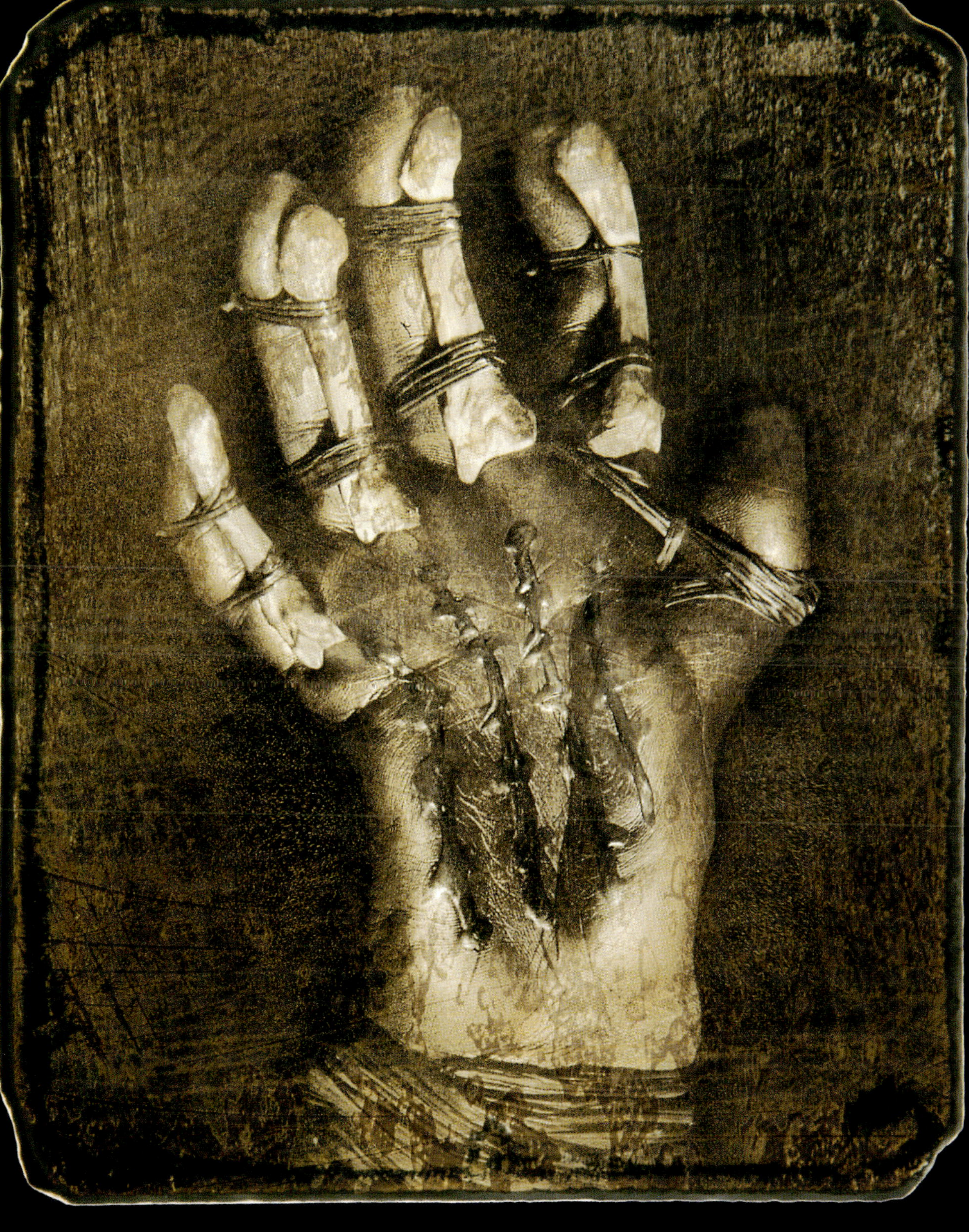

RJ Muna

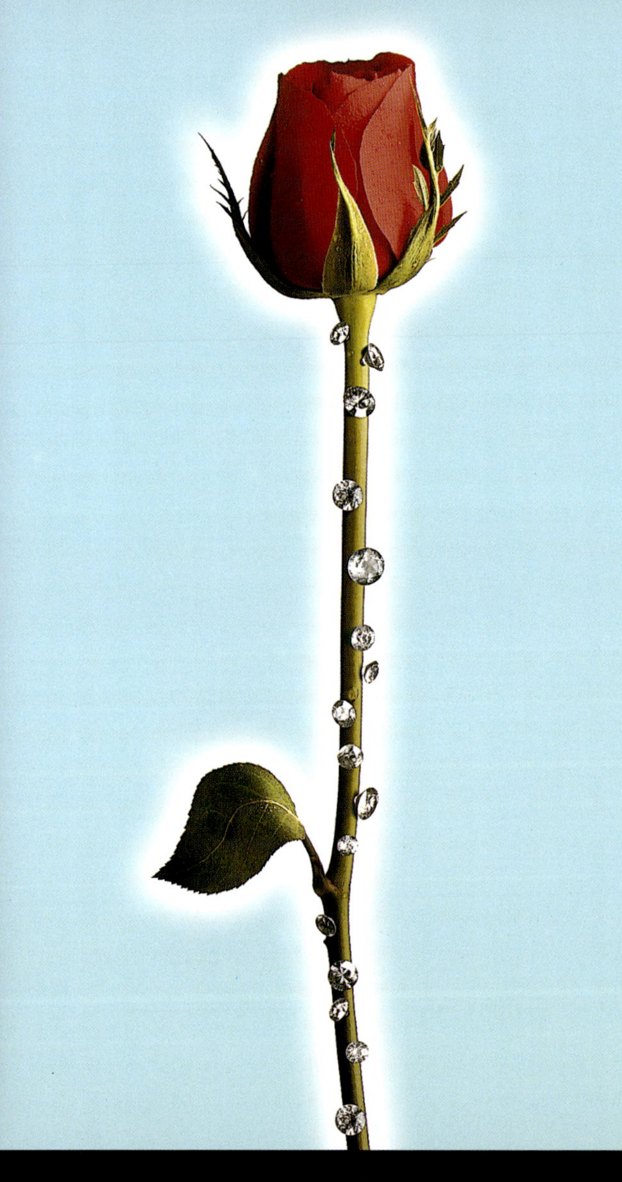

Fernando Zuffo

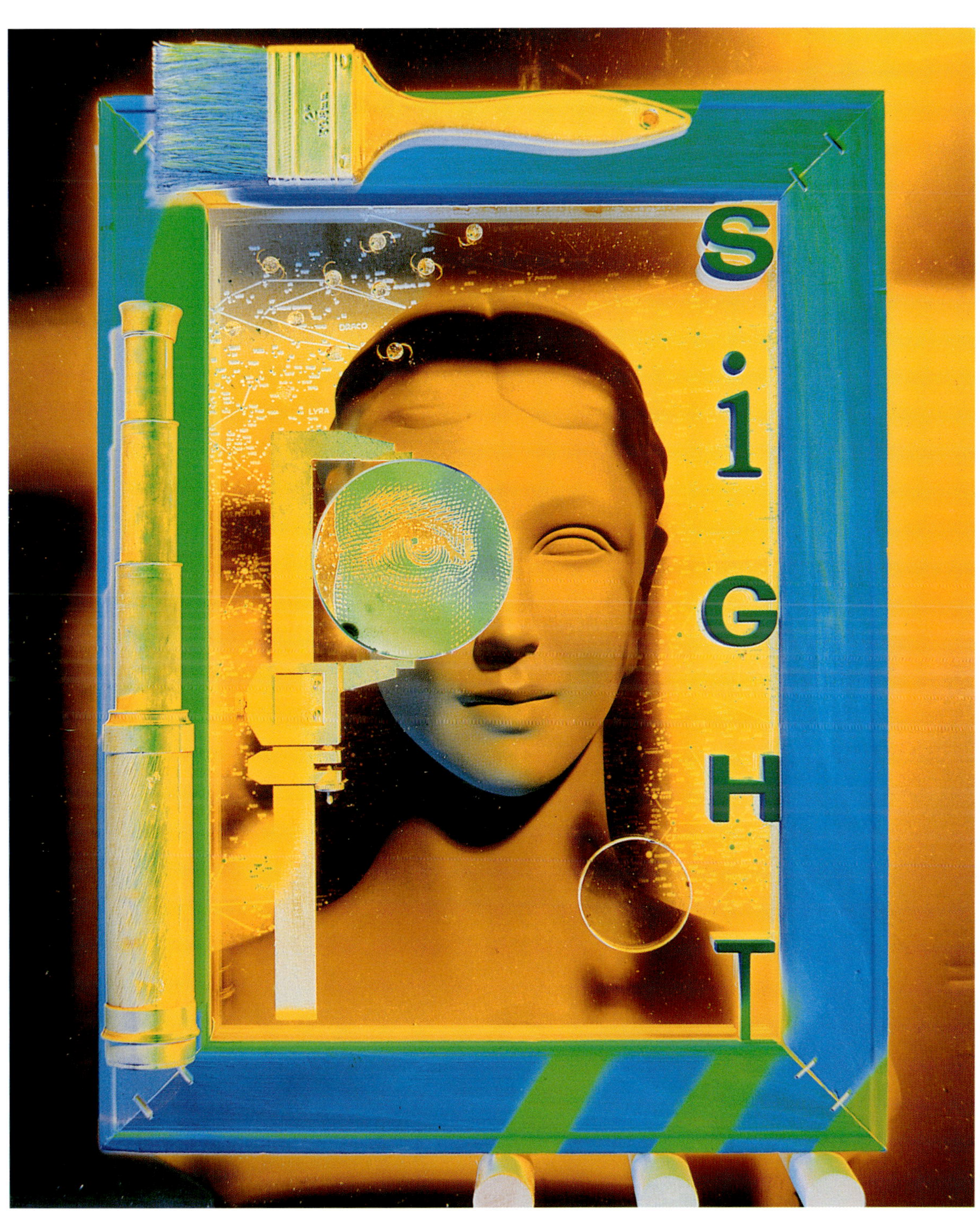

David **G**az

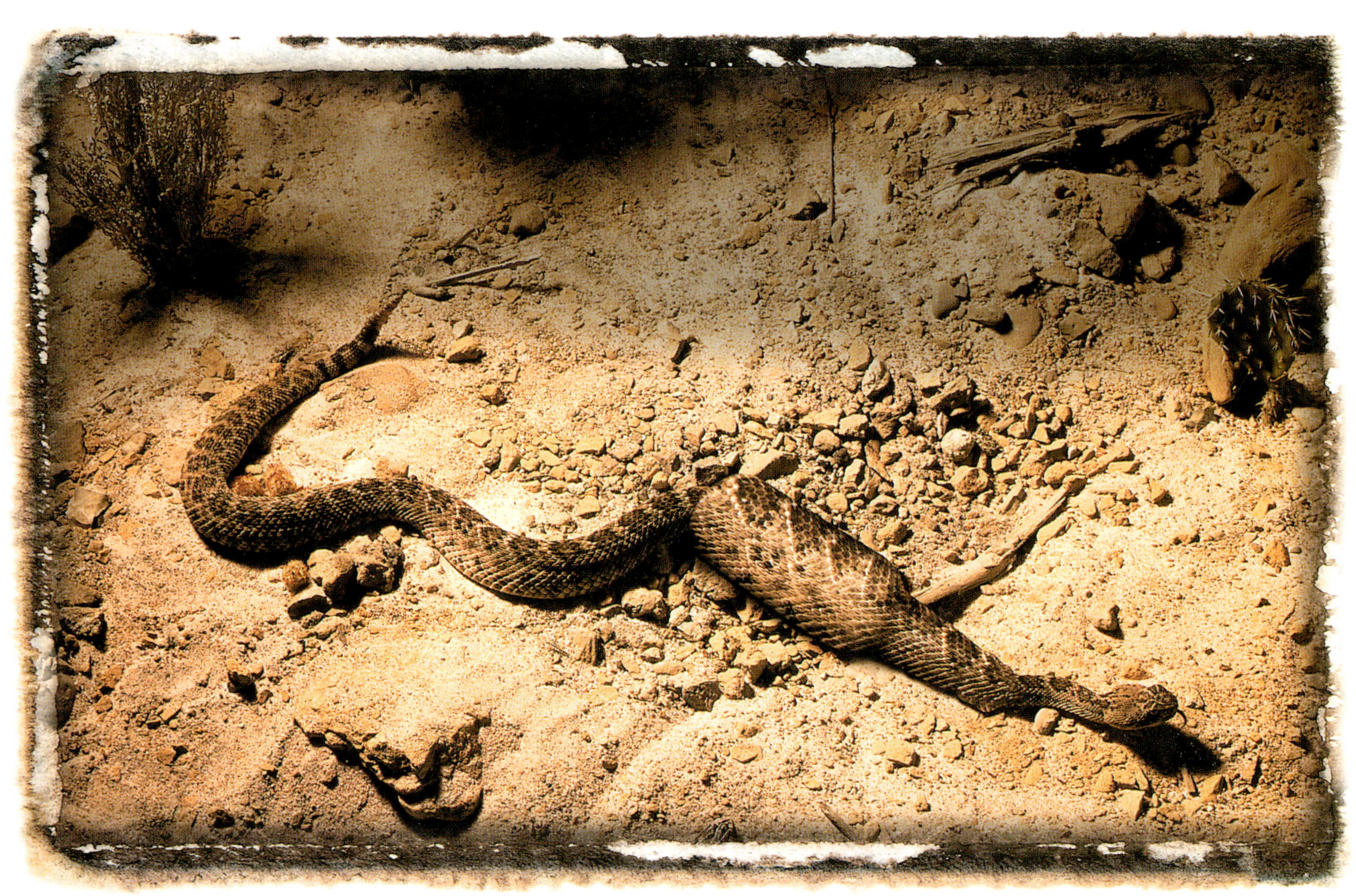

Stuart **B**lock

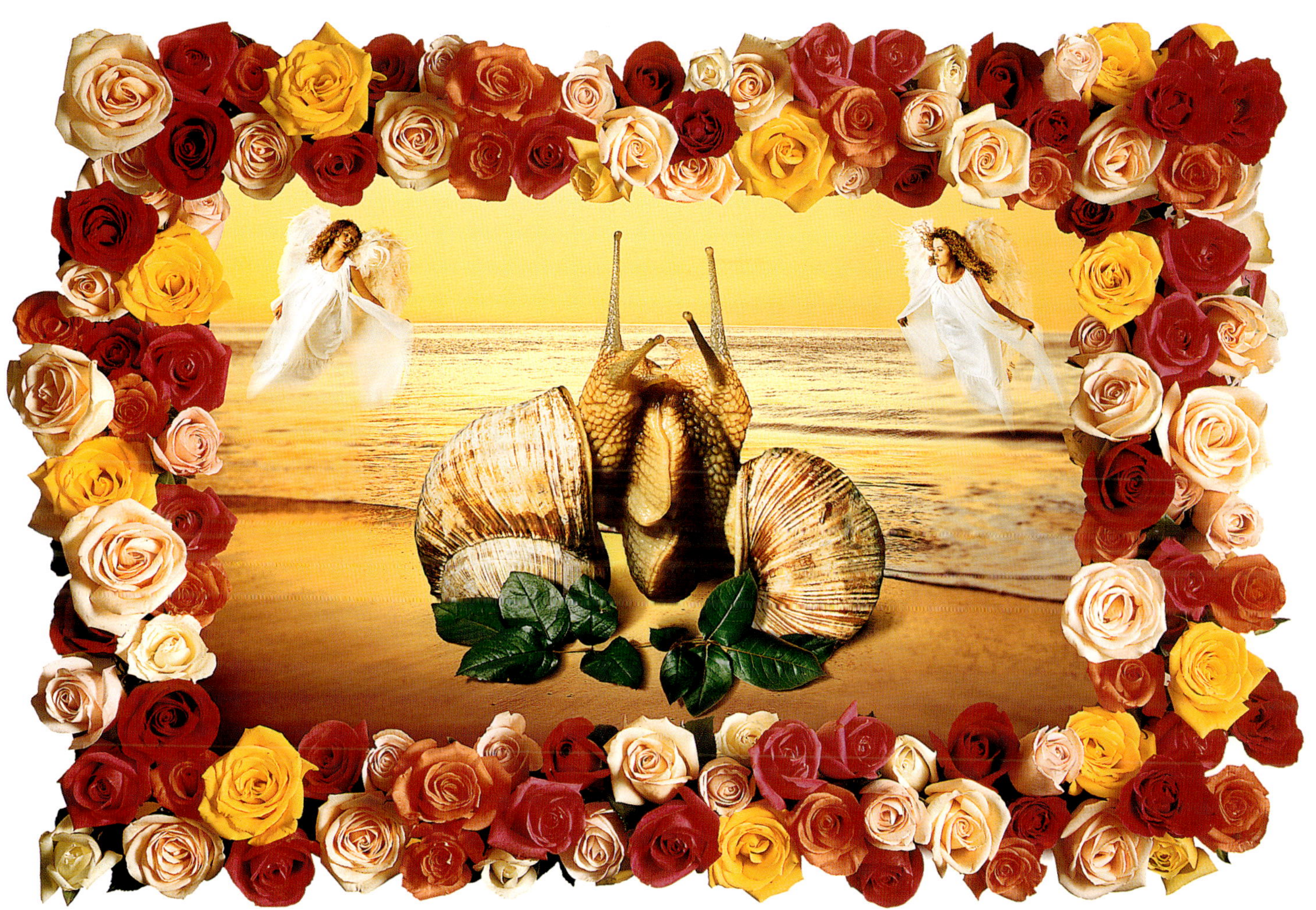

Fernando **Z**uffo

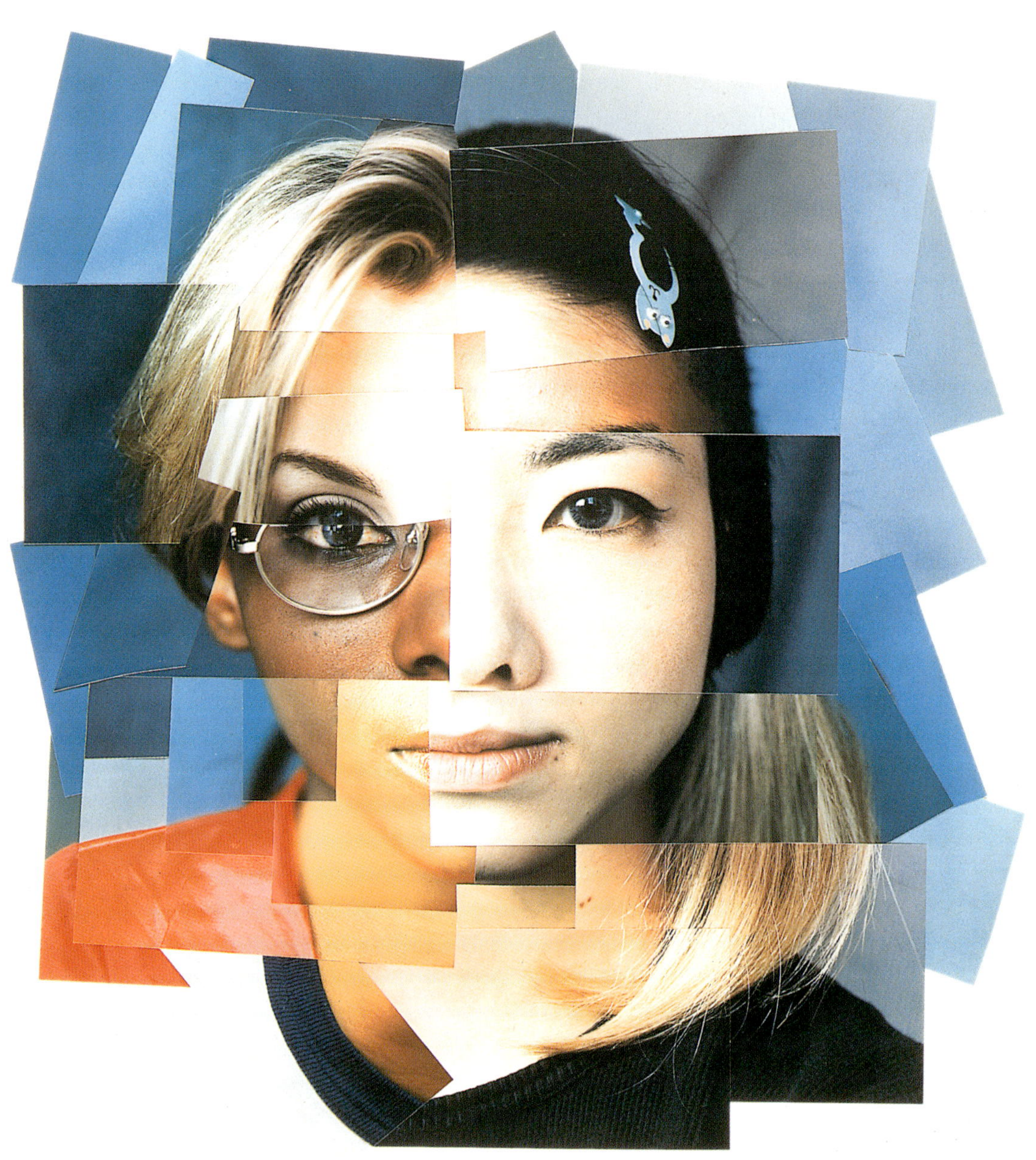

this spread: **J**eremy **W**olff

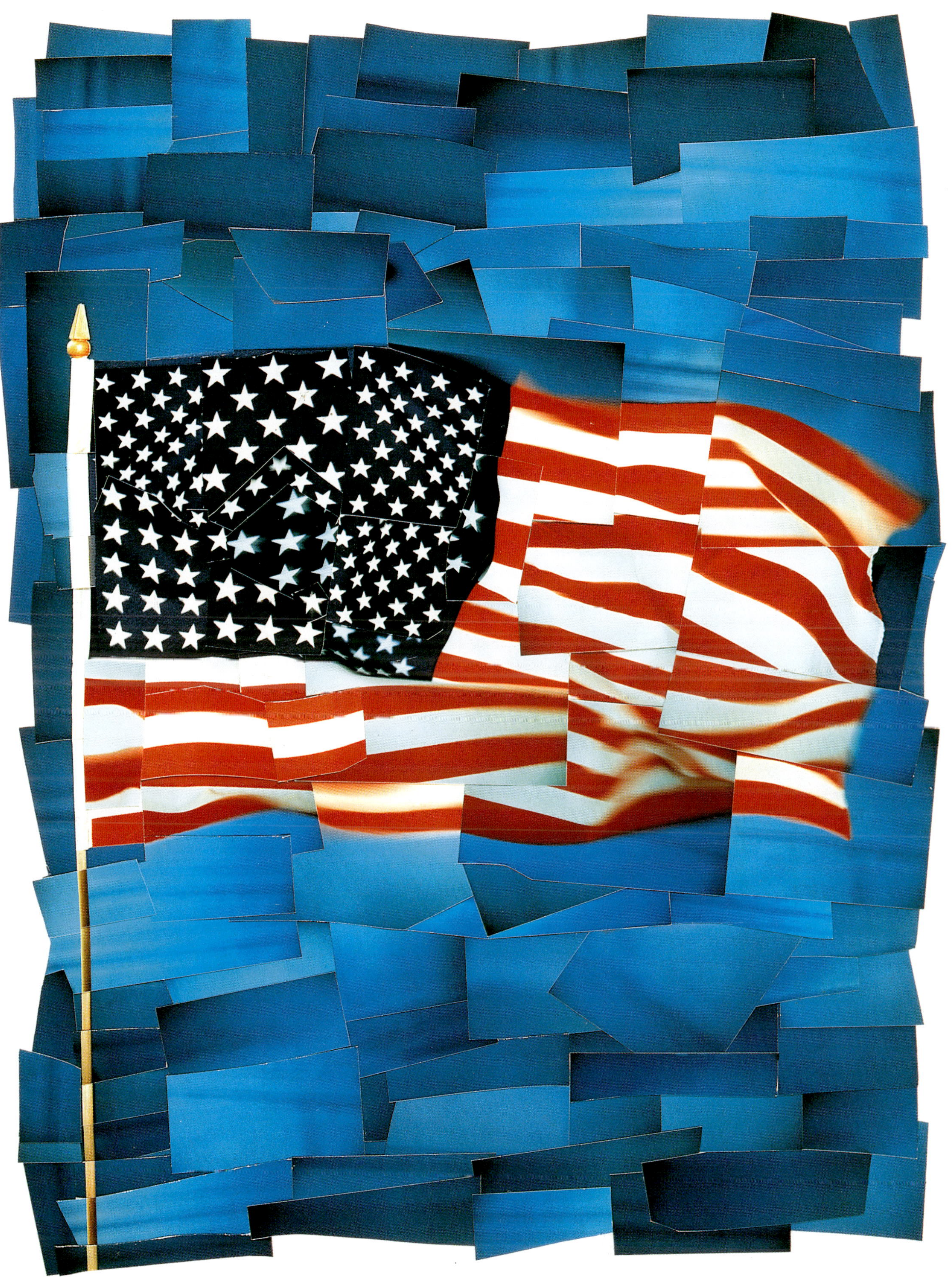

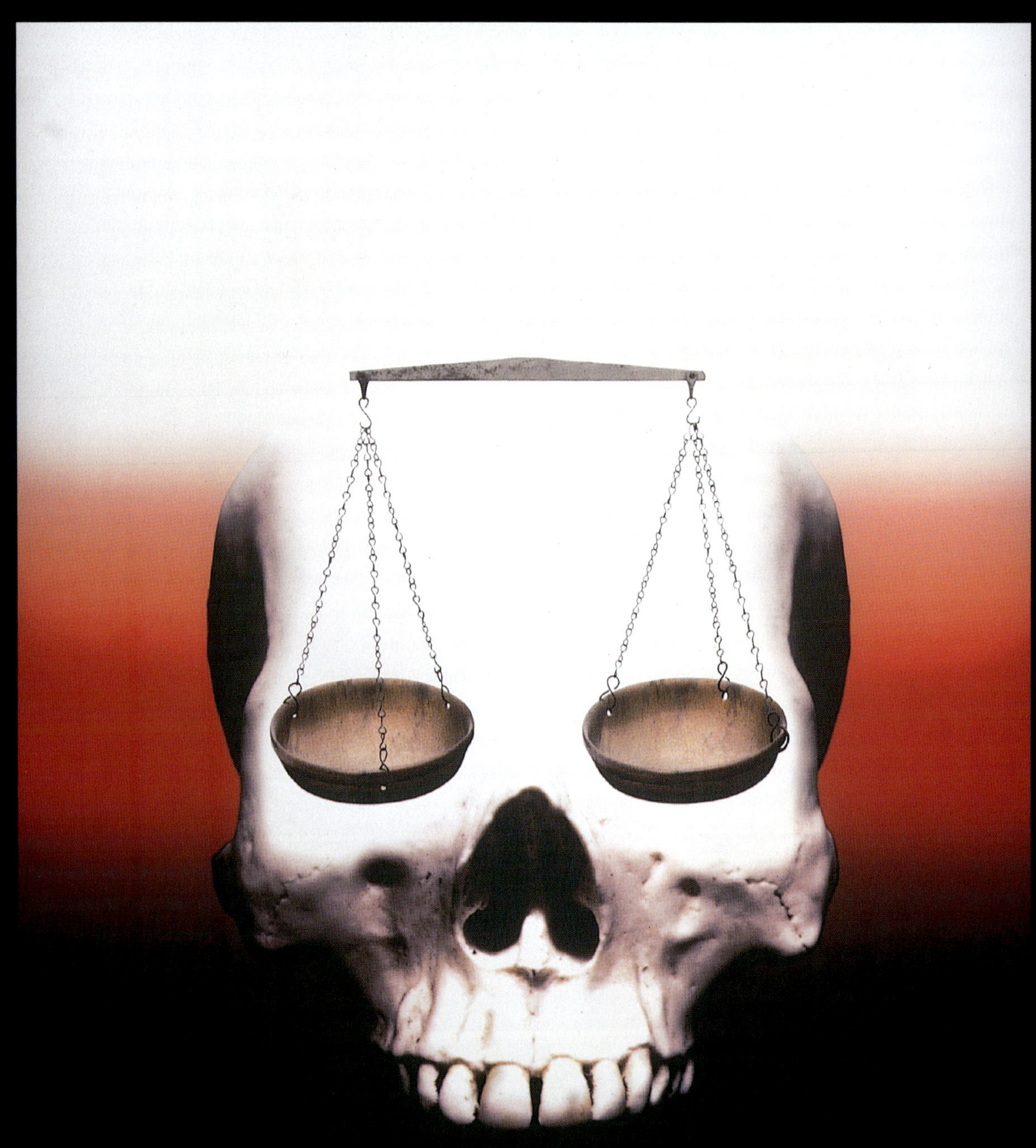

Mirko Ilic

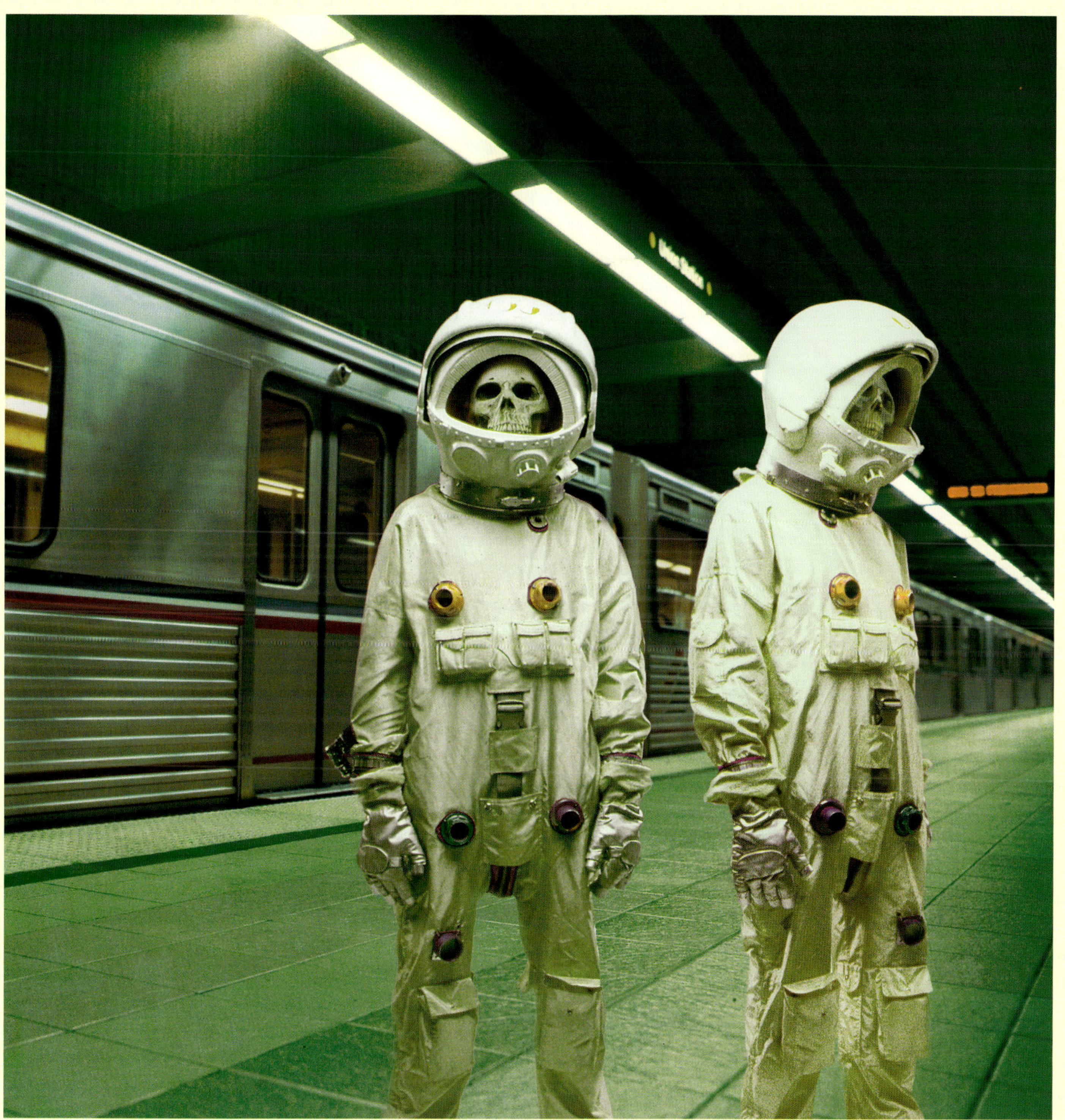

John Eder

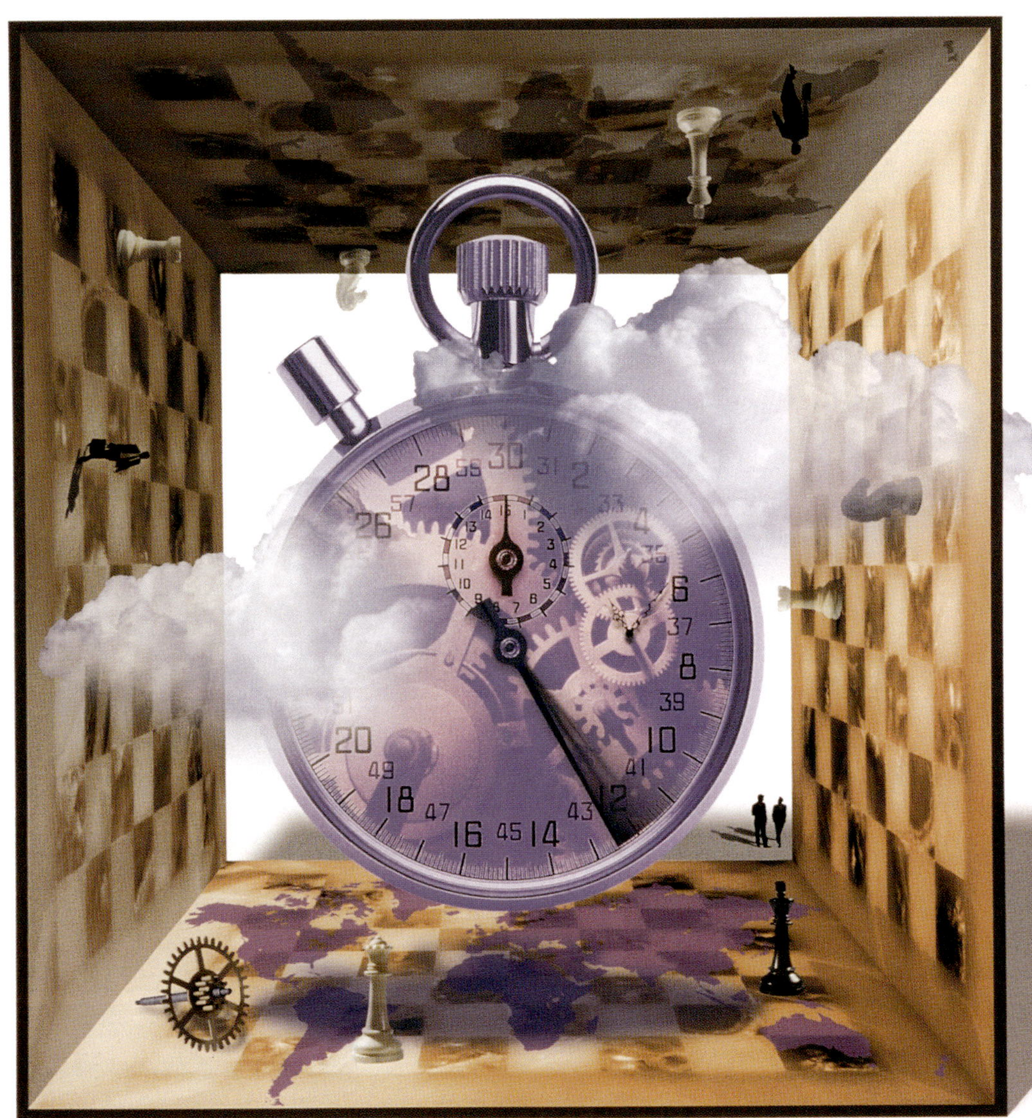

Russ **W**idstrand

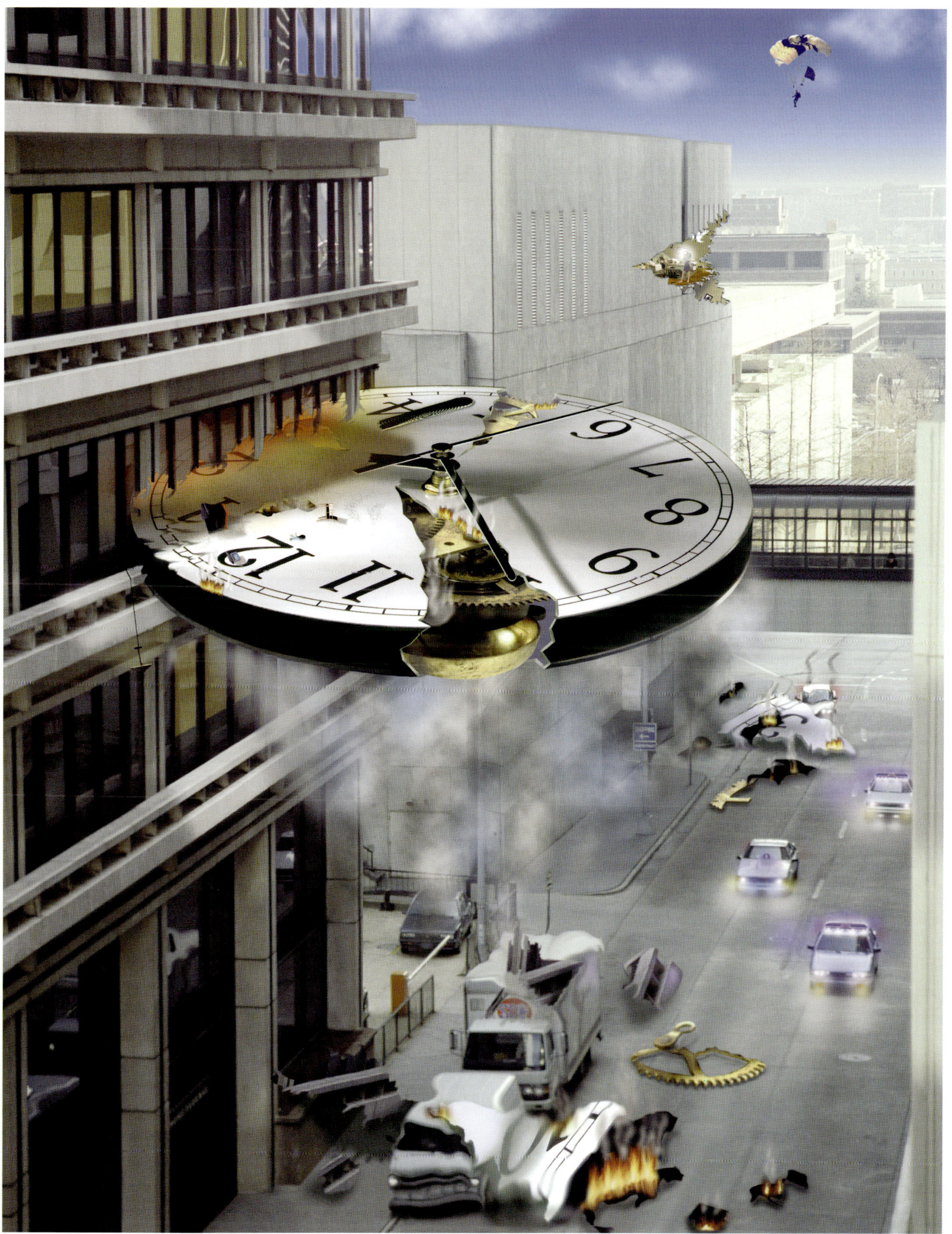

Mike McGlothlen

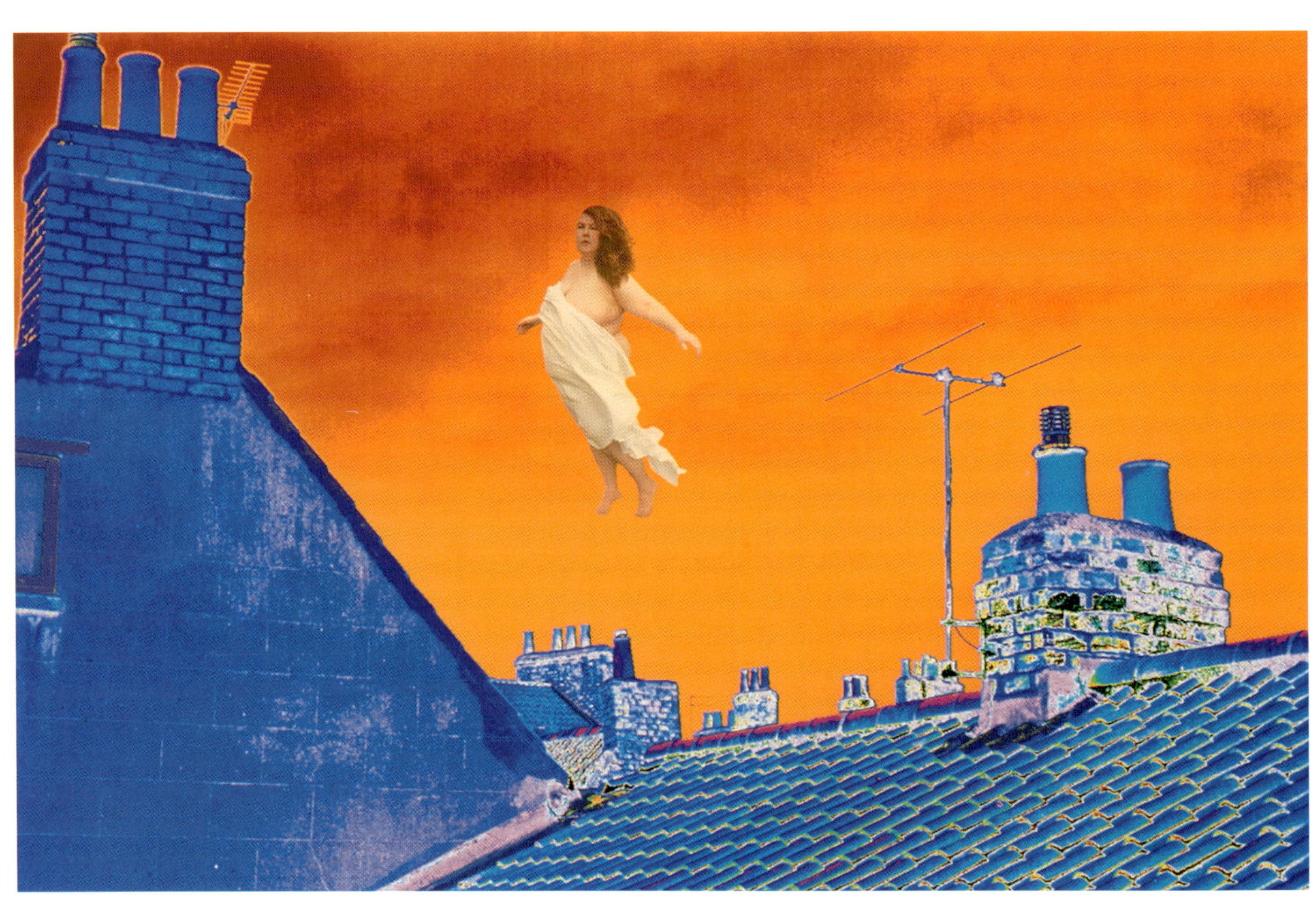

this page: **J**ames **S**tanley **D**augherty opposite: **S**ergio **S**pada

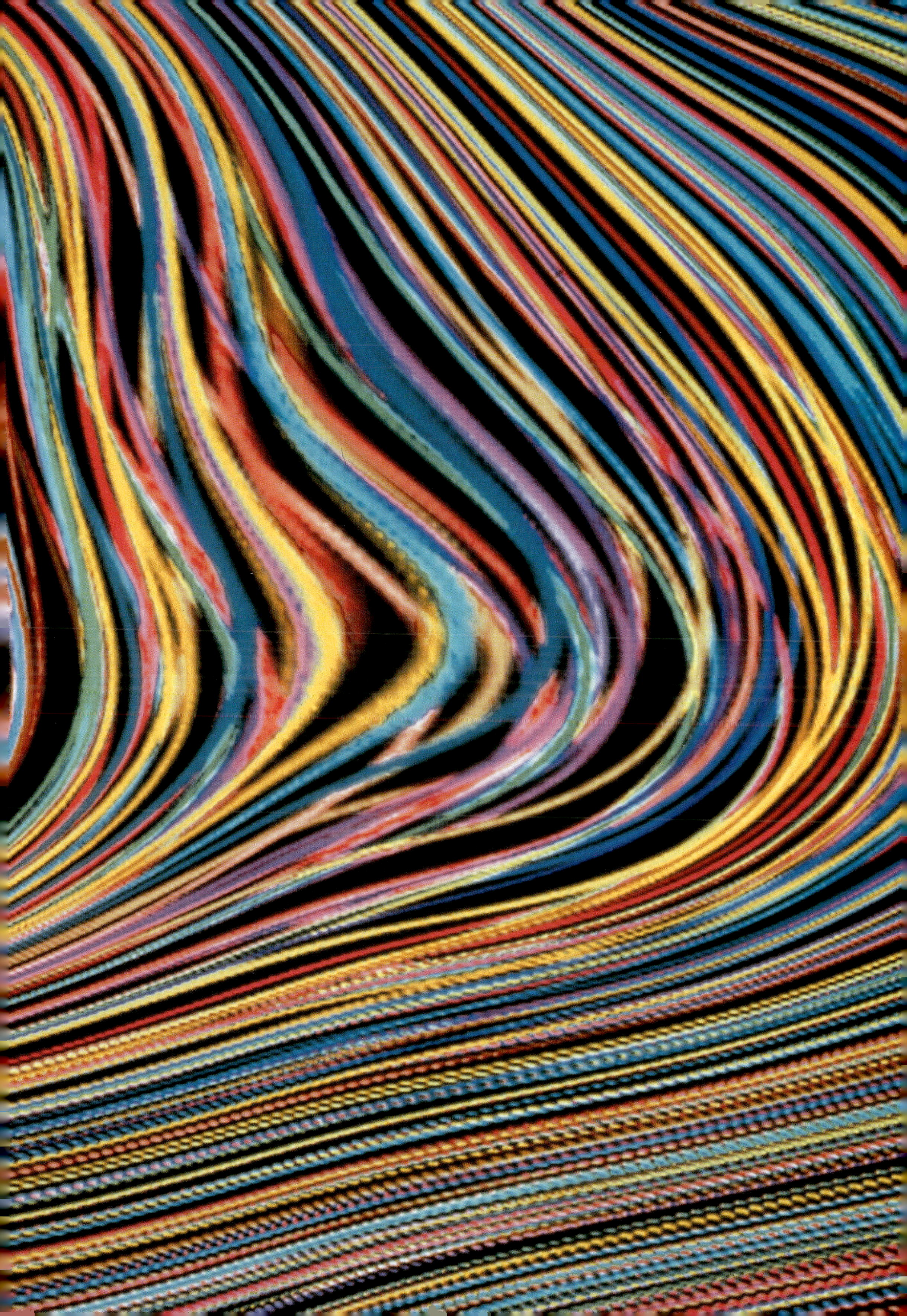

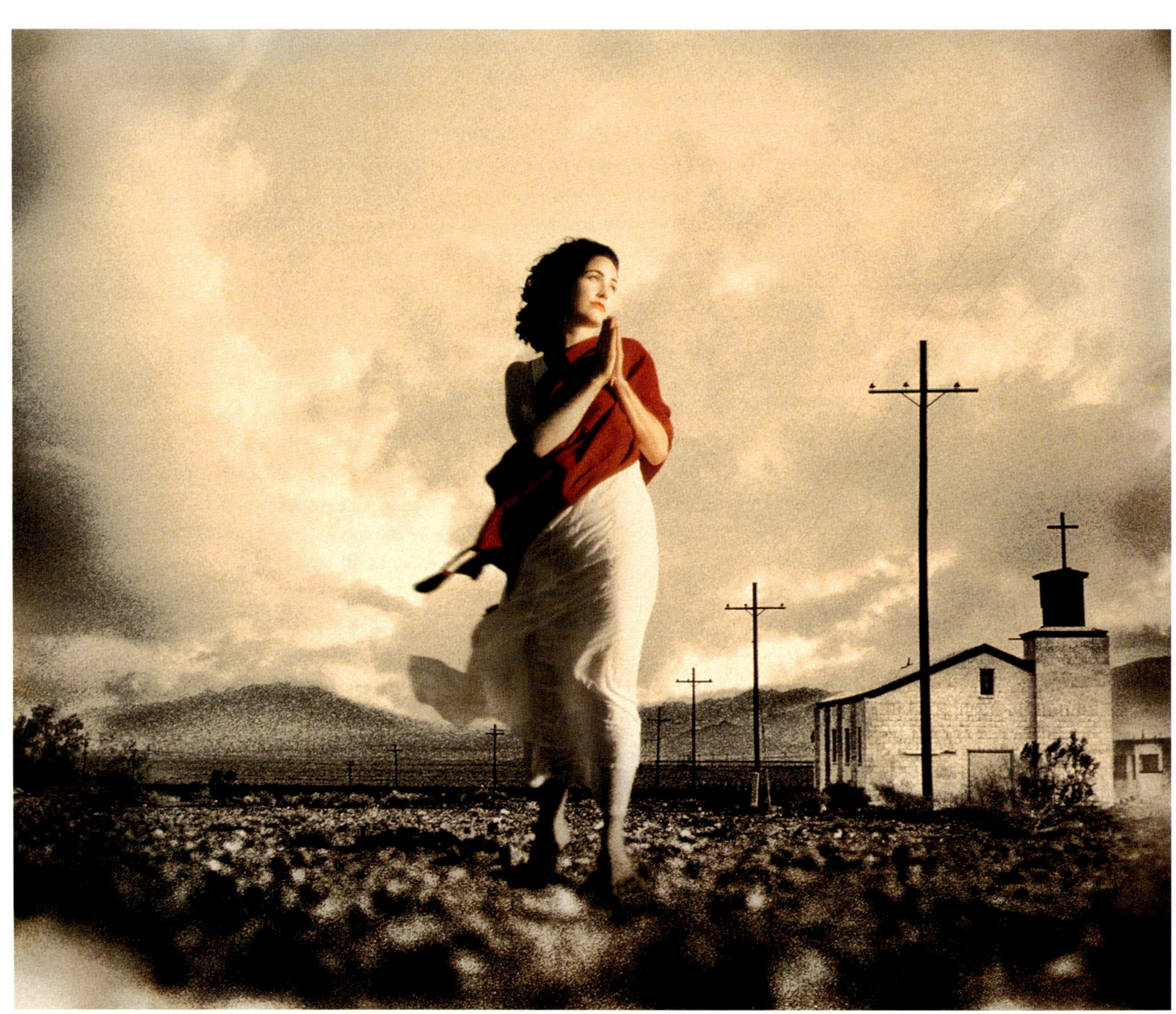

Jim **E**rickson

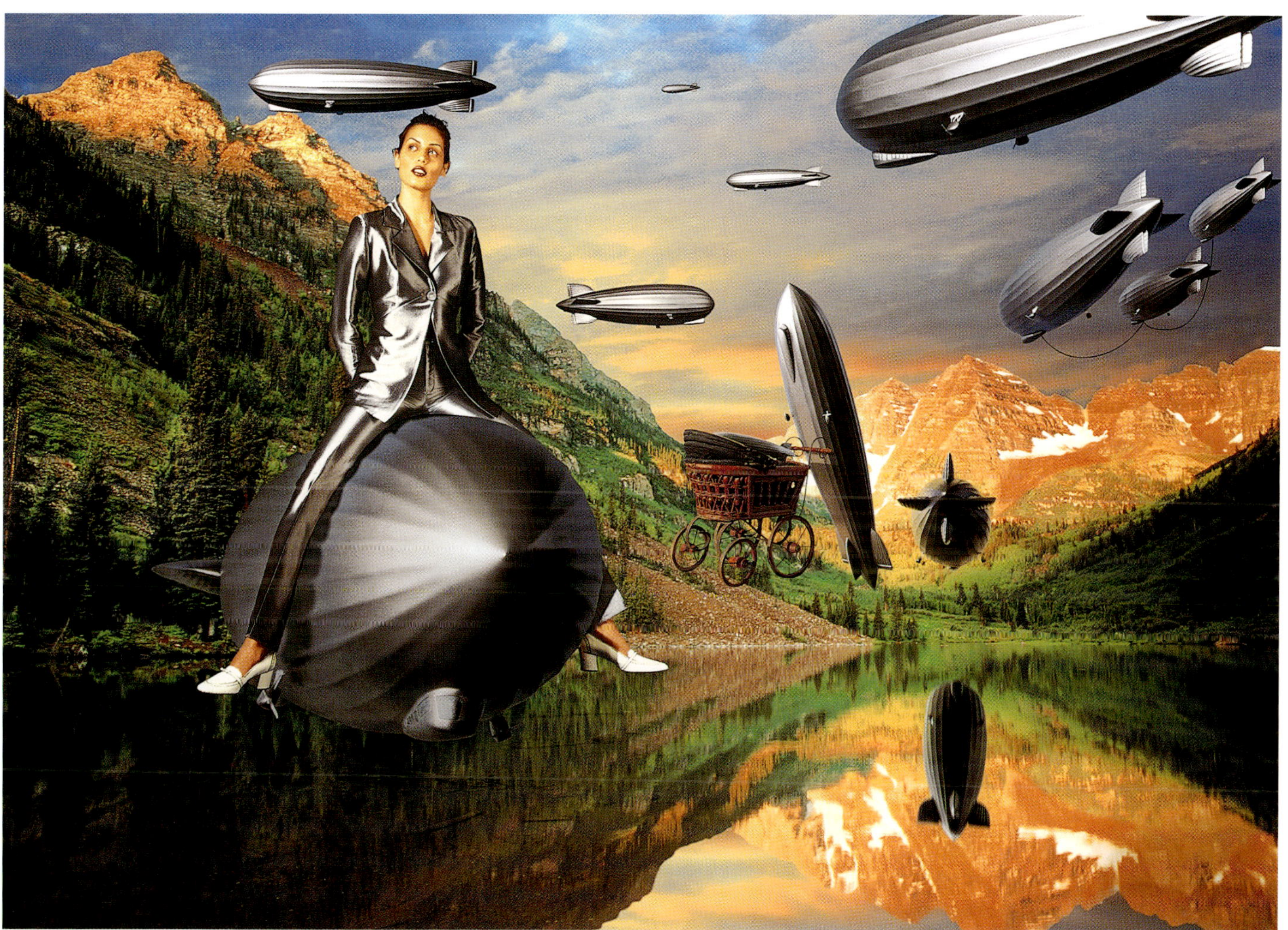

Fernando Zuffo

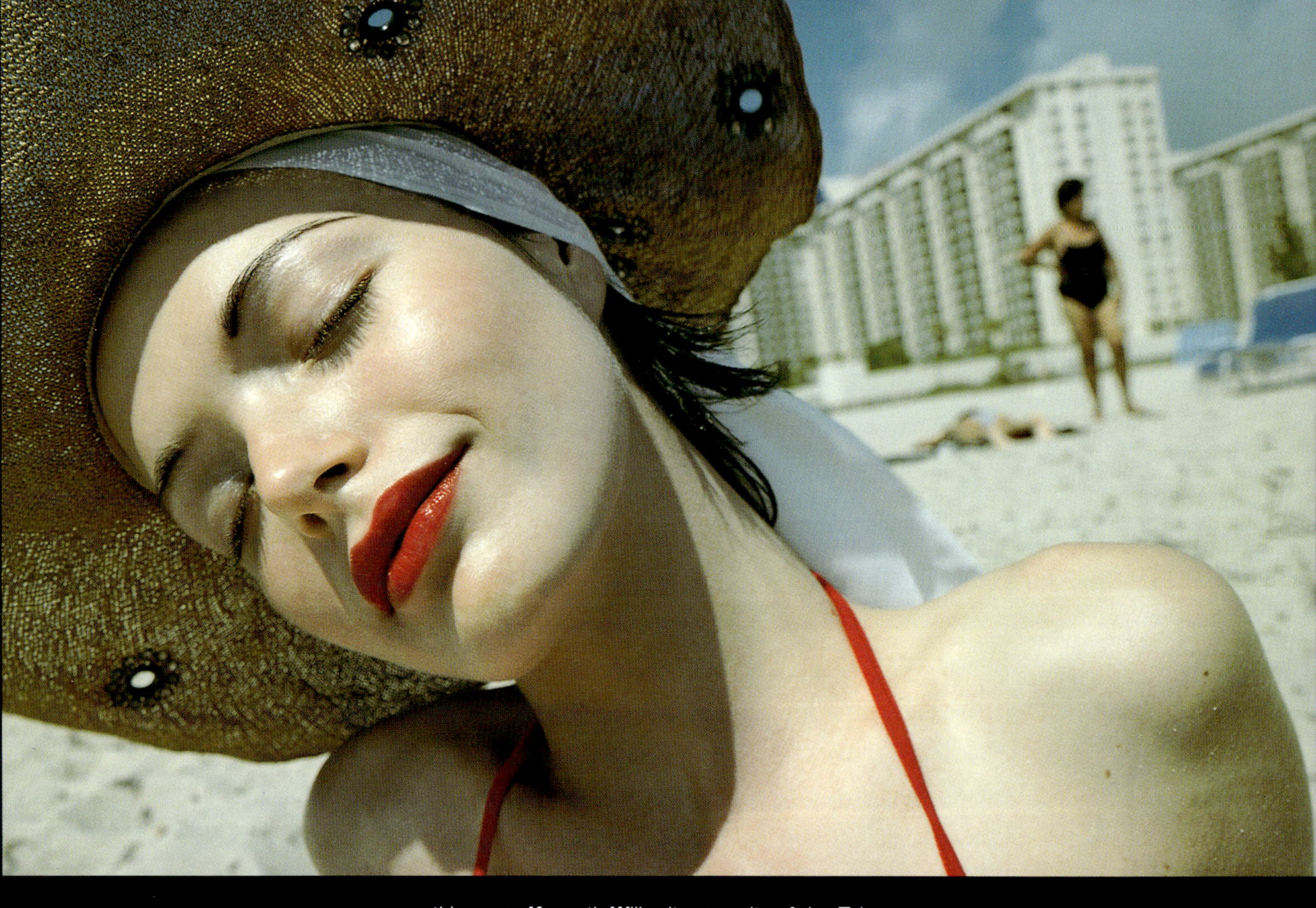

this page: **K**enneth **W**illardt opposite: **J**ohn **E**der

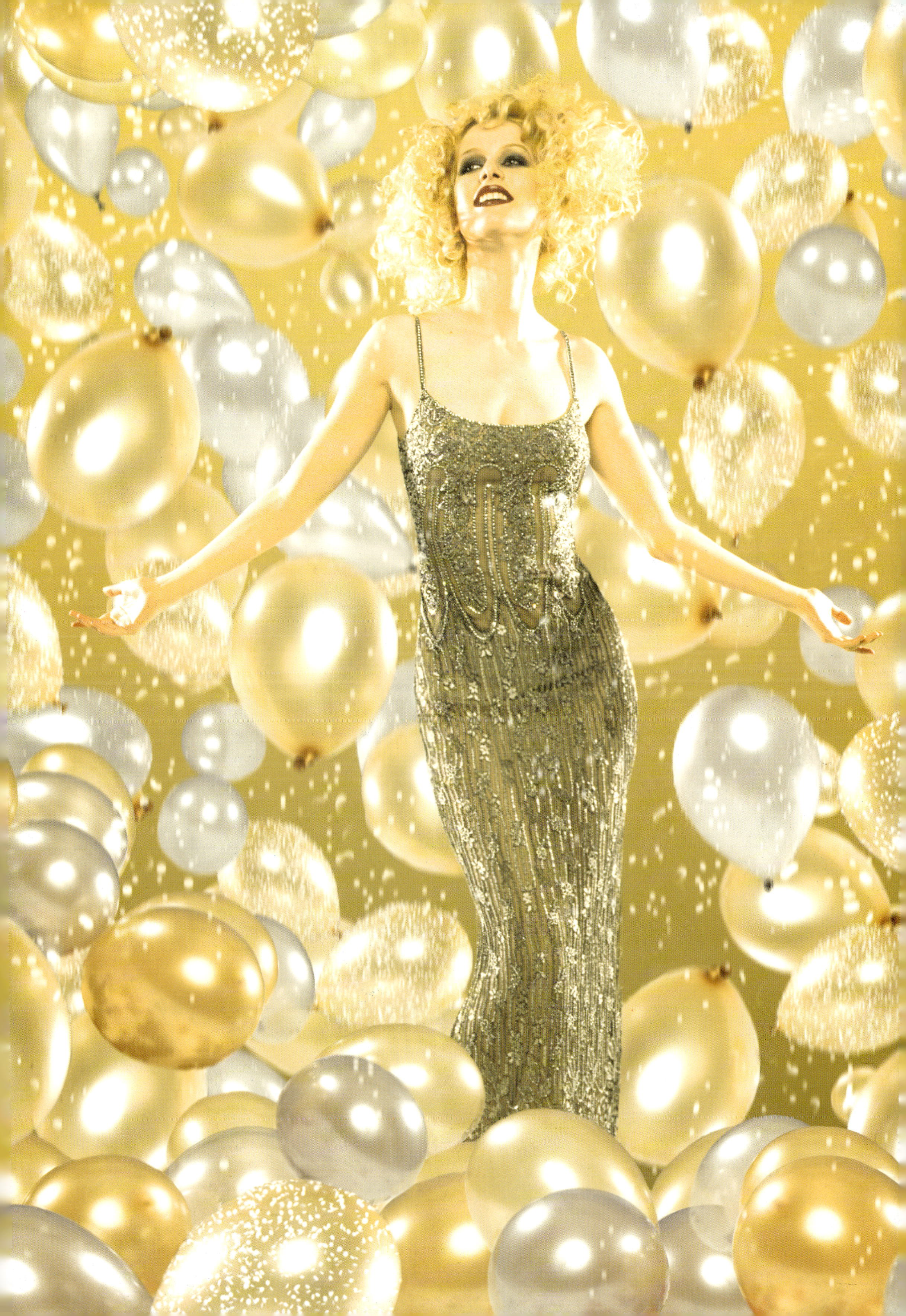

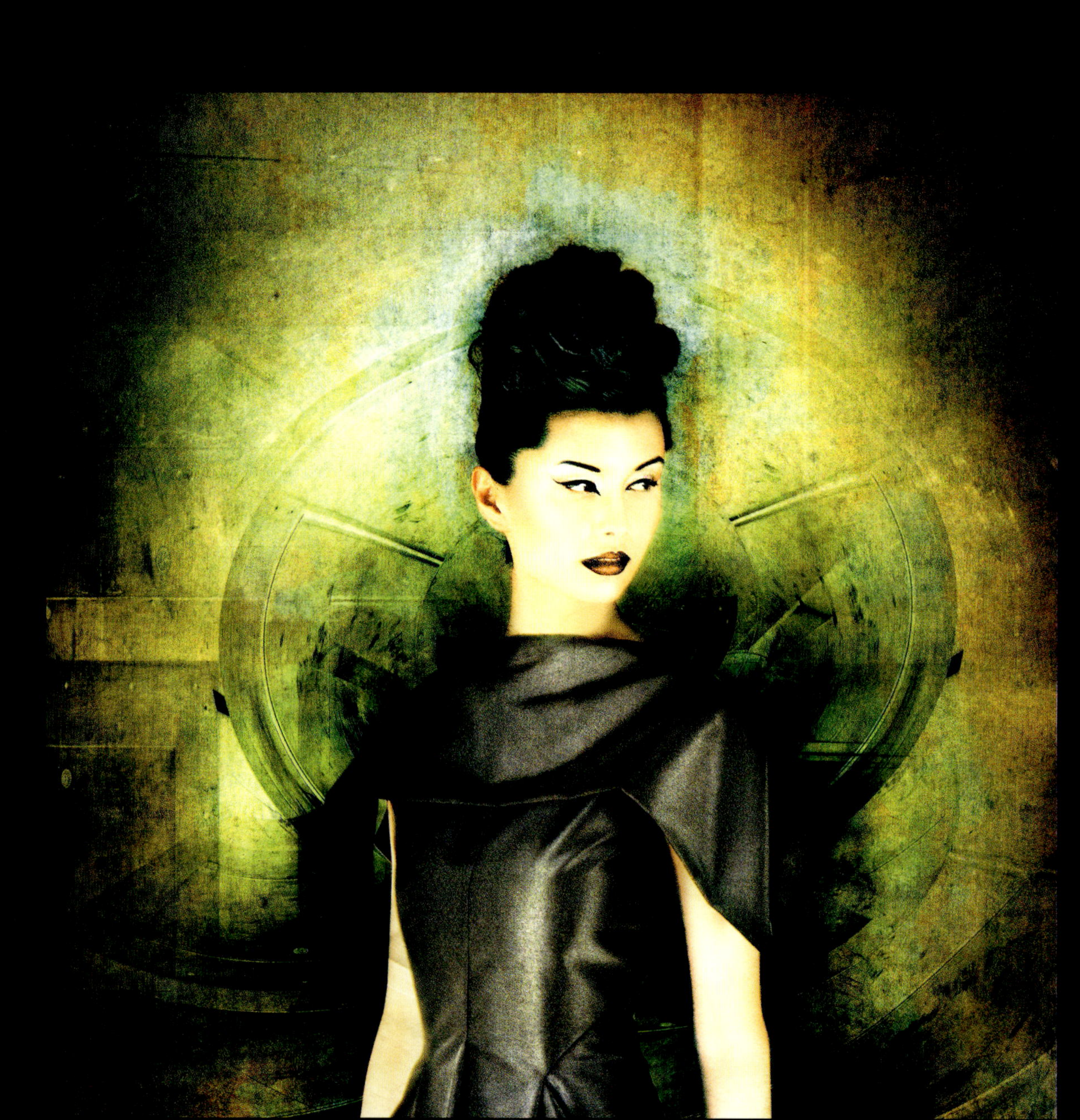

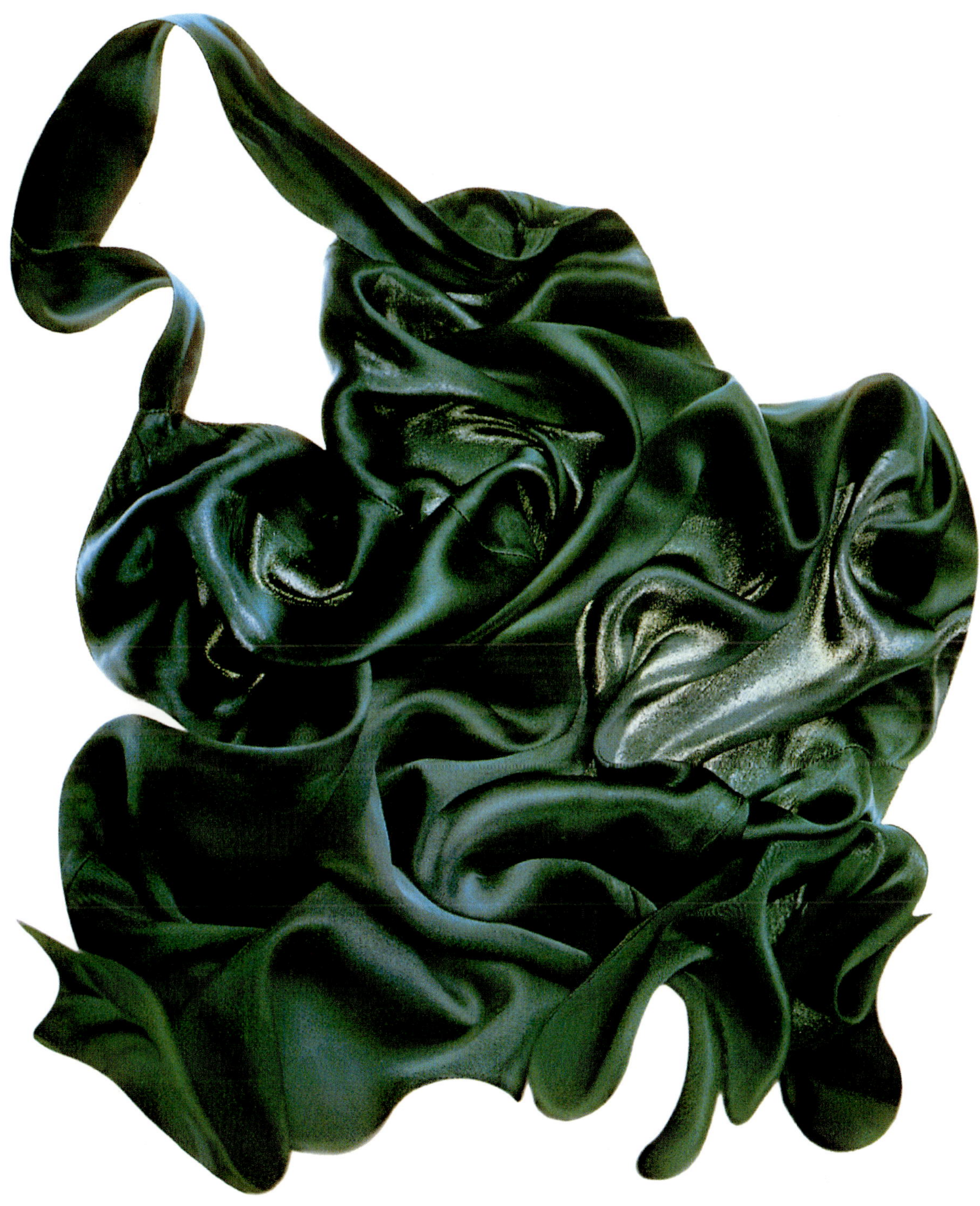

Barry **S**eidman

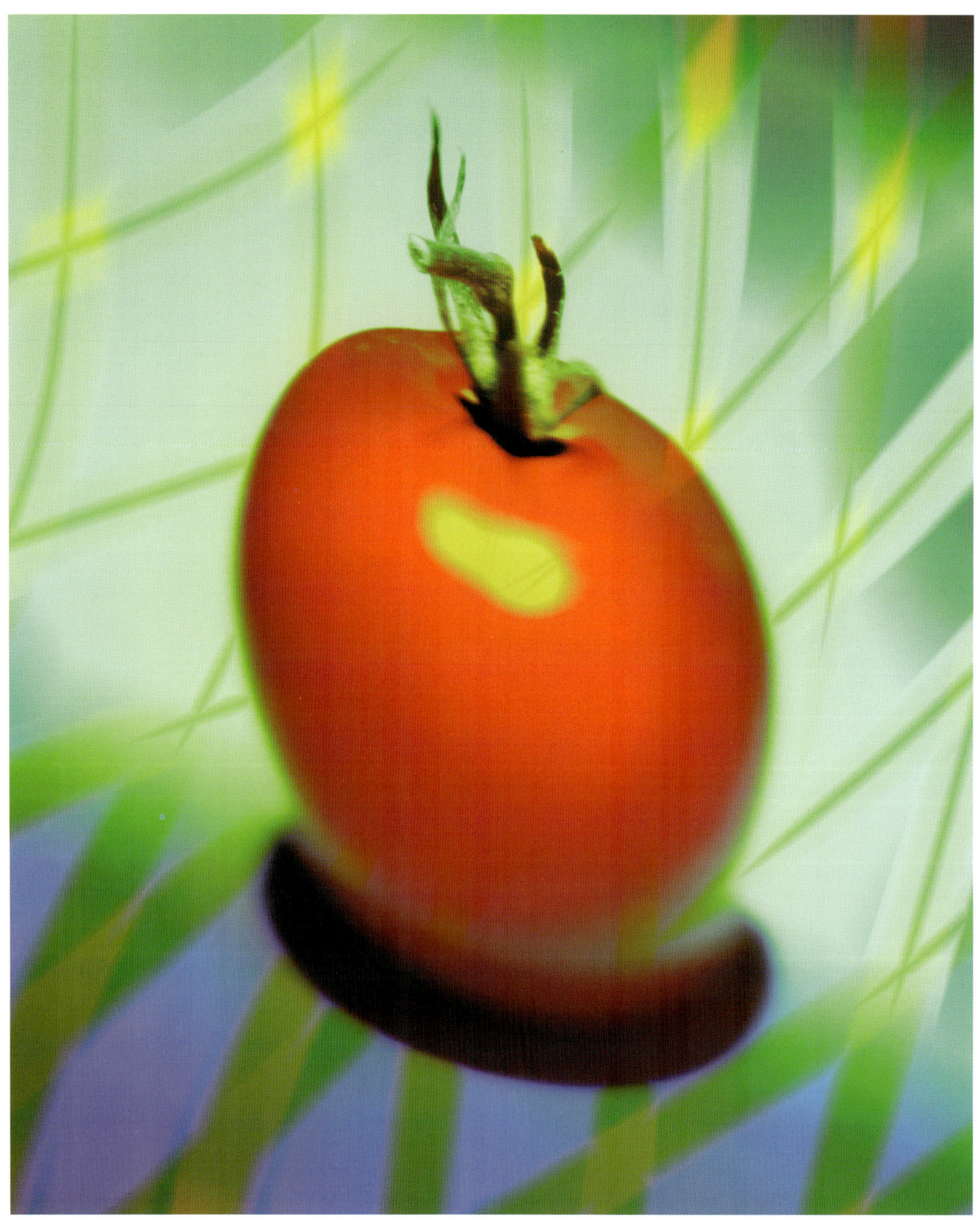

Judy Hermann, Michael Starke

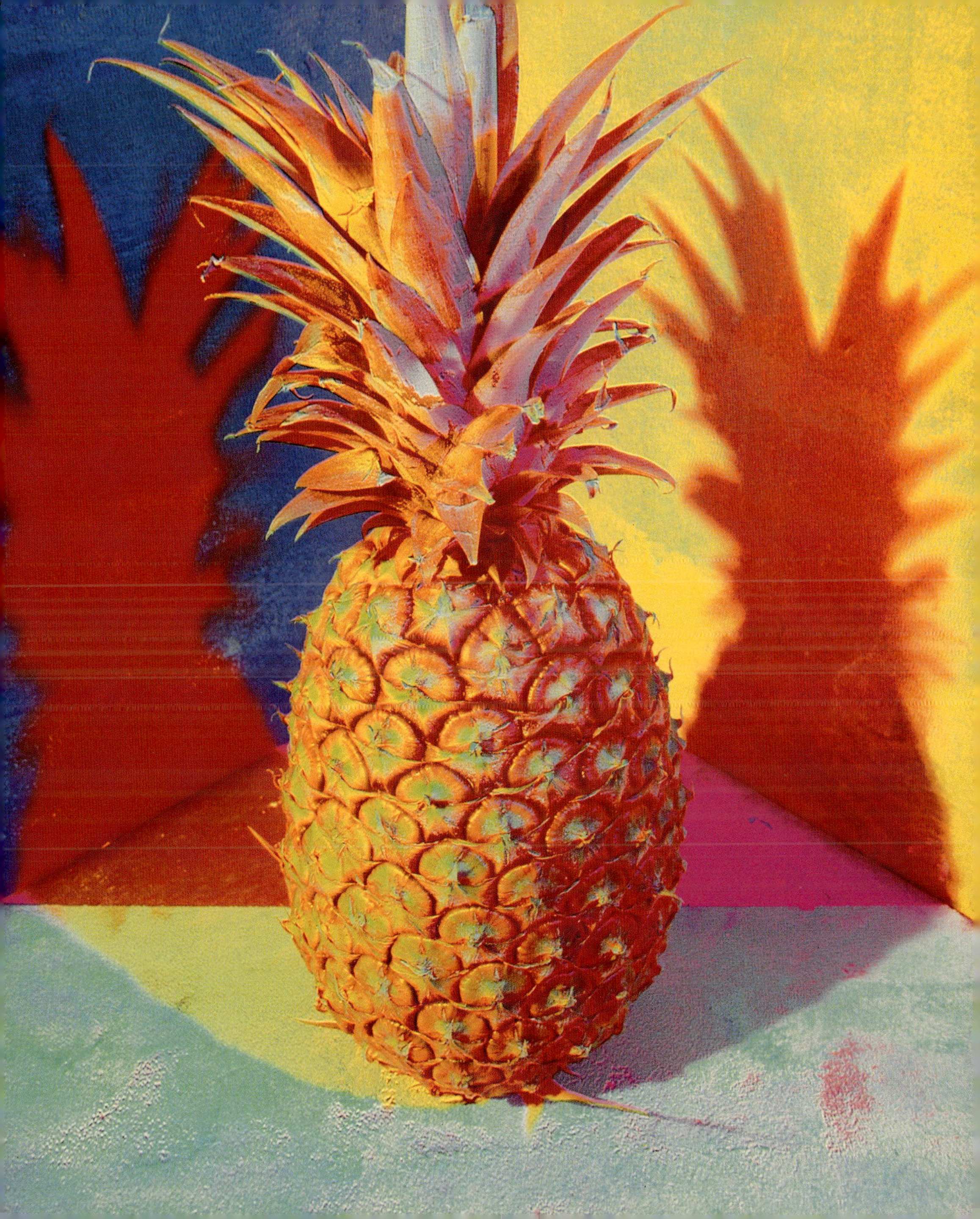

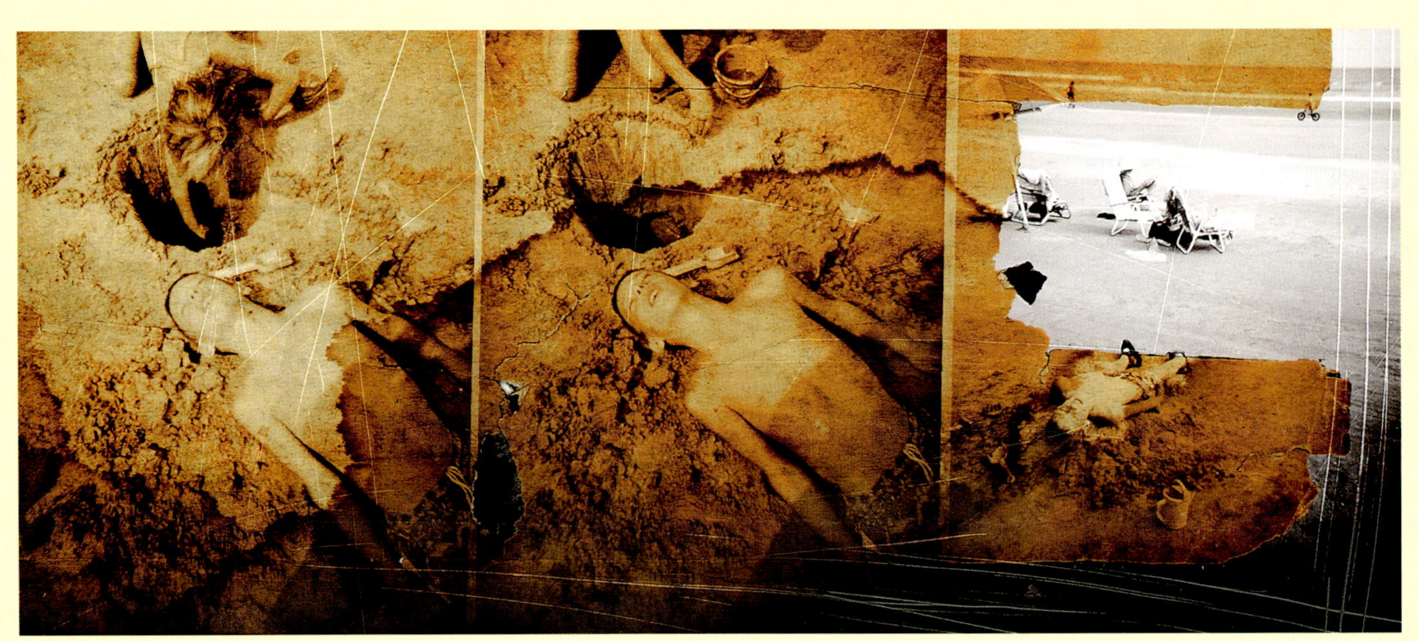

this page: **S**cott **F**erguson opposite: **L**ynn **S**ugarman

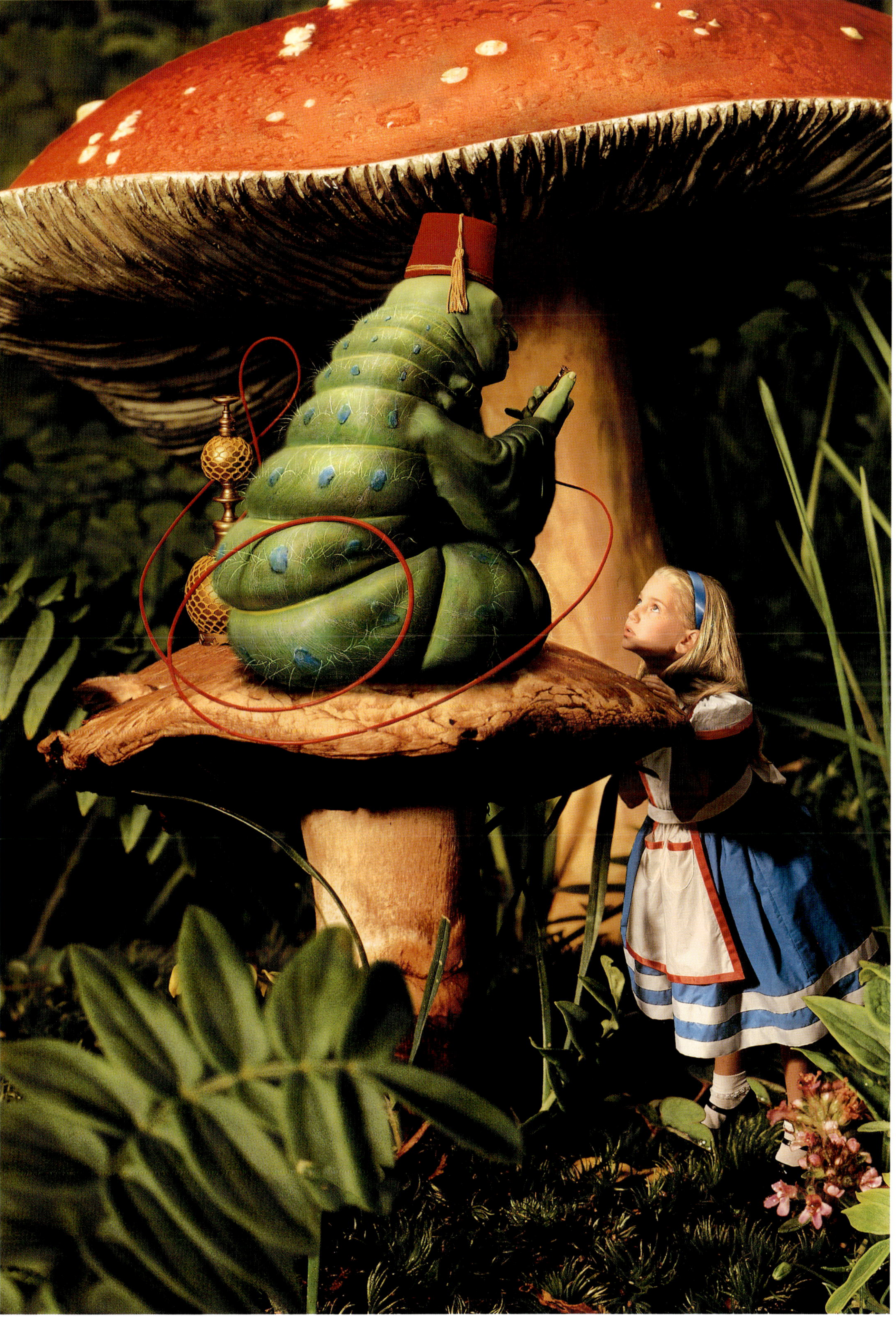

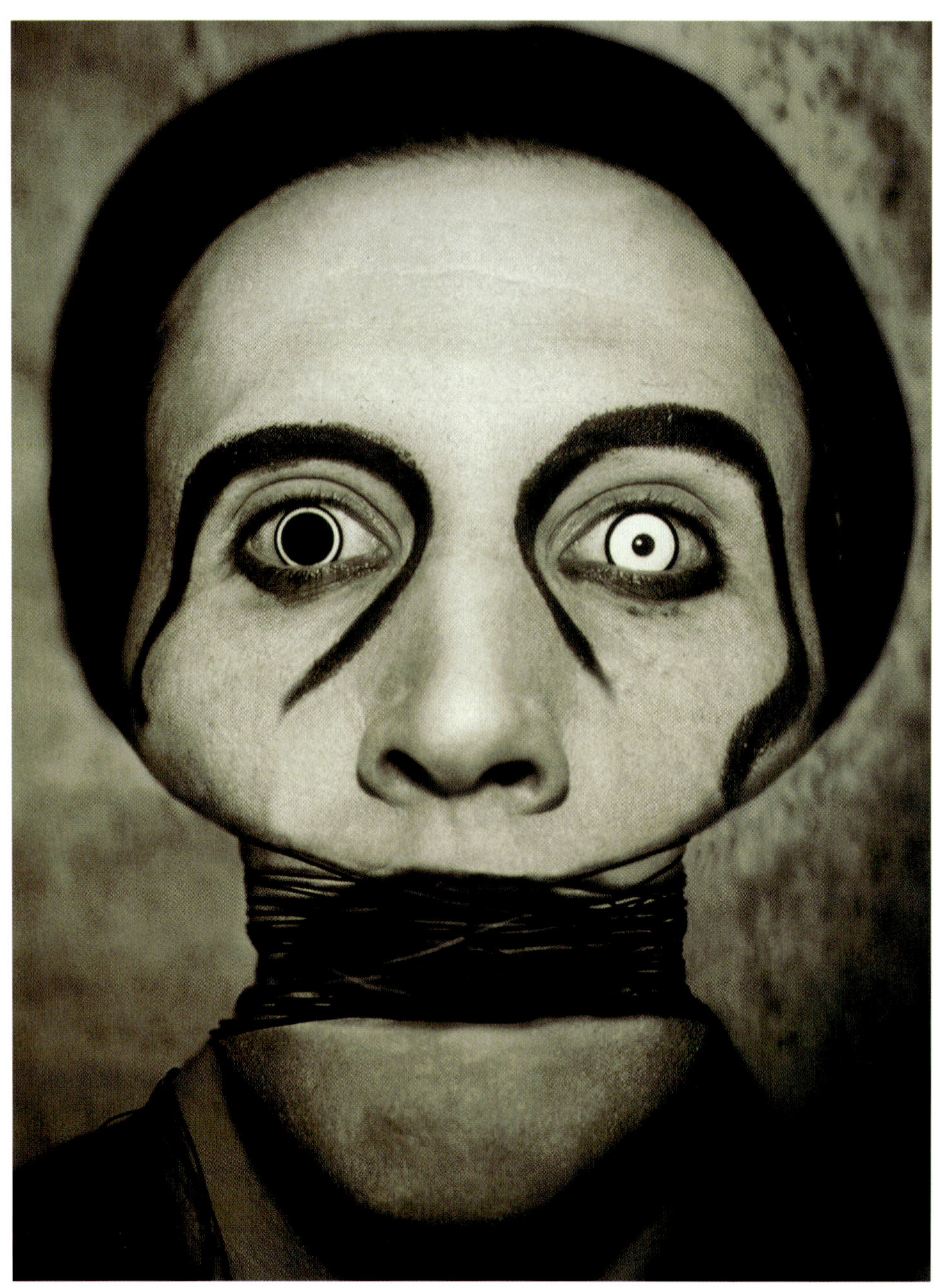

this spread: **M**att **M**ahurin

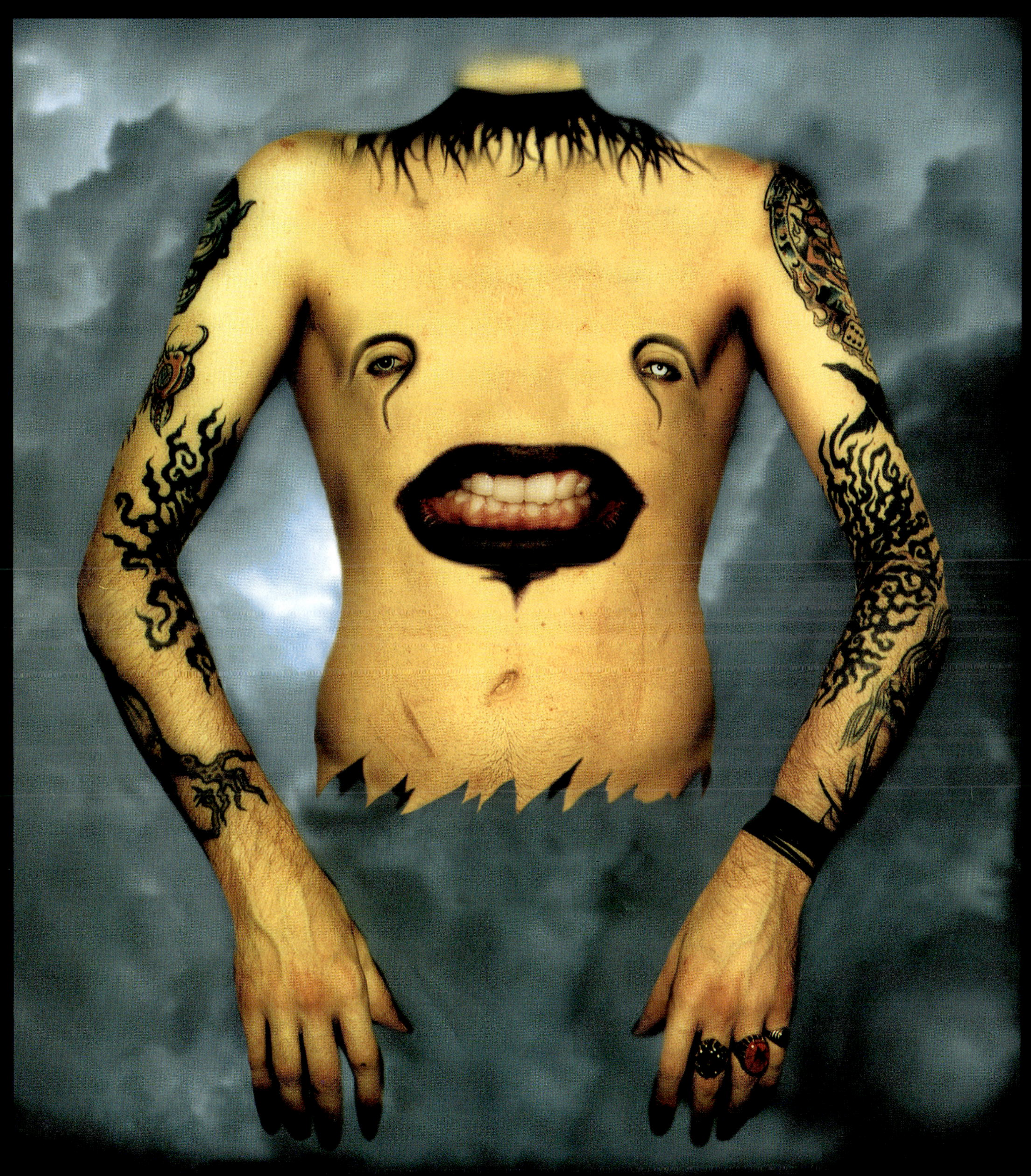

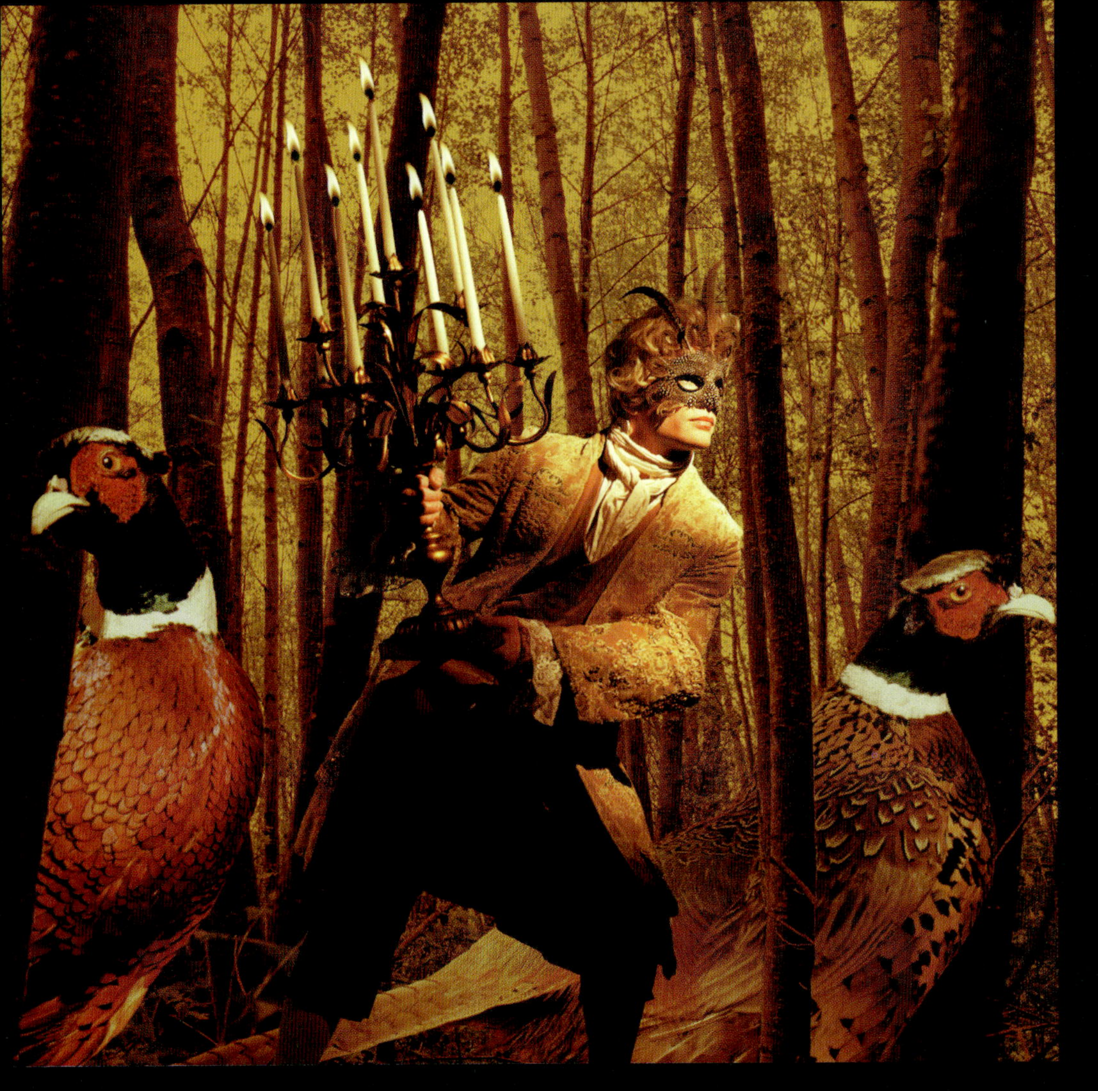

Alan Abrams, Francesca Lacagnina

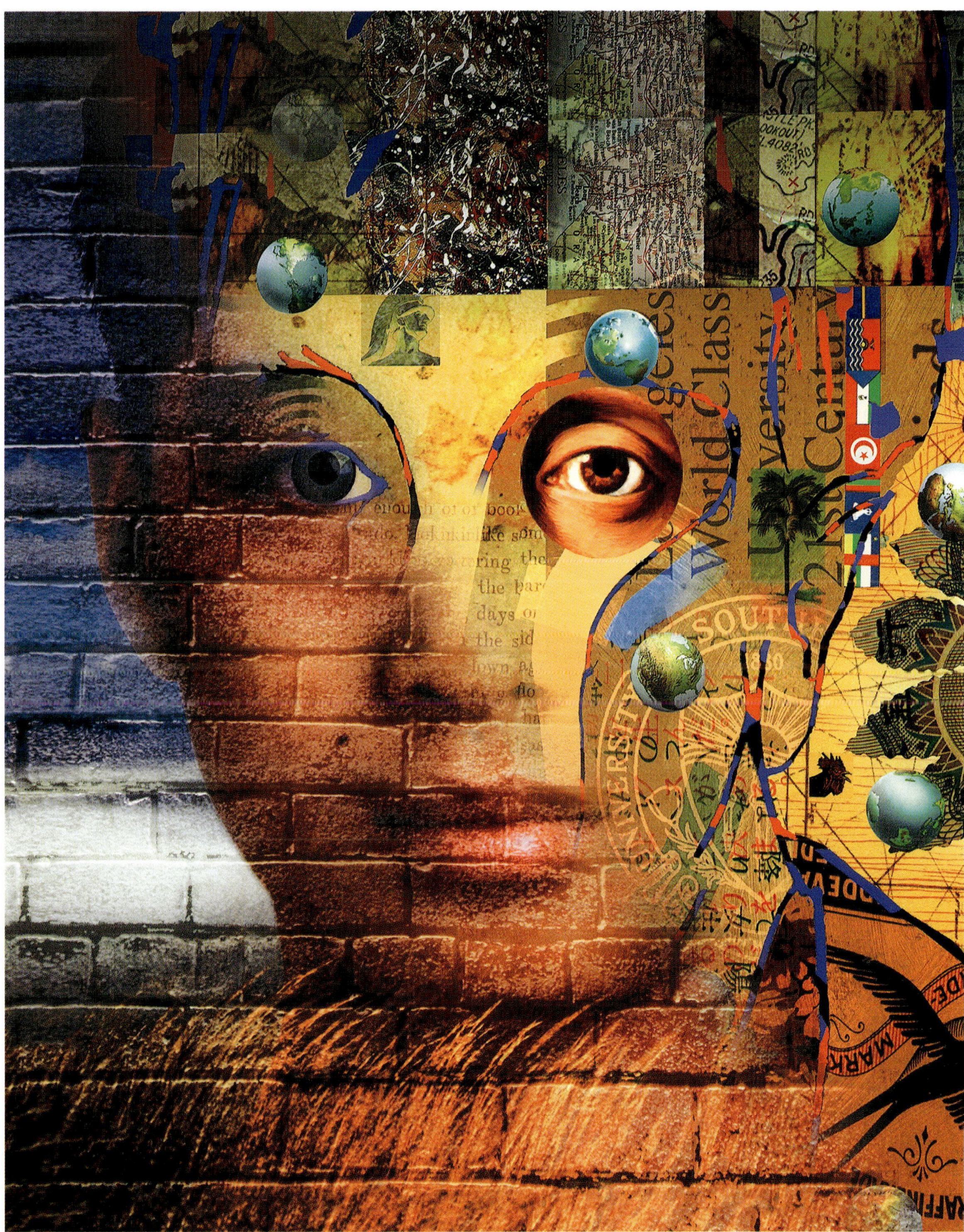

Charly Franklin

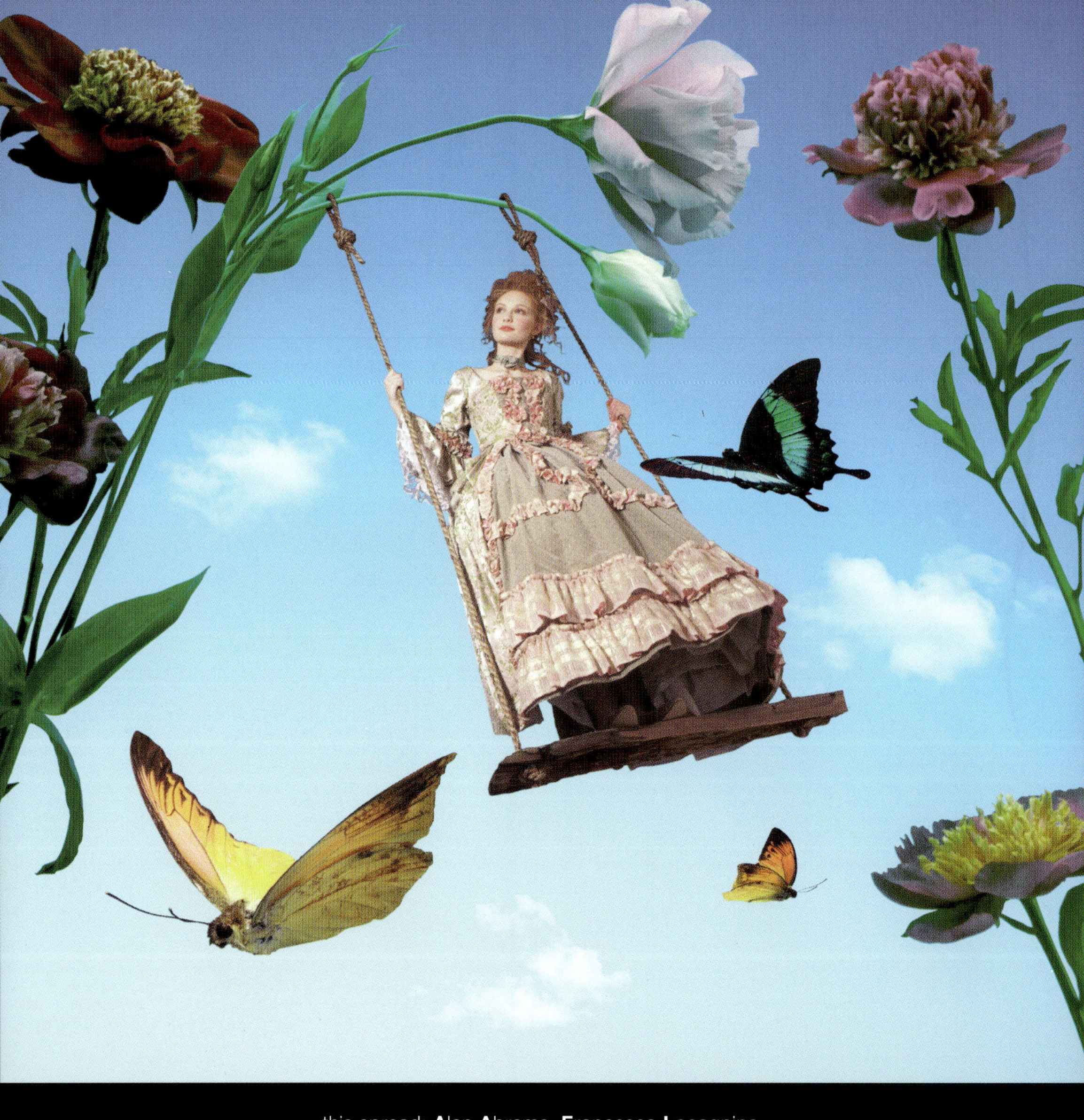

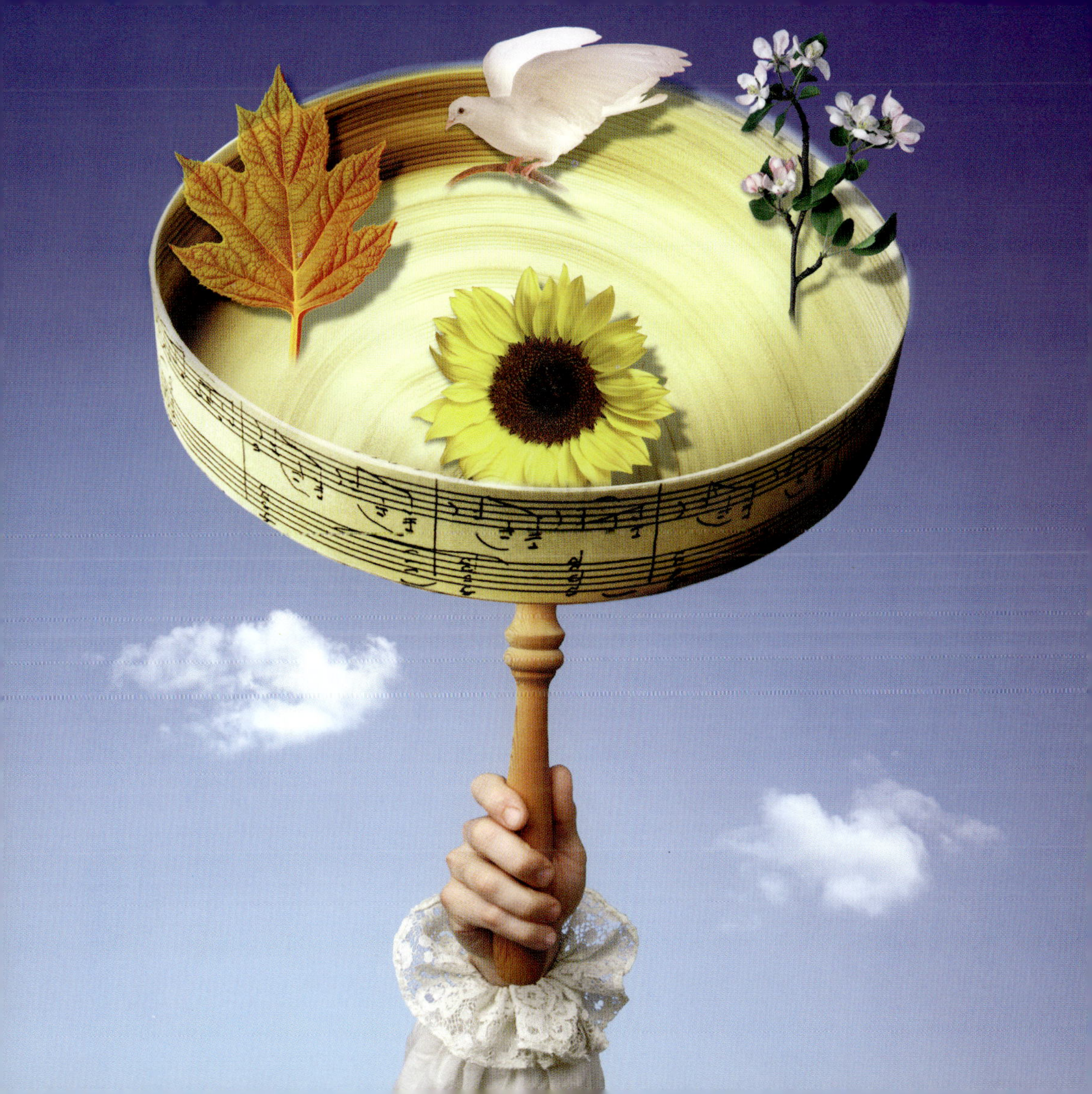

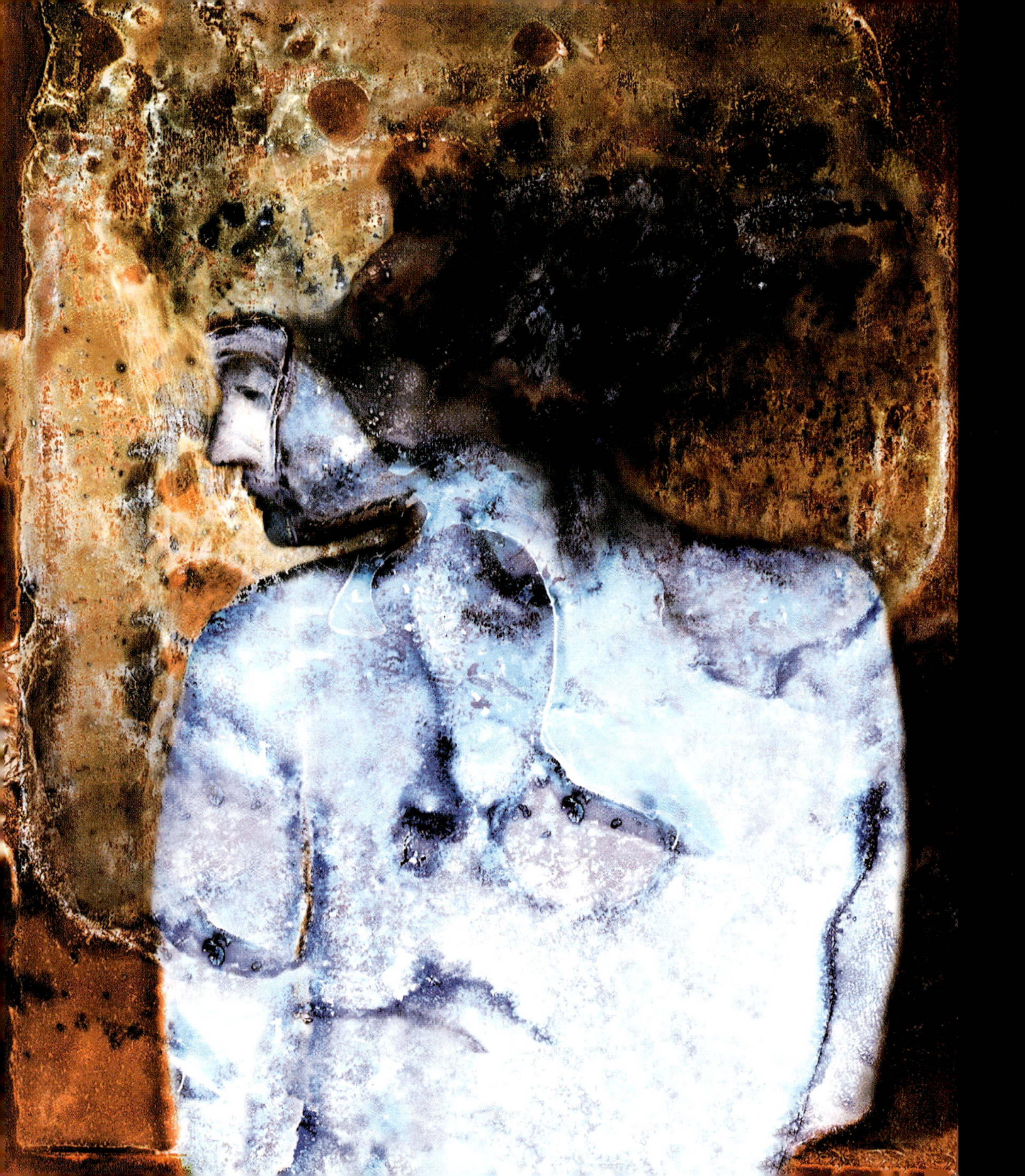

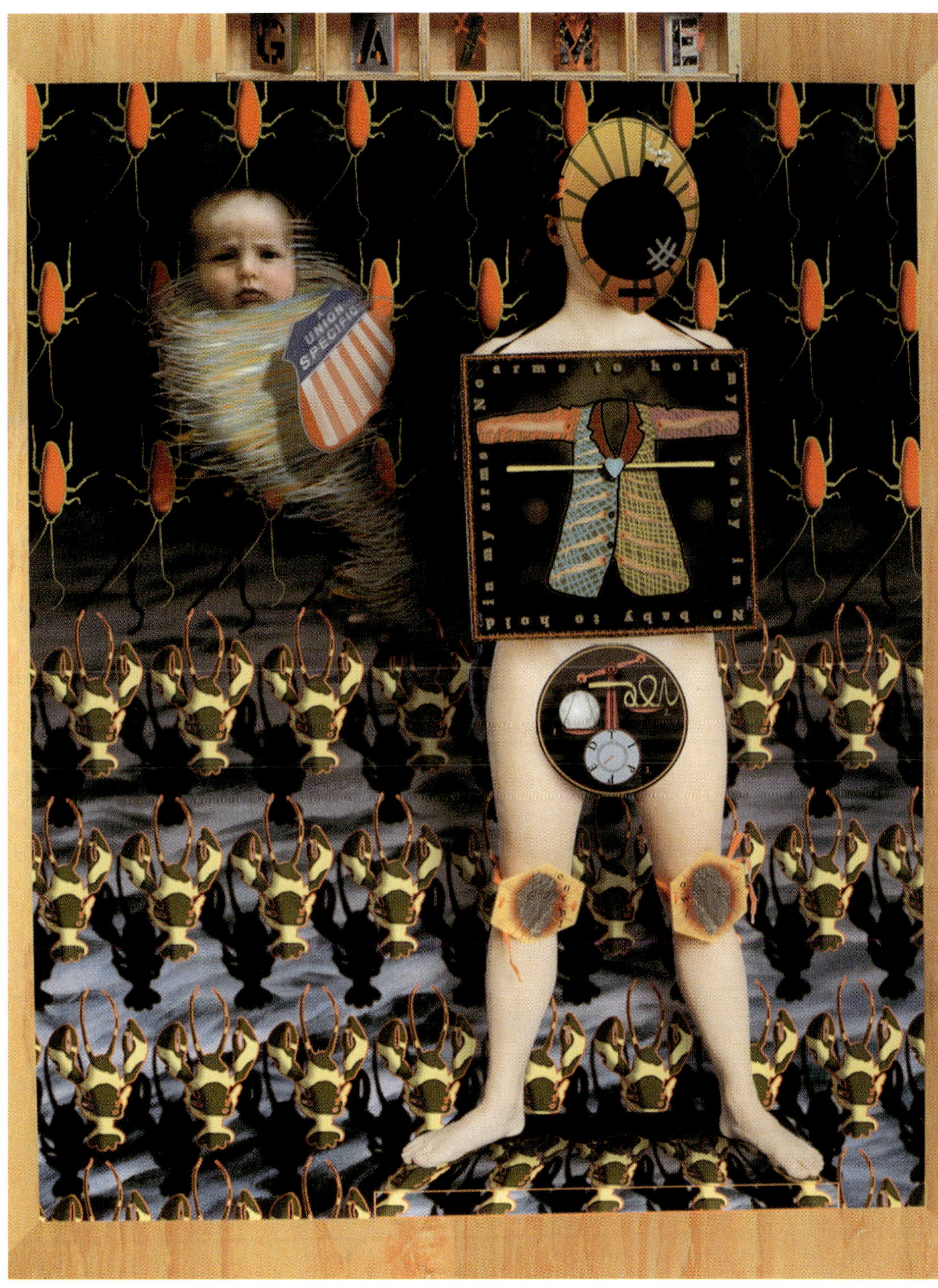

Steven J. Bliss

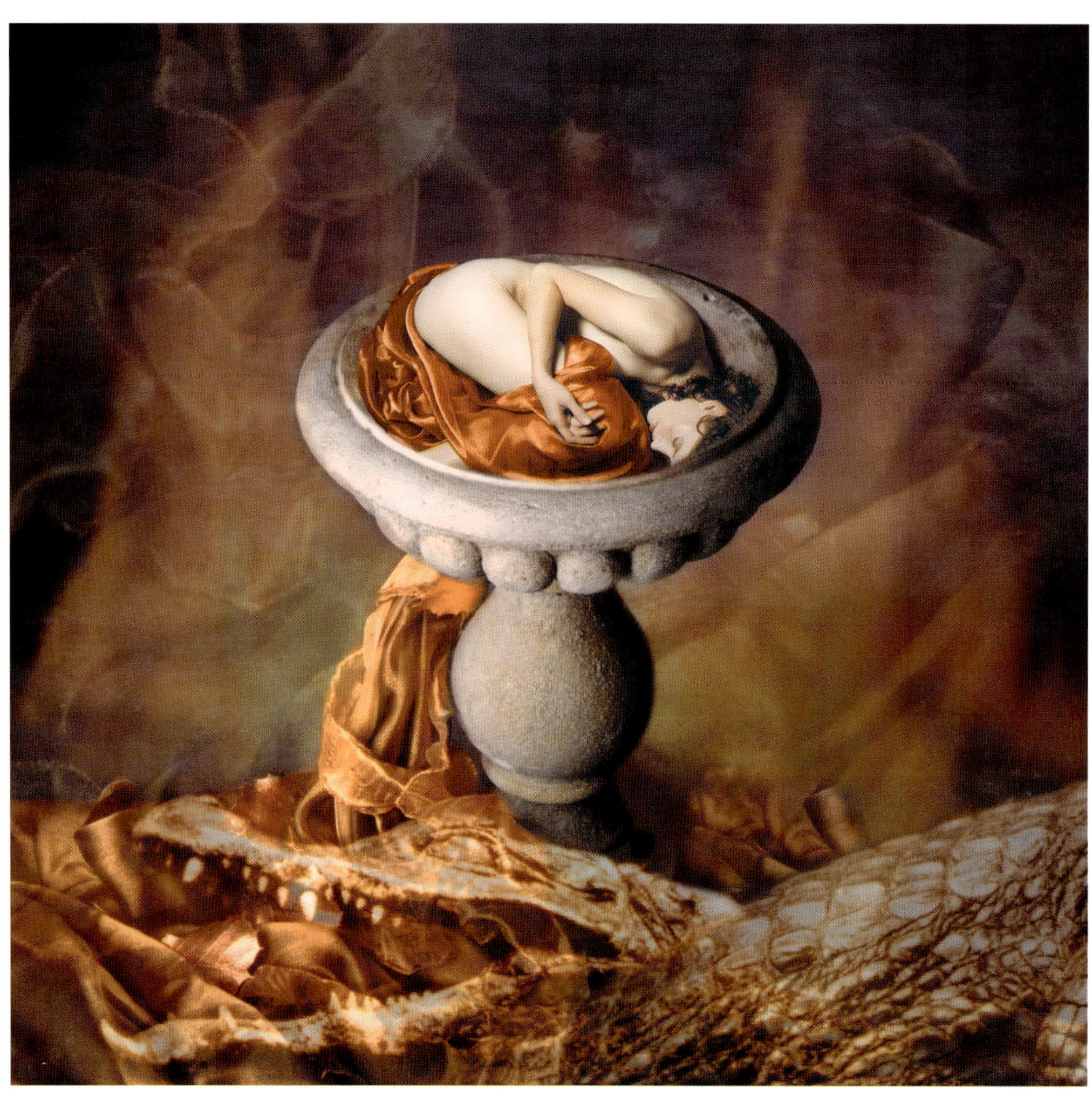

Jules Maclachlan

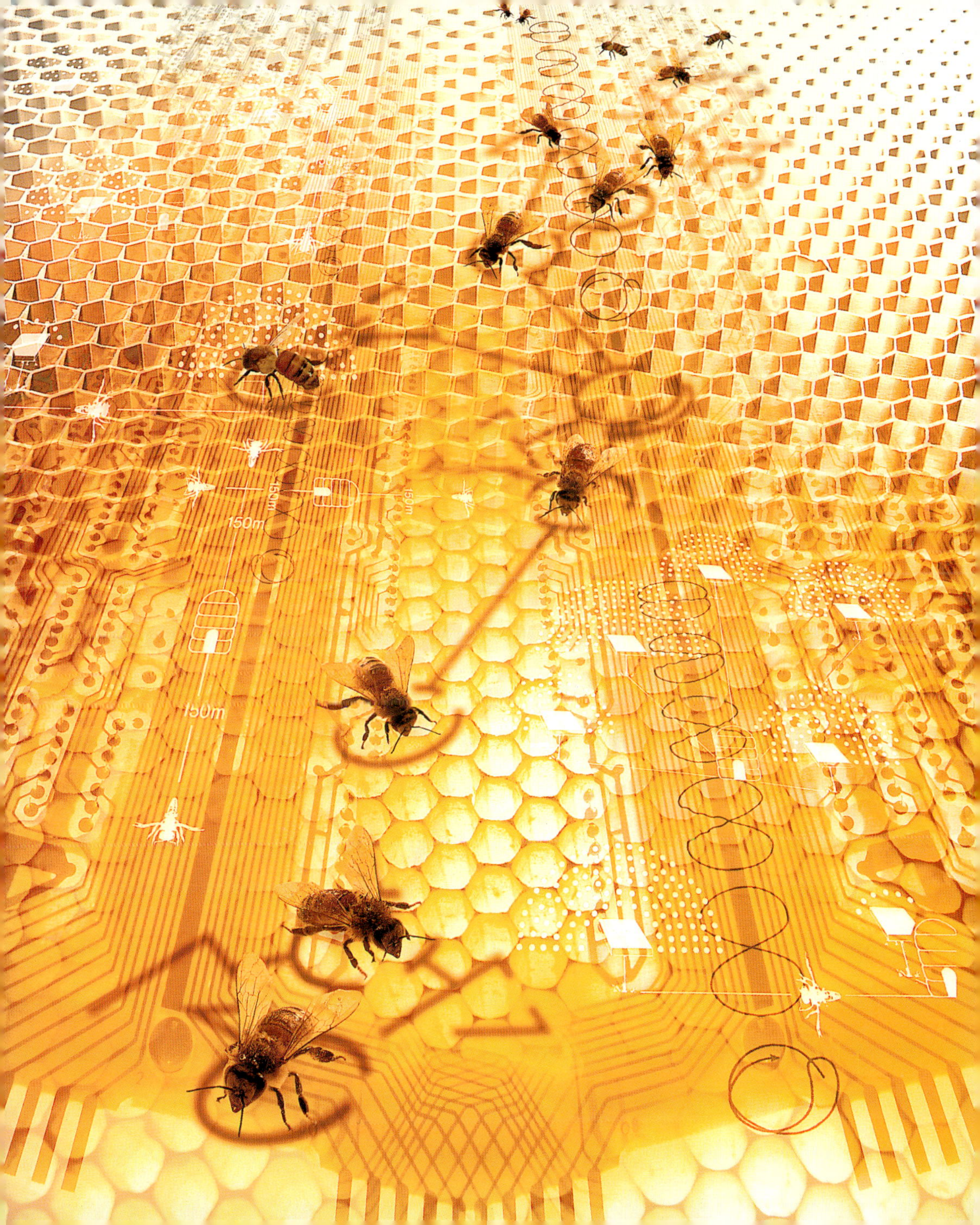

150m
150m
150m
150m

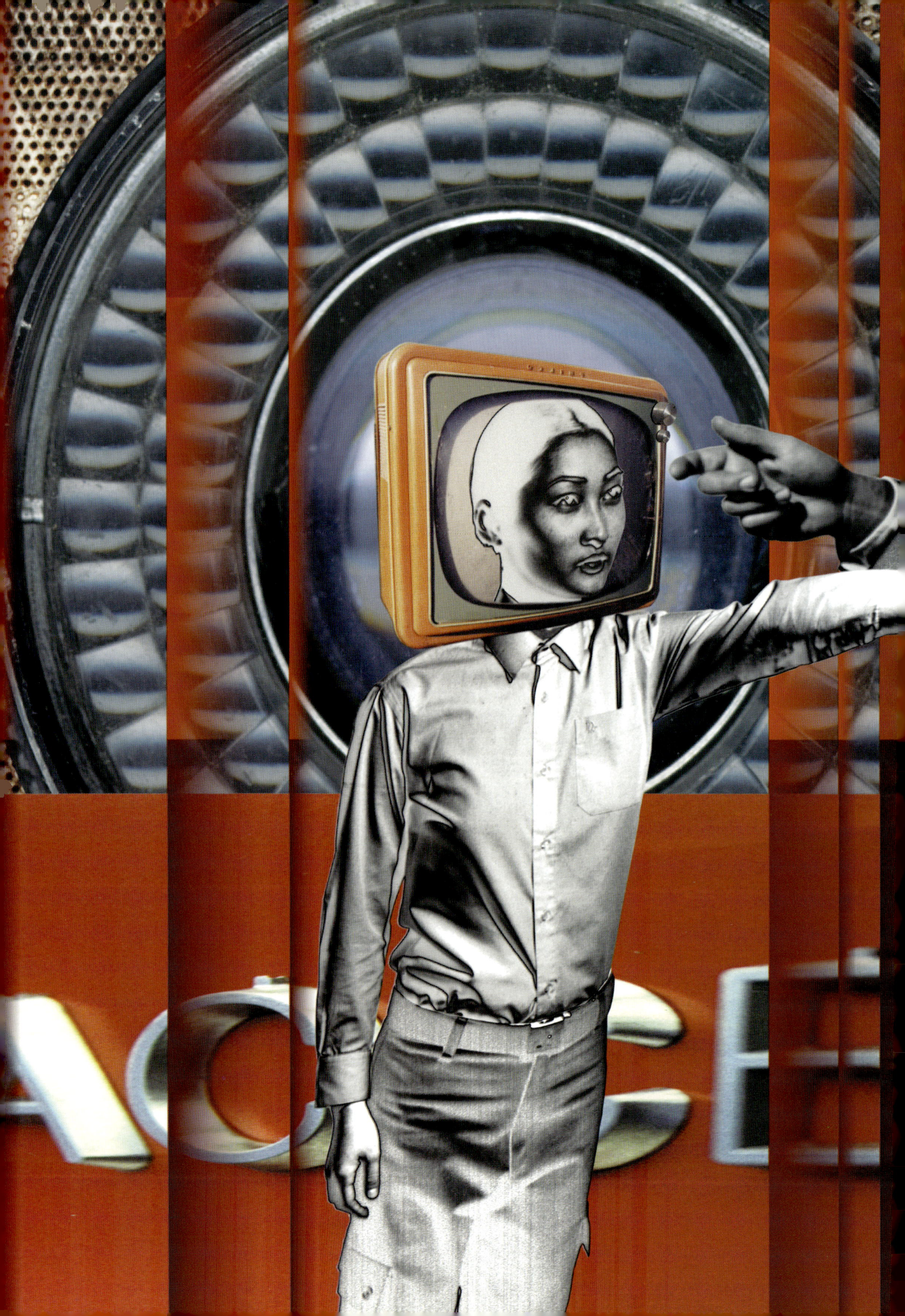

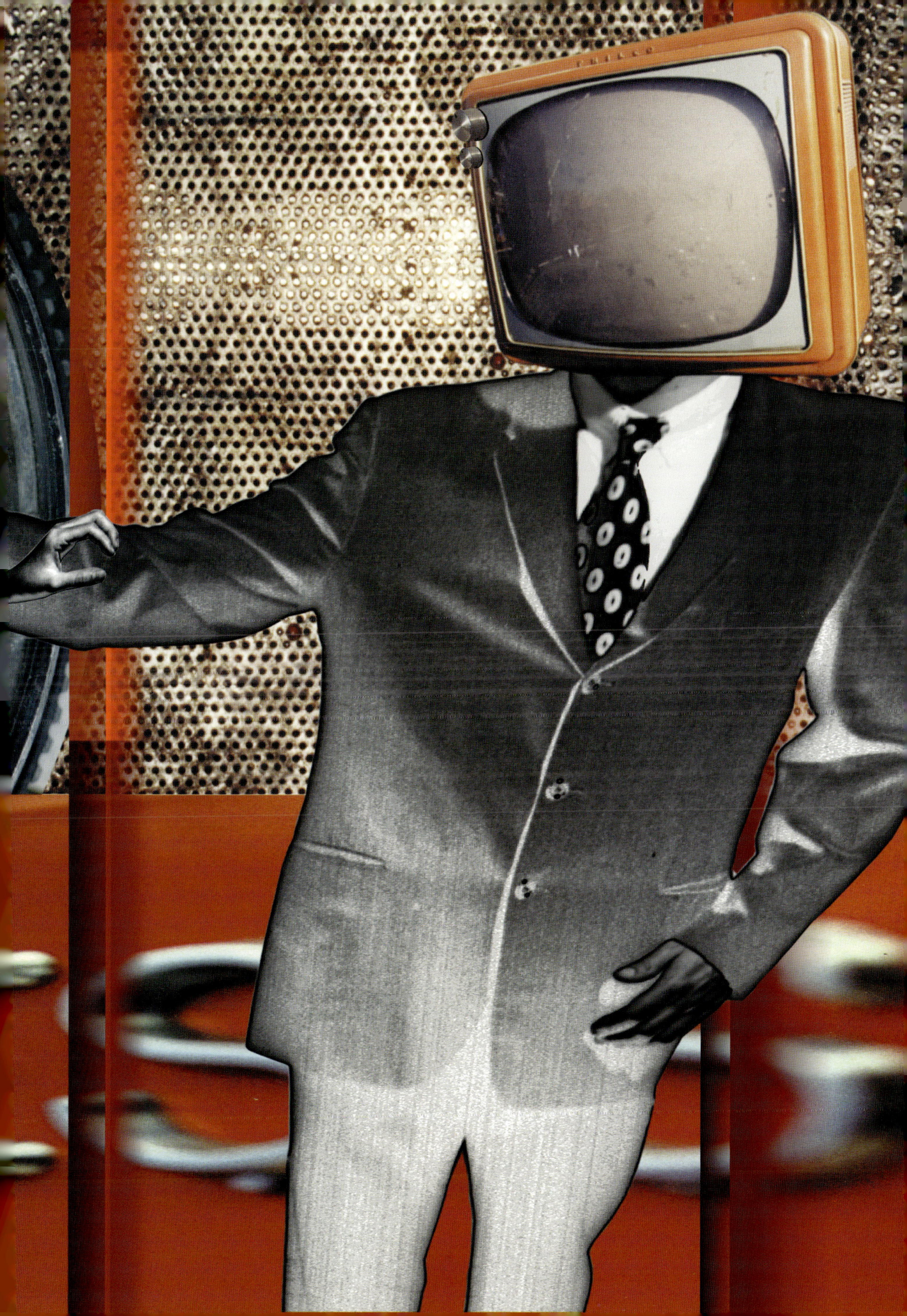

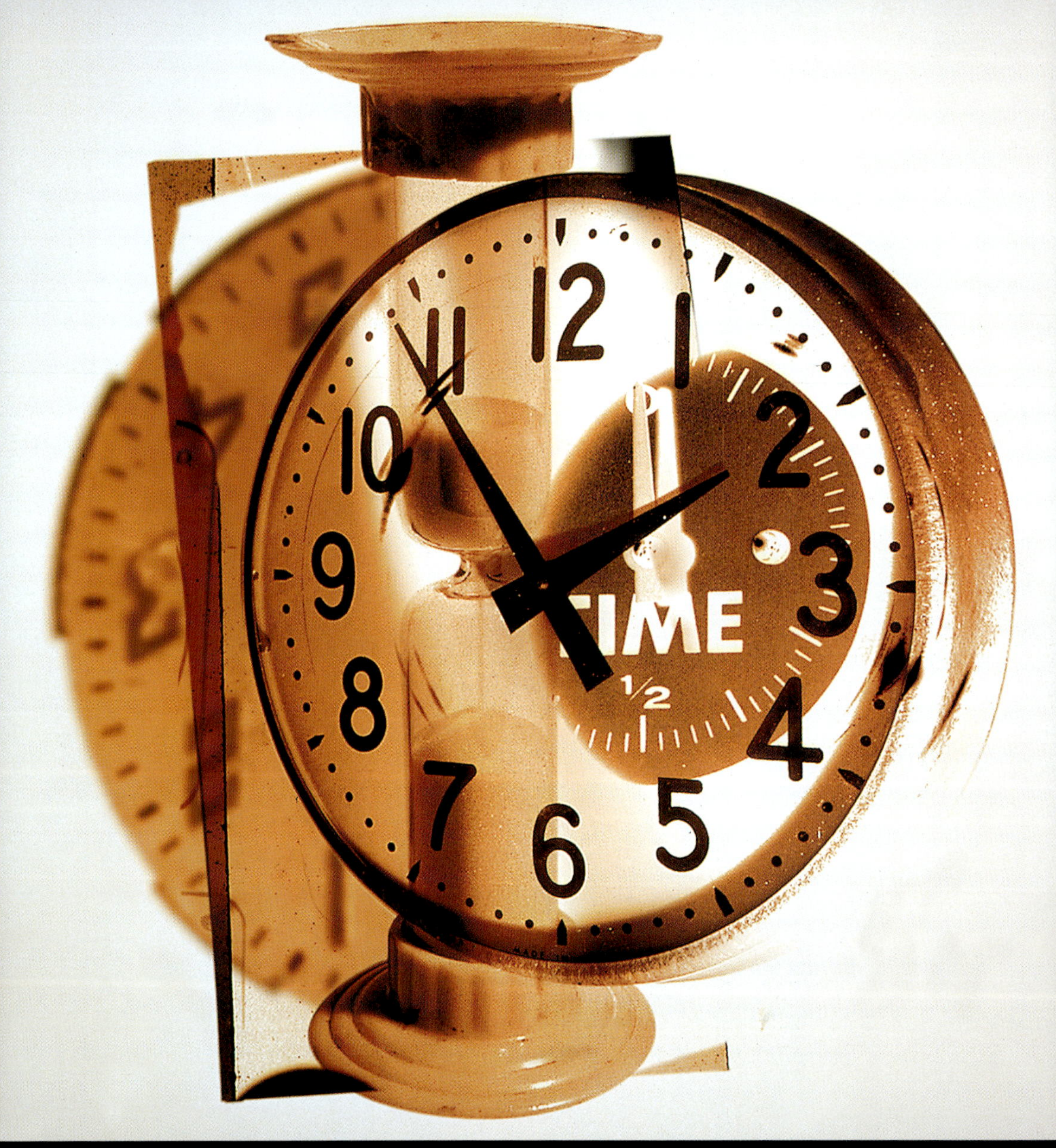

12
1
2
3
4
5
6
7
8
9
10
11
TIME
1/2

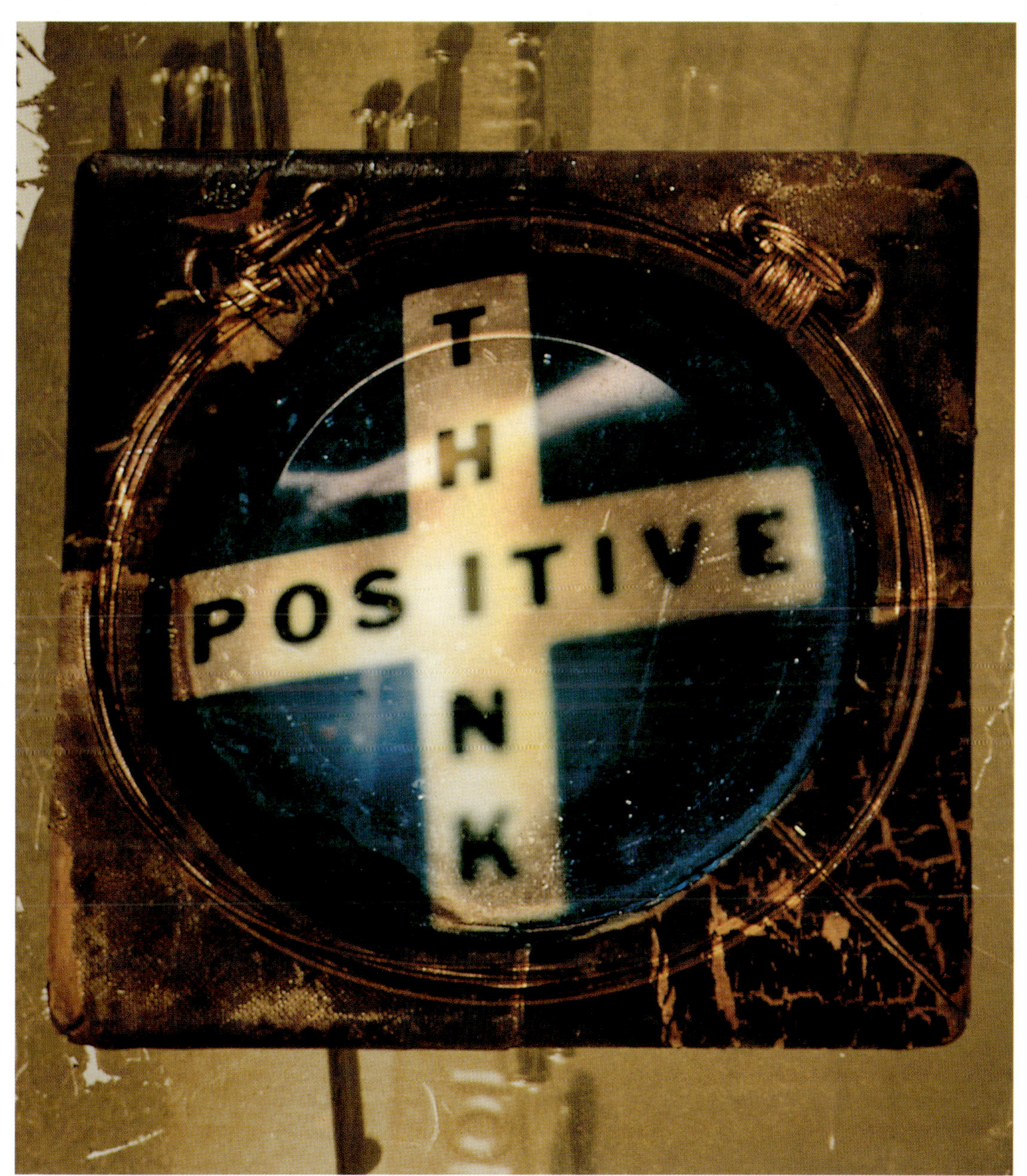
THINK
POSITIVE

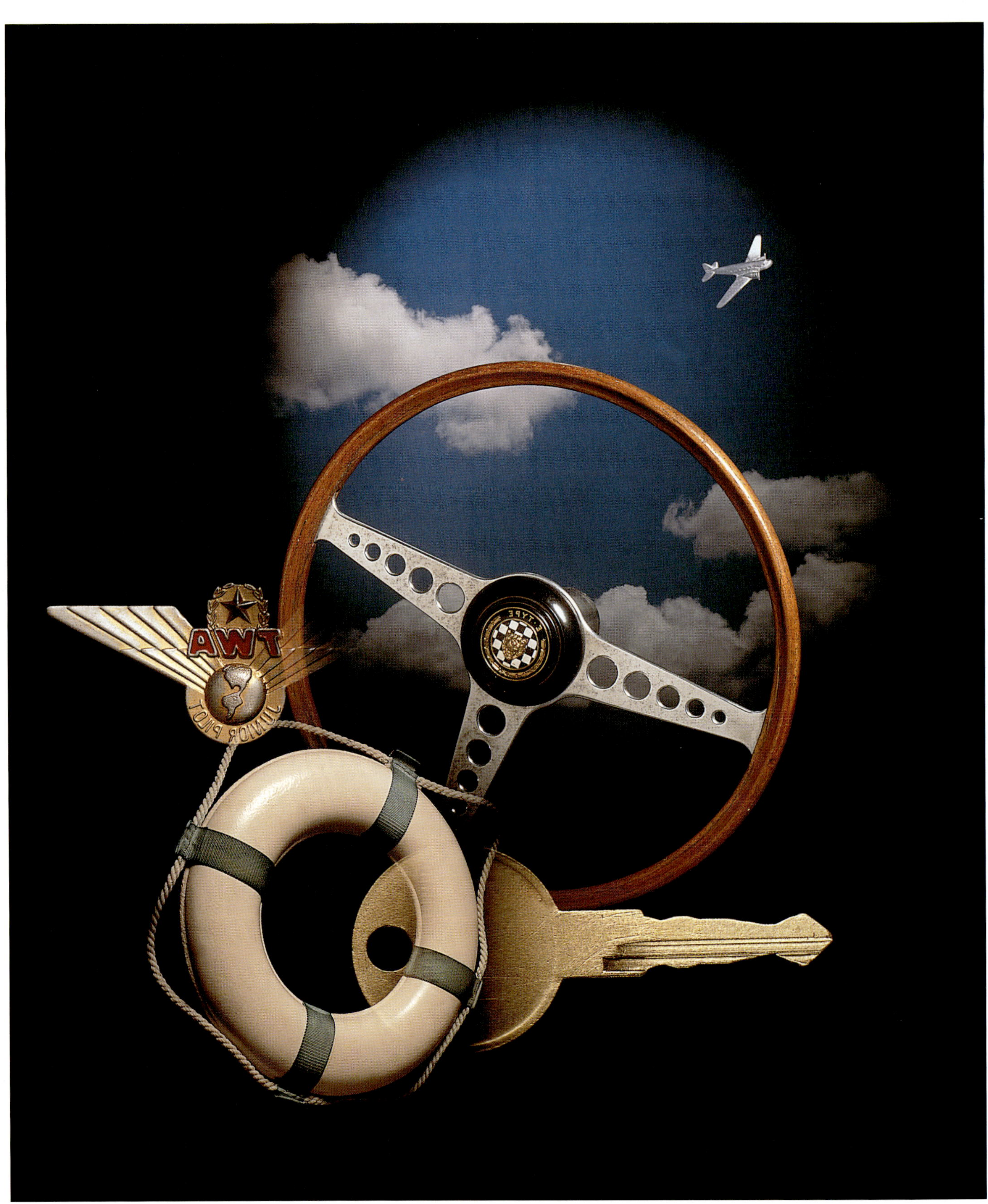

this and following spread: **H**ugh **K**retschmer

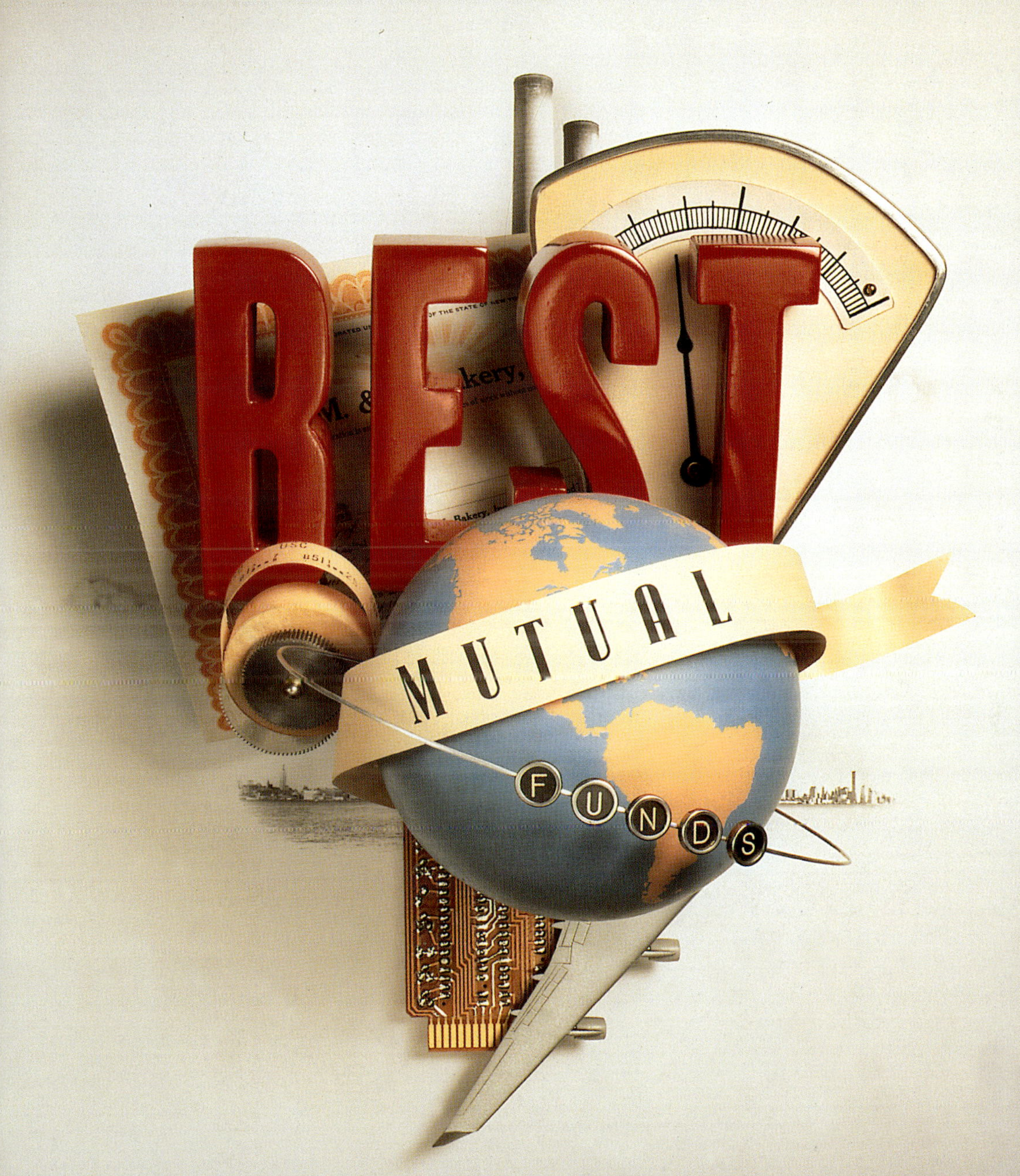

BEST
MUTUAL
FUNDS

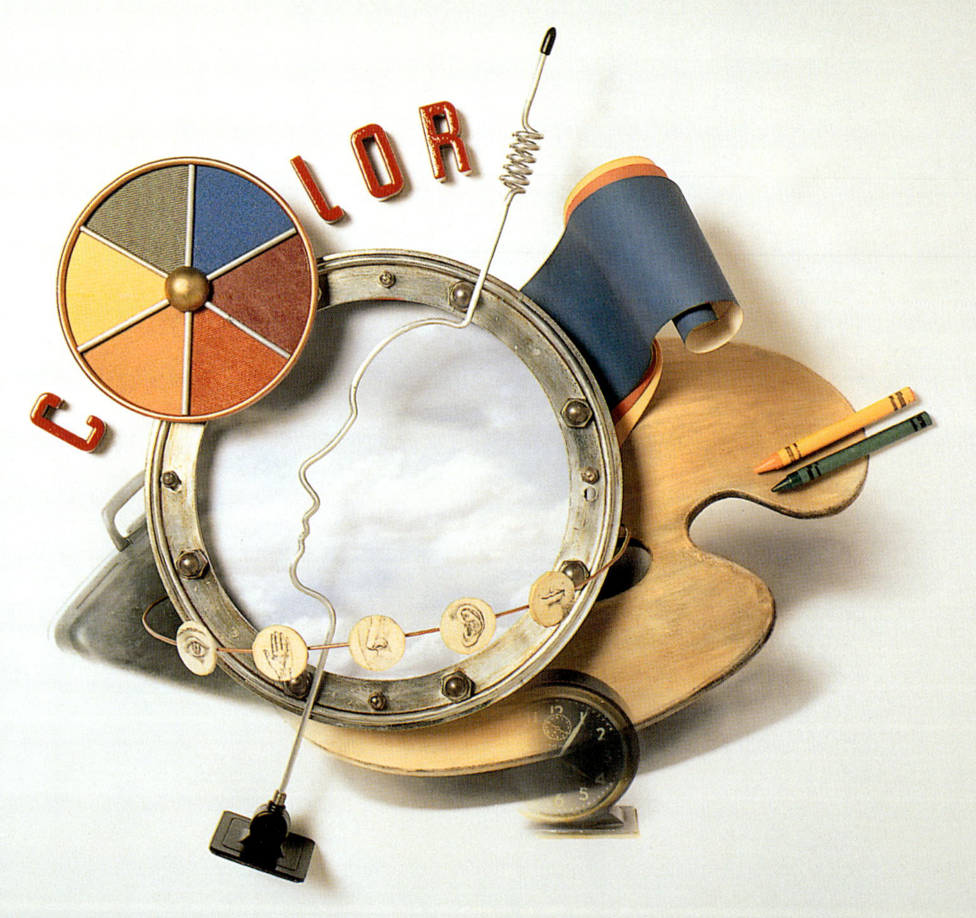

C
LOR

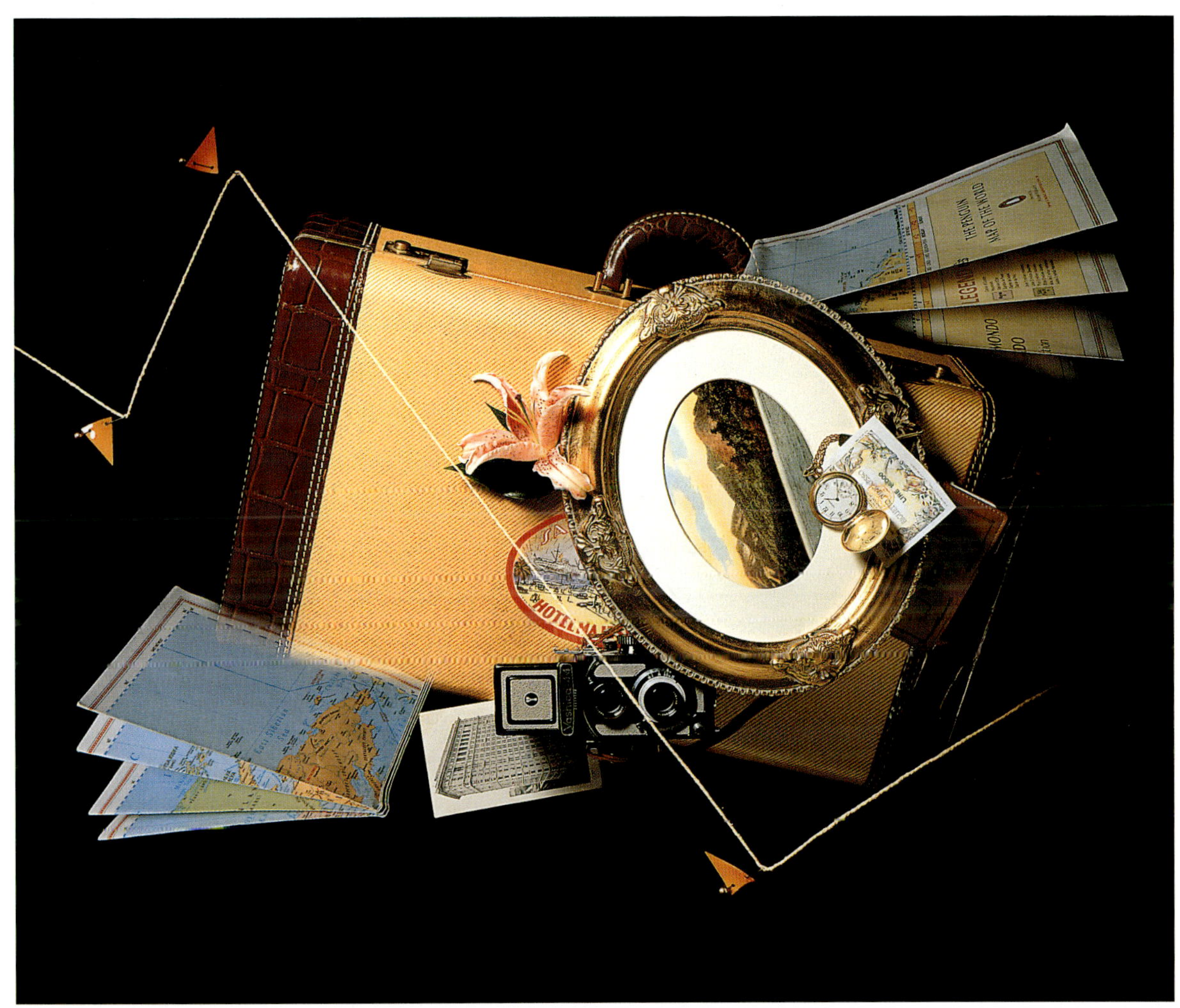

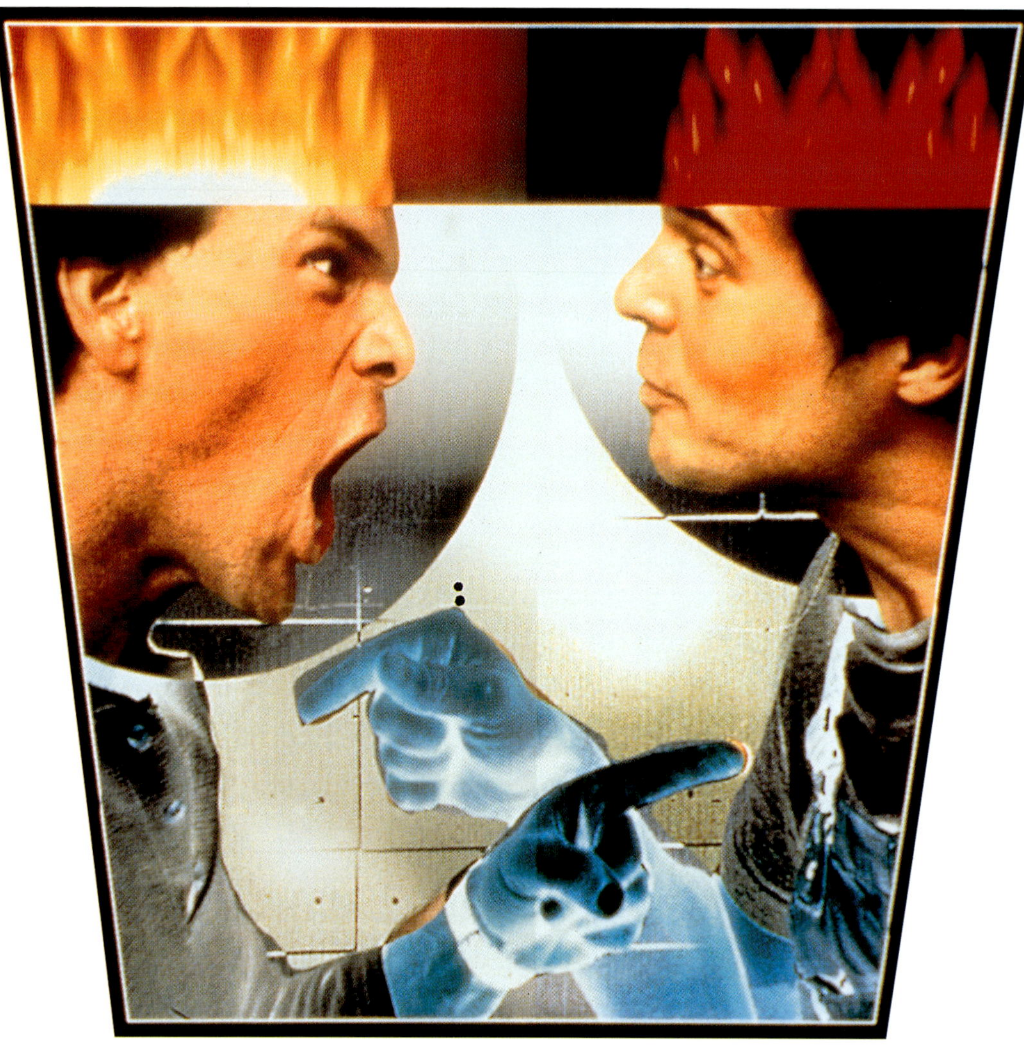

this spread: **J**ohn **R**itter

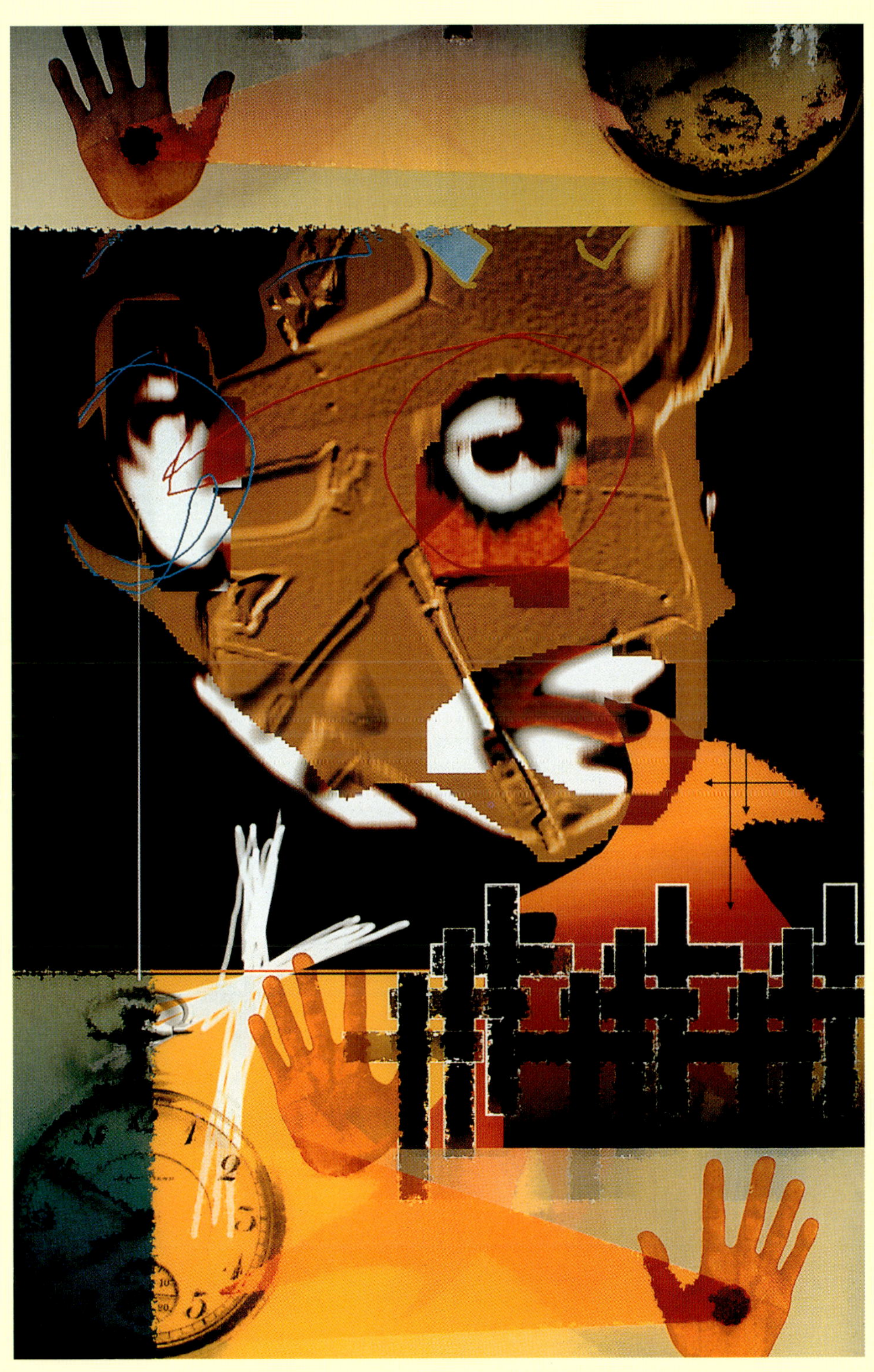

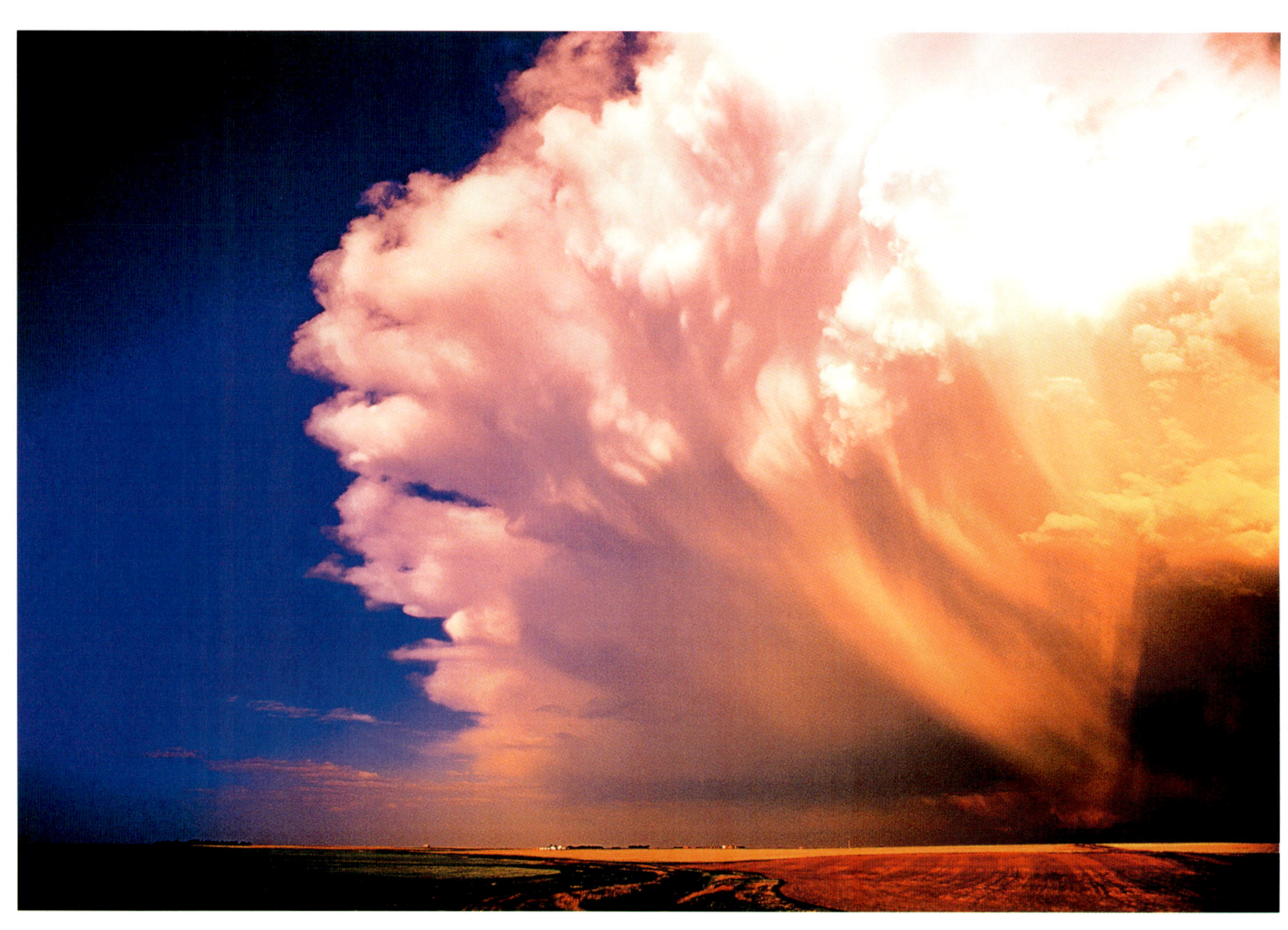

Douglas **E**. **W**alker

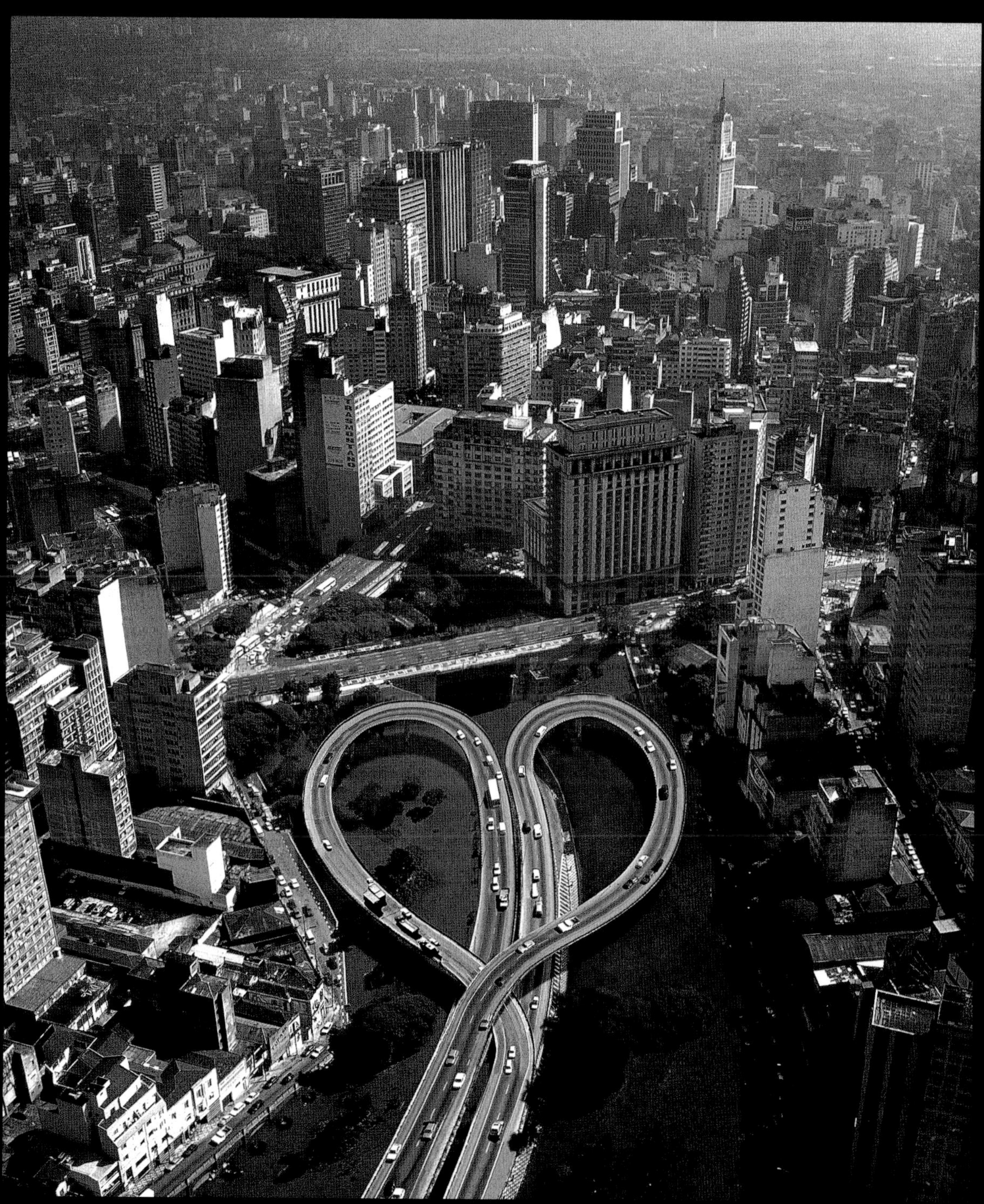

Fernando **Z**uffo

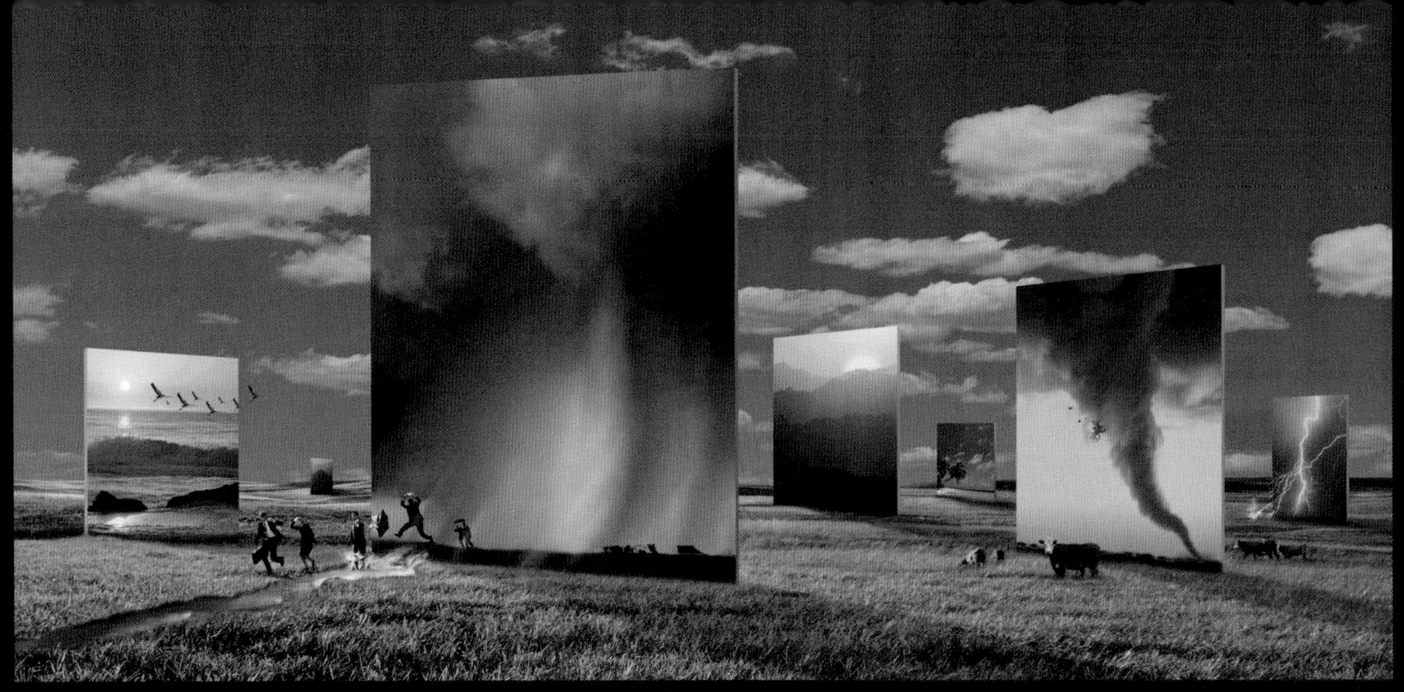

Steve Hix

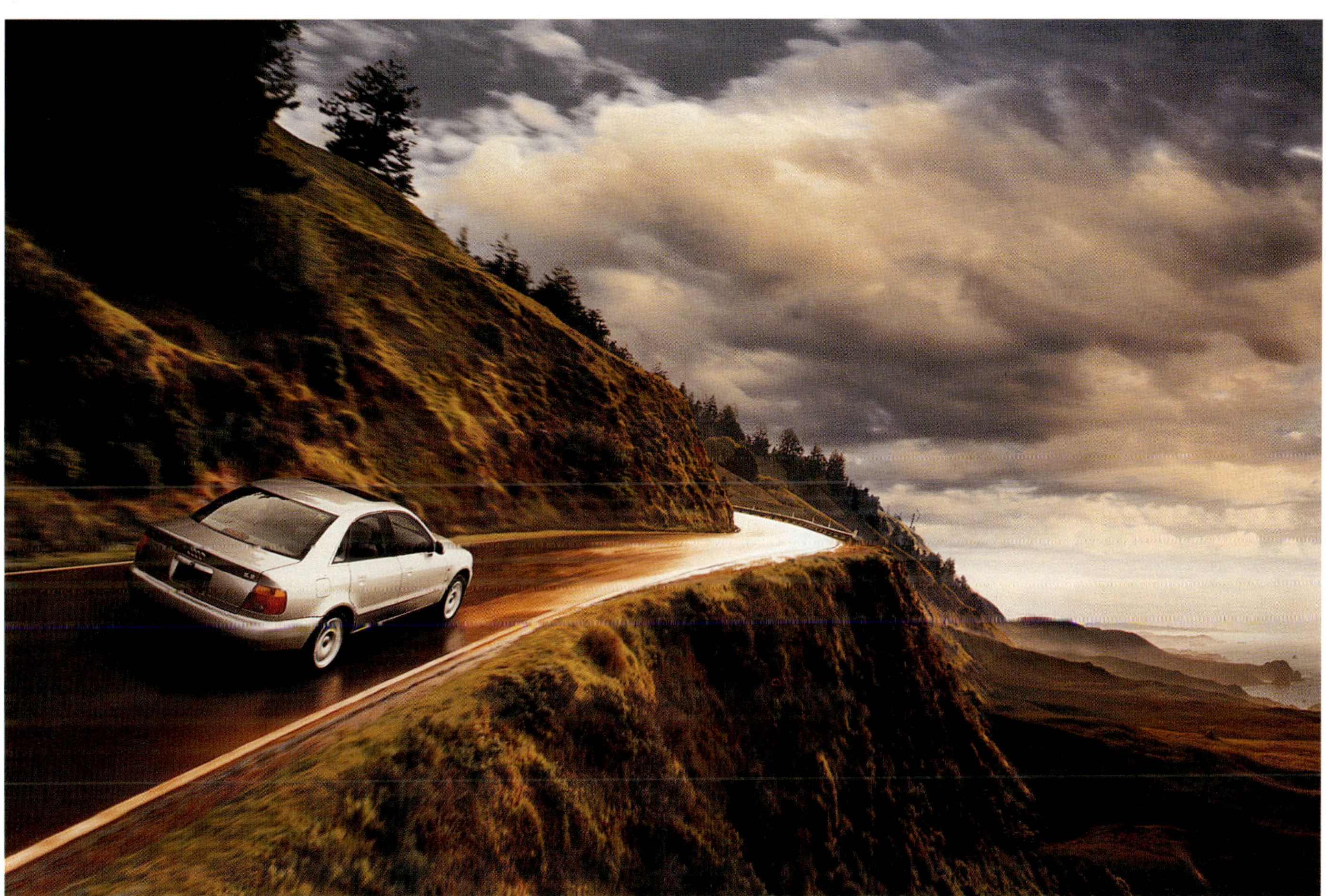

Jim **E**rickson

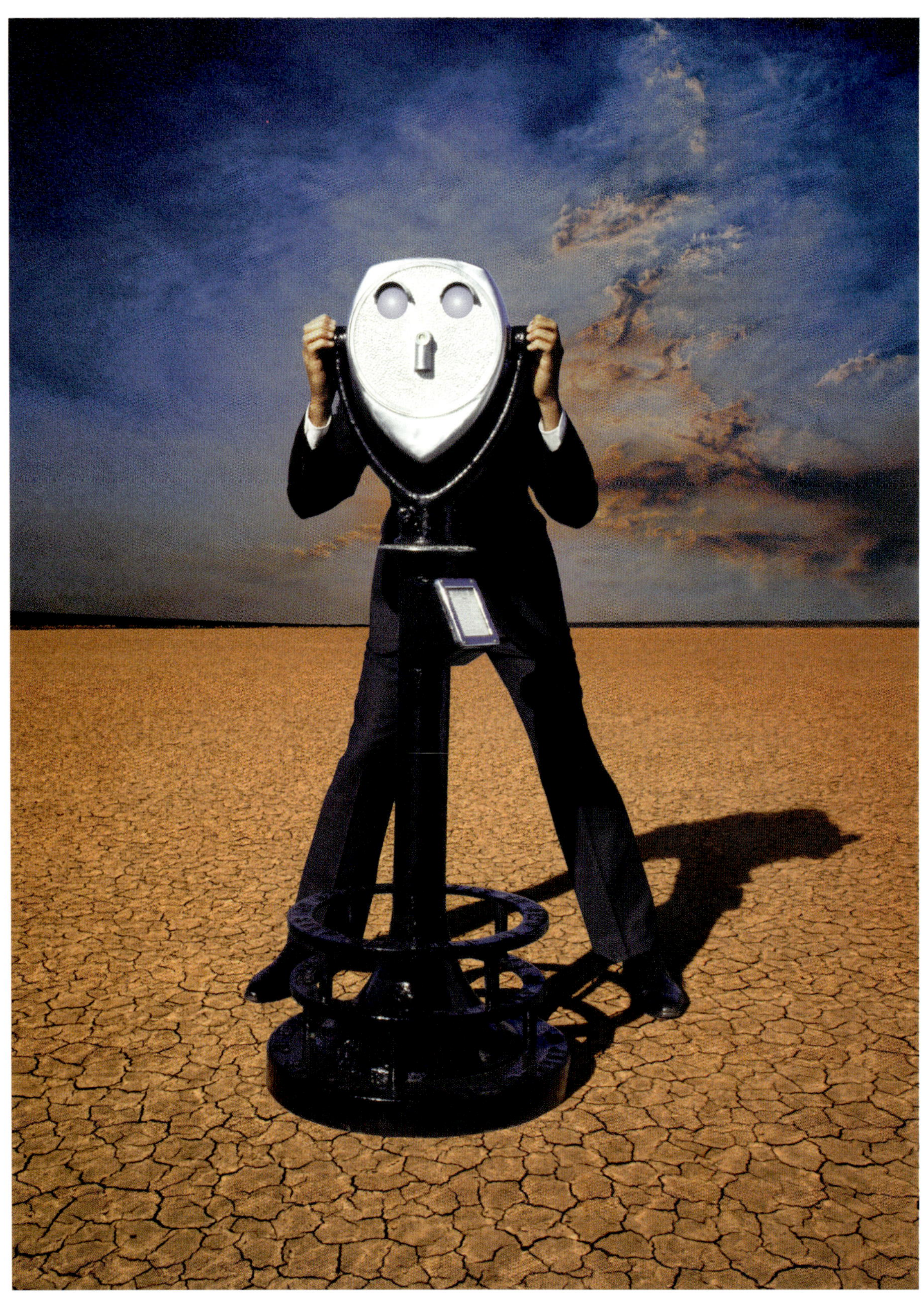

Charly Franklin

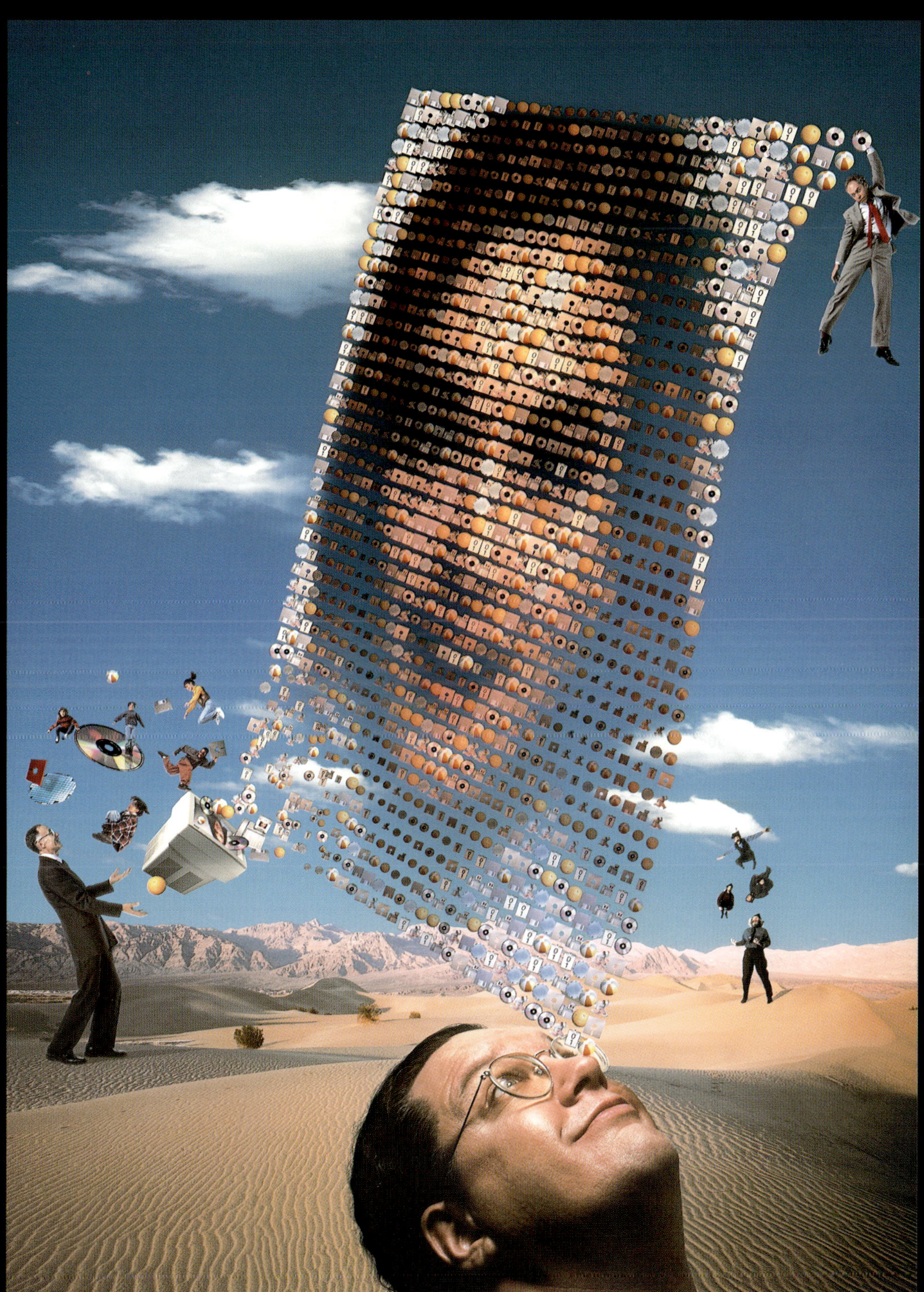

Ryszard Horowitz

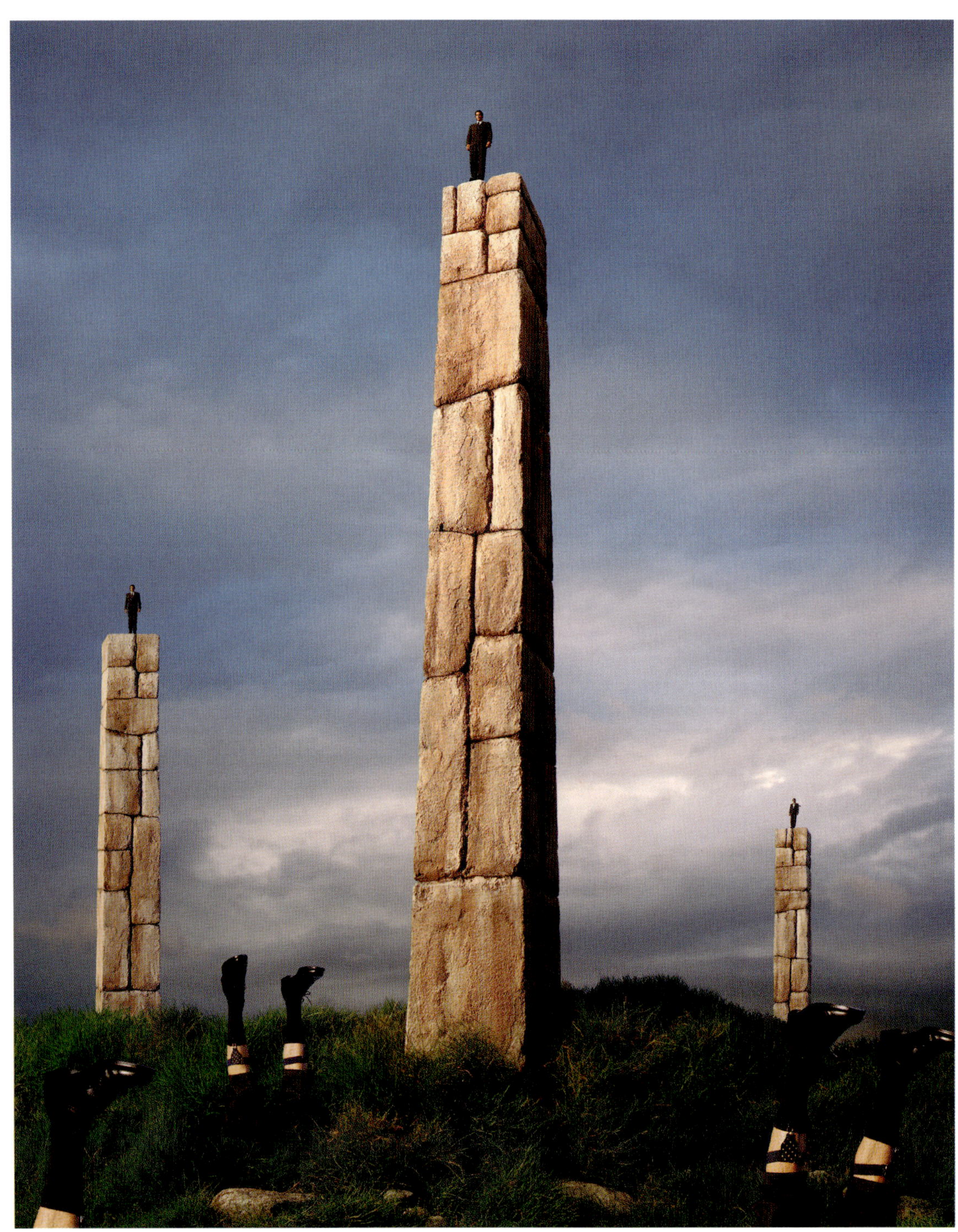

Glen Wexler

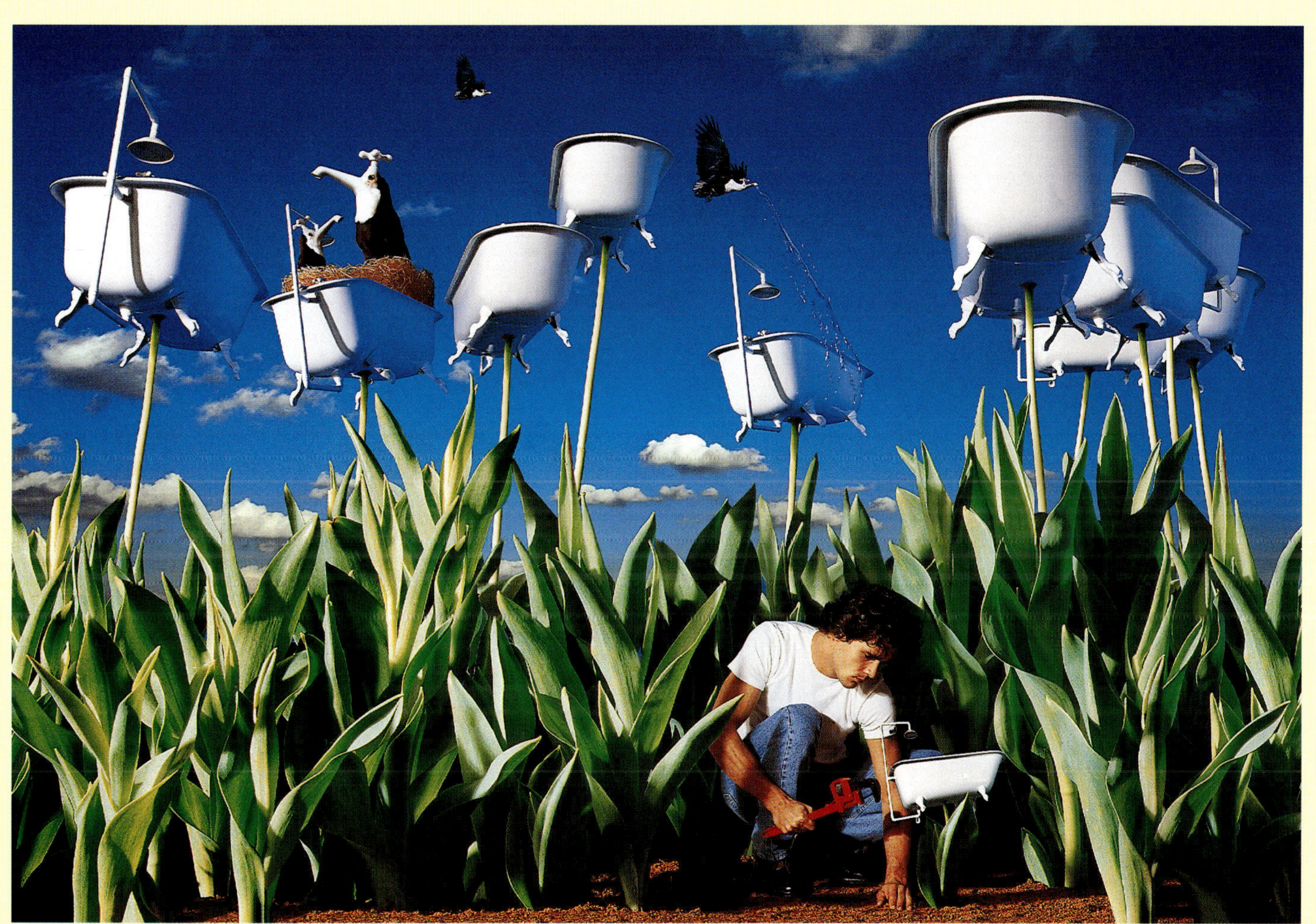

Fernando Zuffo

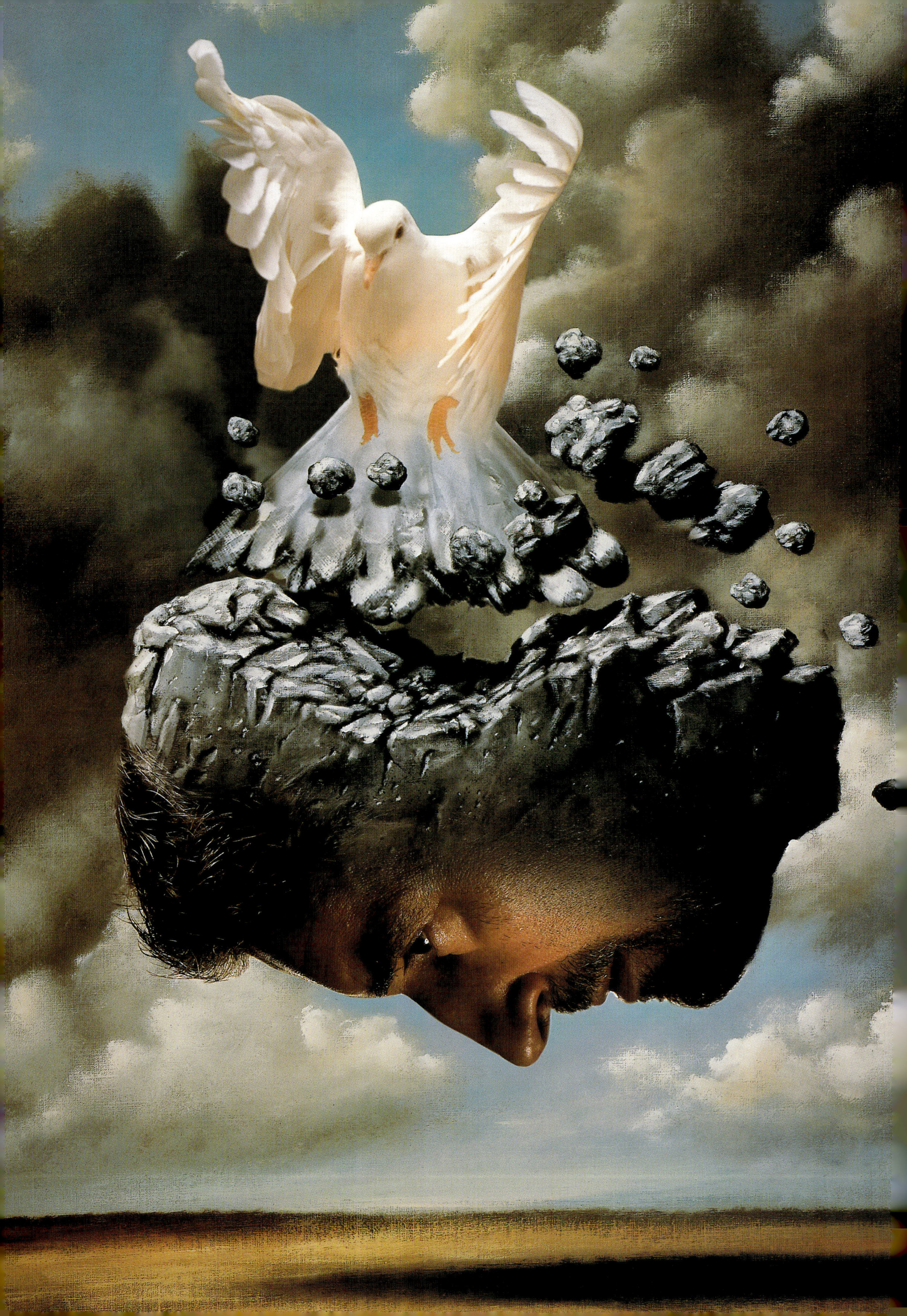

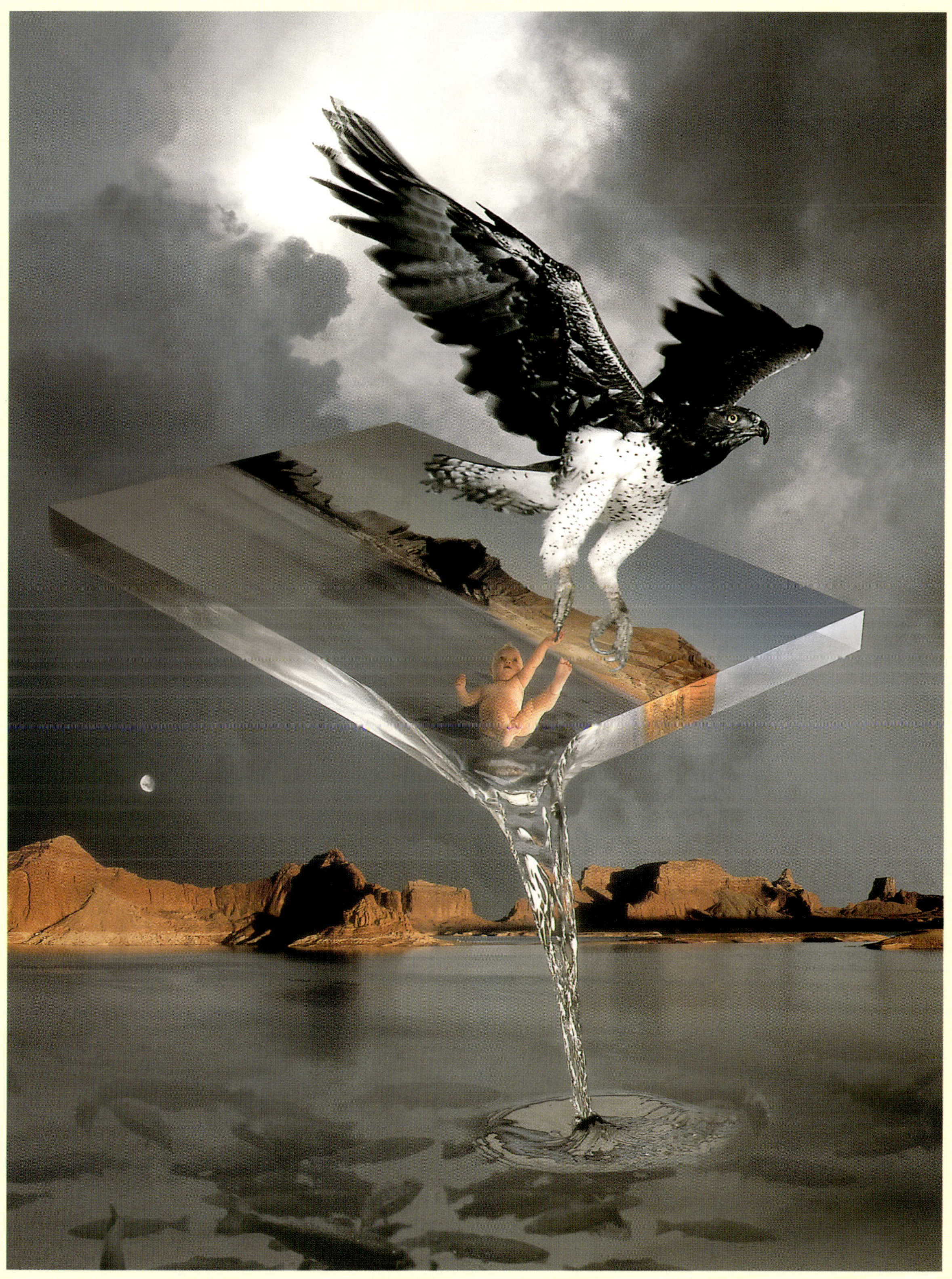

this spread: **R**yszard **H**orowitz

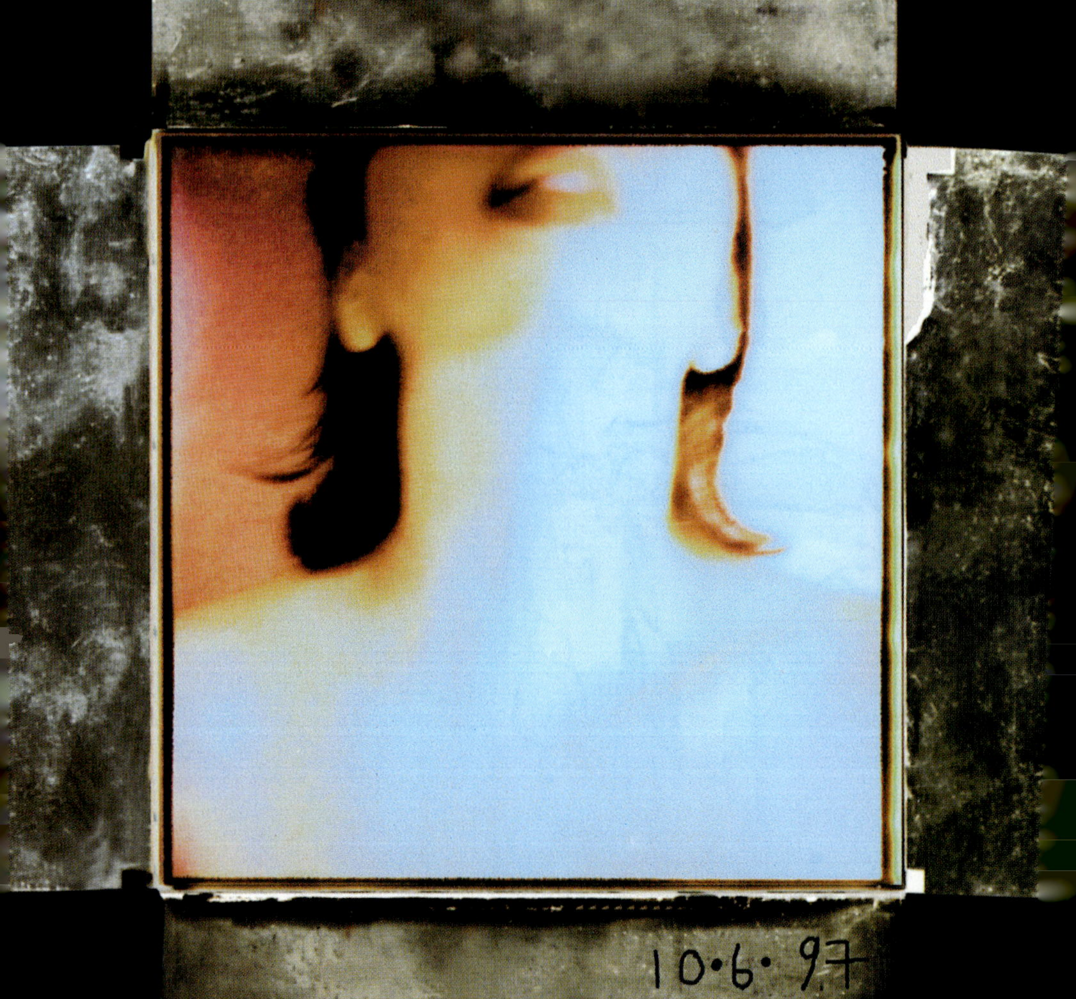
10·6·97

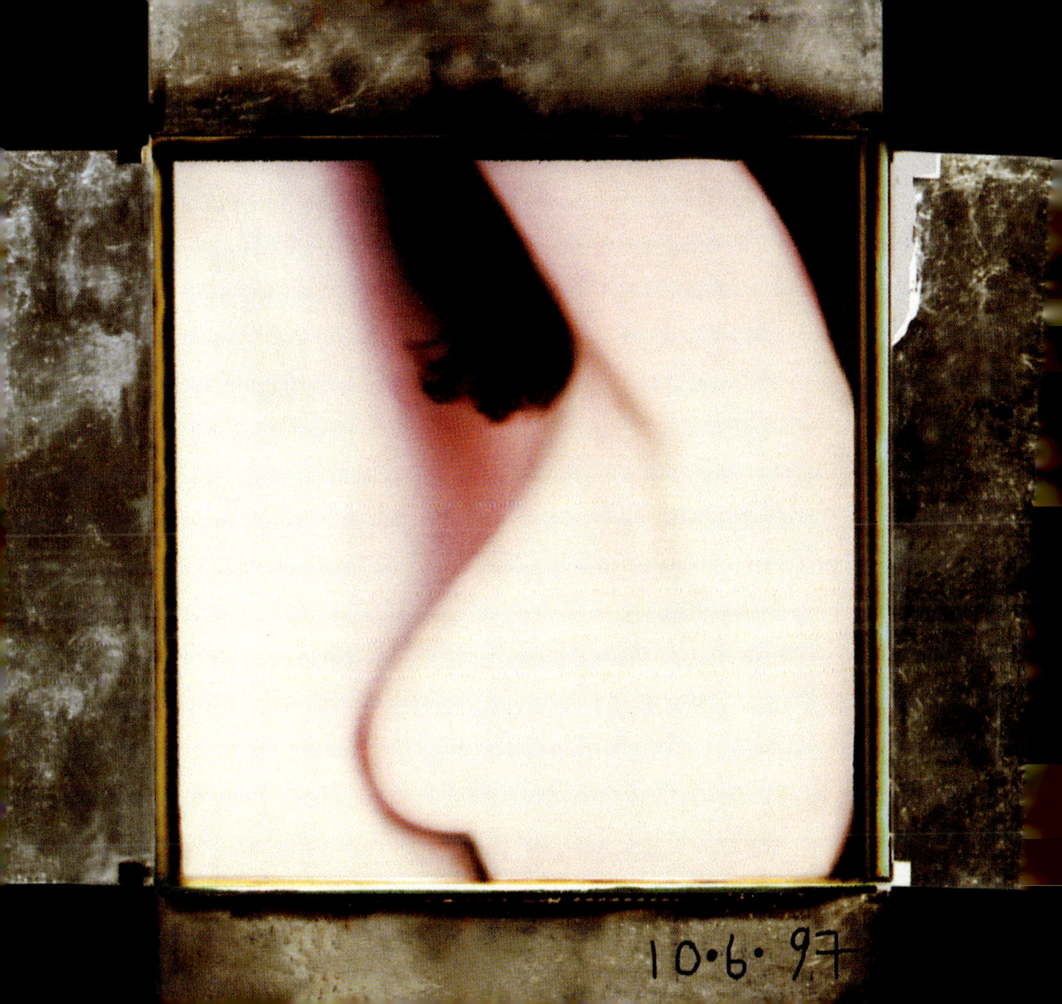
10·6·97

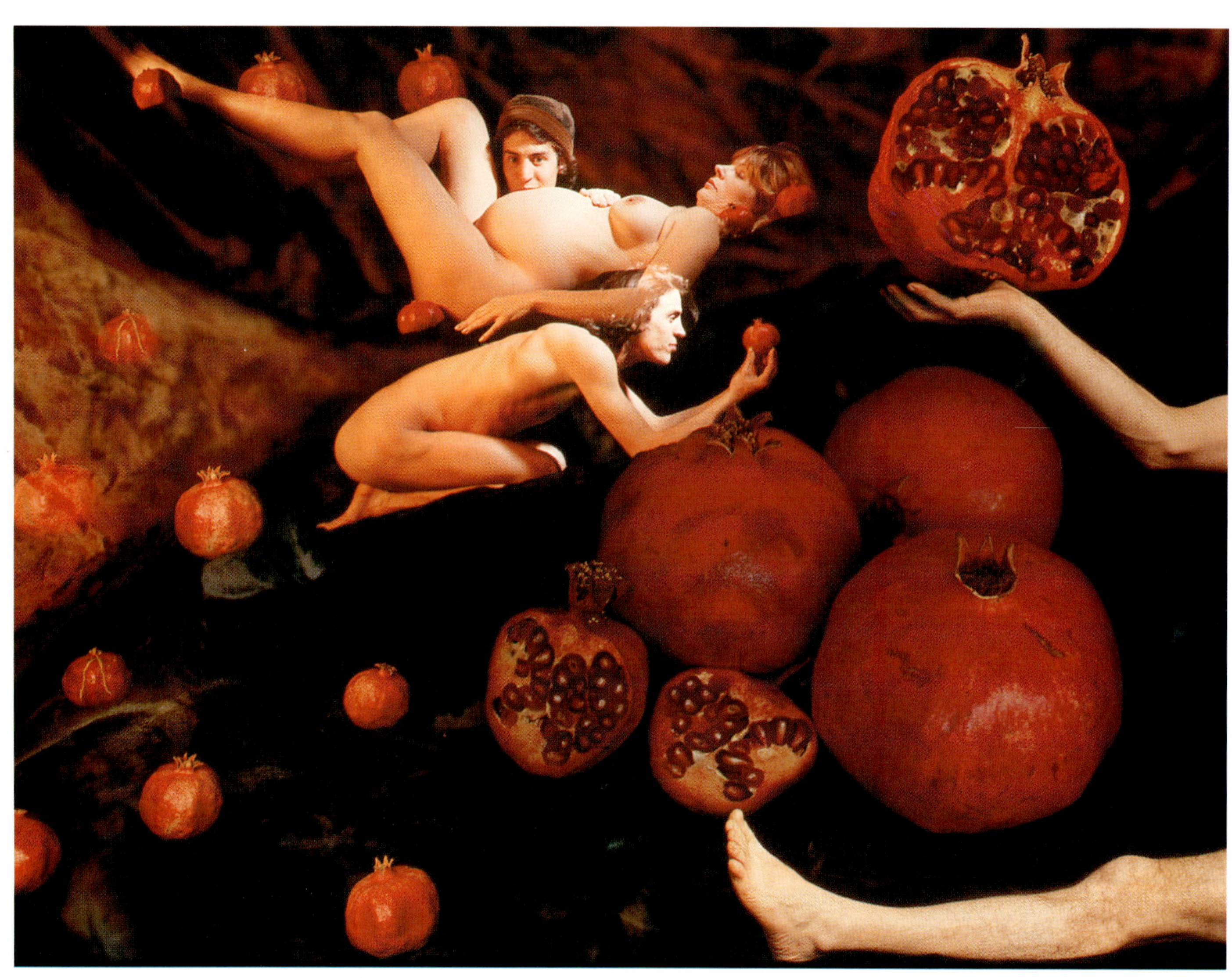

Zvia **S**adja

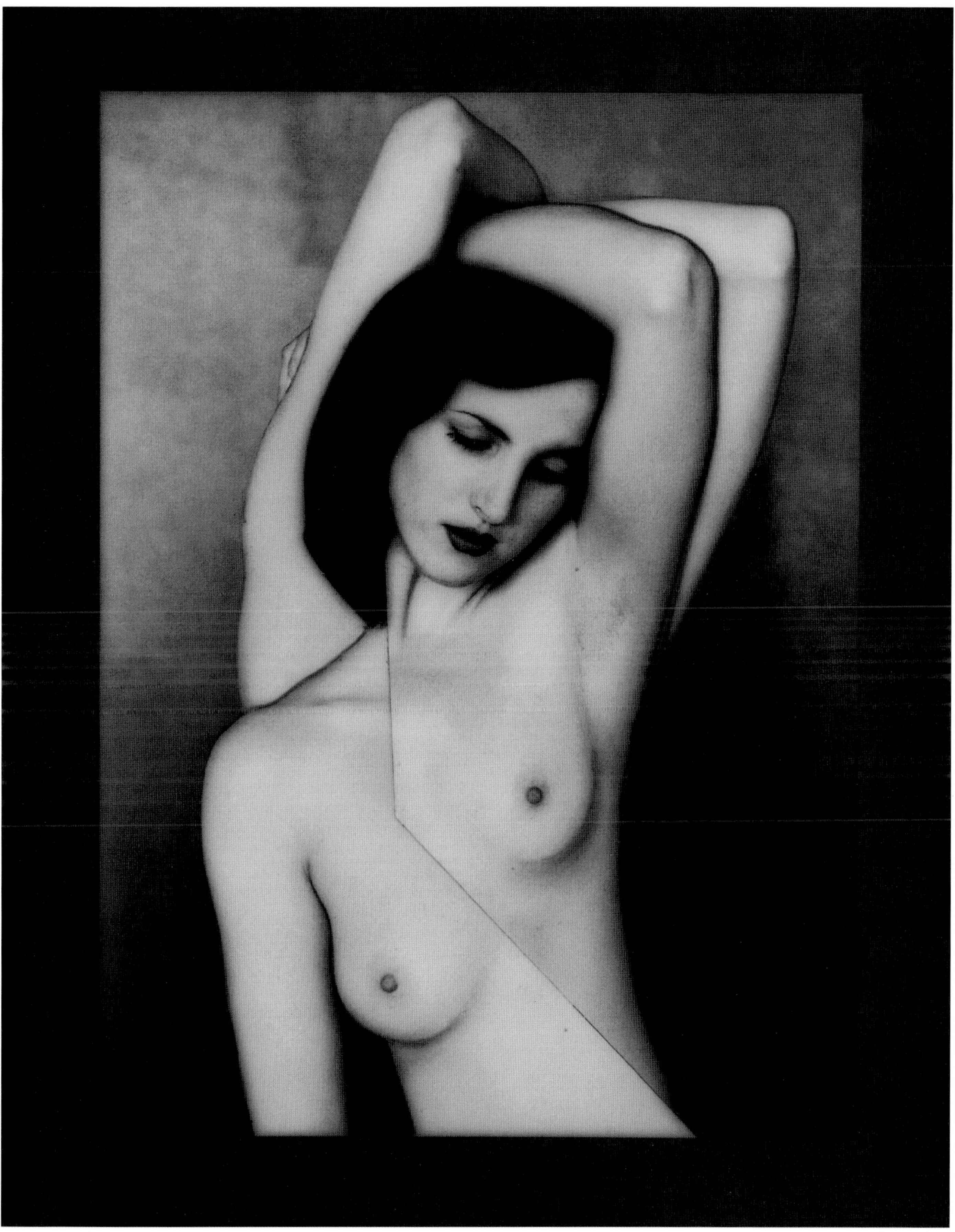

Adrian **V**an **V**alen

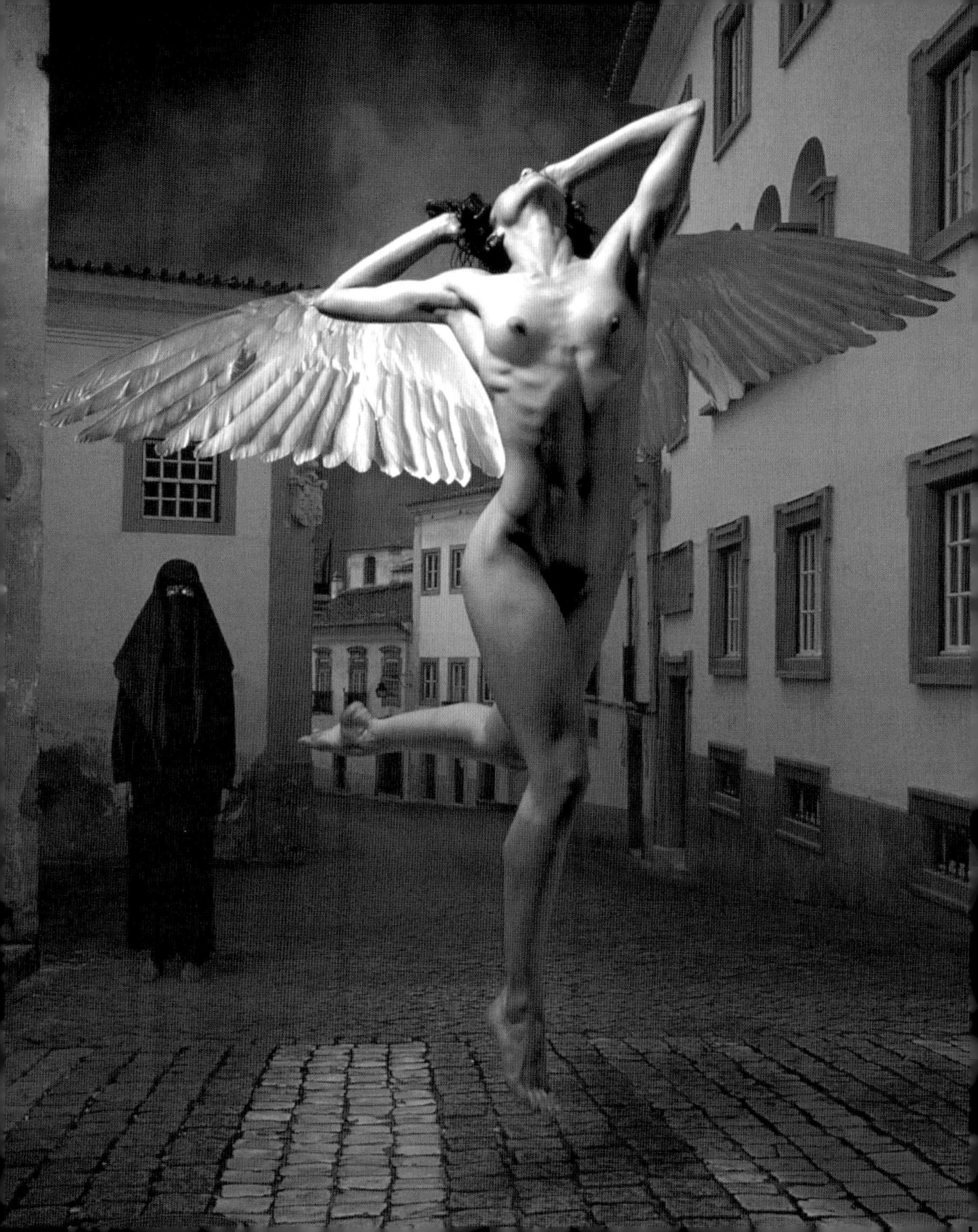

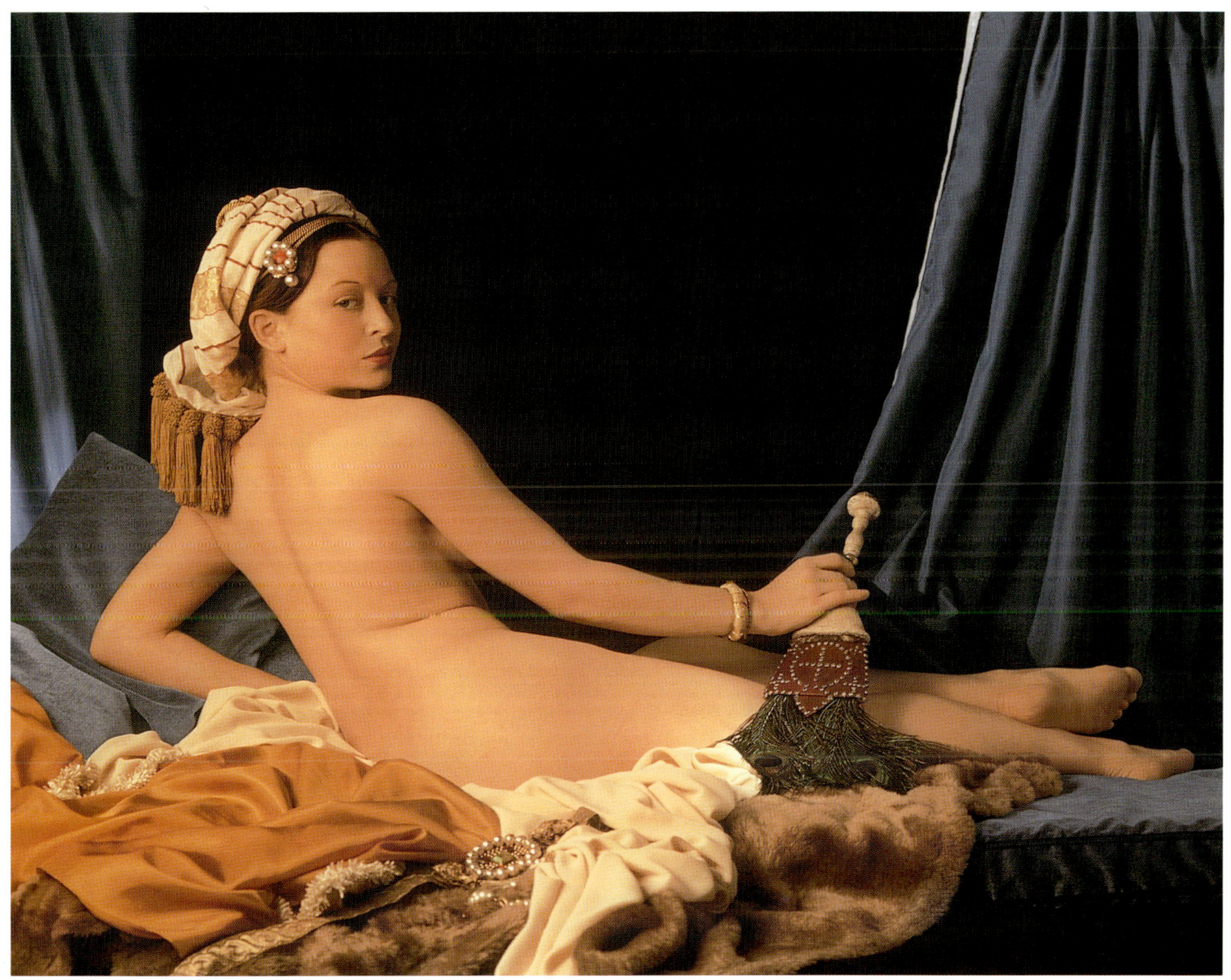

Marco **P**rozzo

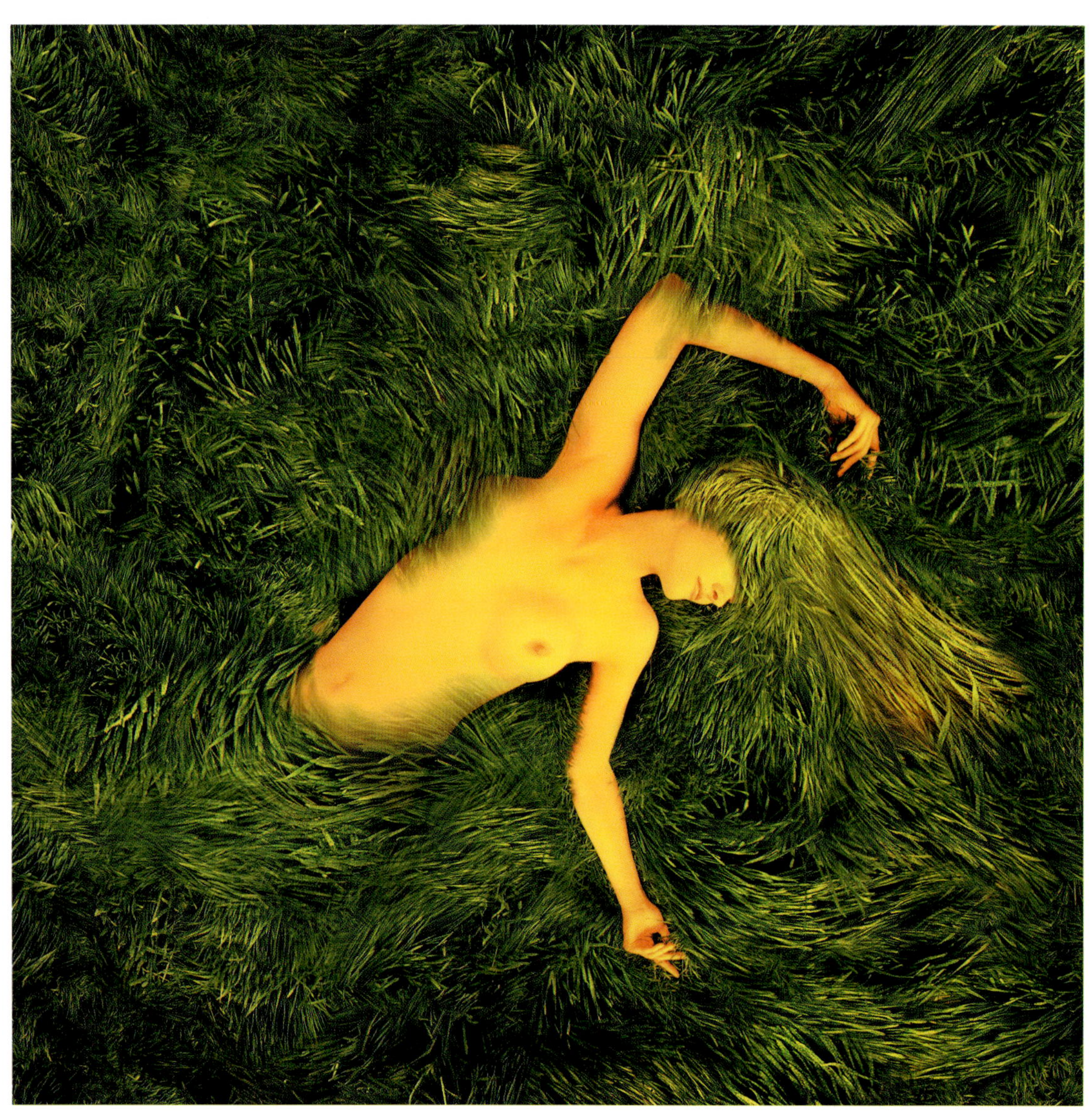

Sanjay **K**othari

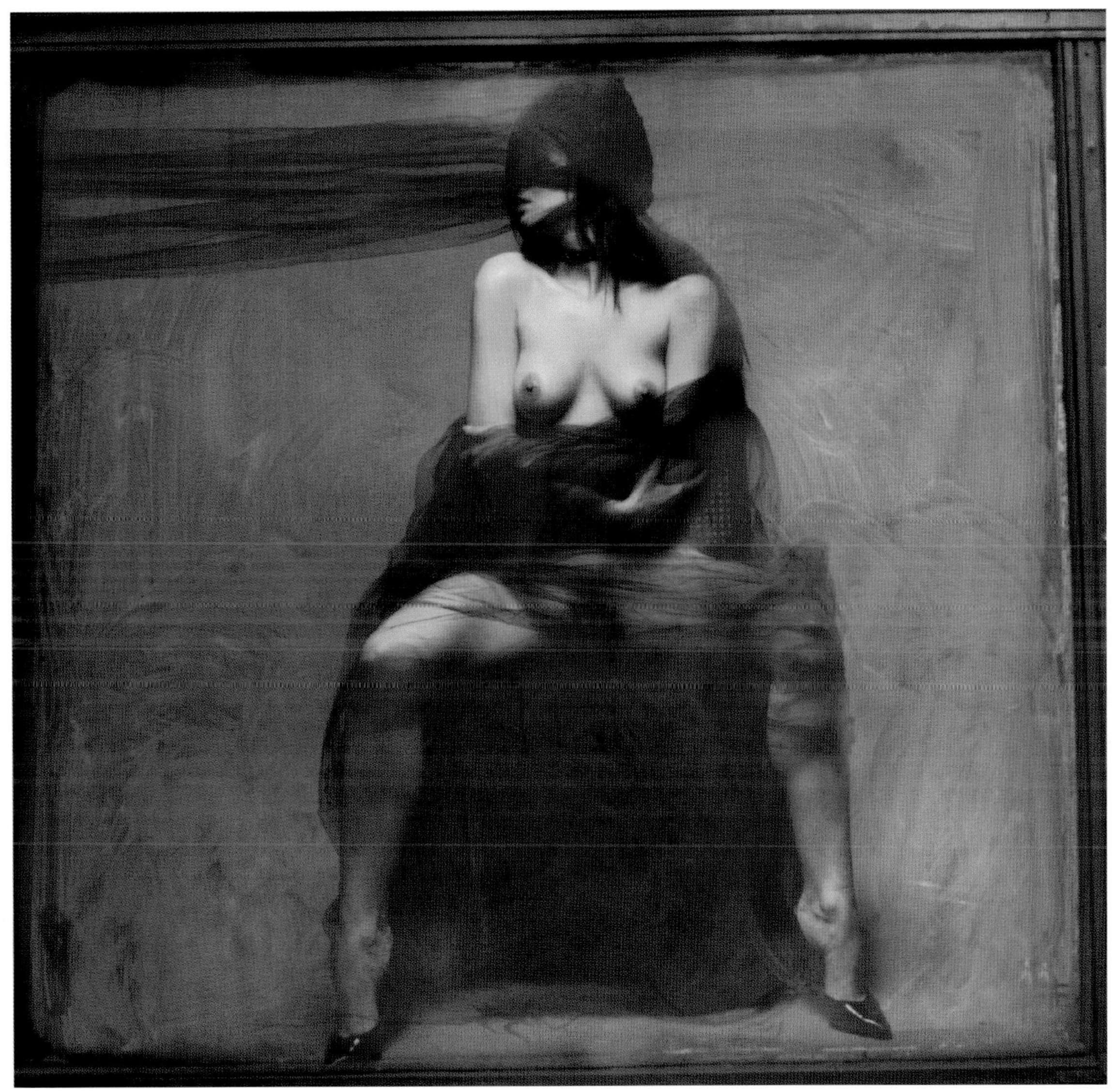

Roy **V**olkmann

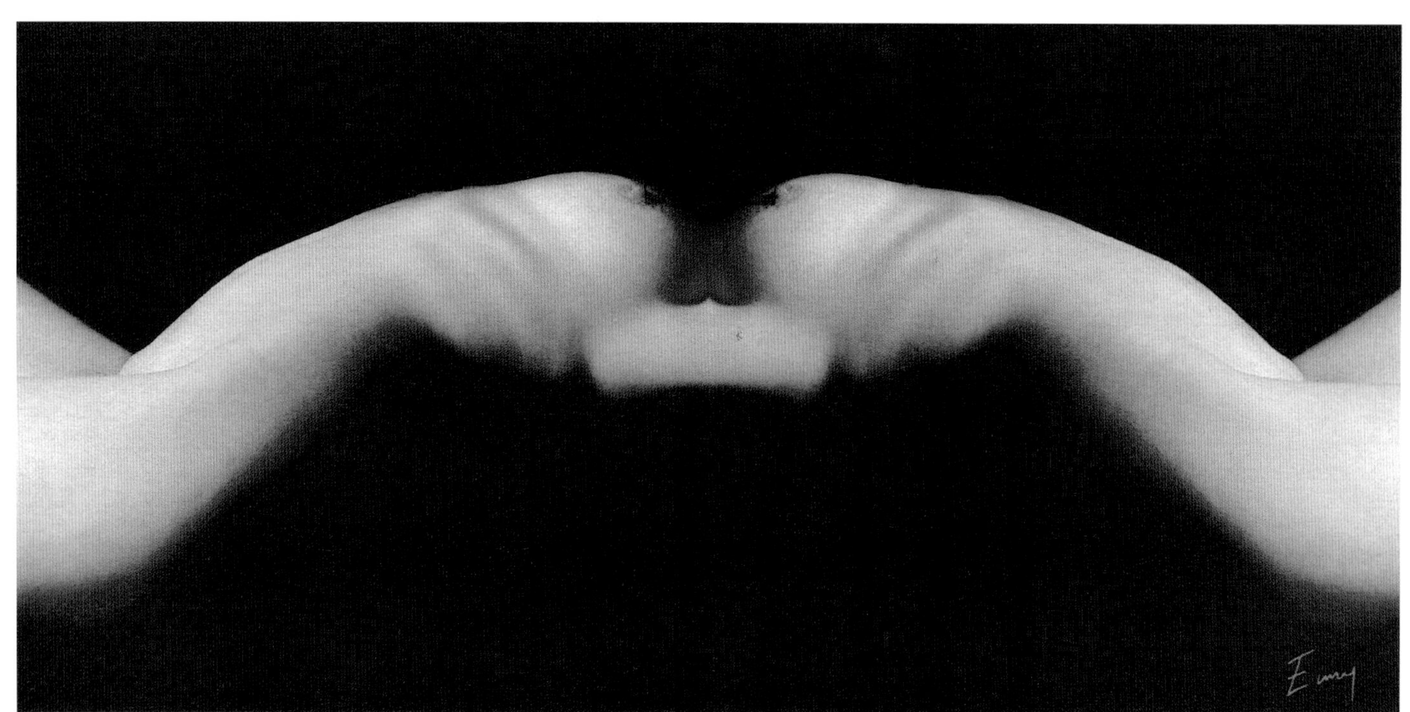

Emy **K**at

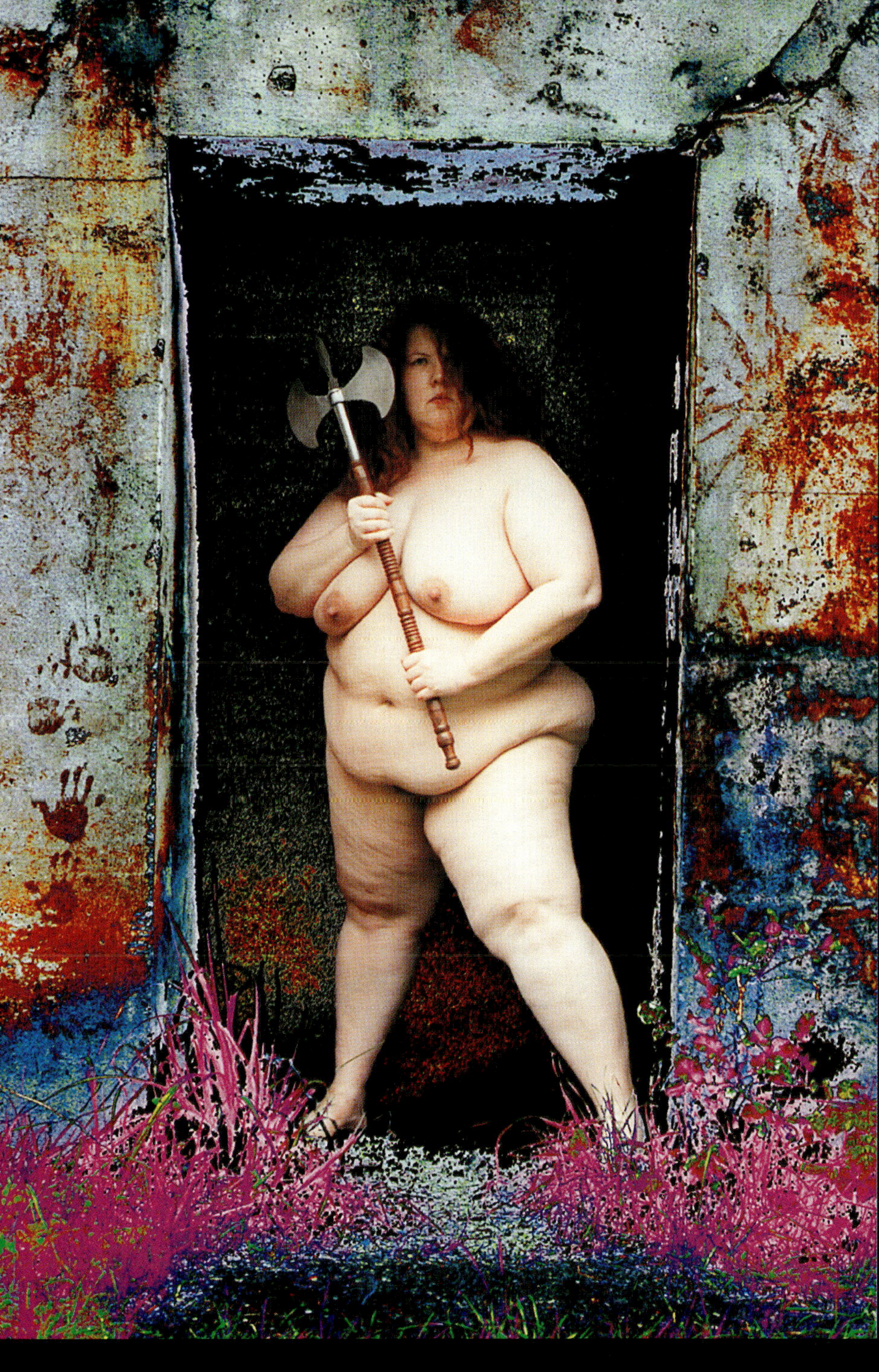

this and following page: **J**ames **S**tanley **D**augherty

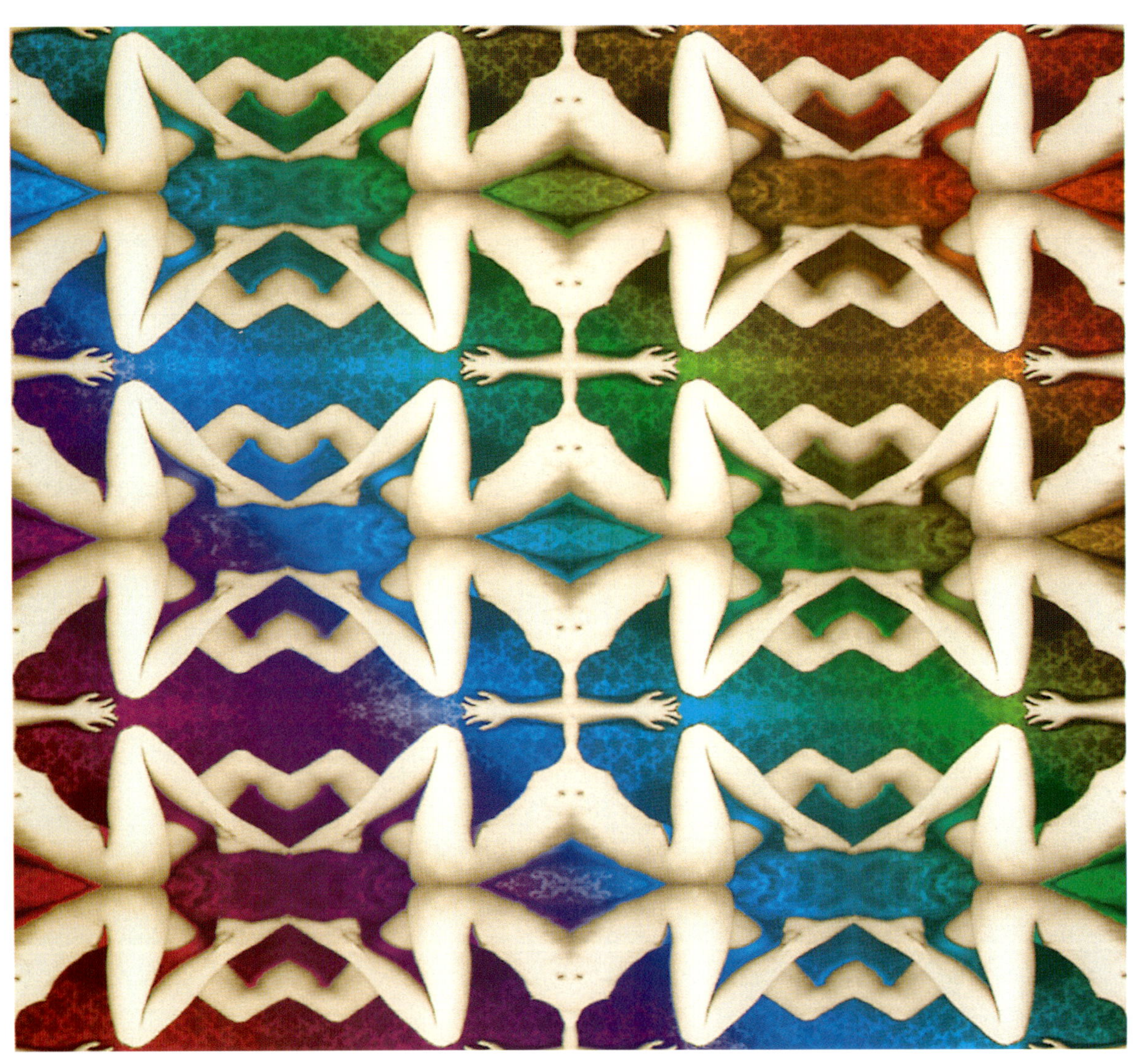

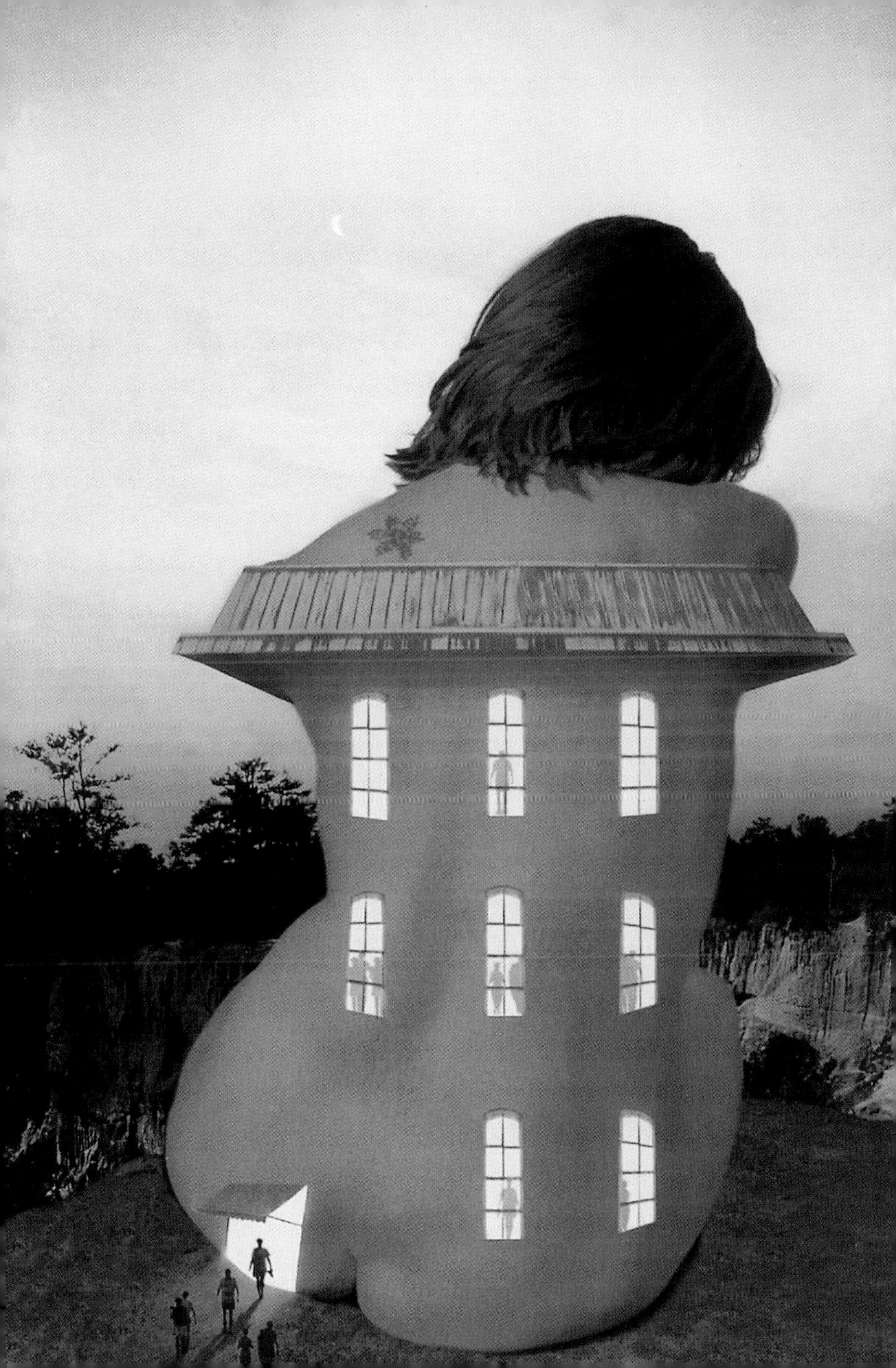

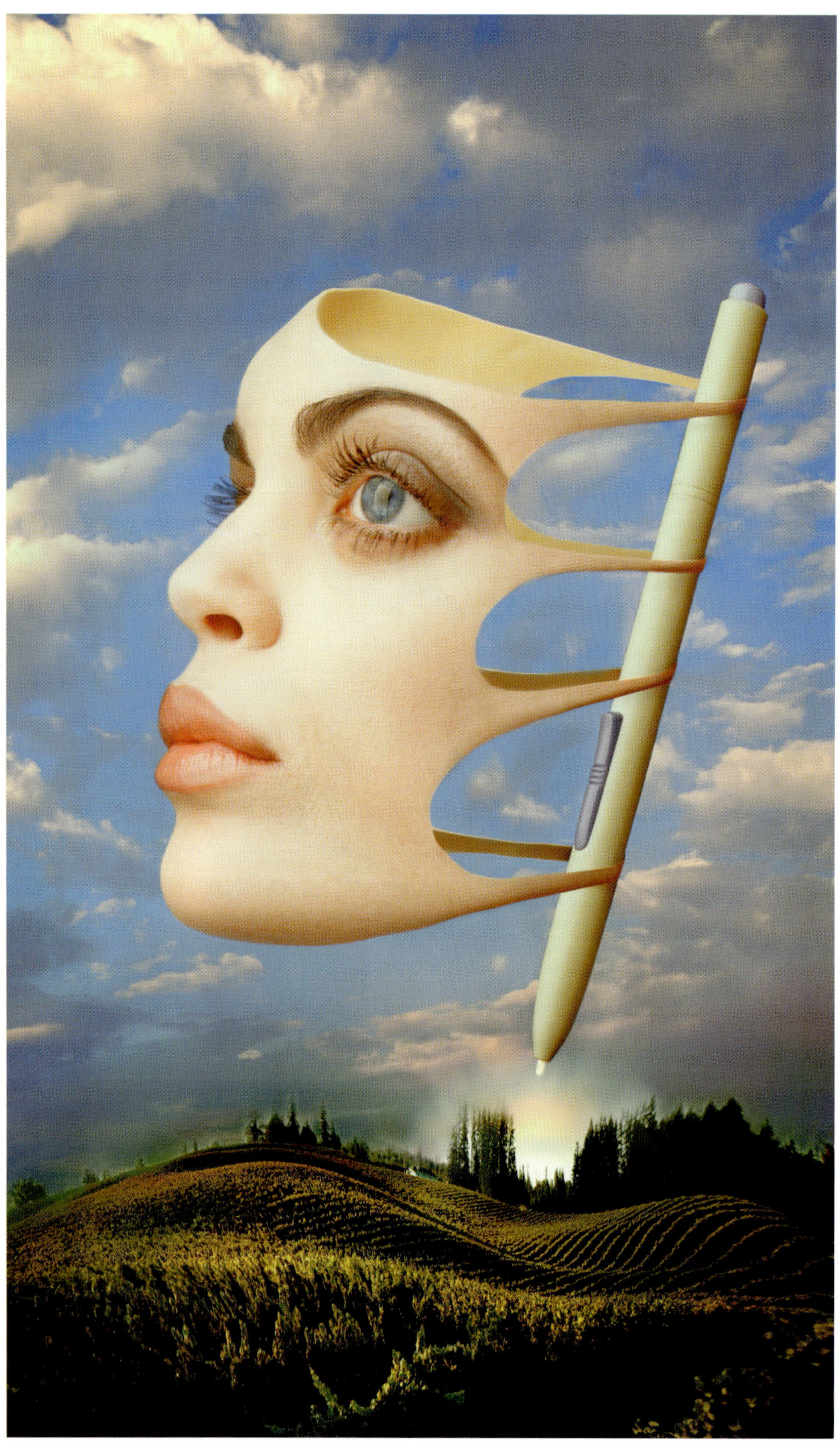

Gerald **B**ybee

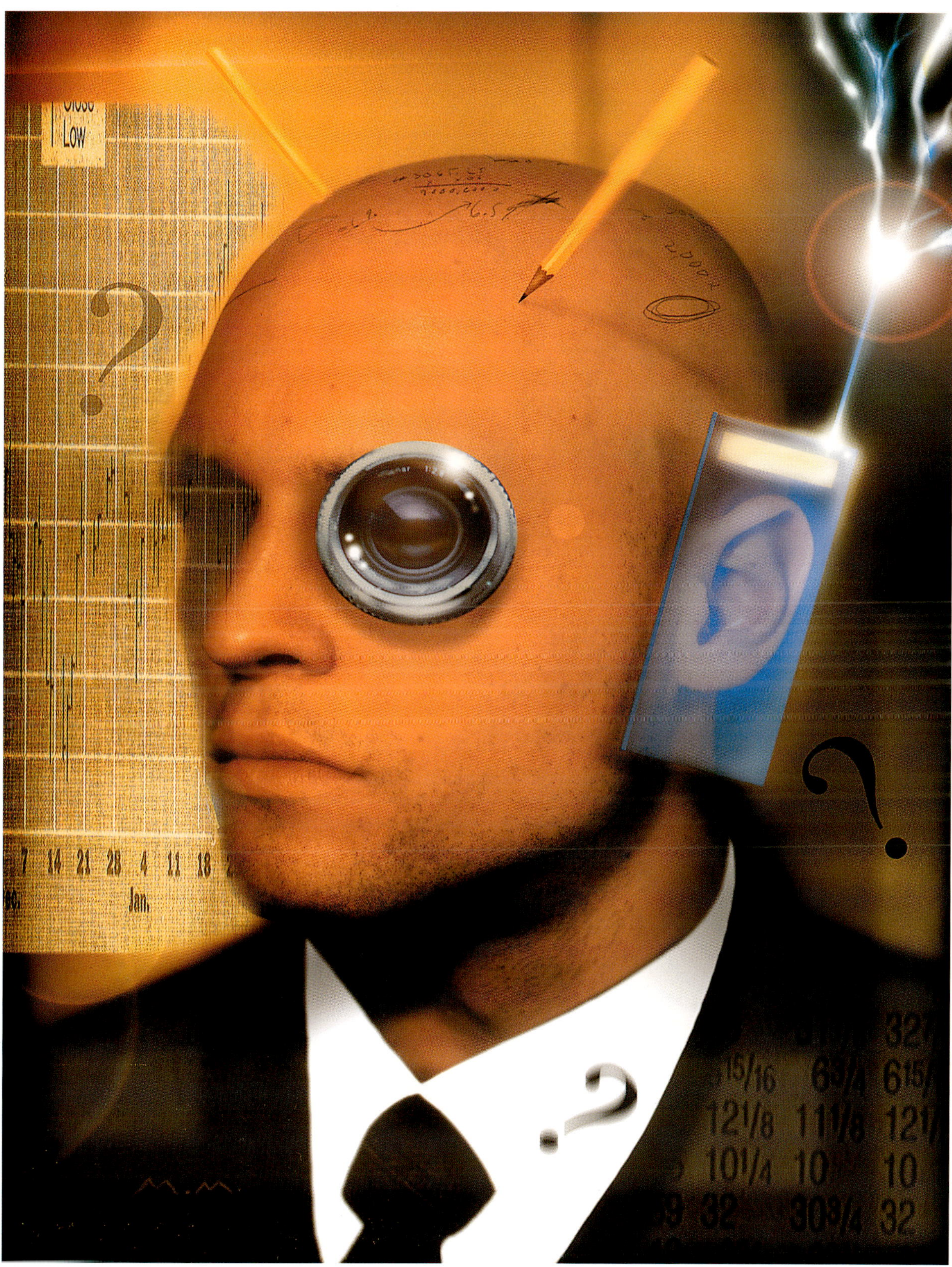

Matt Mahurin

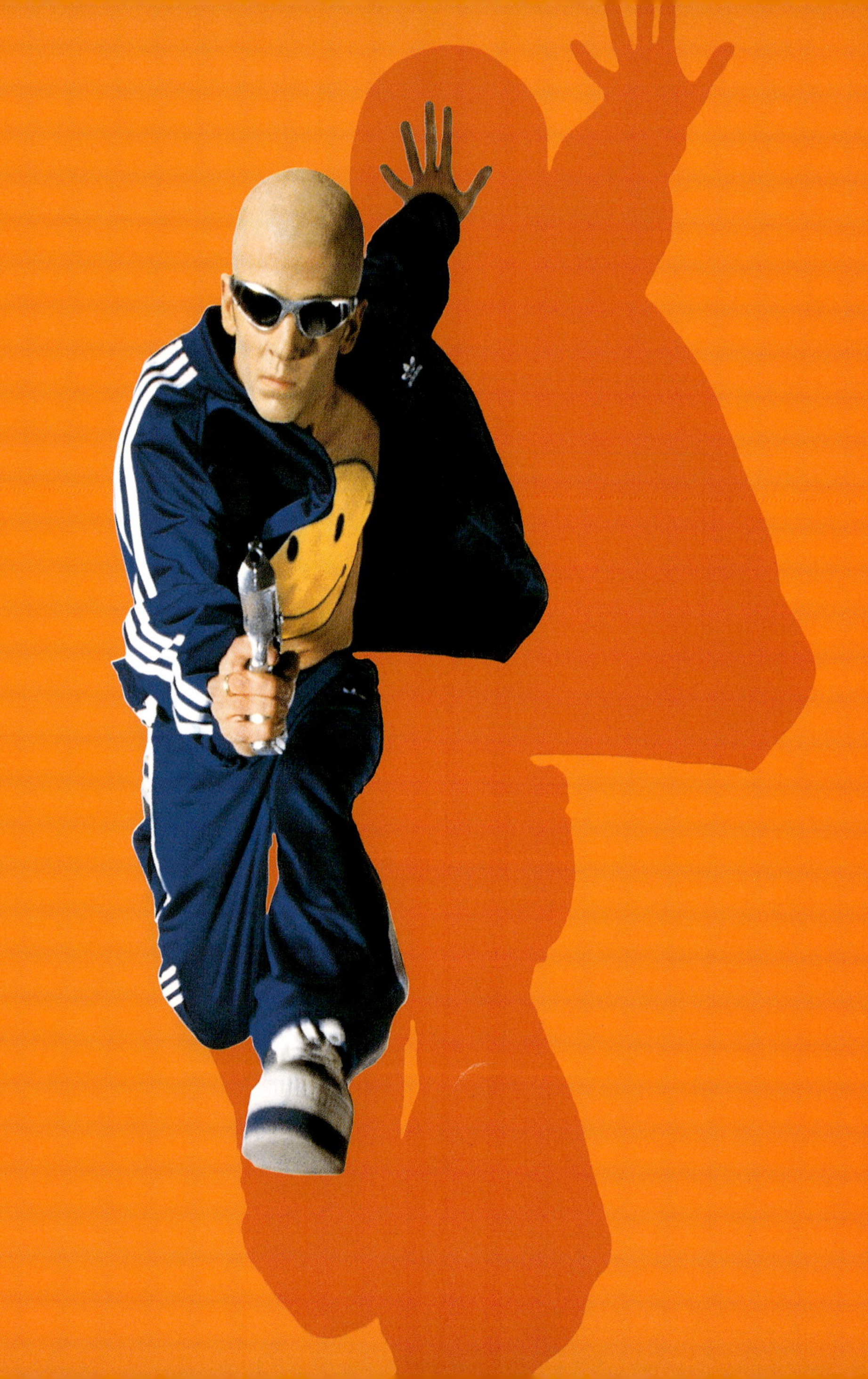

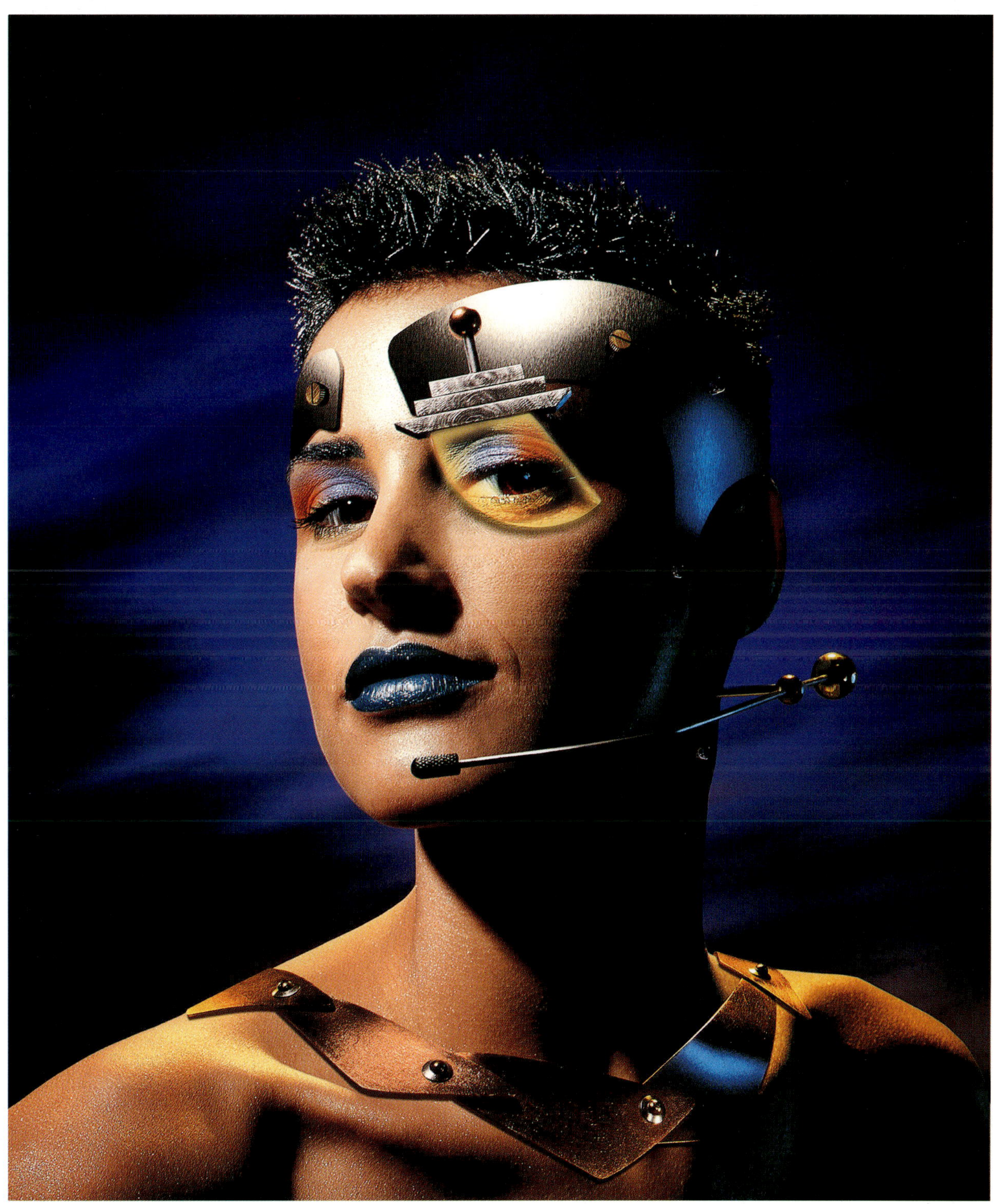

James **P**orto

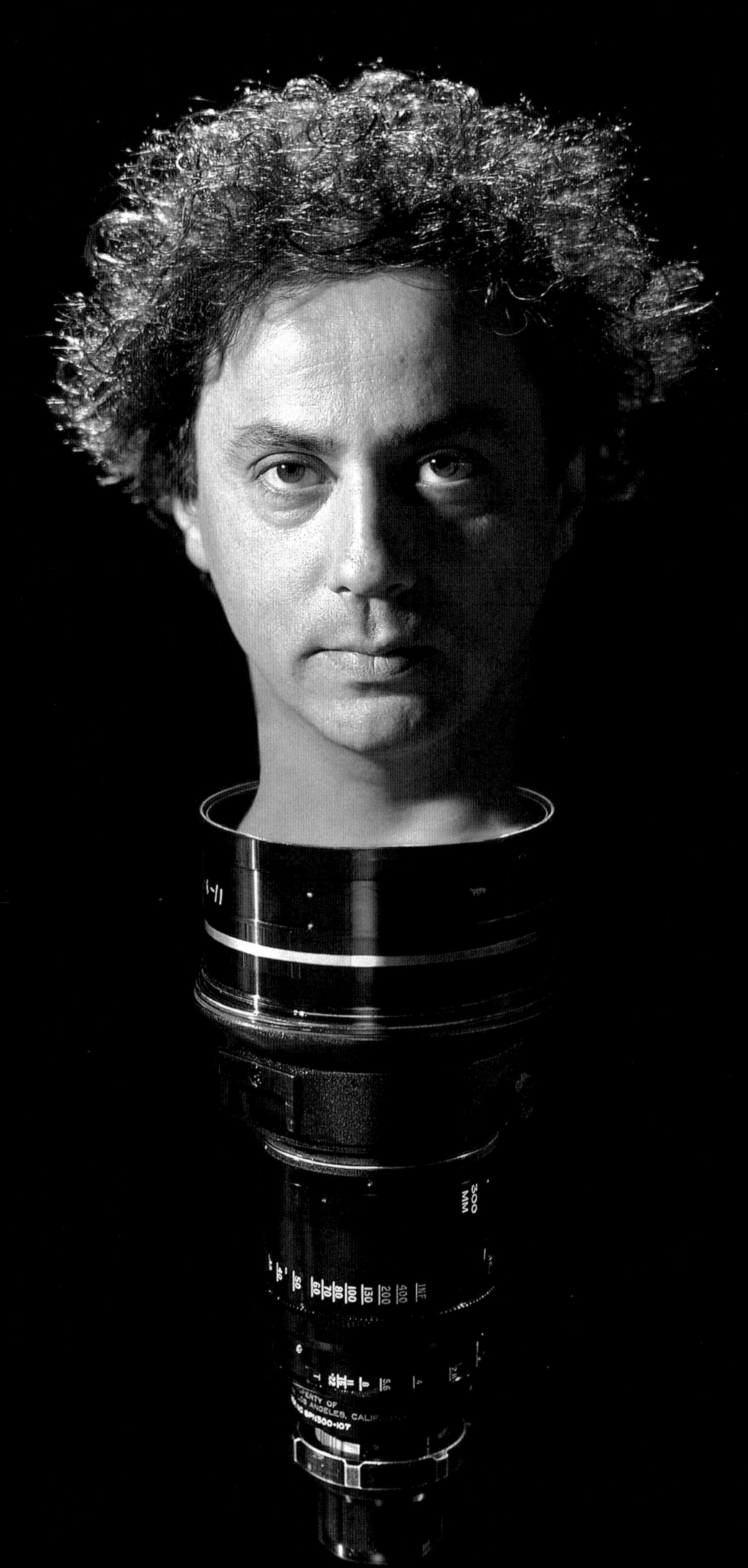
300 MM
INF
400
200
130
100
80
70
60
50
52
PROPERTY OF
ANGELES, CALIF.
SPN300-107

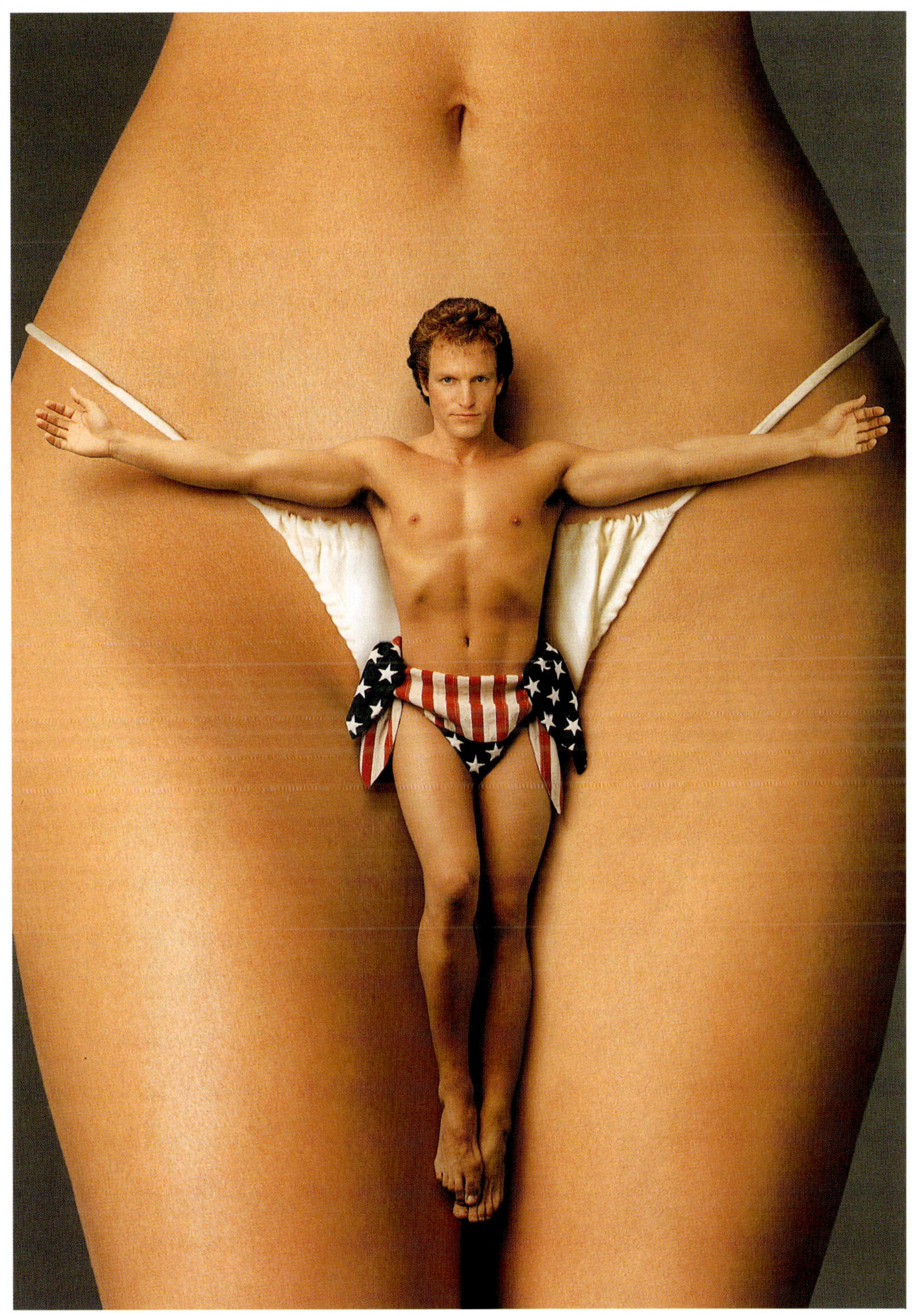

opposite: **P**eter **S**orel this page: **S**ydney **B**aldwin

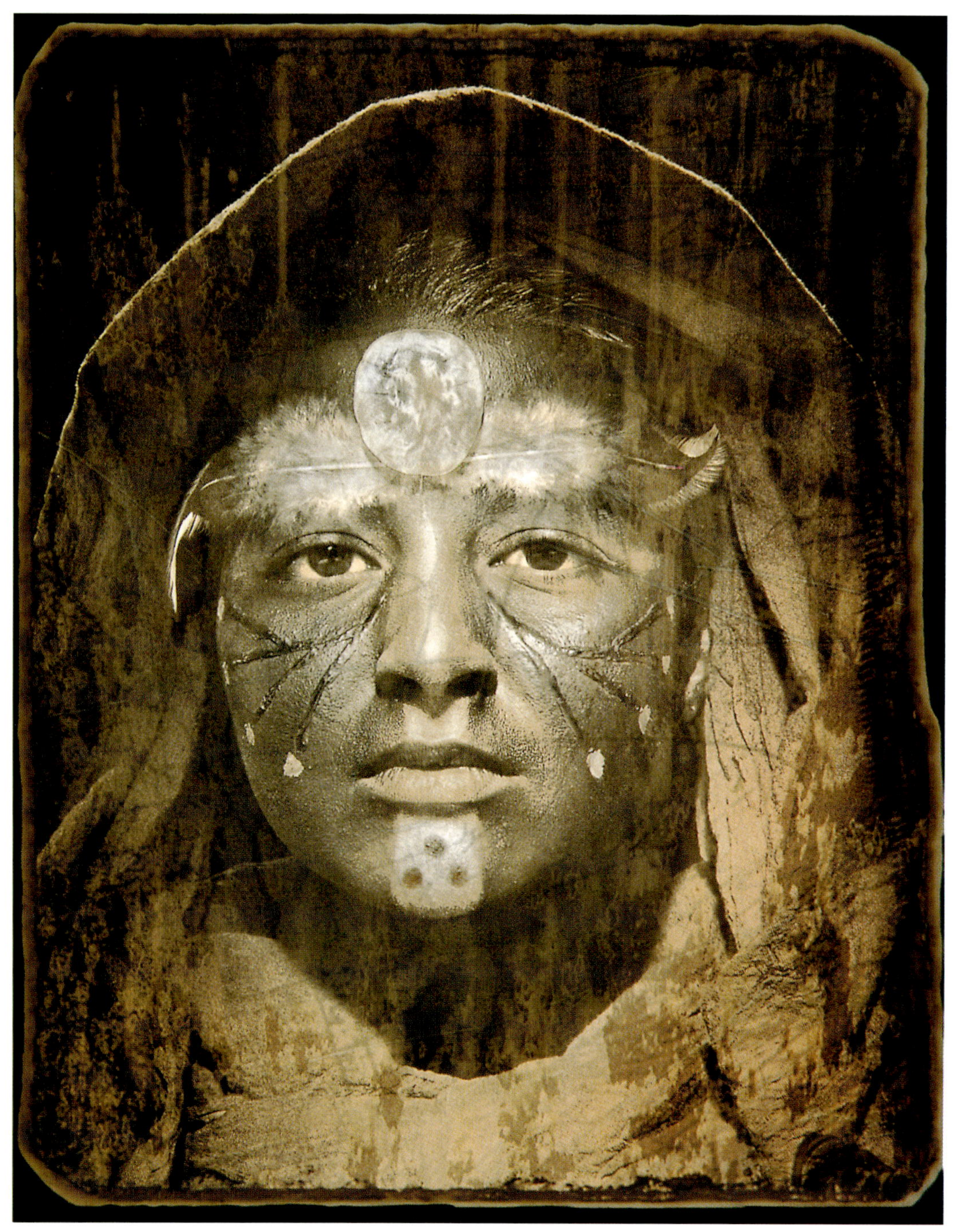

RJ Muna

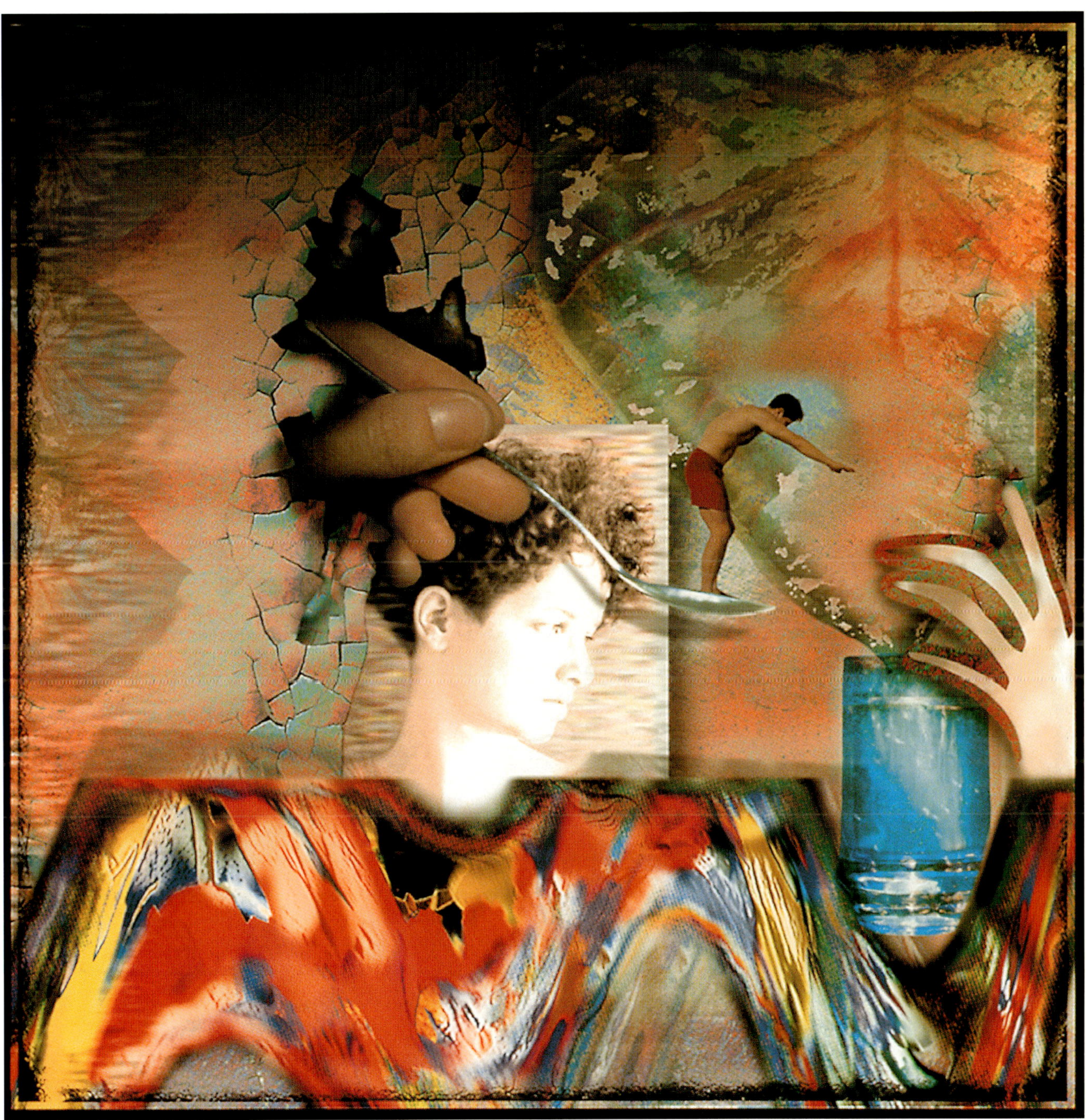

Christiane Scholl

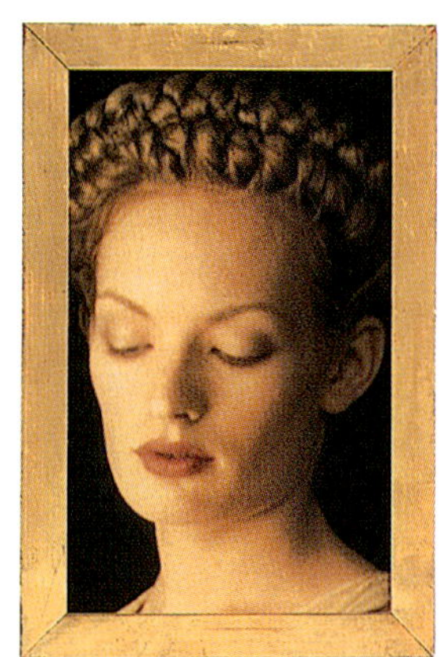
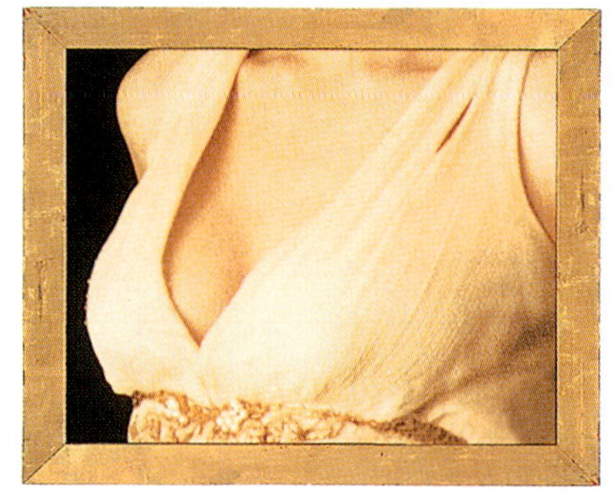
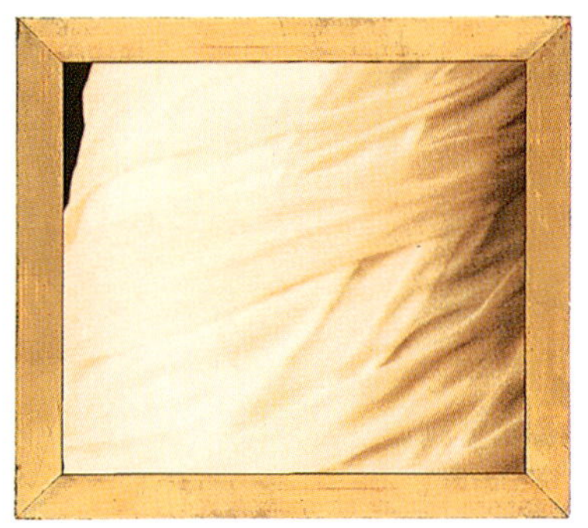
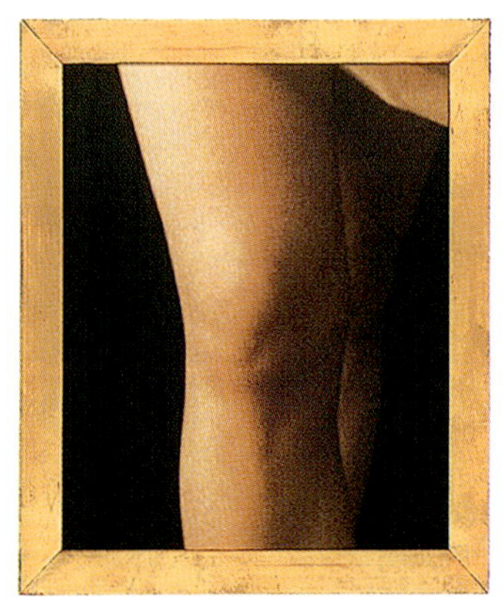
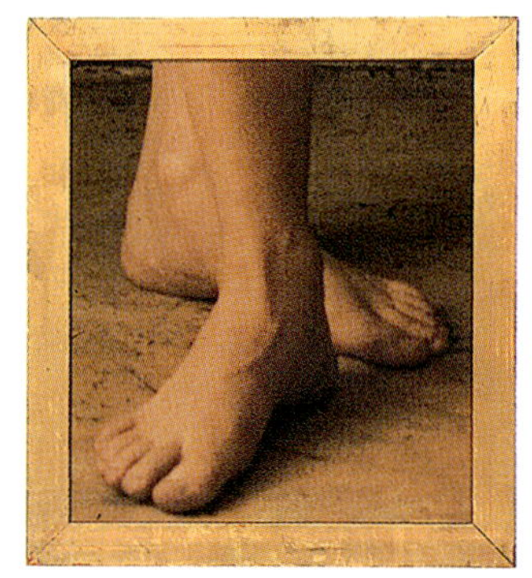

Marco Prozzo

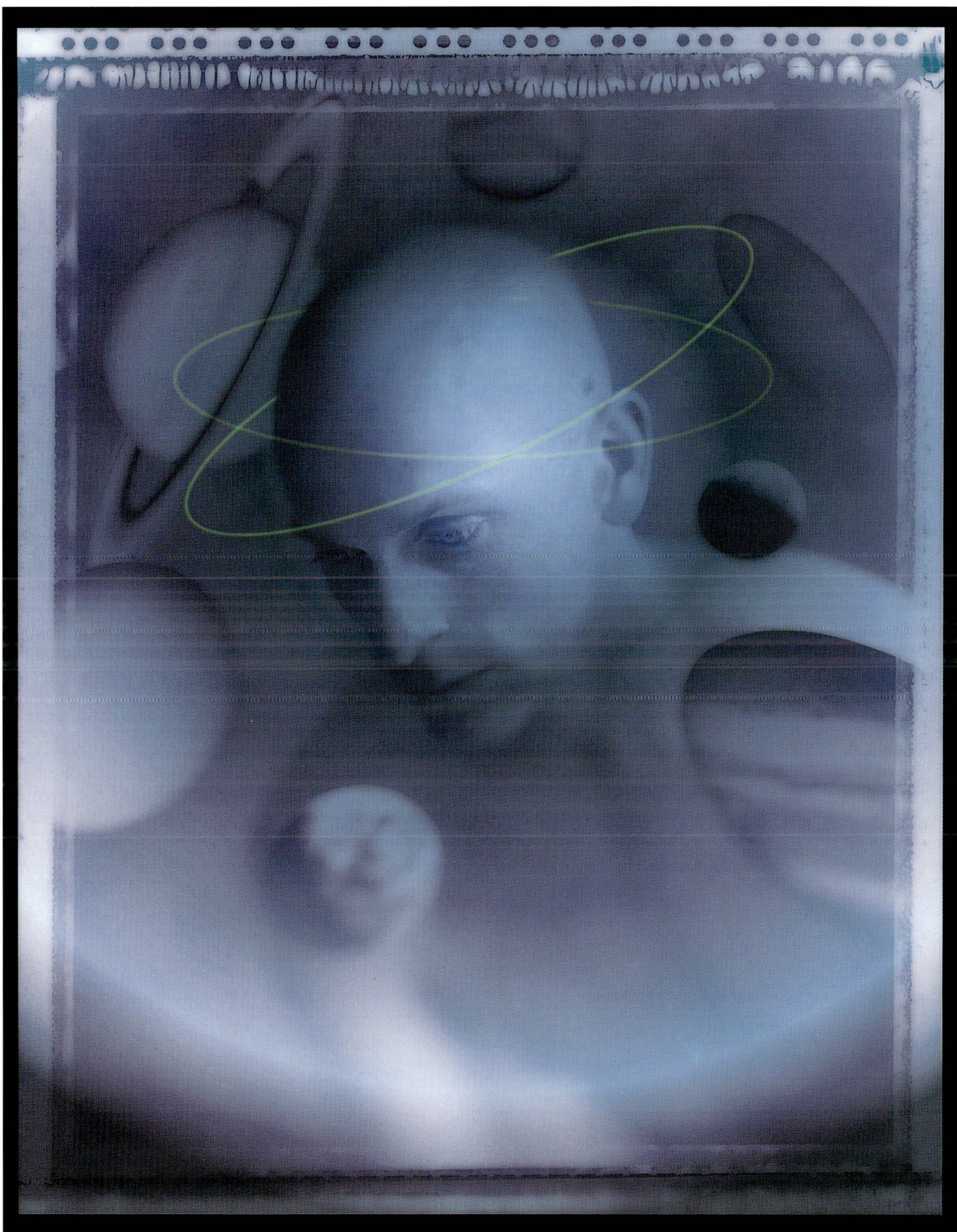

Scott Ferguson

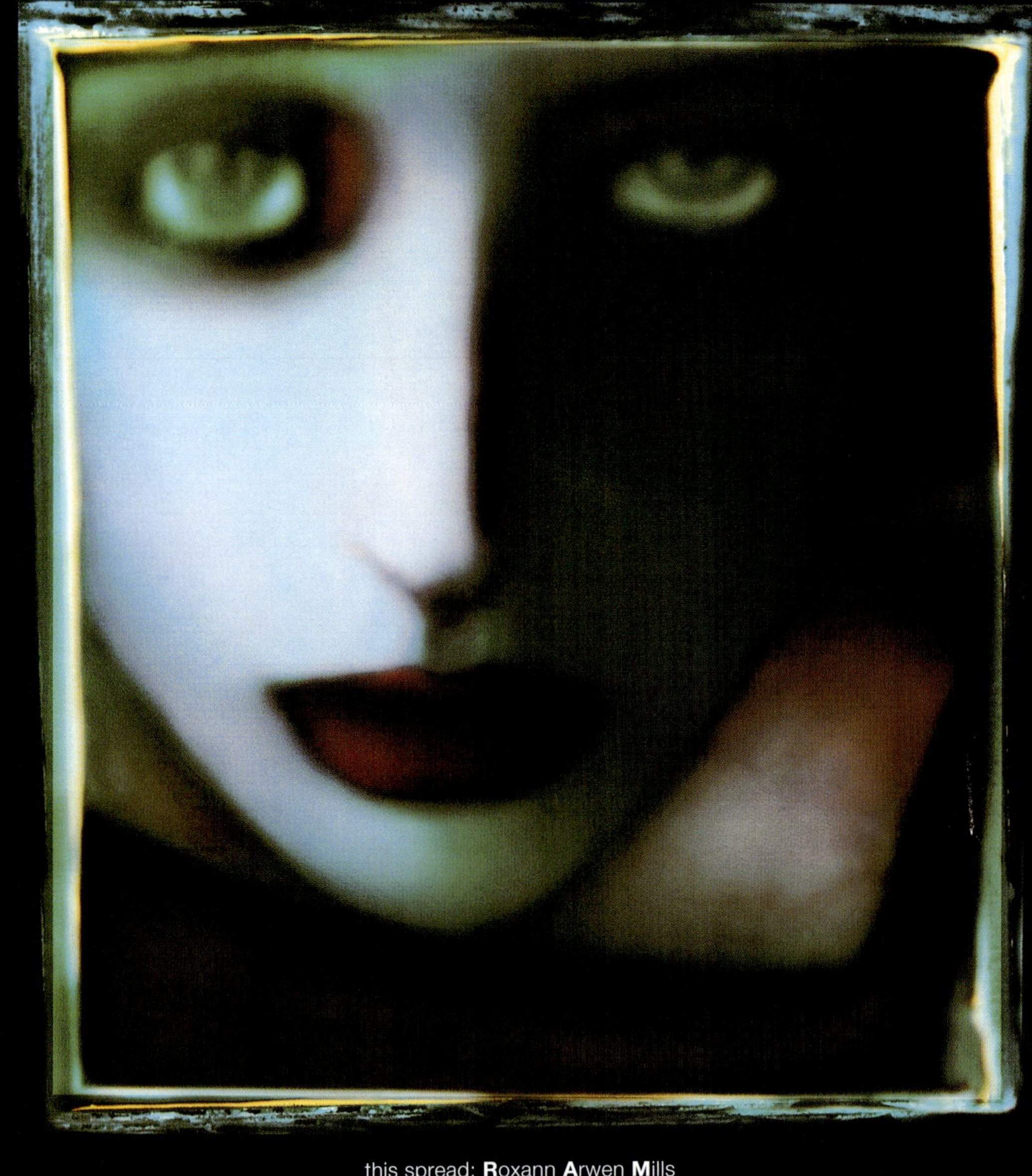

this spread: **Roxann Arwen Mills**

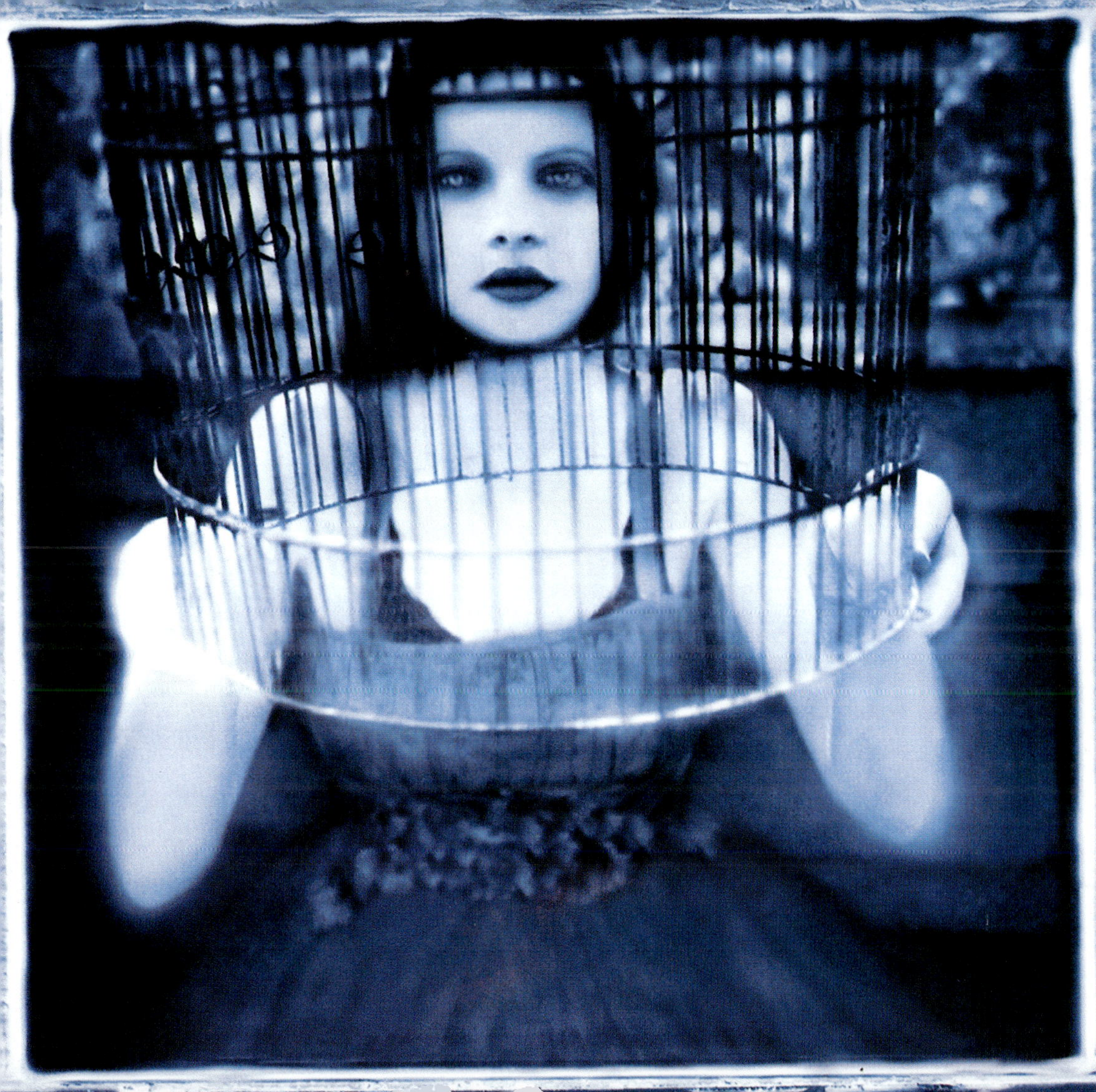

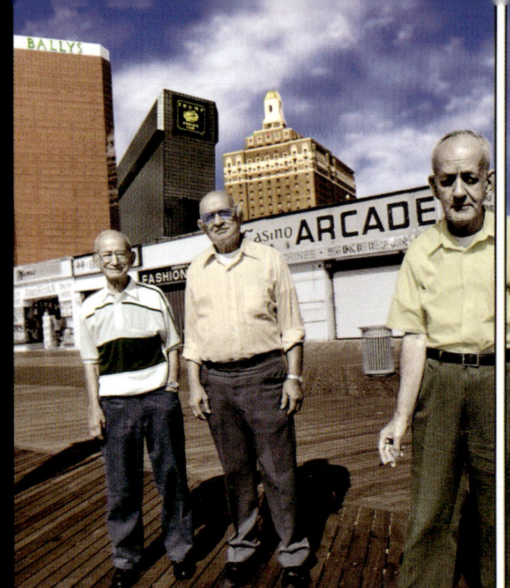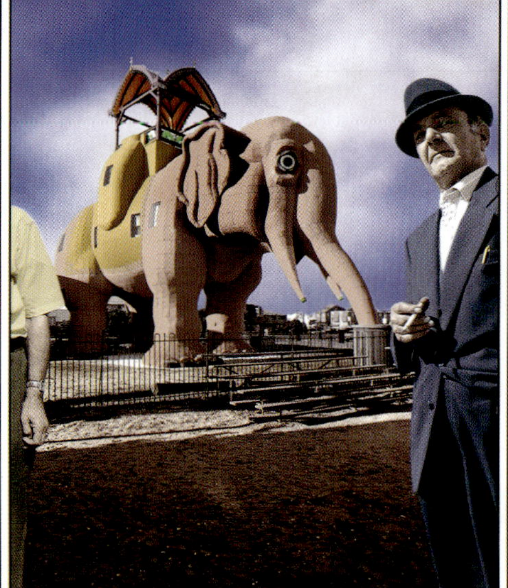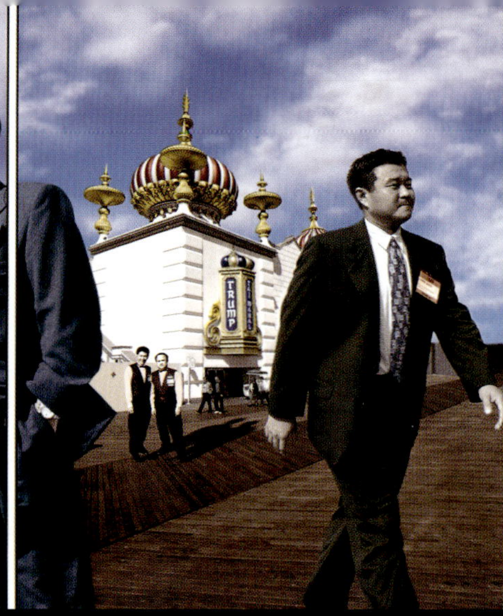

this spread: **D**avid **S**. **W**aitz

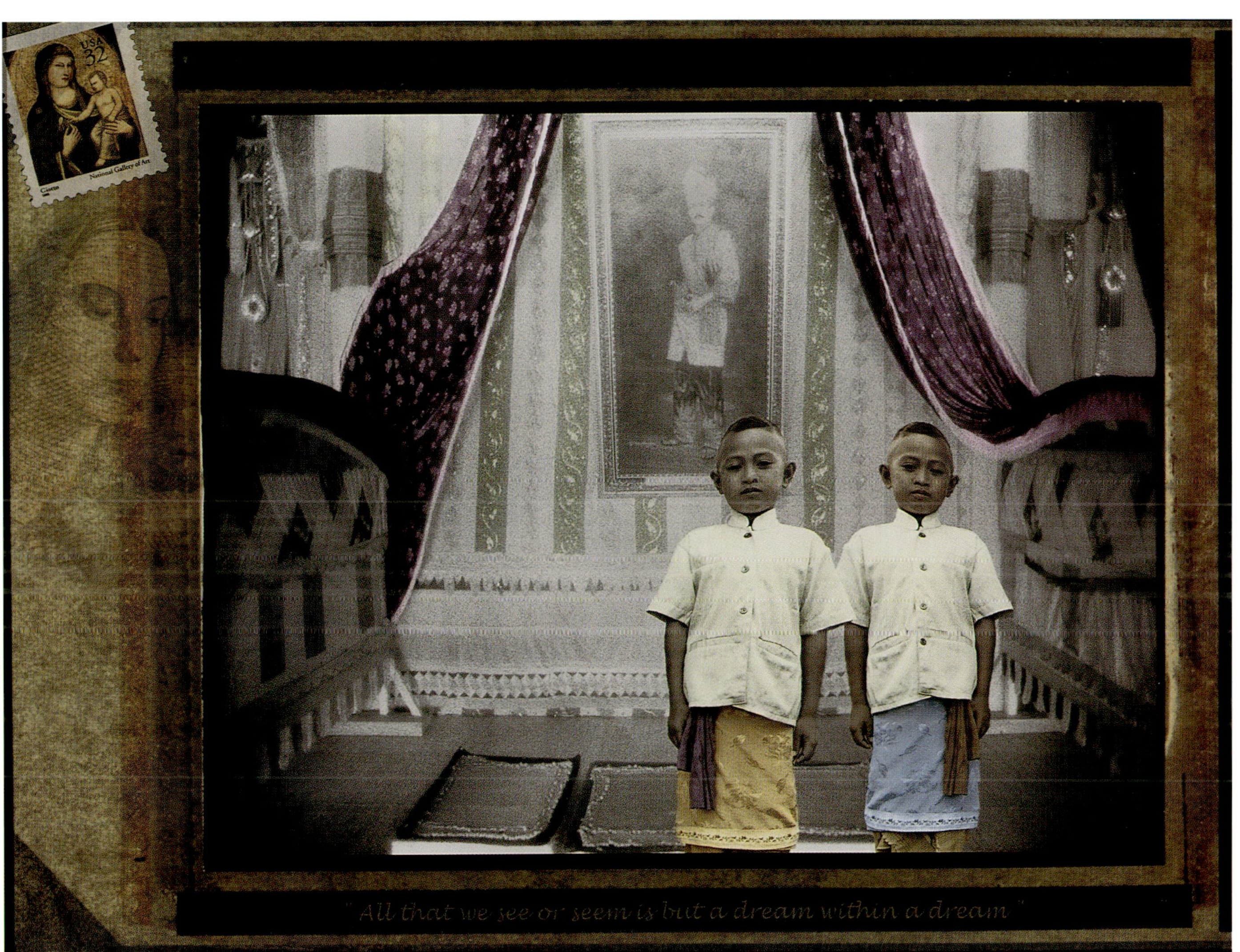

" All that we see or seem is but a dream within a dream "

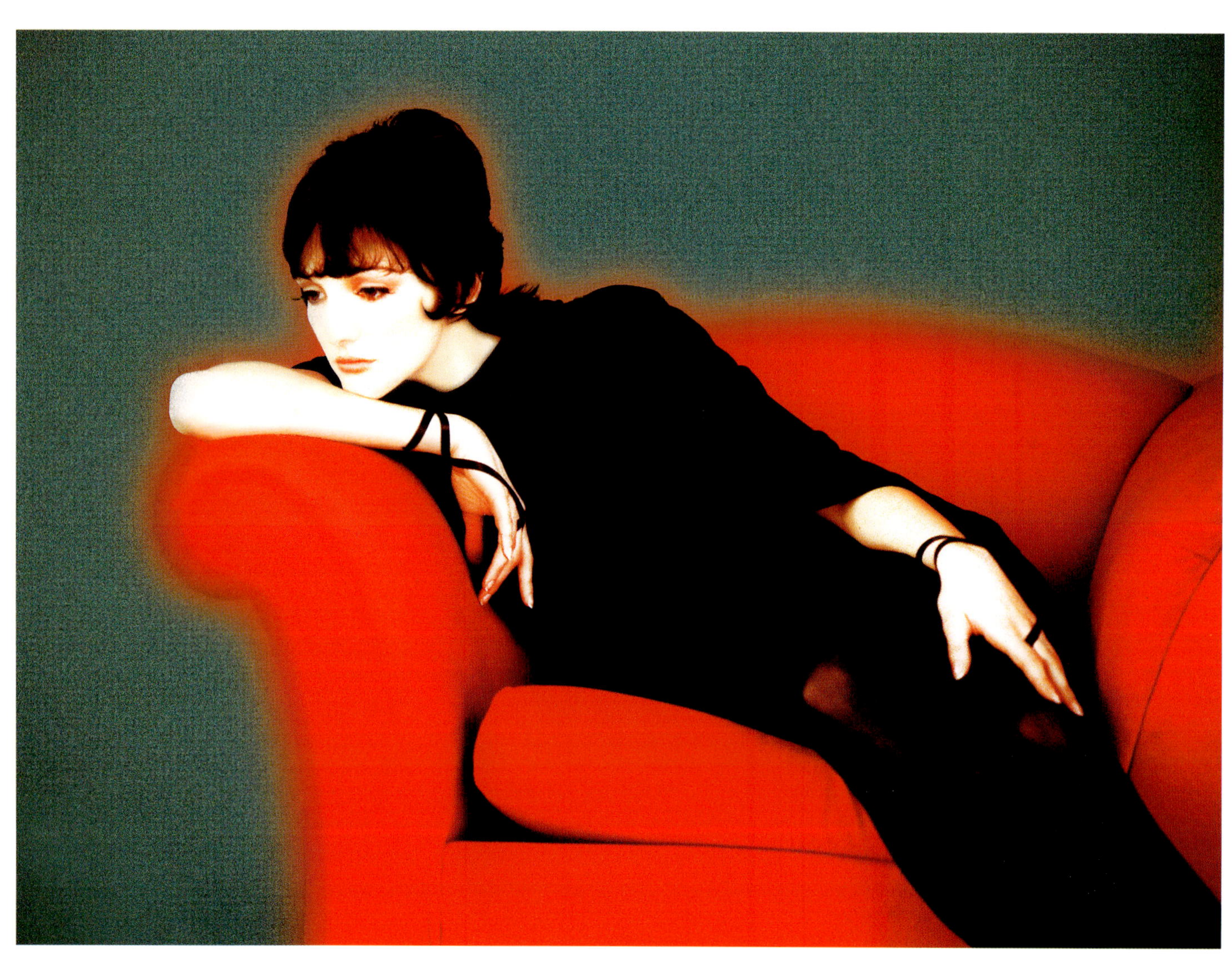

this spread: **S**anjay **K**othari

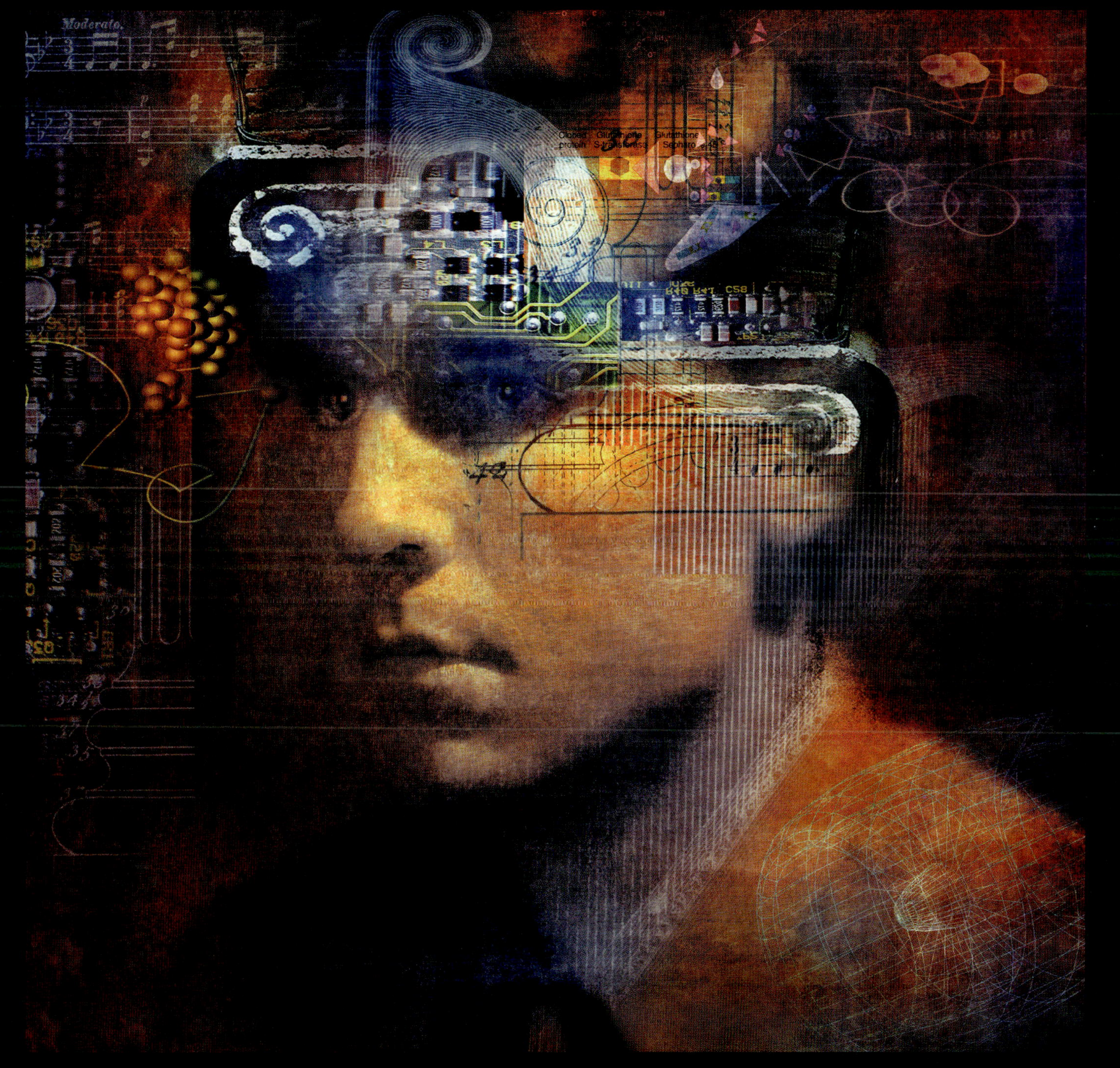

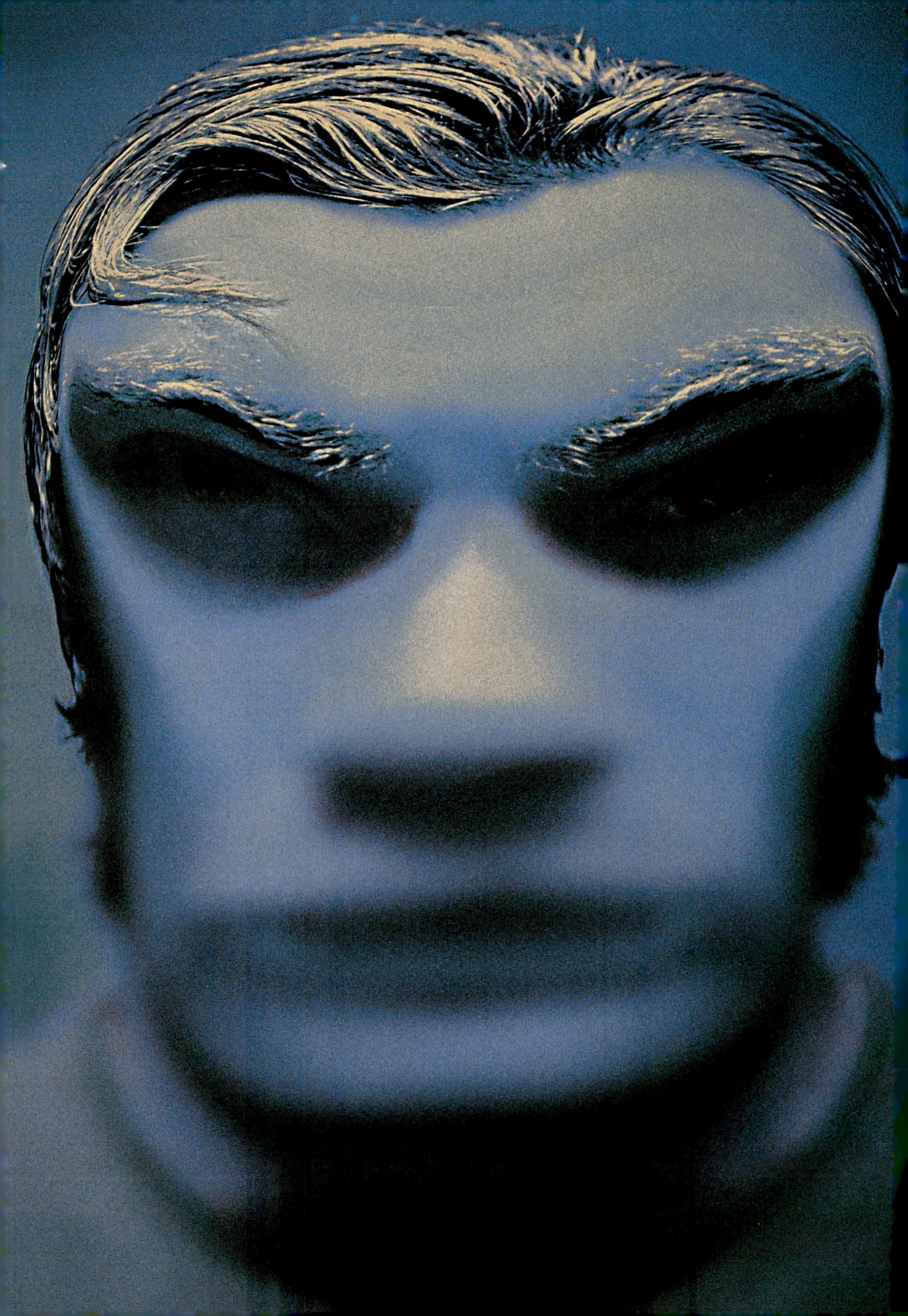

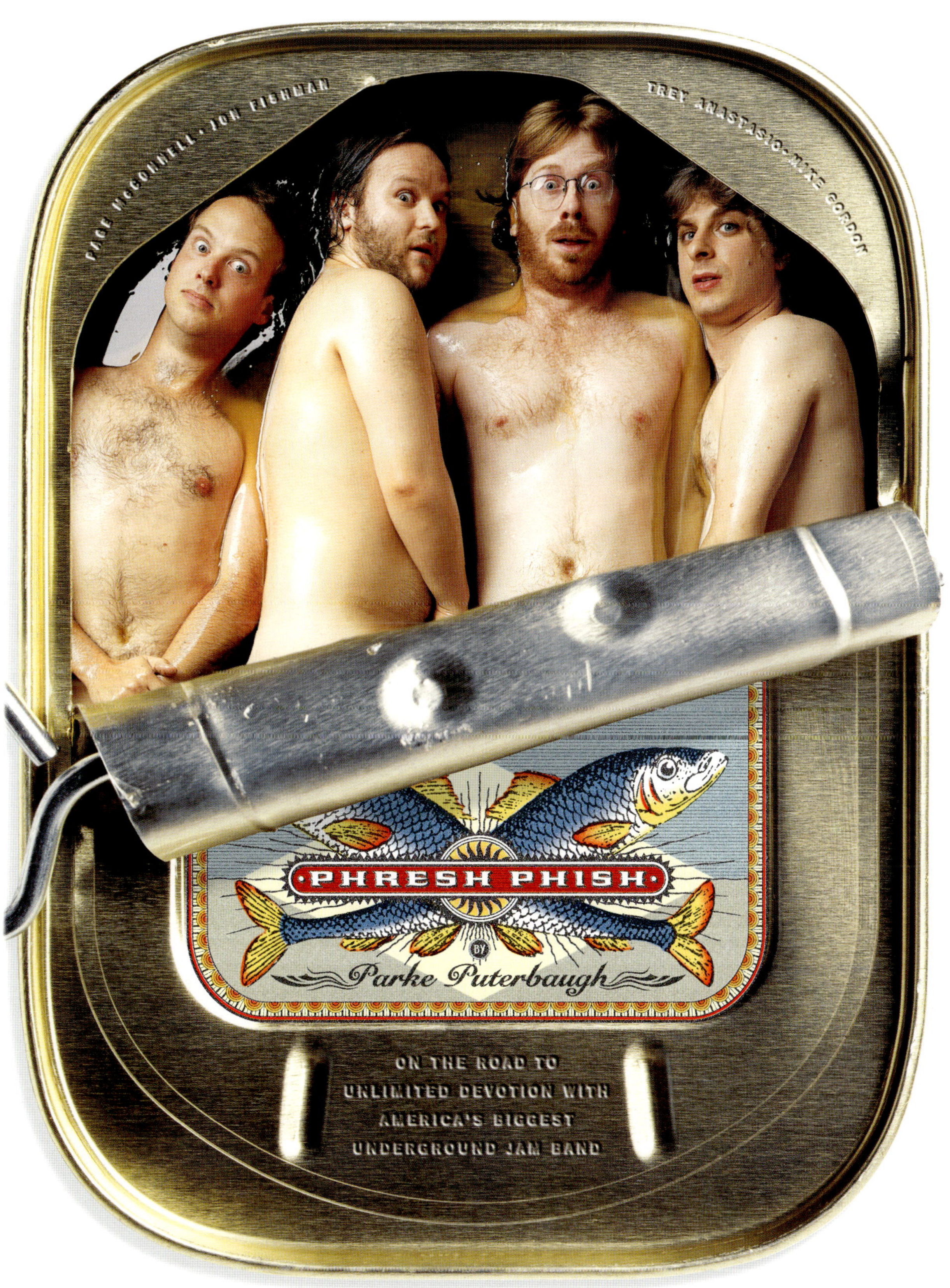

opposite: **M**ir **L**ada this page: **M**ark **S**eliger

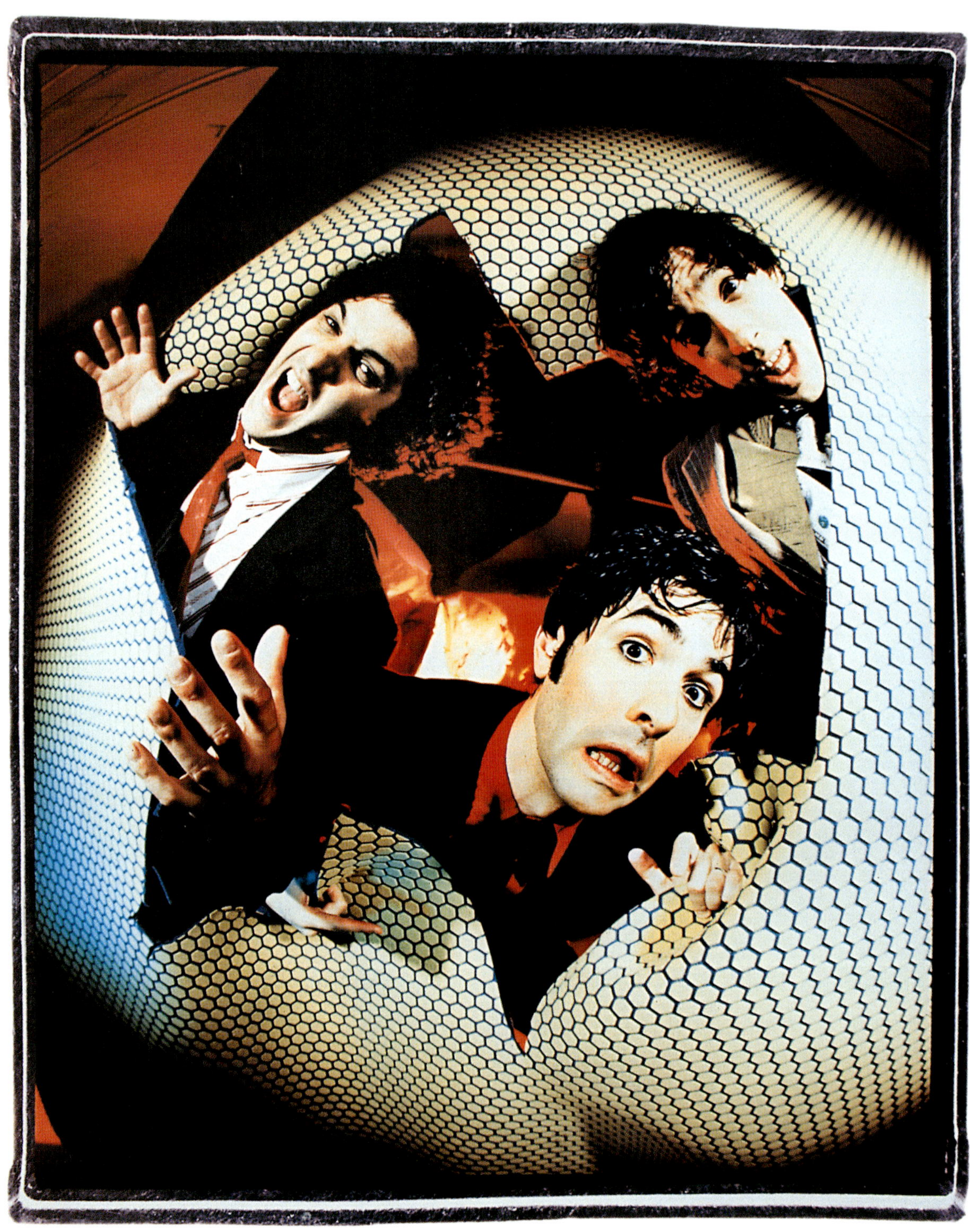

this page: **R**afael **F**uchs opposite: **M**ir **L**ada

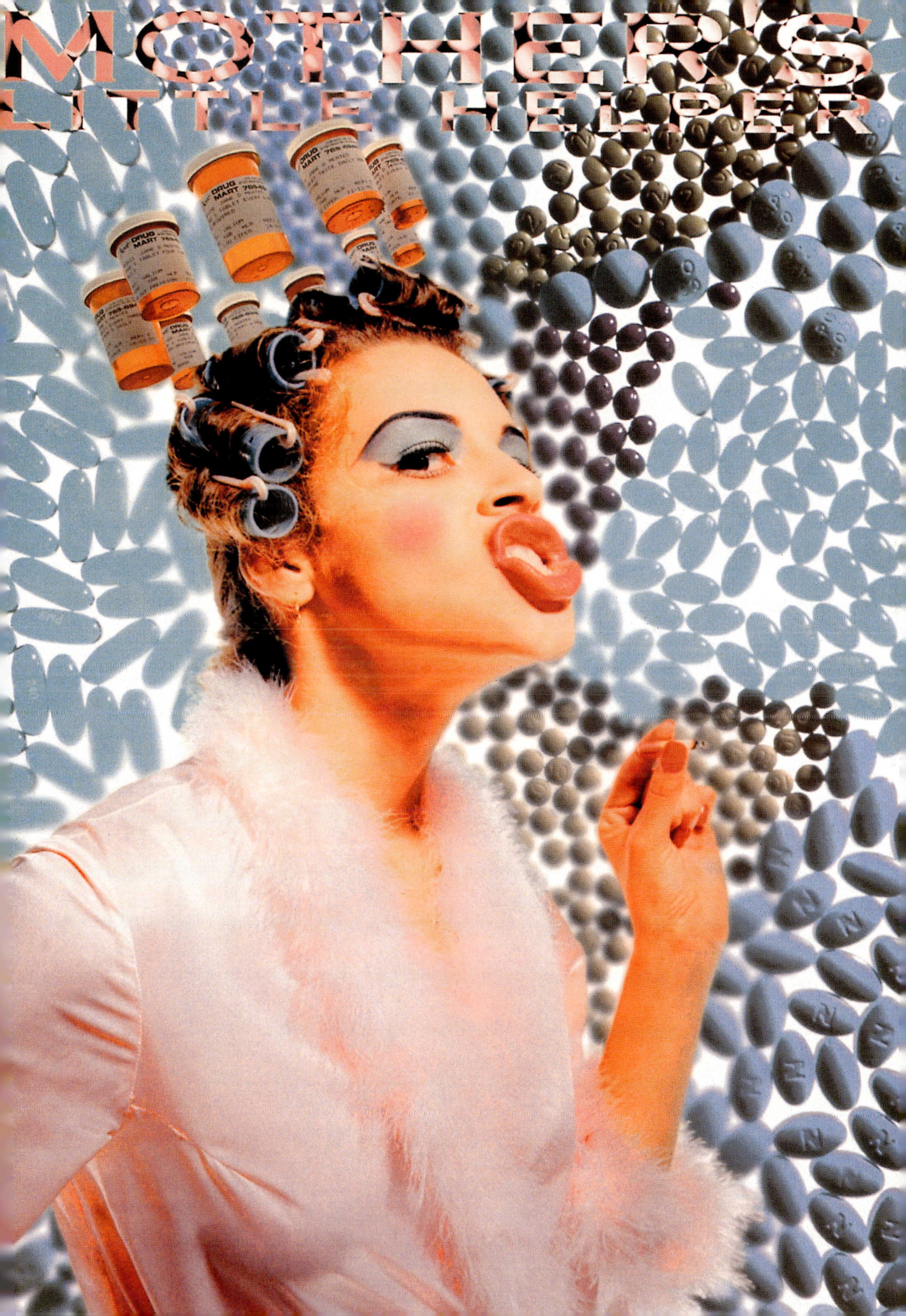

MOTHER'S
LITTLE HELPER

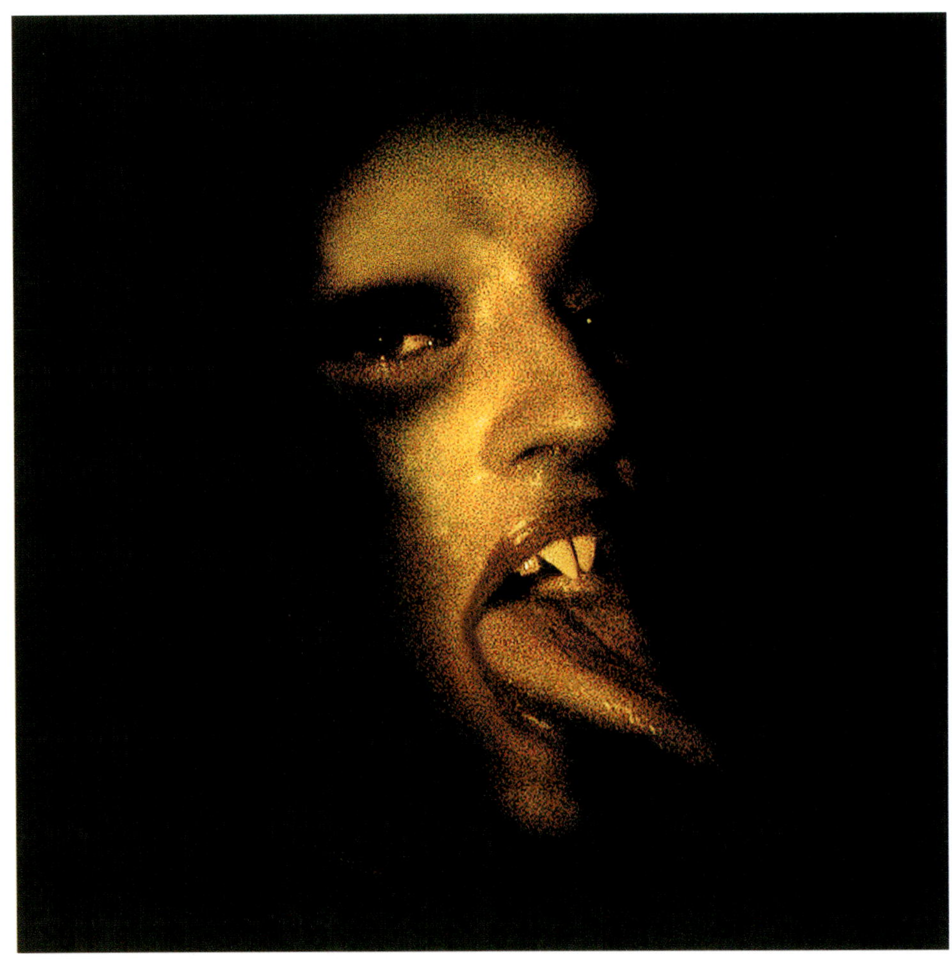

this spread: **E**ric **V**an **D**en **B**rulle

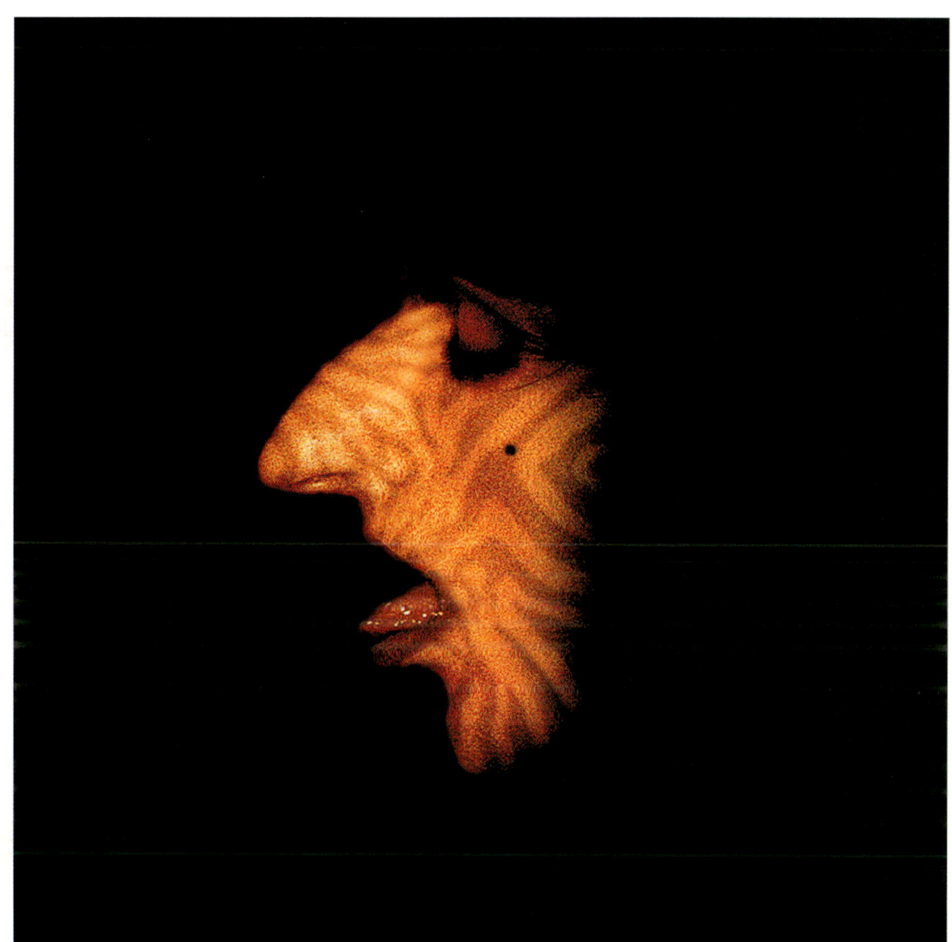

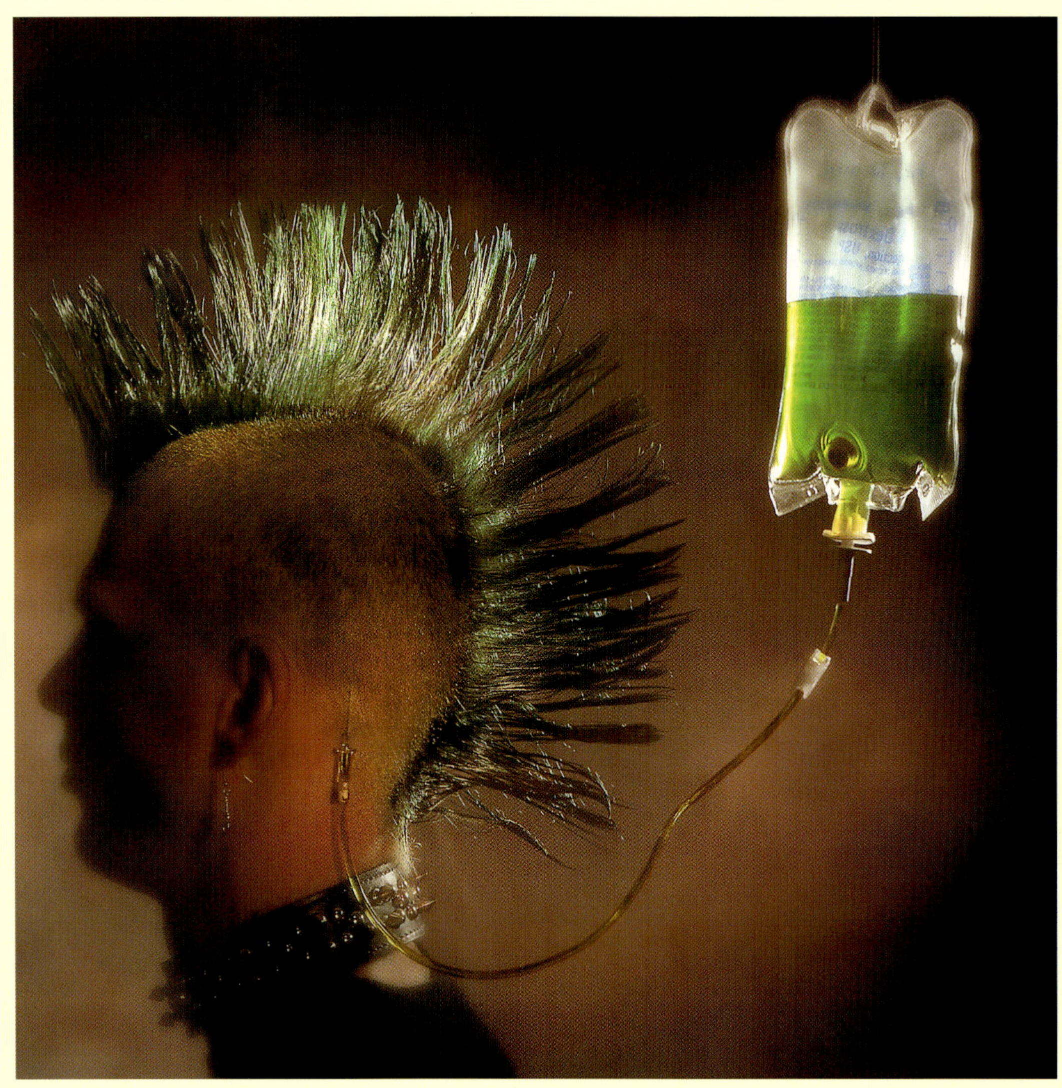

Bruce DeBoer

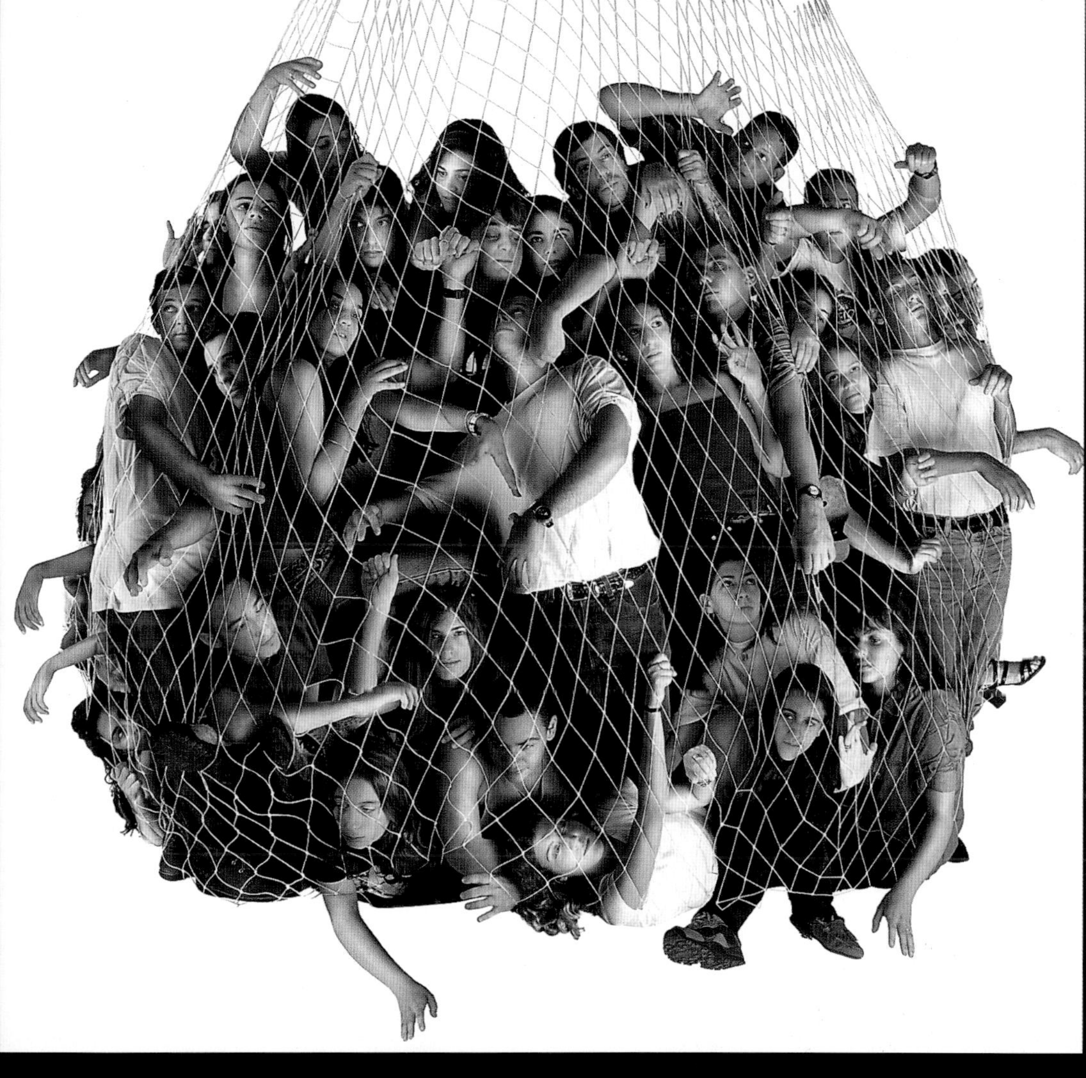

Fernando **Z**uffo

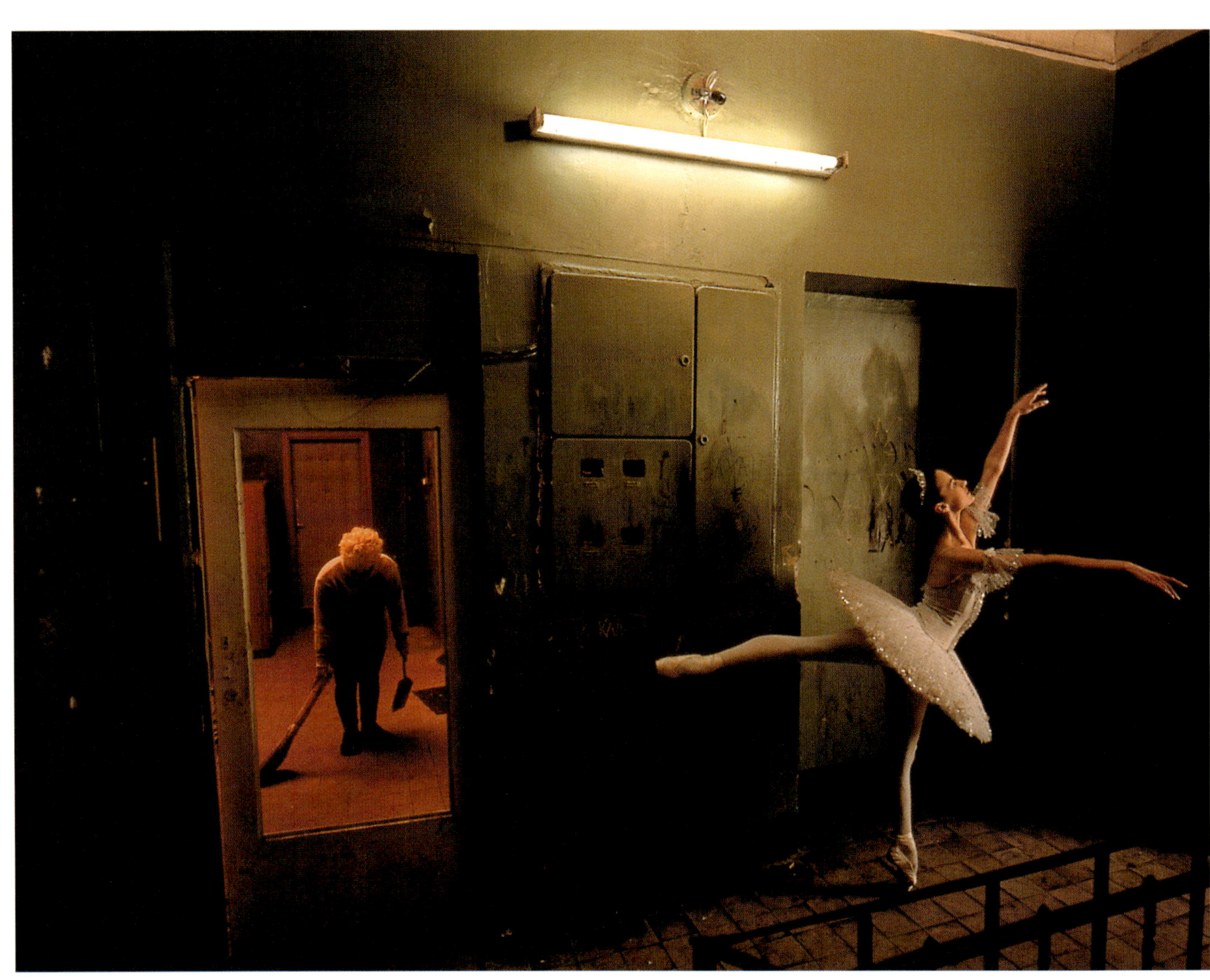

this spread, following page: **J**oe **M**c**N**ally

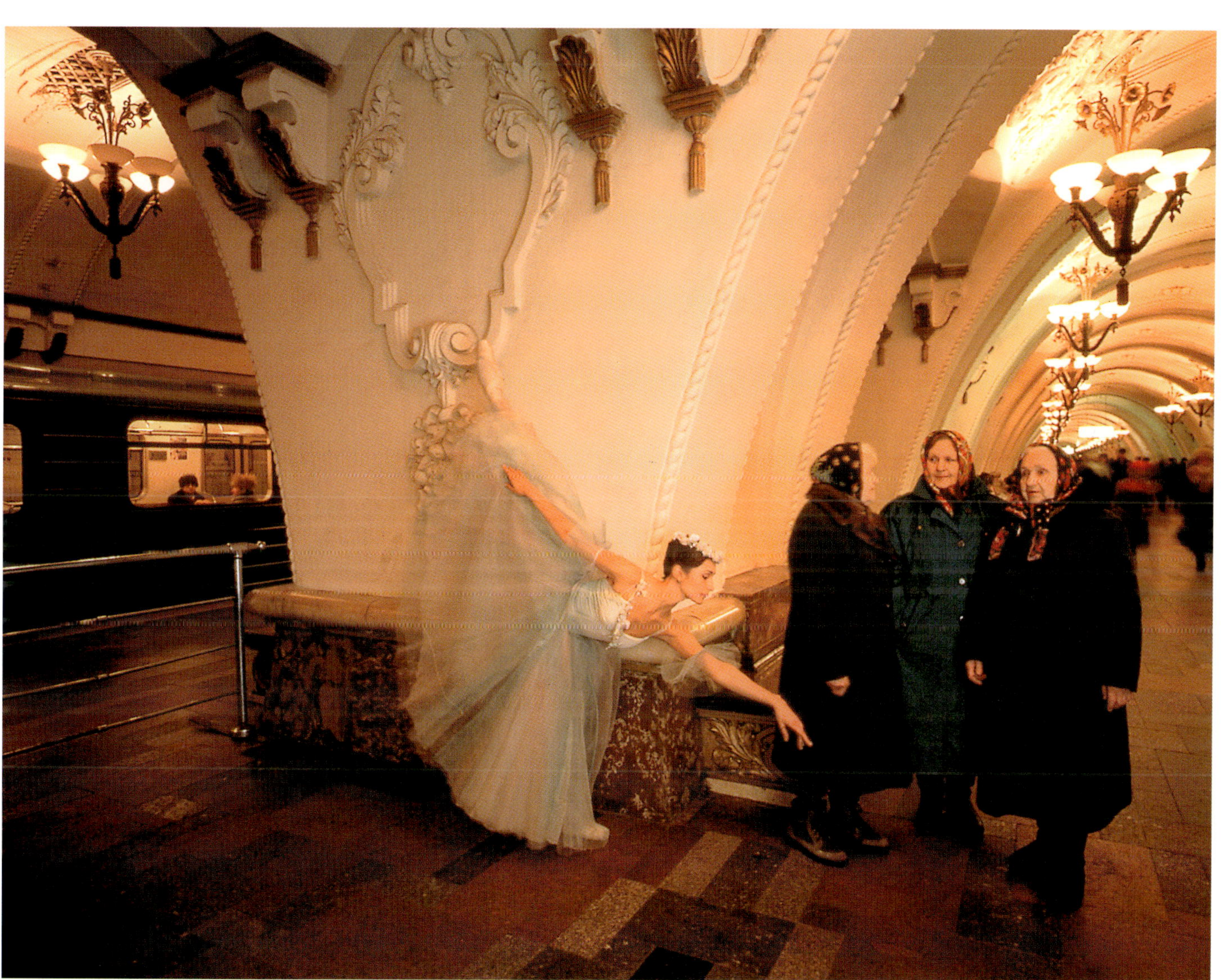

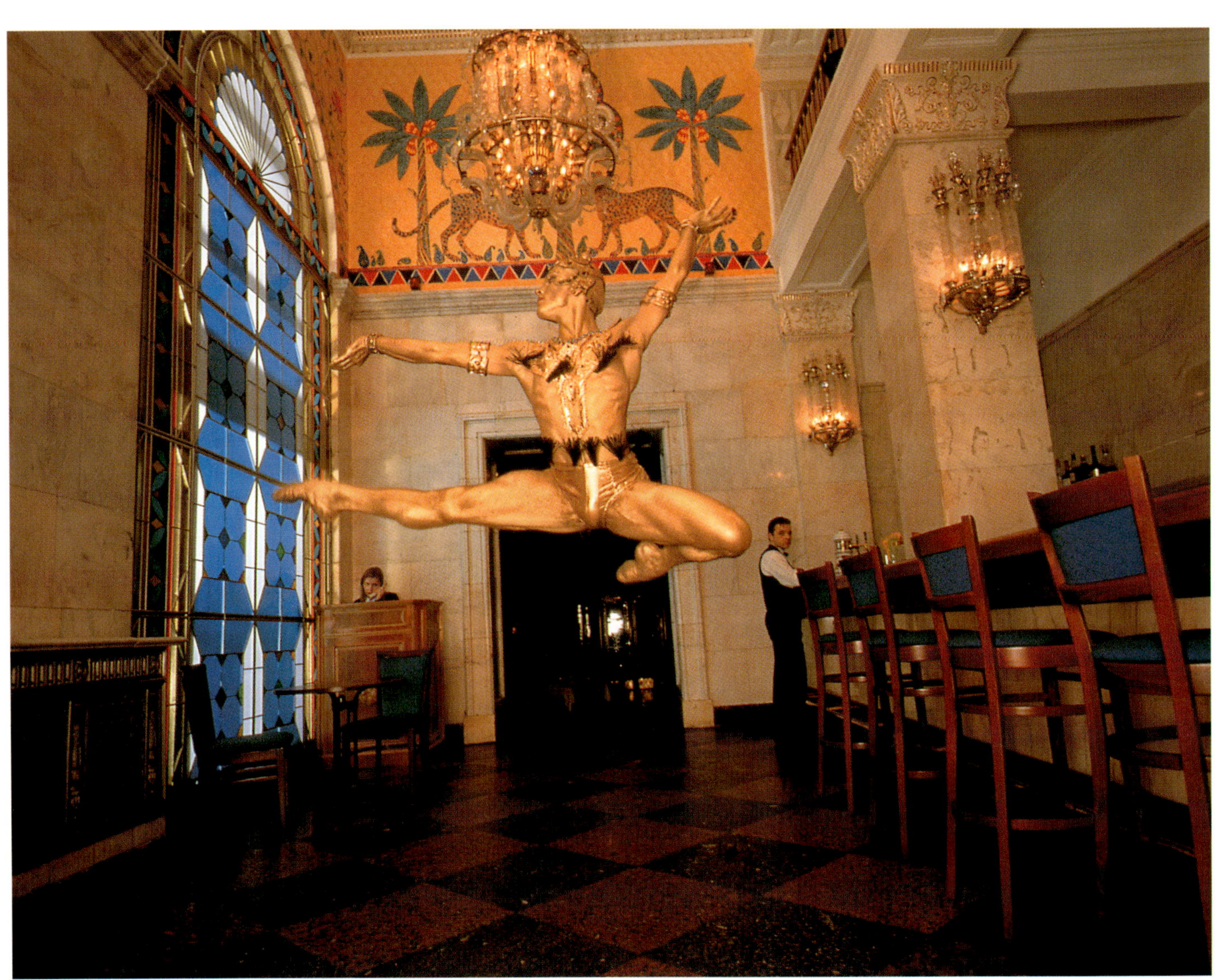

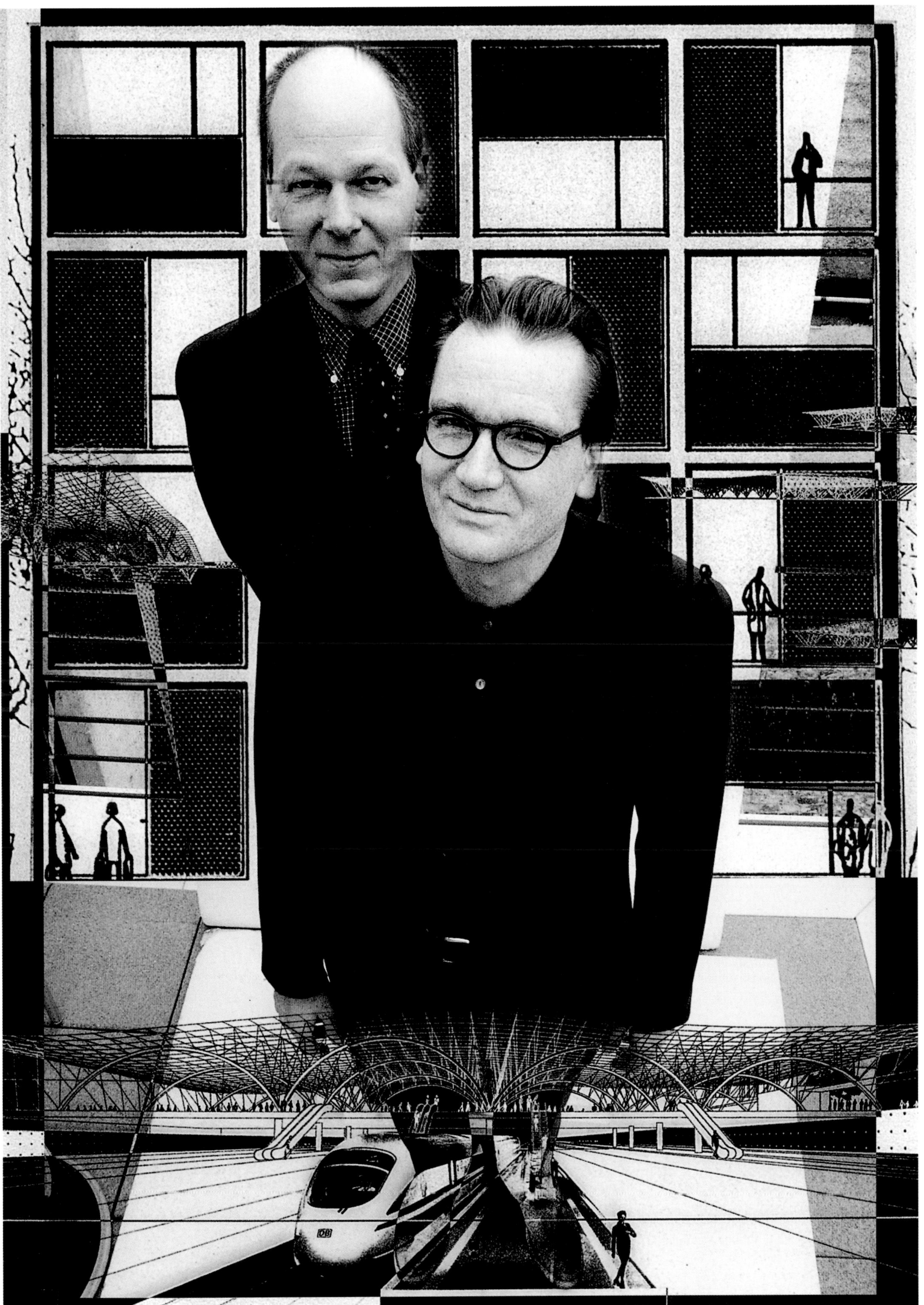

Michale **E**ibes, **K**laus **H**agmeier

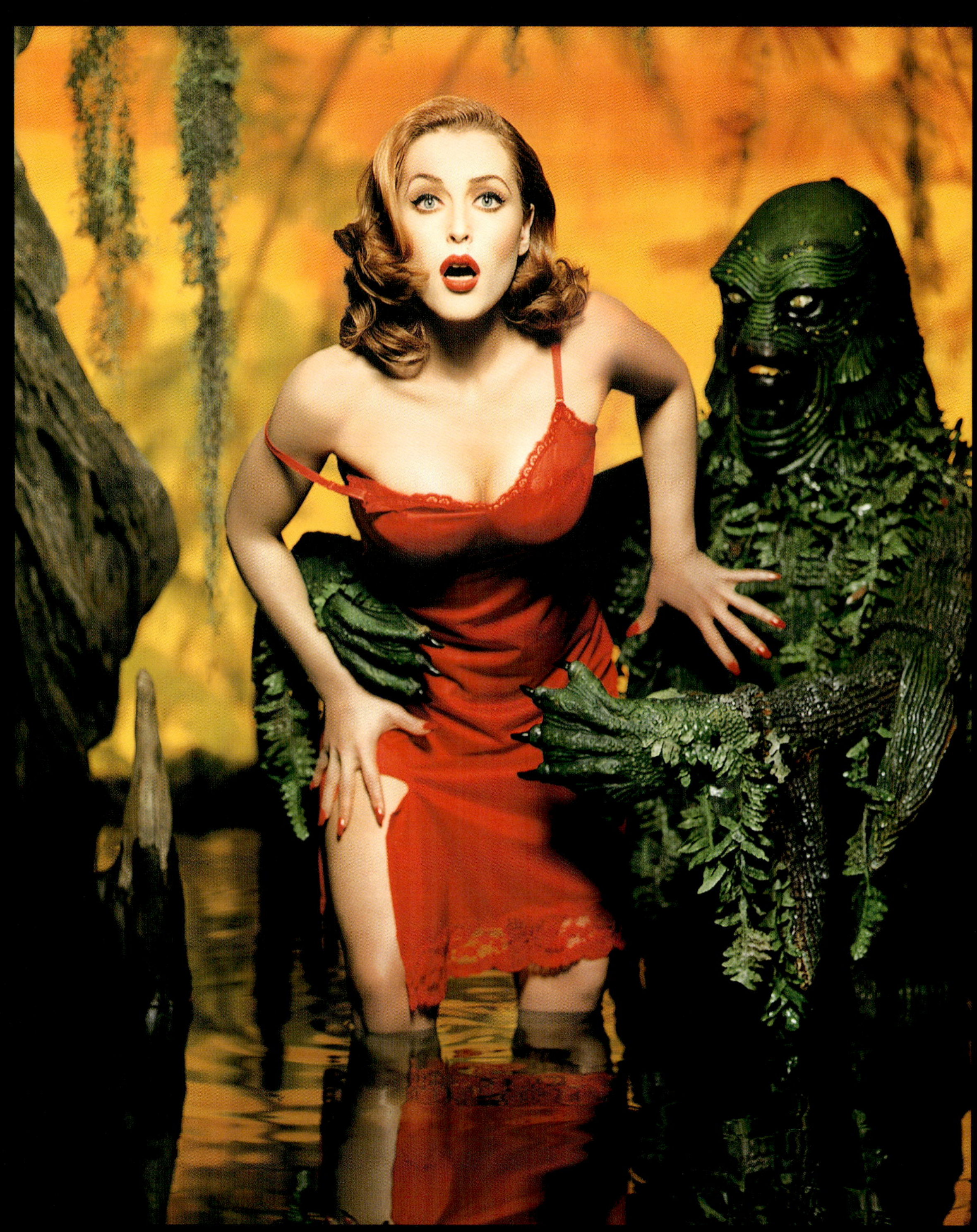

Matthew Rolston

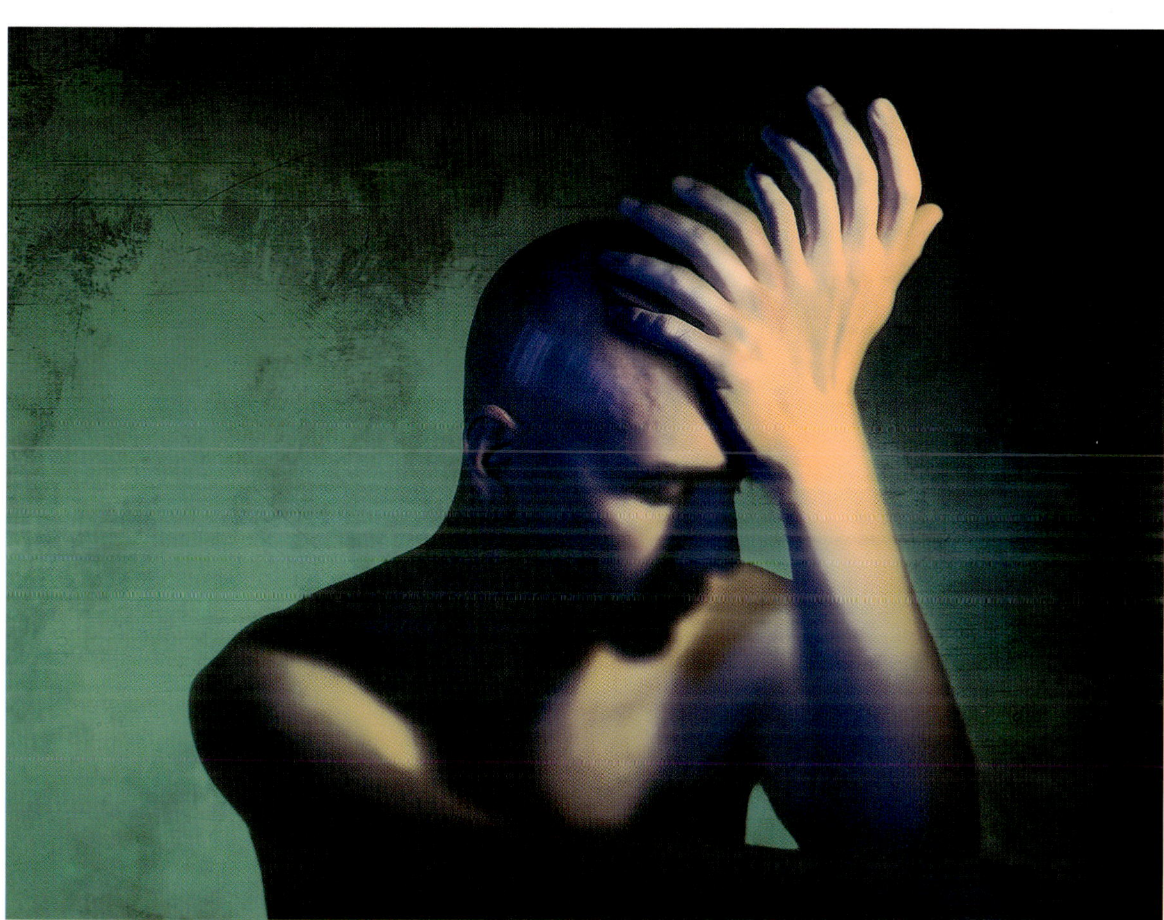

Doug Landreth

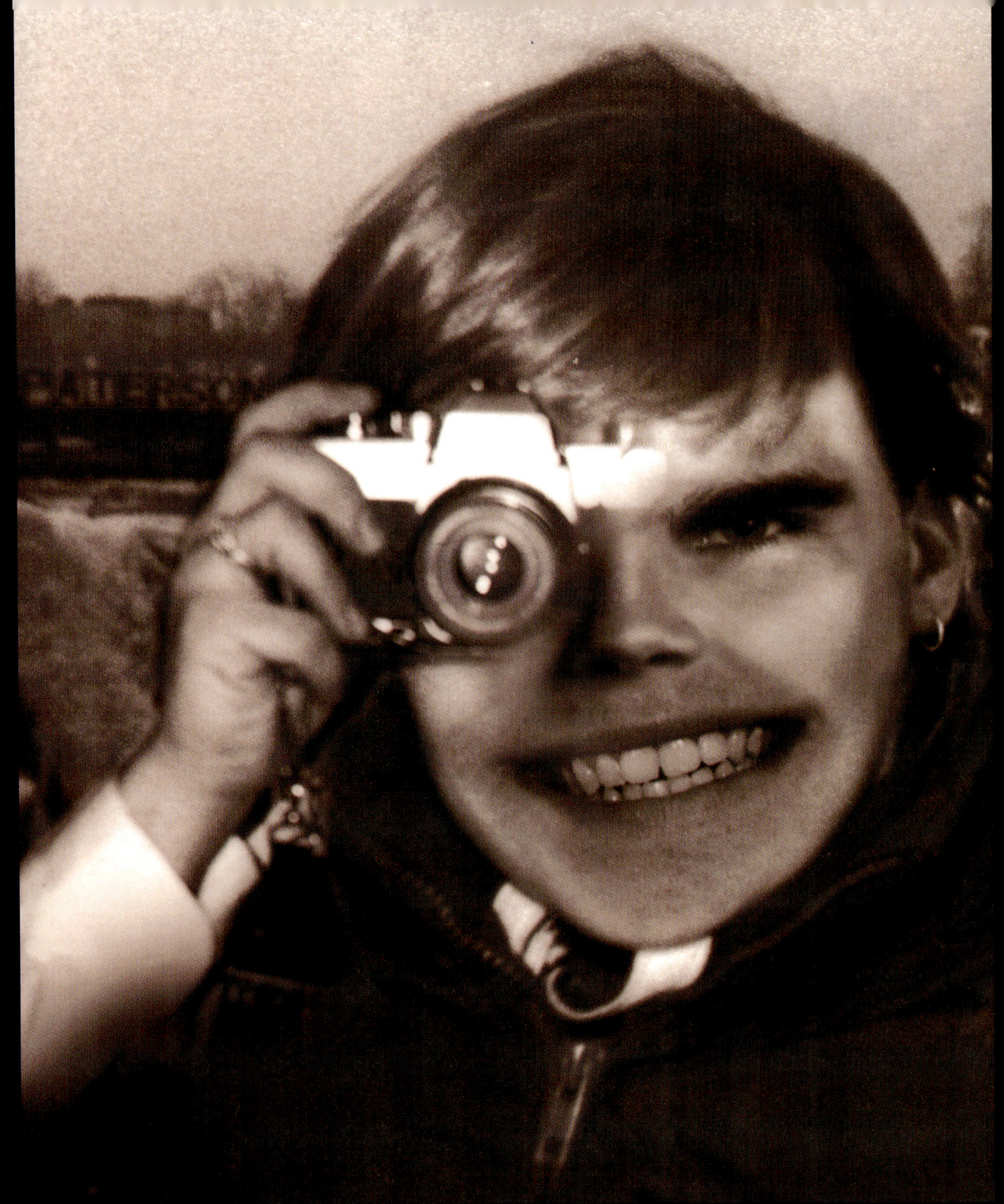

Greg **Z**ukowski

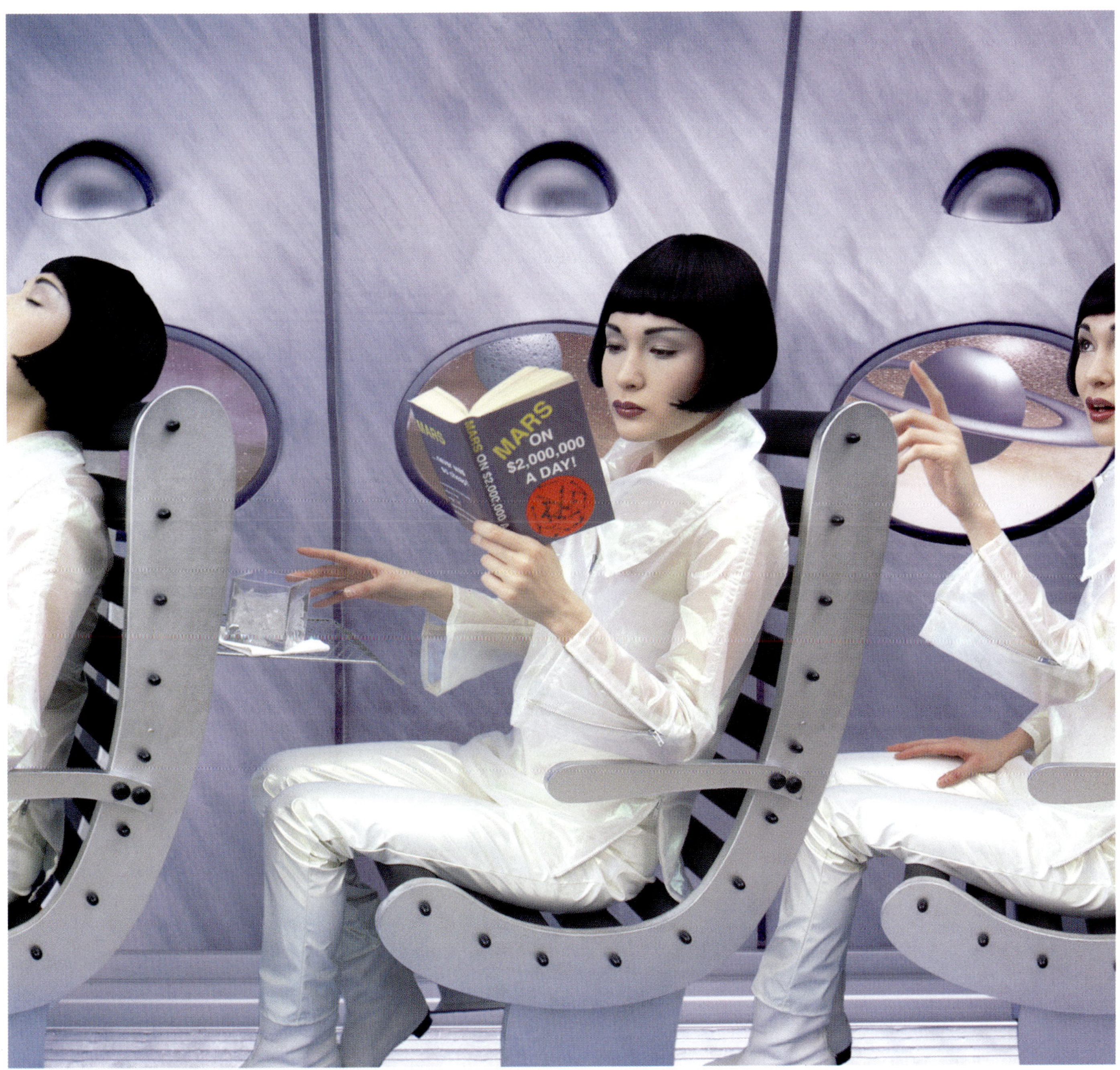

Alan Abrams, Francesca Lacagnina

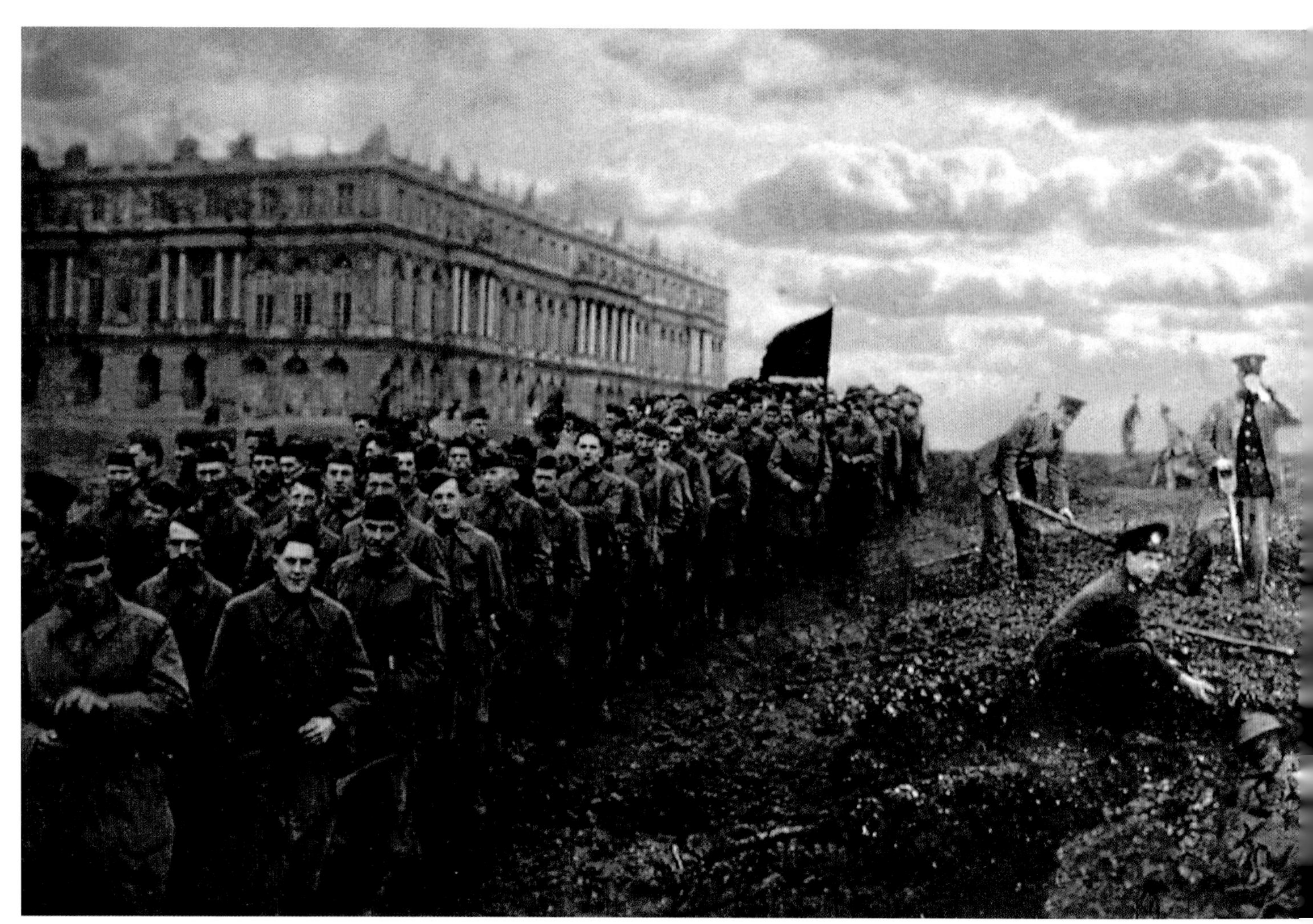

Charles Brackman

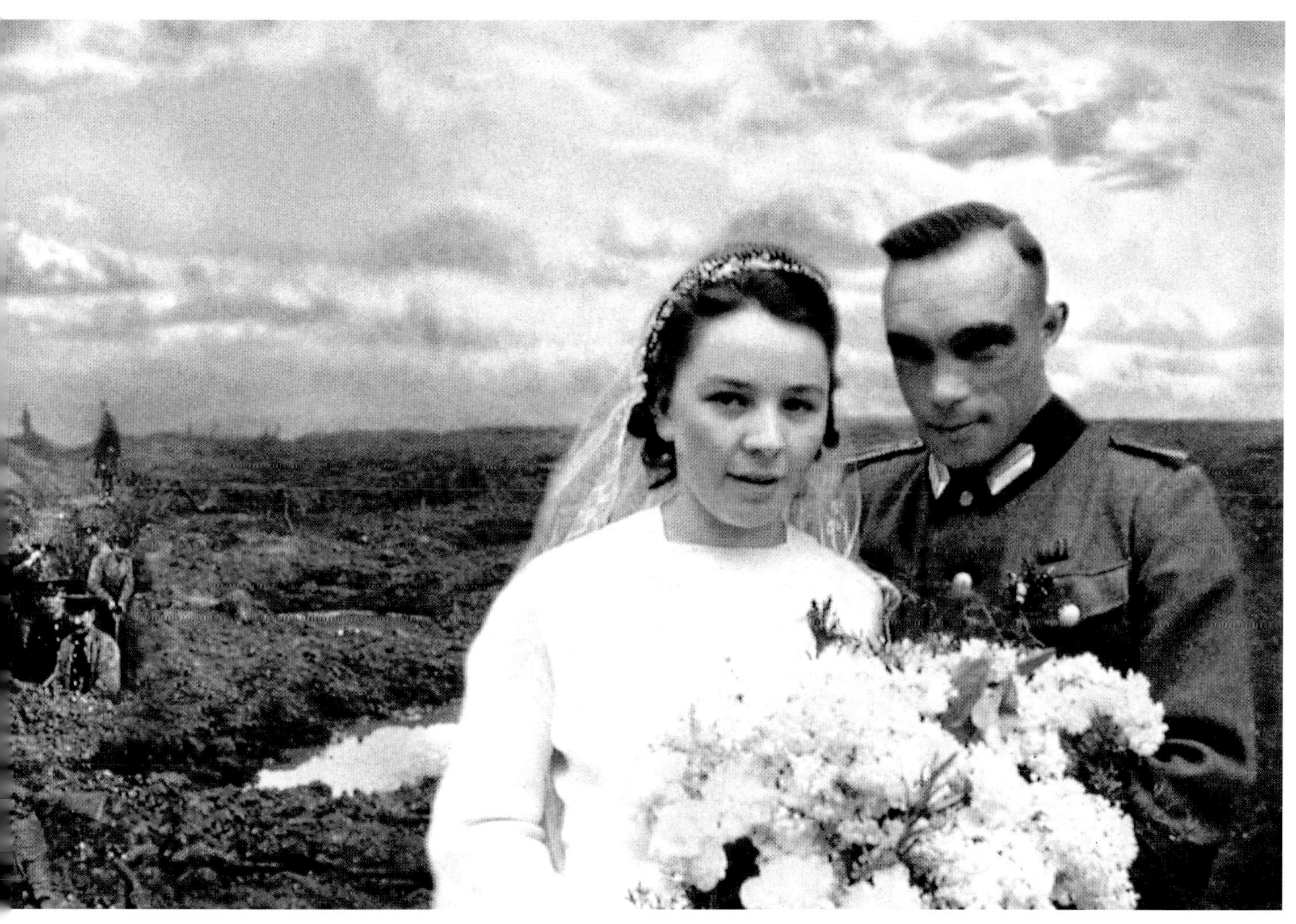

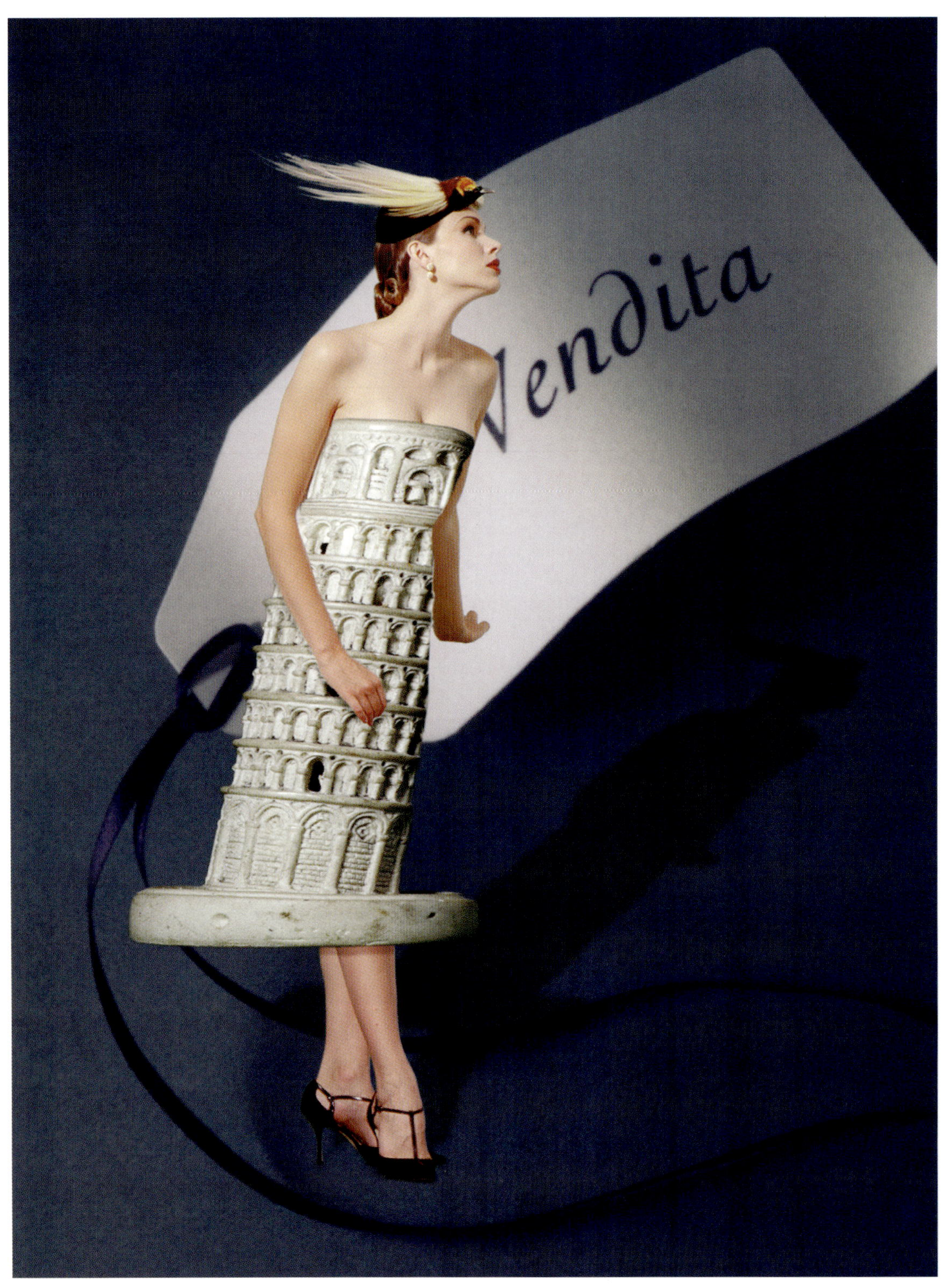

this page: **A**lan **A**brams, **F**rancesca **L**acagnina opposite: **F**ernando **Z**uffo

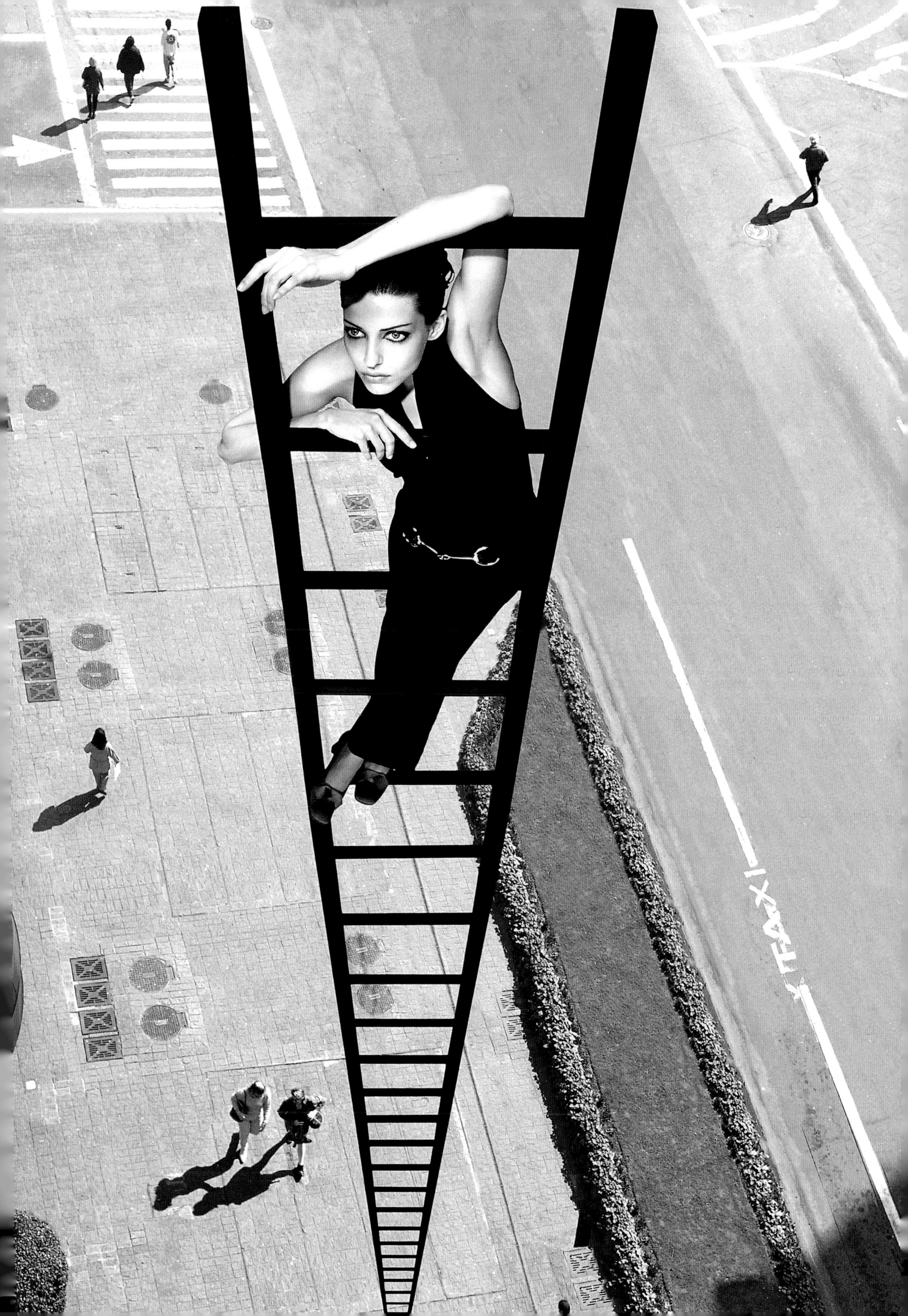

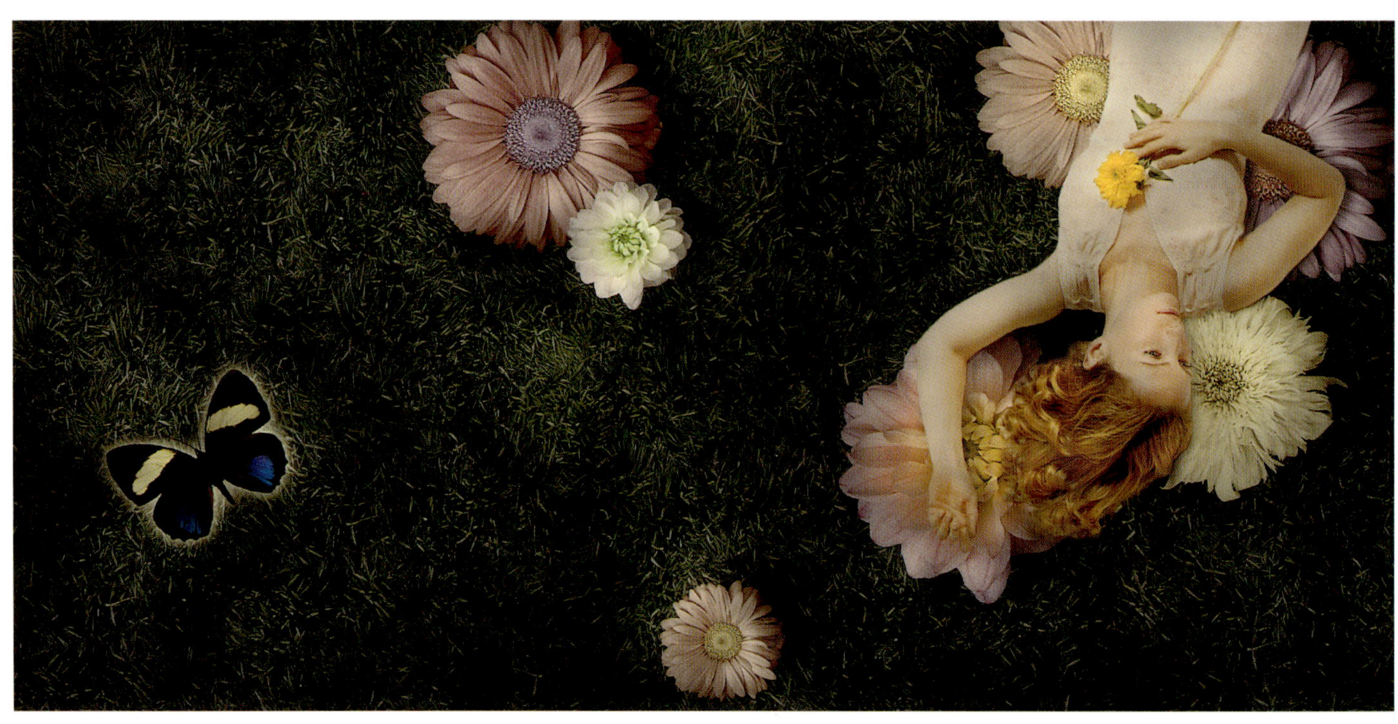

this page: **D**avid **W**aitz opposite: **D**an **L**im

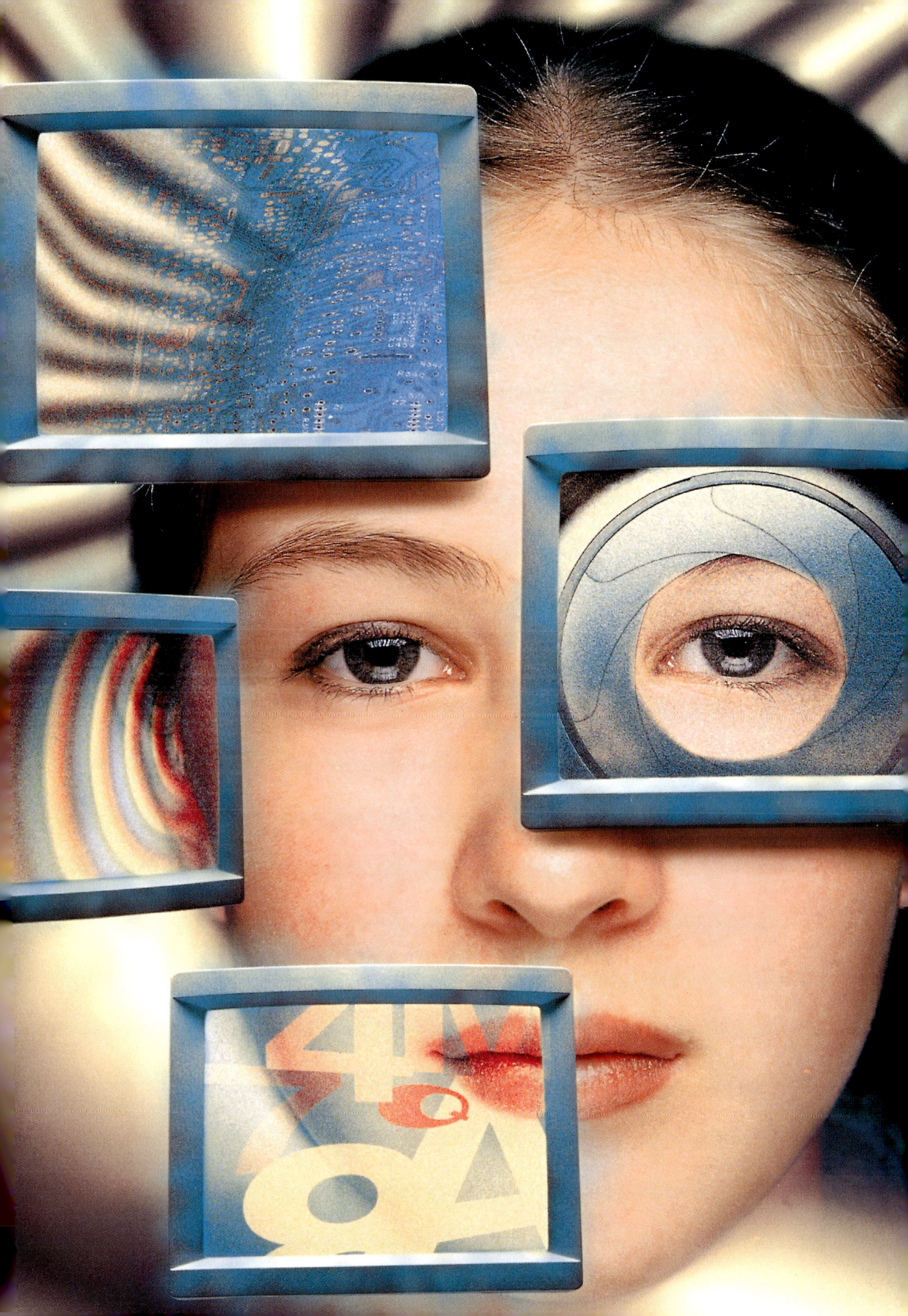

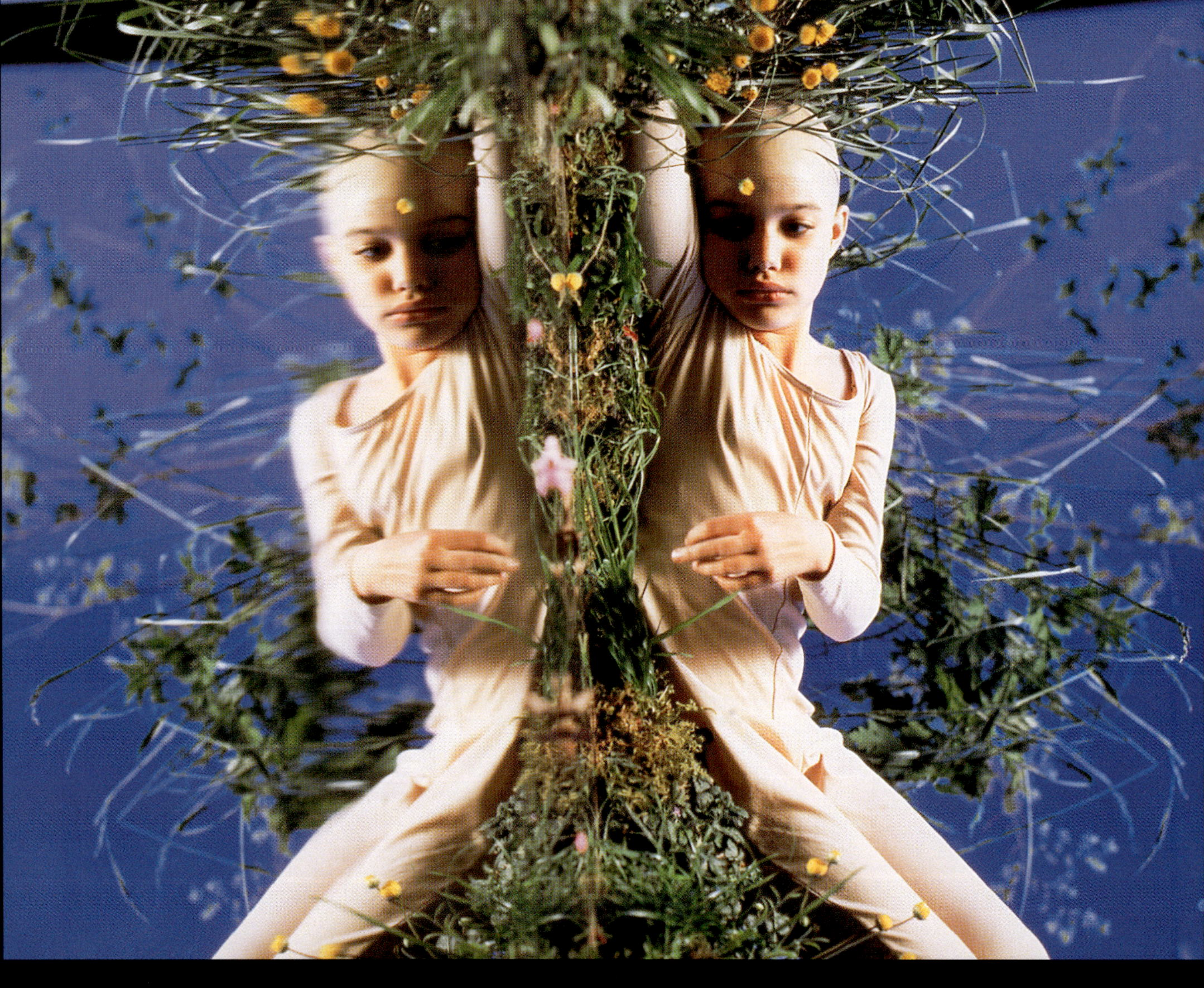

this spread: **H**ugh **H**ales-**T**ooke

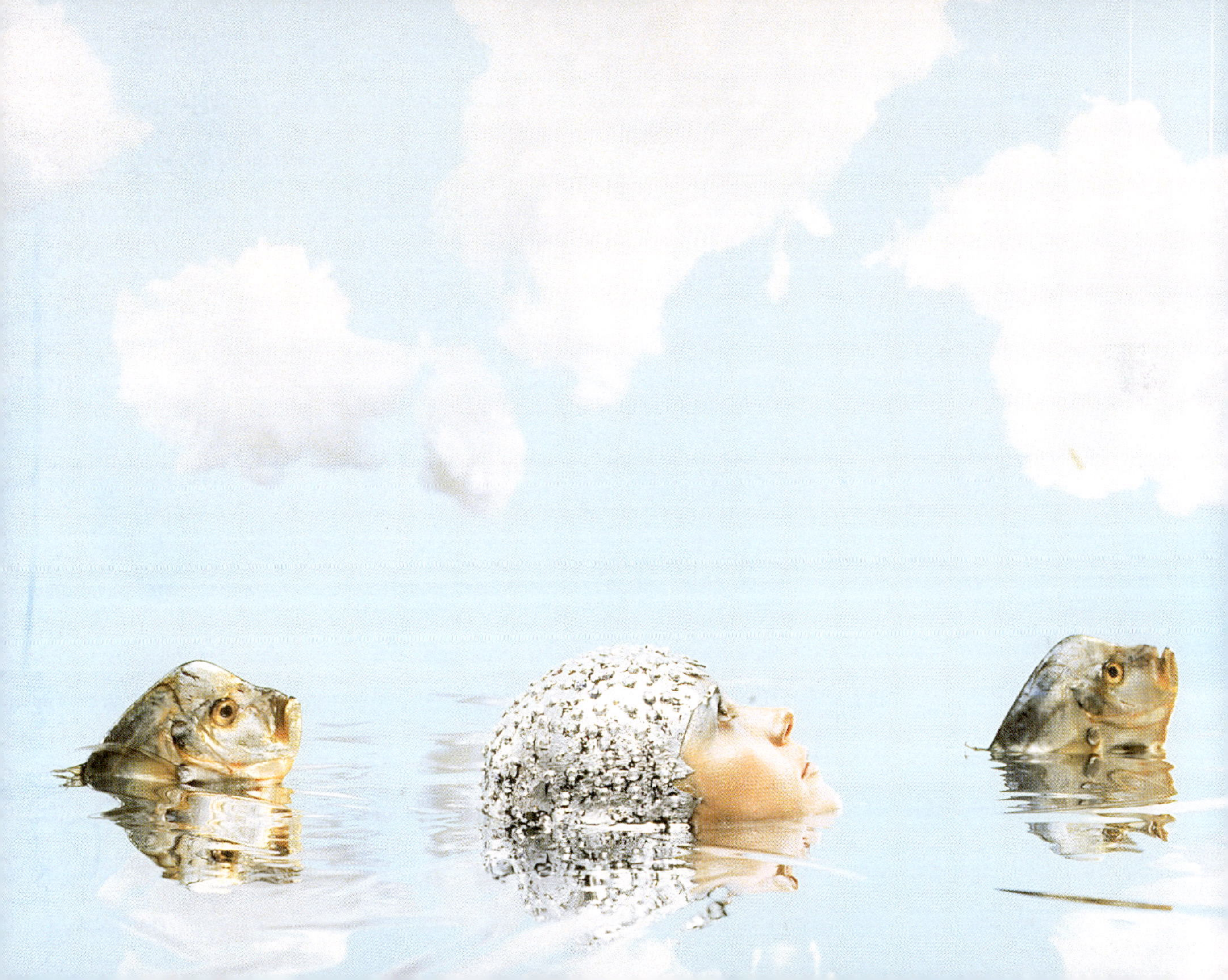

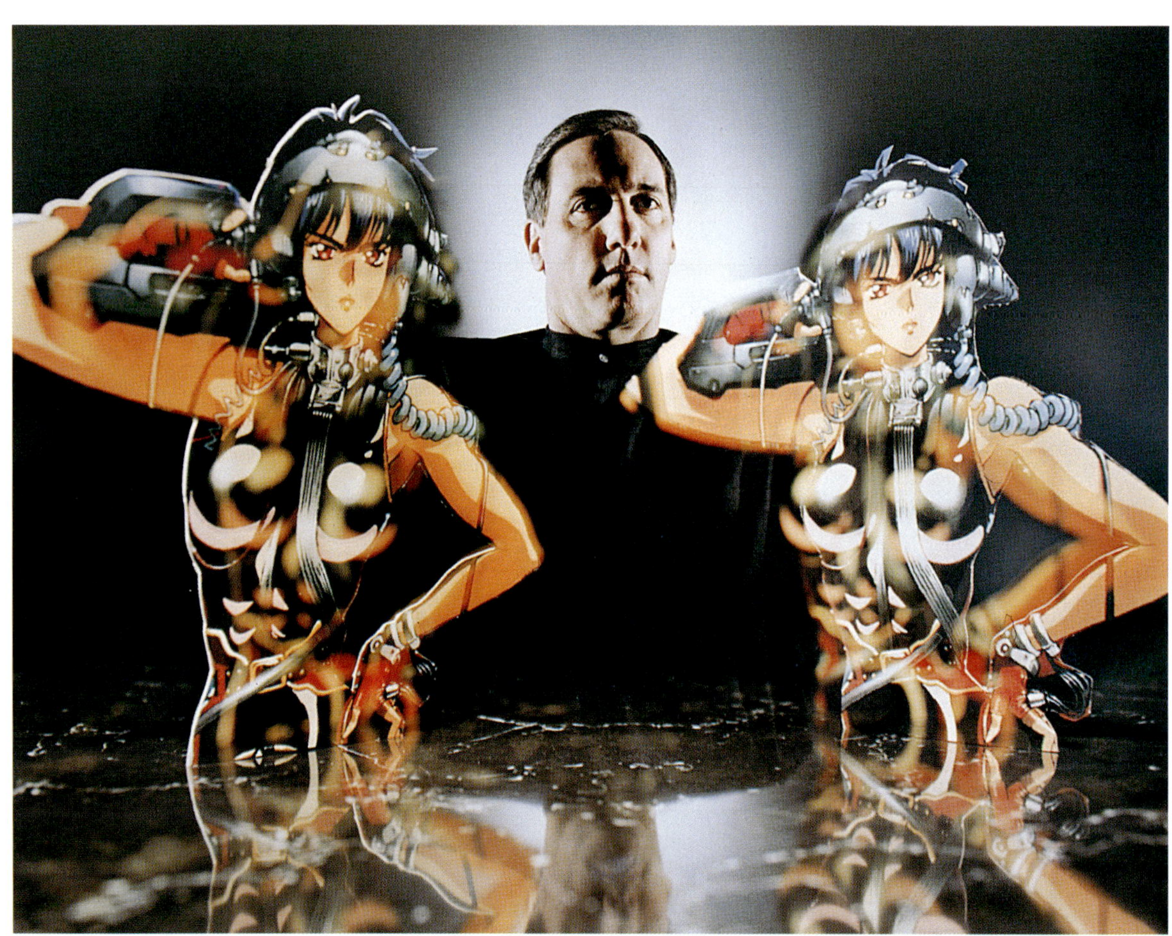

Rafael Fuchs

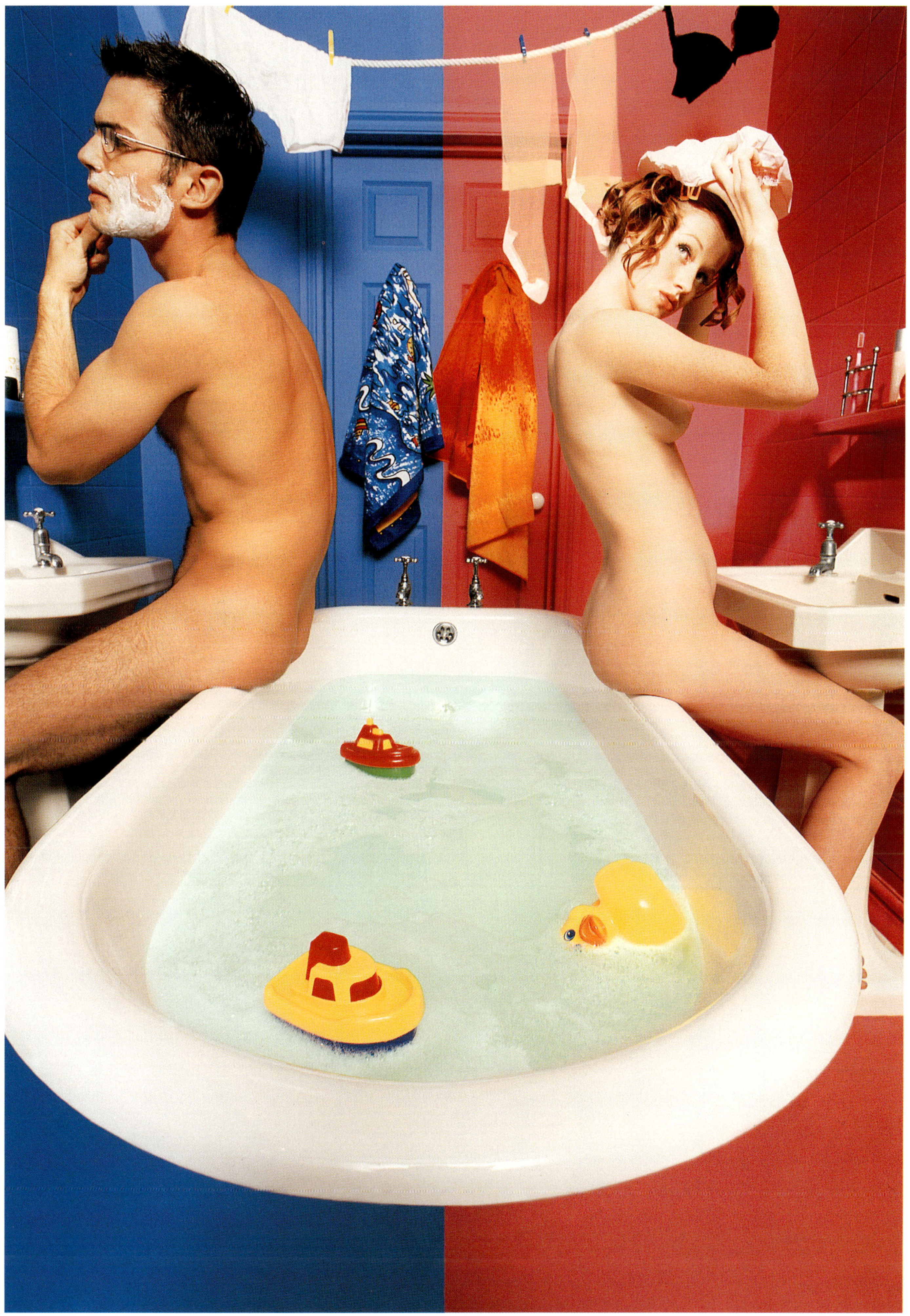

Frank Herholdt

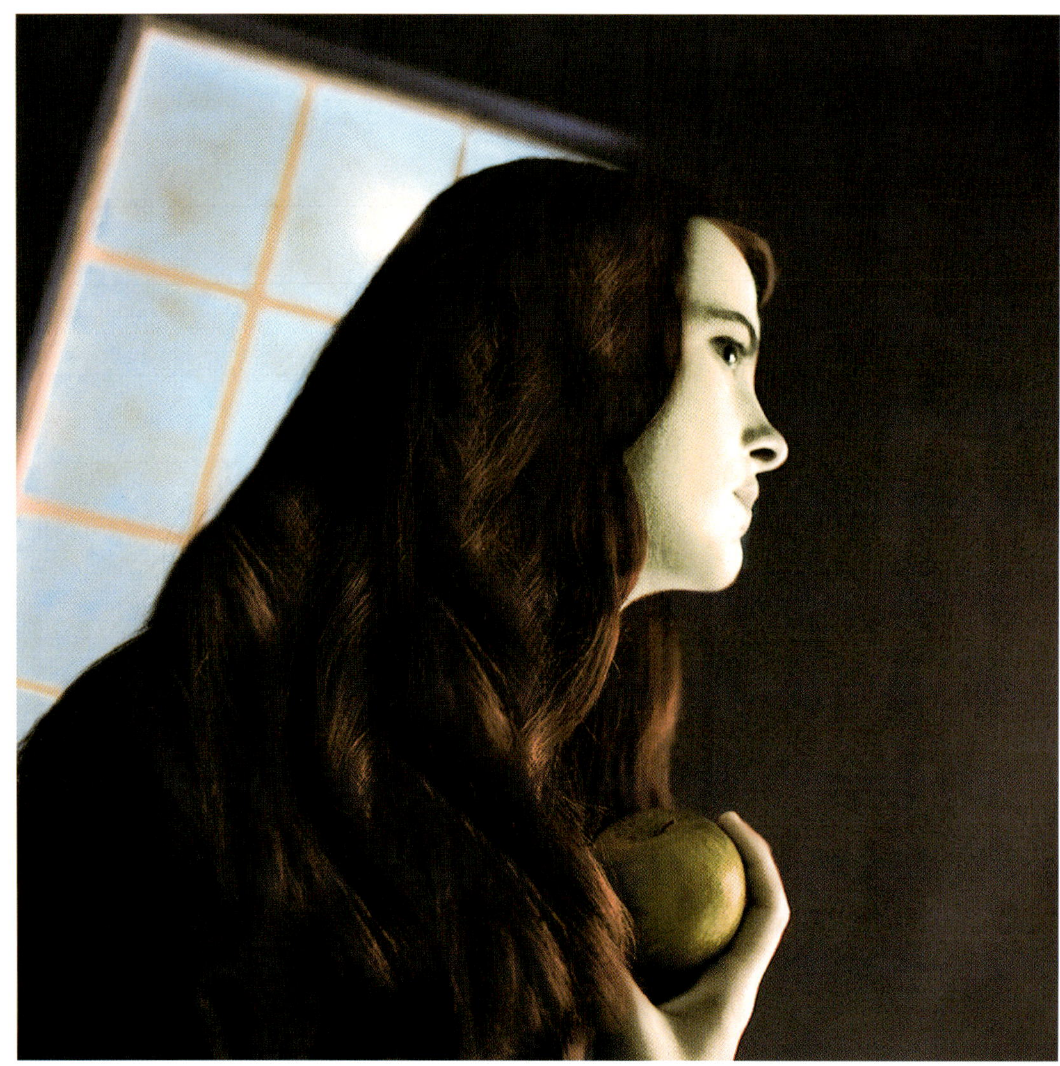

Roxann Arwen Mills

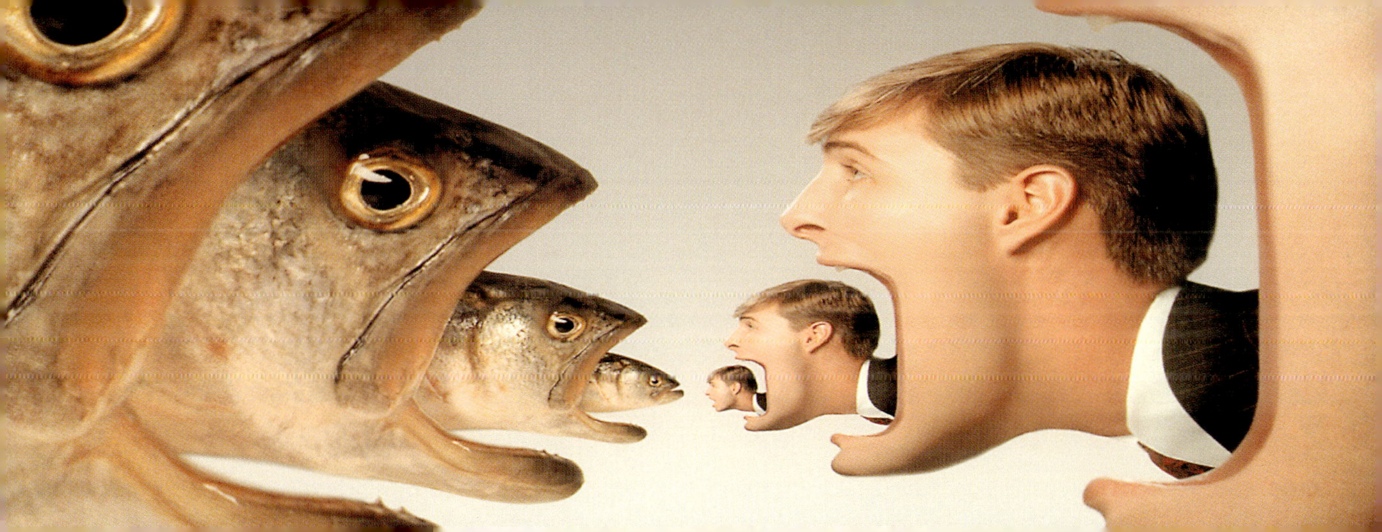

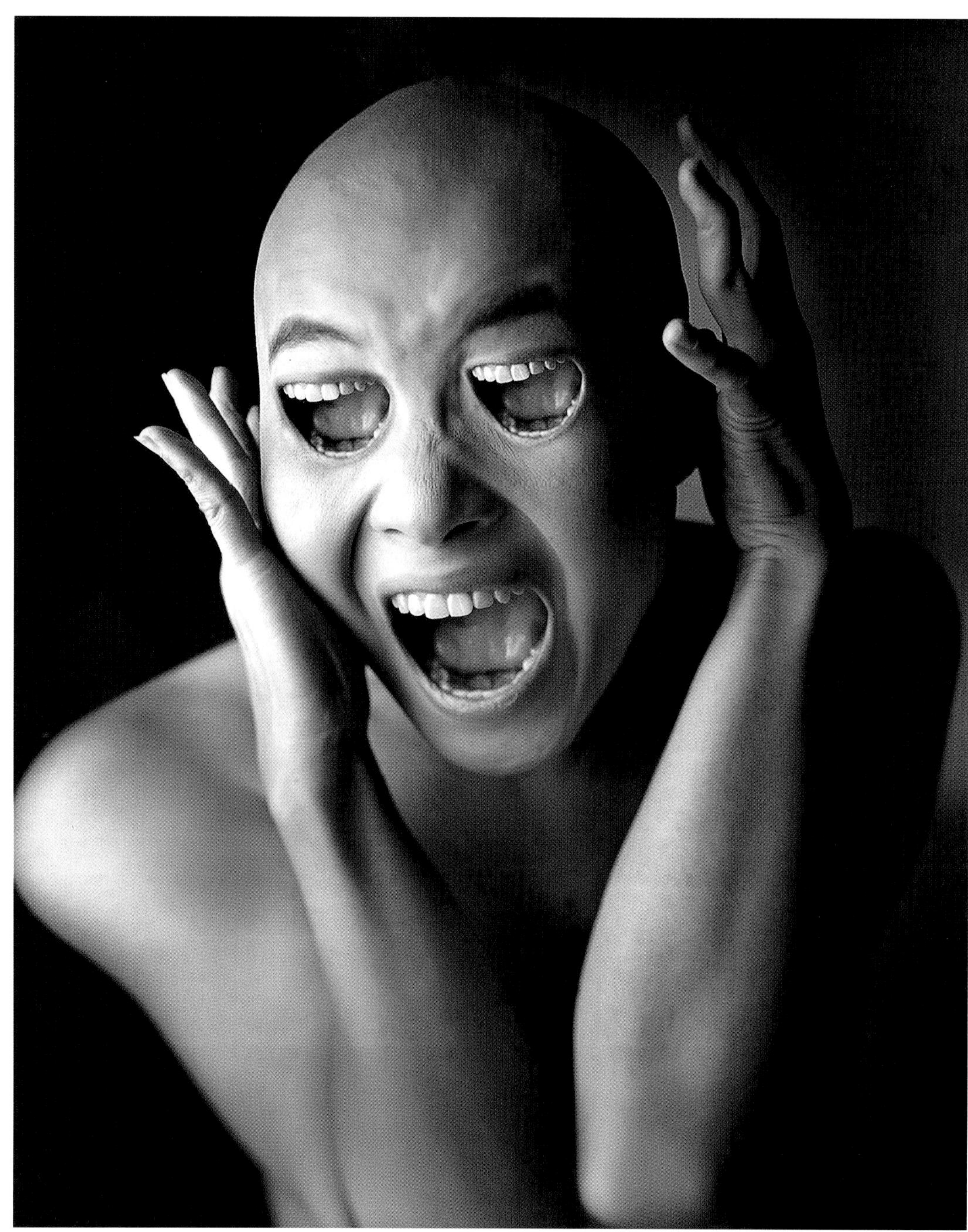

this spread: **G**erald **B**ybee

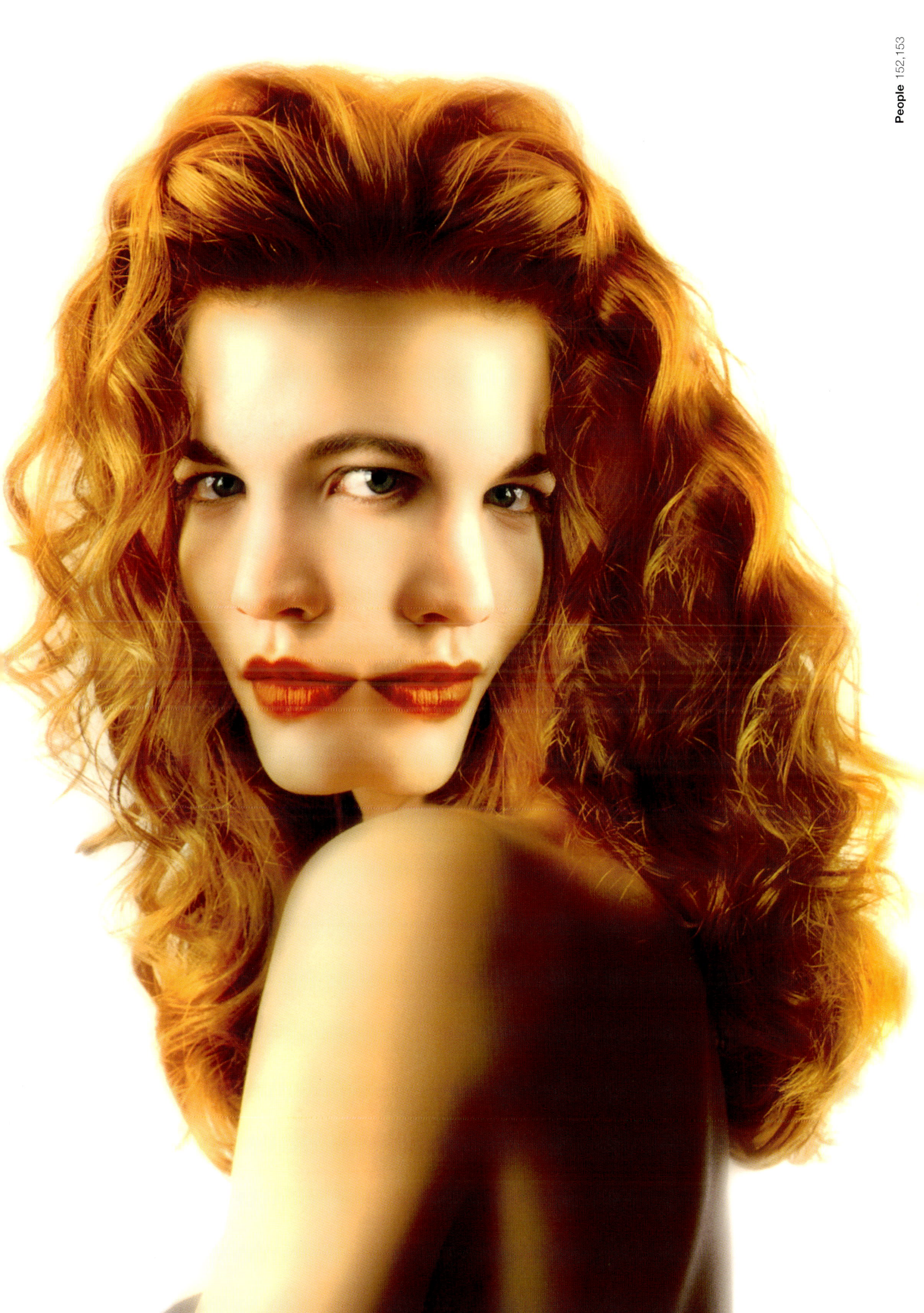

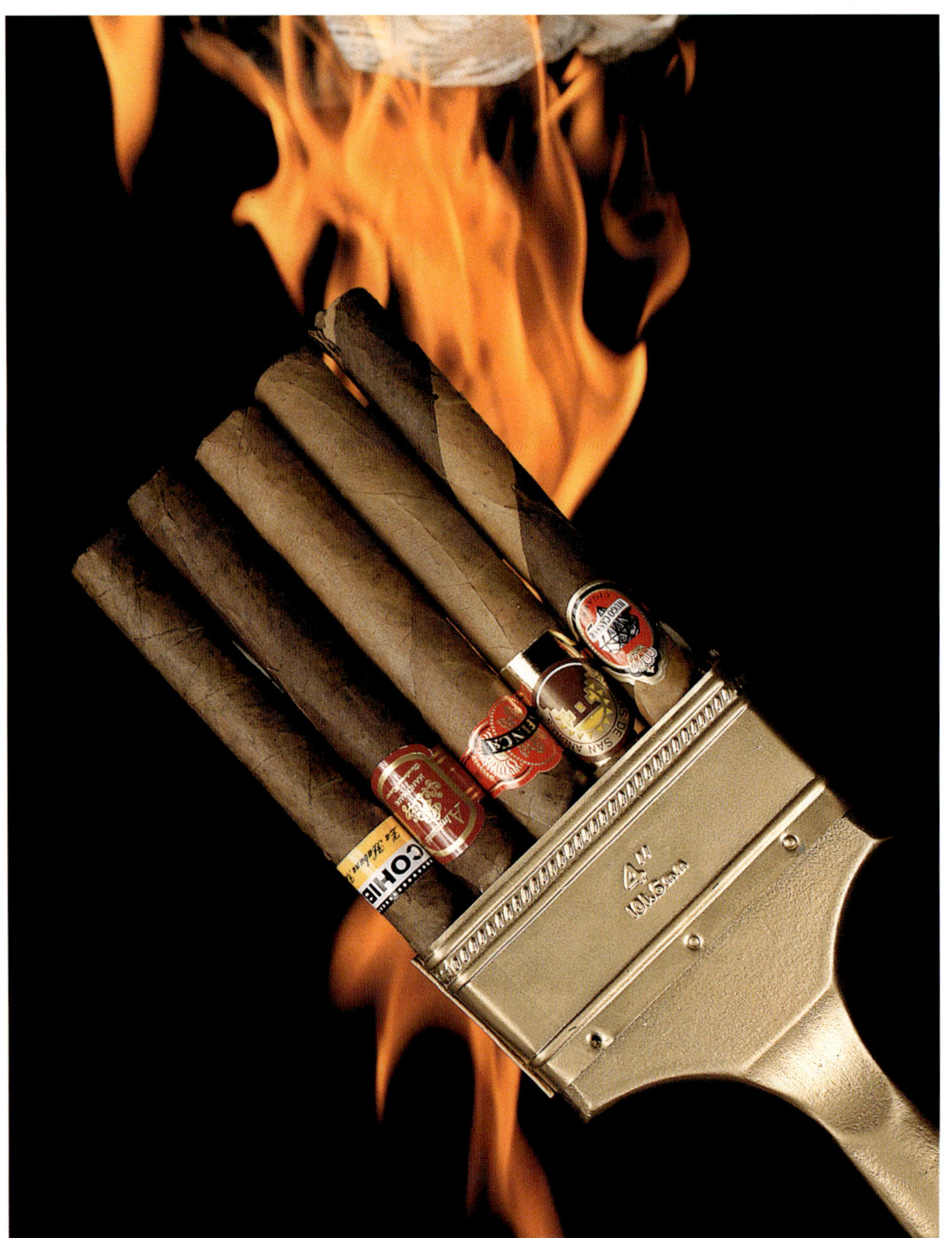

Bruce Curtis

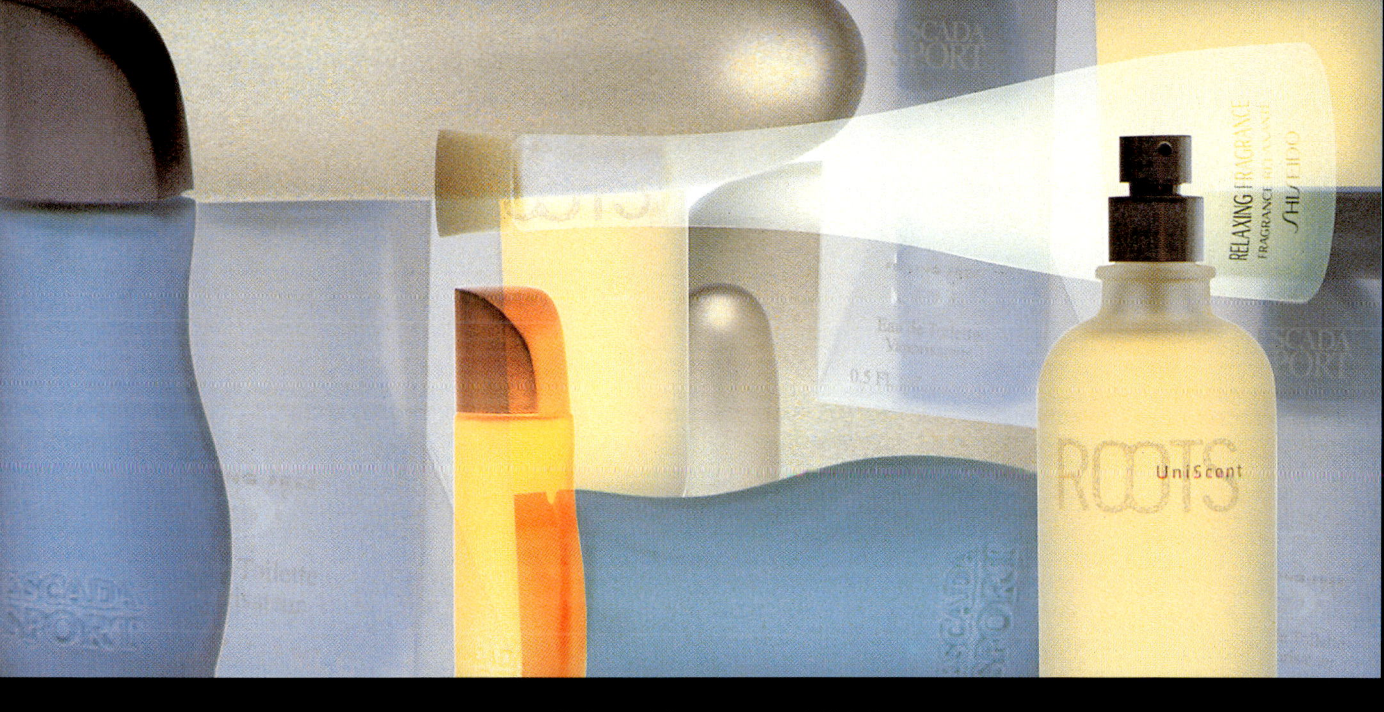

this page: **M**ir **L**ada following spread: **D**irk **K**arsten

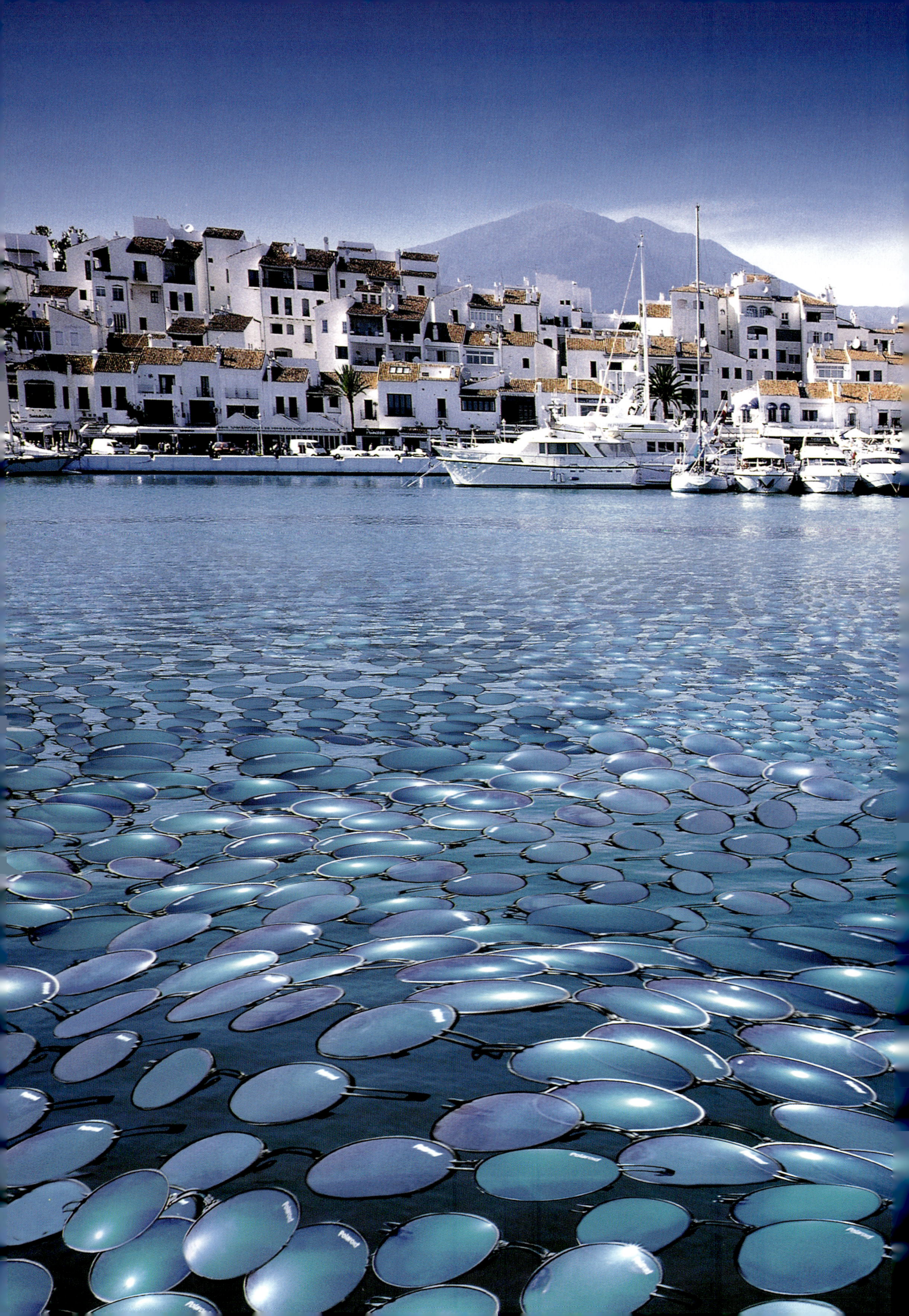

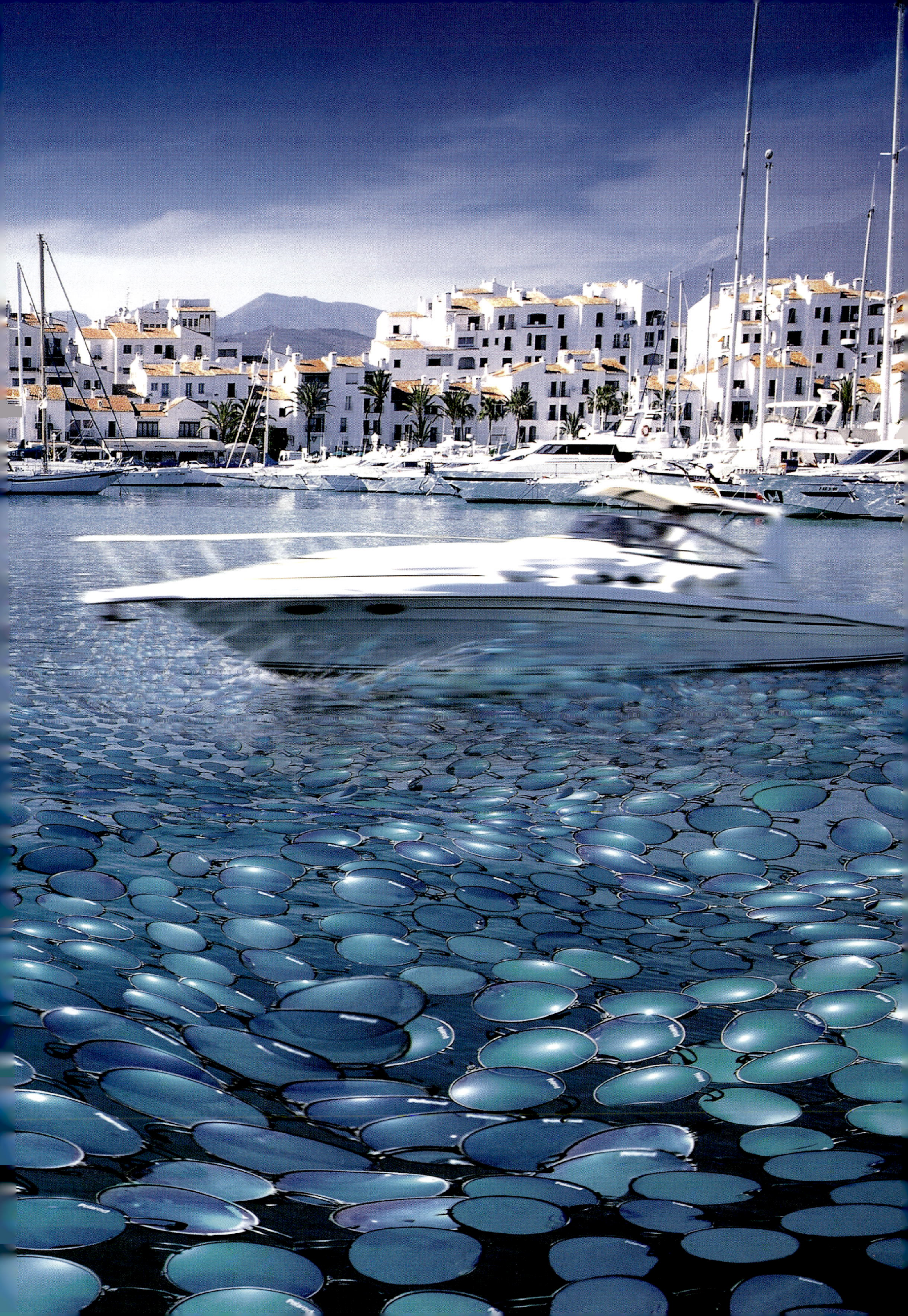

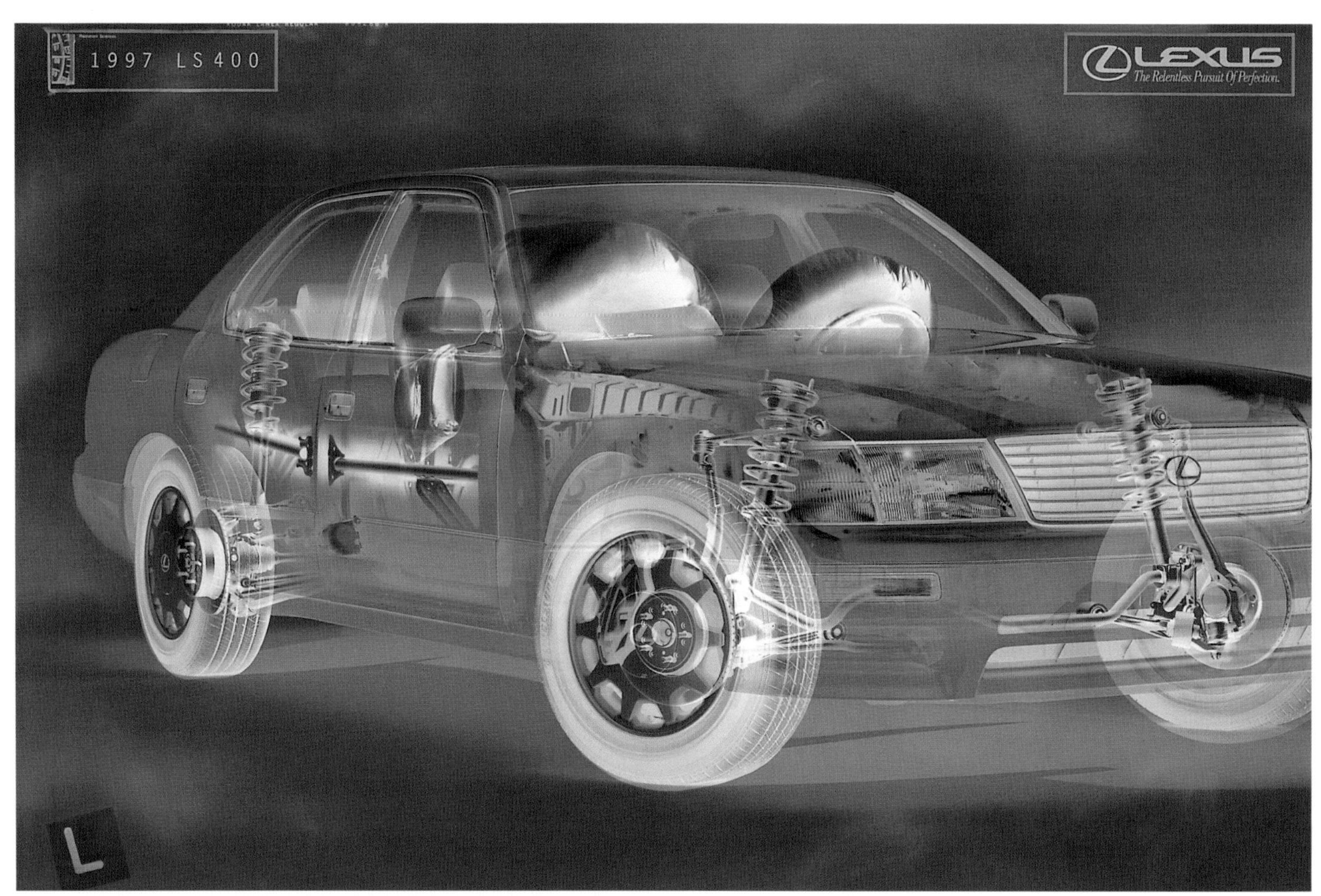

this page: **C**raig **C**utler opposite: **R**yszard **H**orowitz

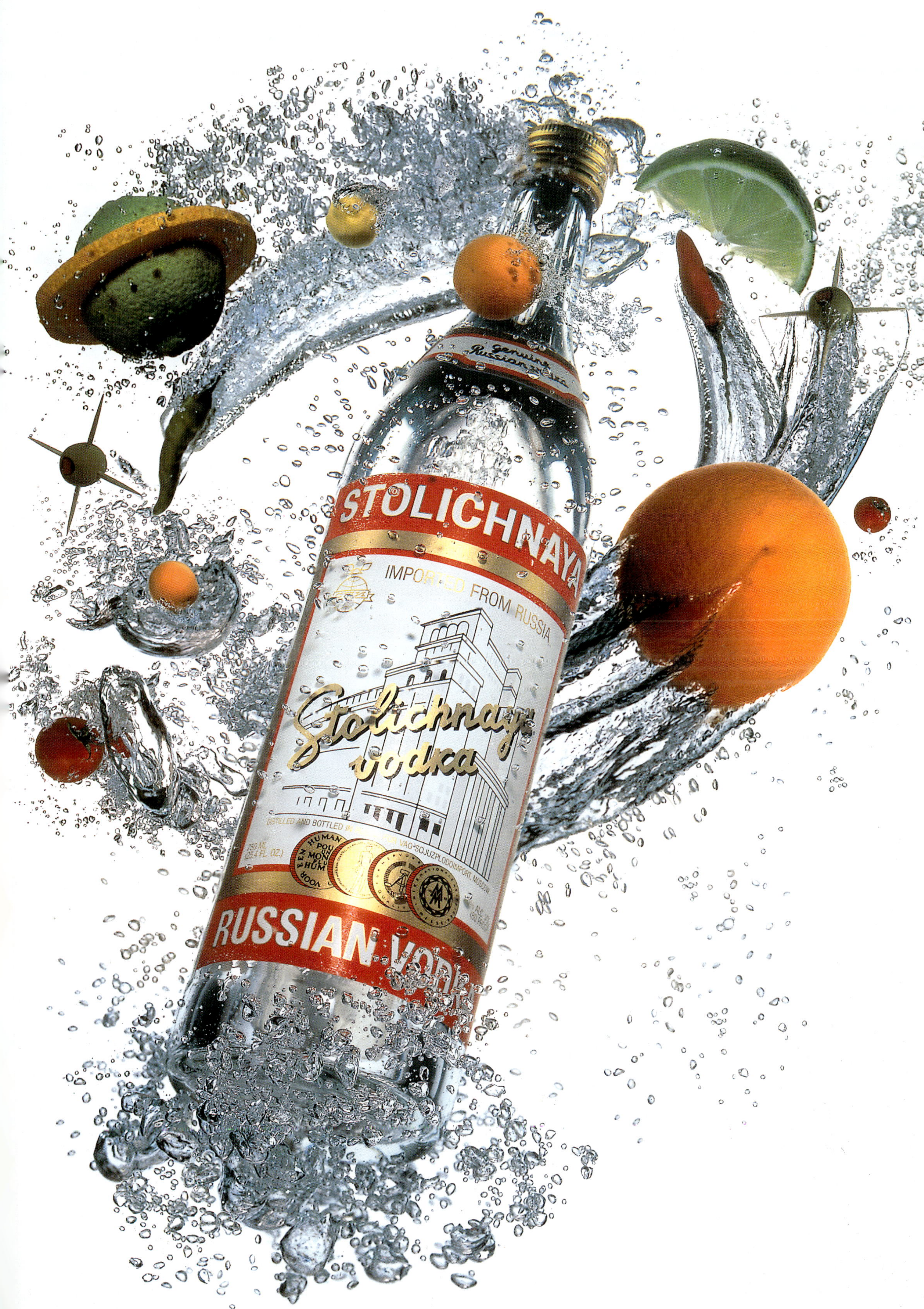

Genuine
Russian
STOLICHNAYA
IMPORTED FROM RUSSIA
Stolichnaya
vodka
DISTILLED AND BOTTLED IN
VAO-SOJUZPLODOIMPORT, MOSCOW
750 ML
(25.4 FL. OZ.)
HUMAN
POU
EN MON
HÛM
VOOR
ALC. 40%
(80 PROOF)
RUSSIAN VODKA

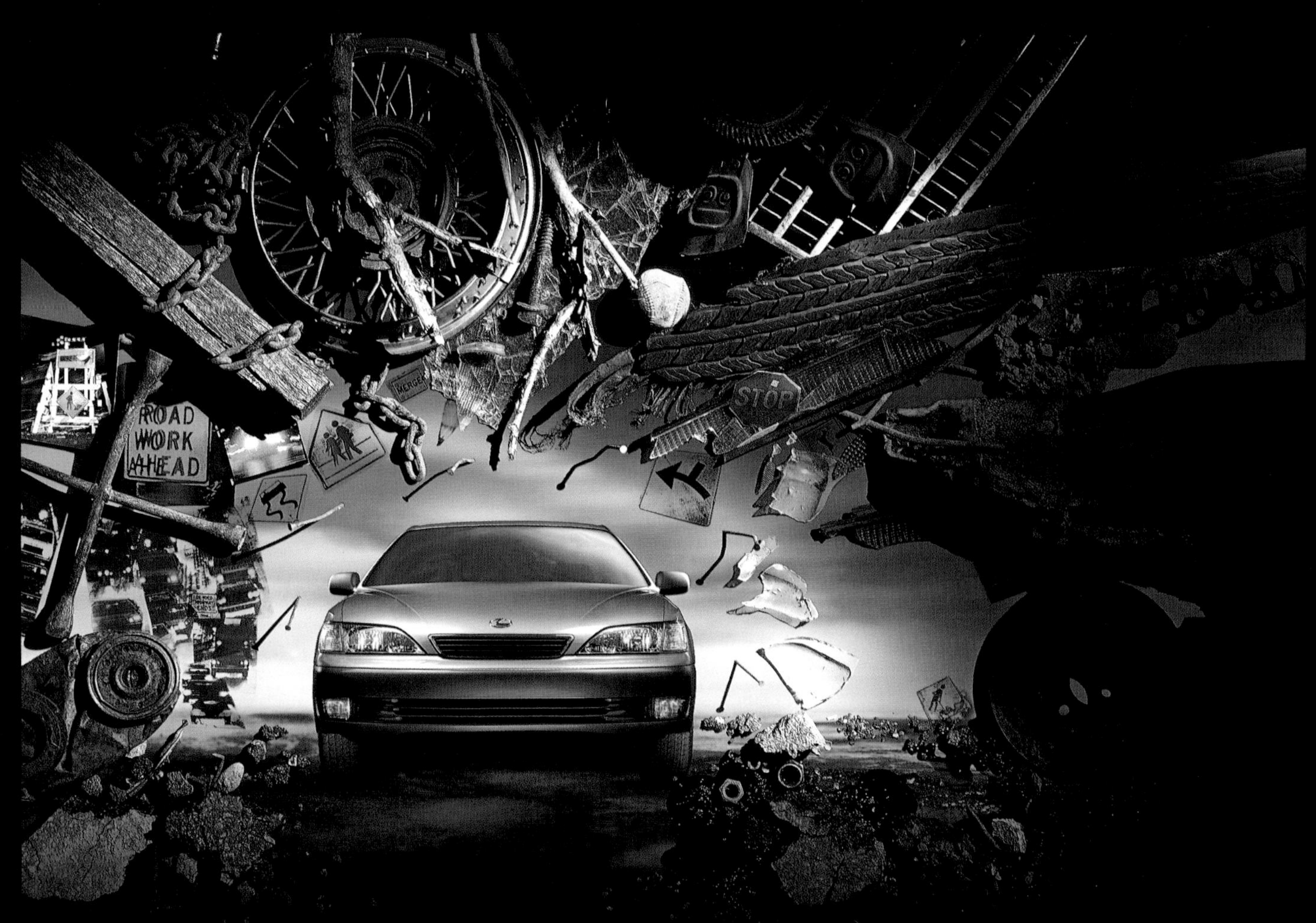

Hans Neleman

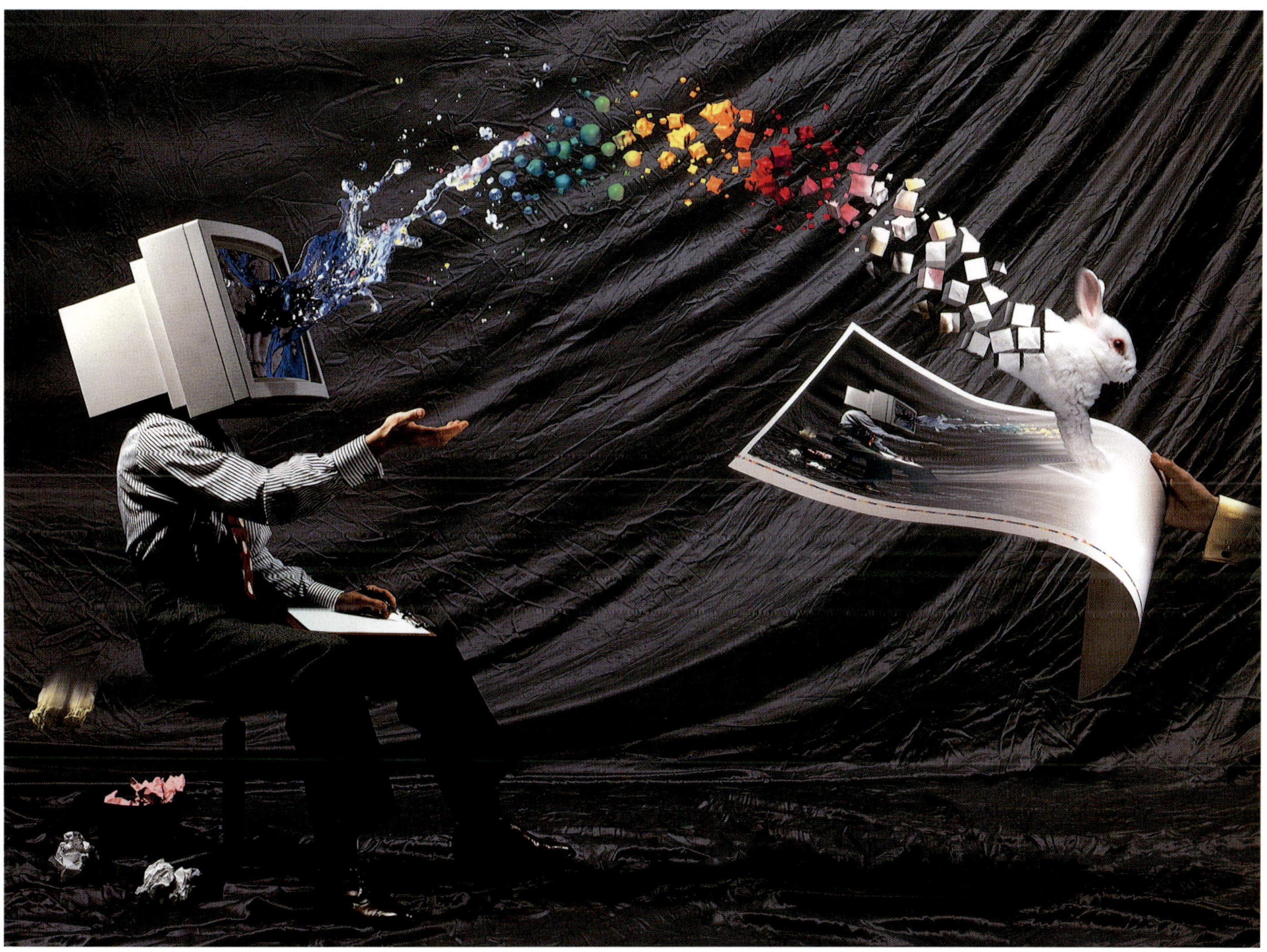

Ryszard **H**orowitz

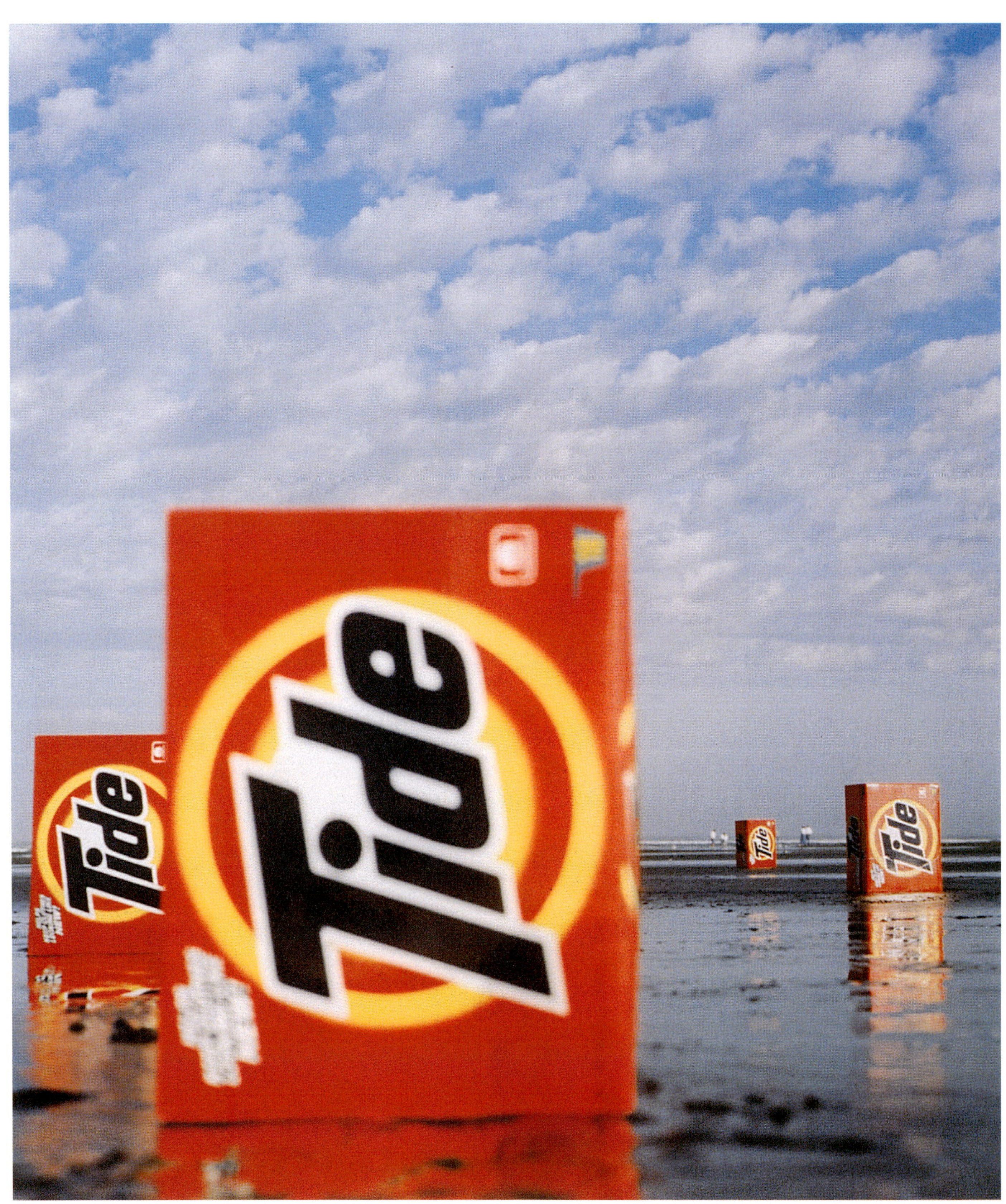

Suzanne **O**pton

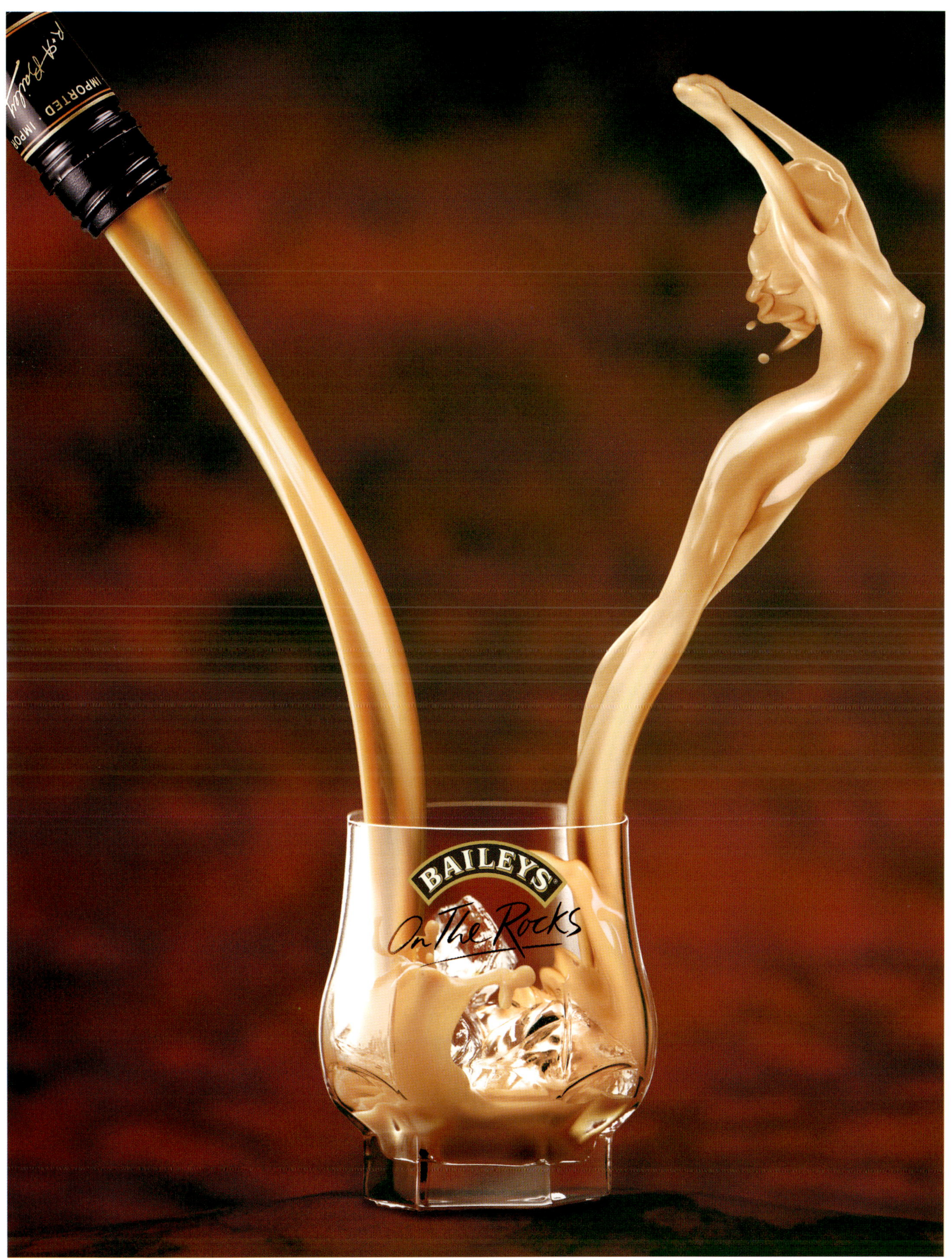

C. I. Choi

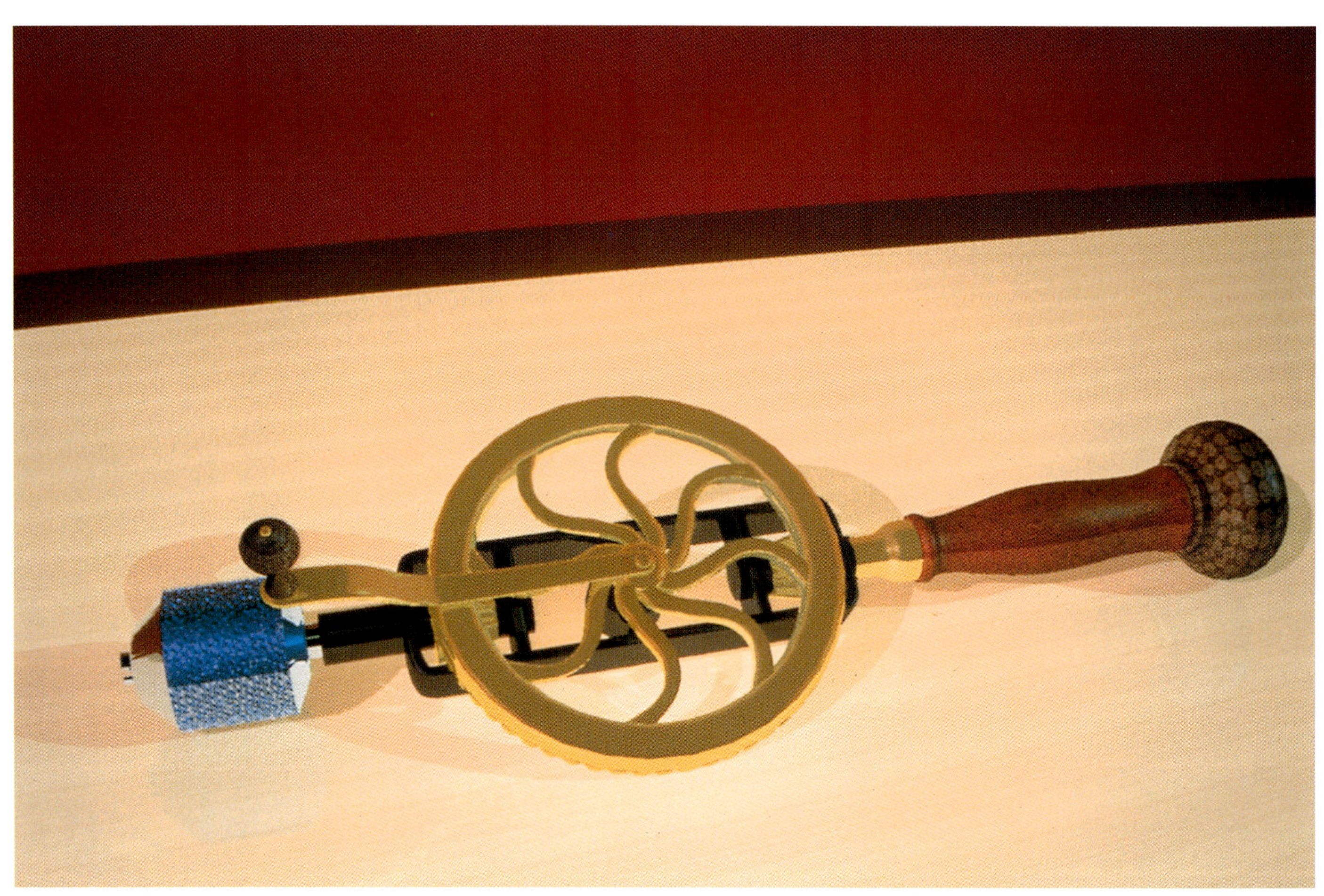

this spread: **B**yron **M**orris

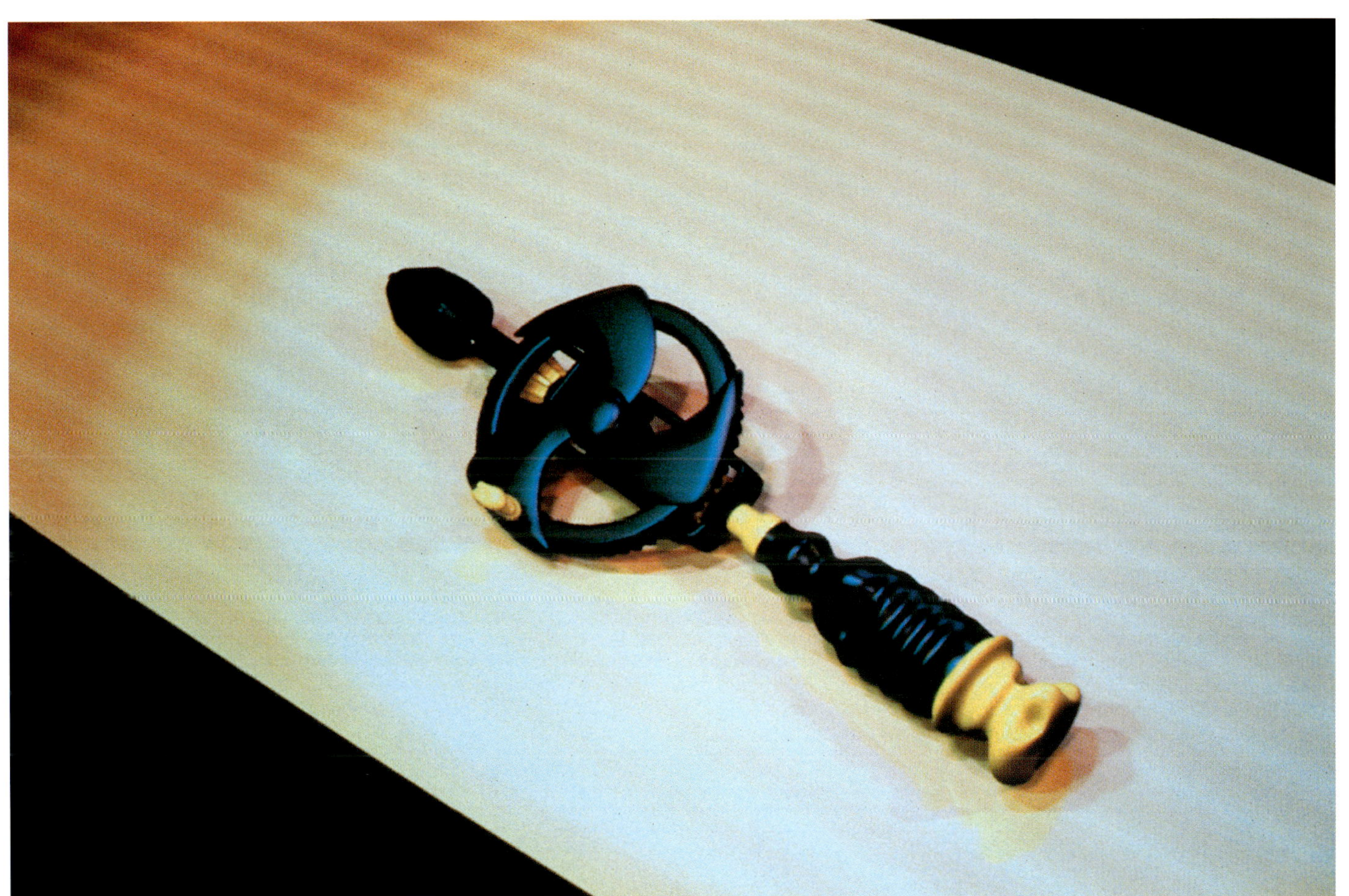

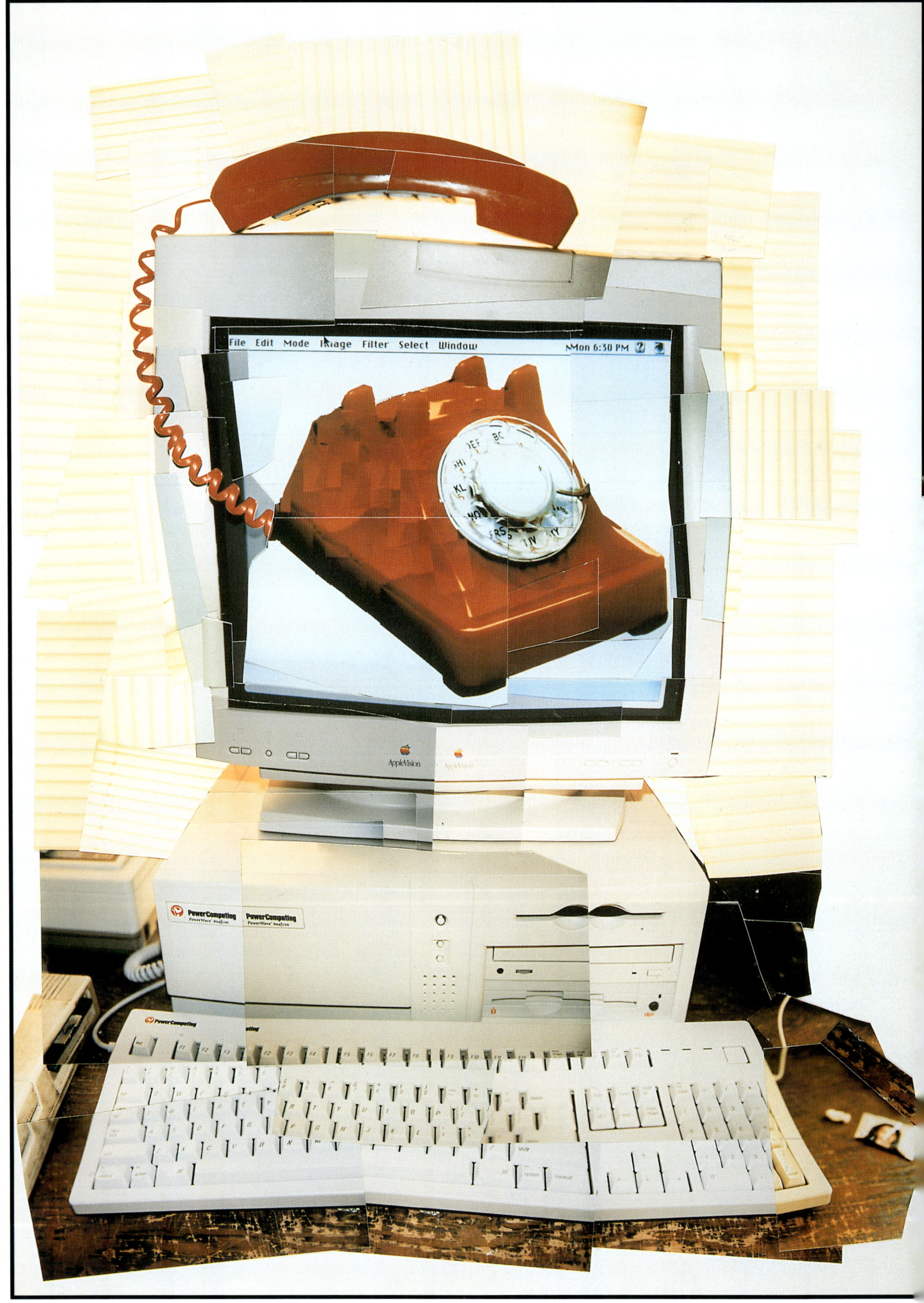
File Edit Mode Image Filter Select Window
Mon 6:30 PM
AppleVision
PowerComputing

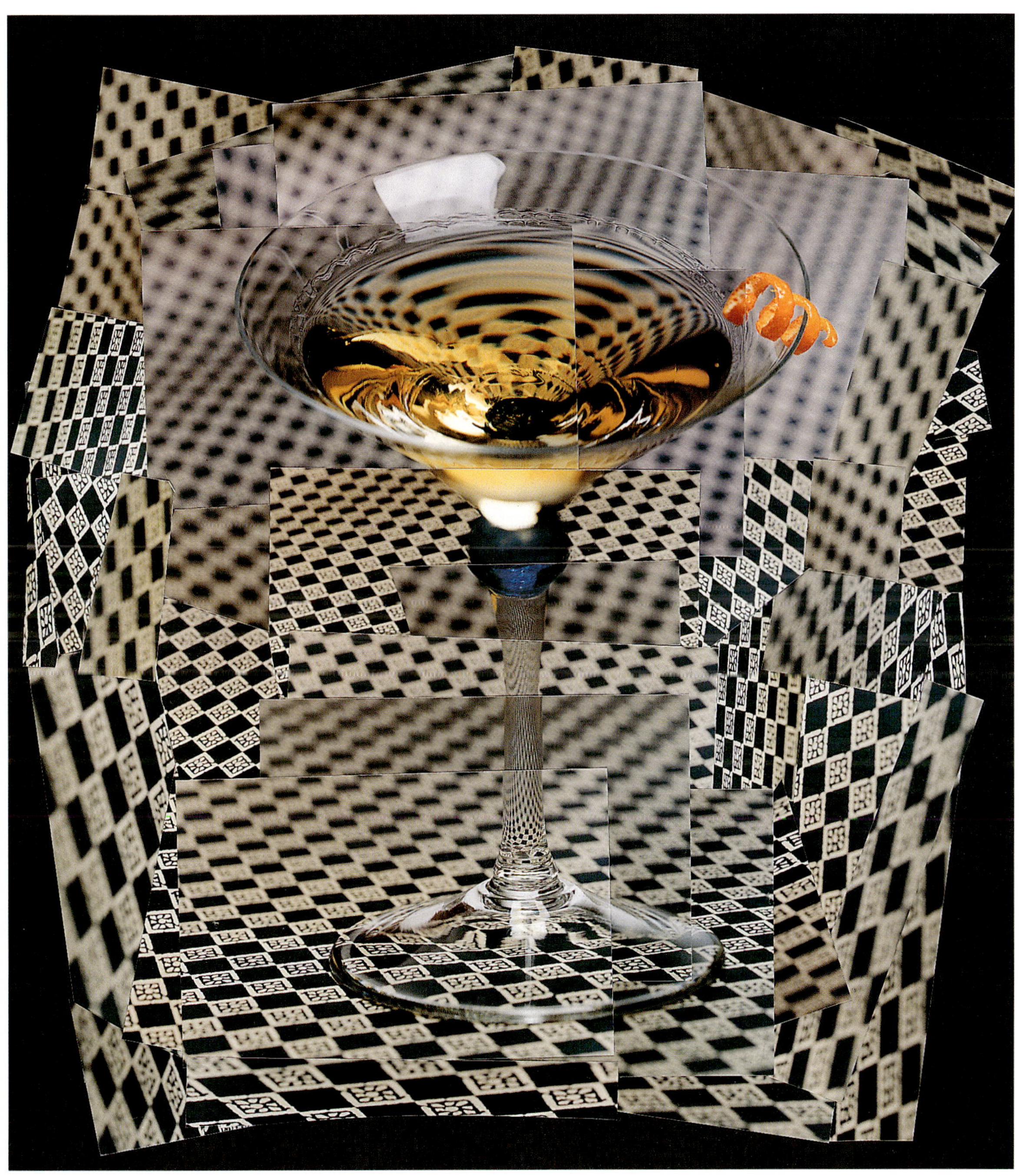

this spread: **J**eremy **W**olff

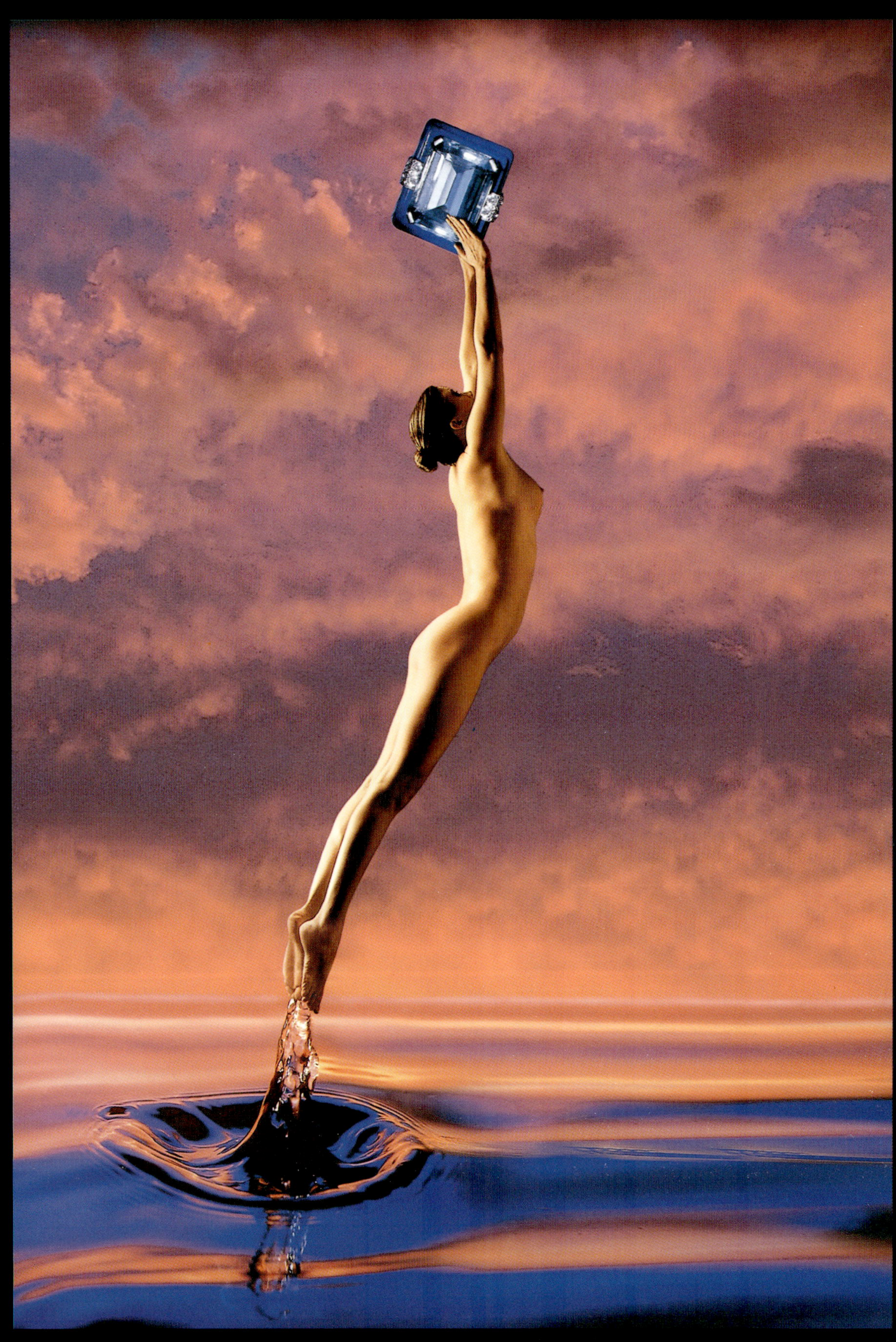

Ryszard **H**orowitz

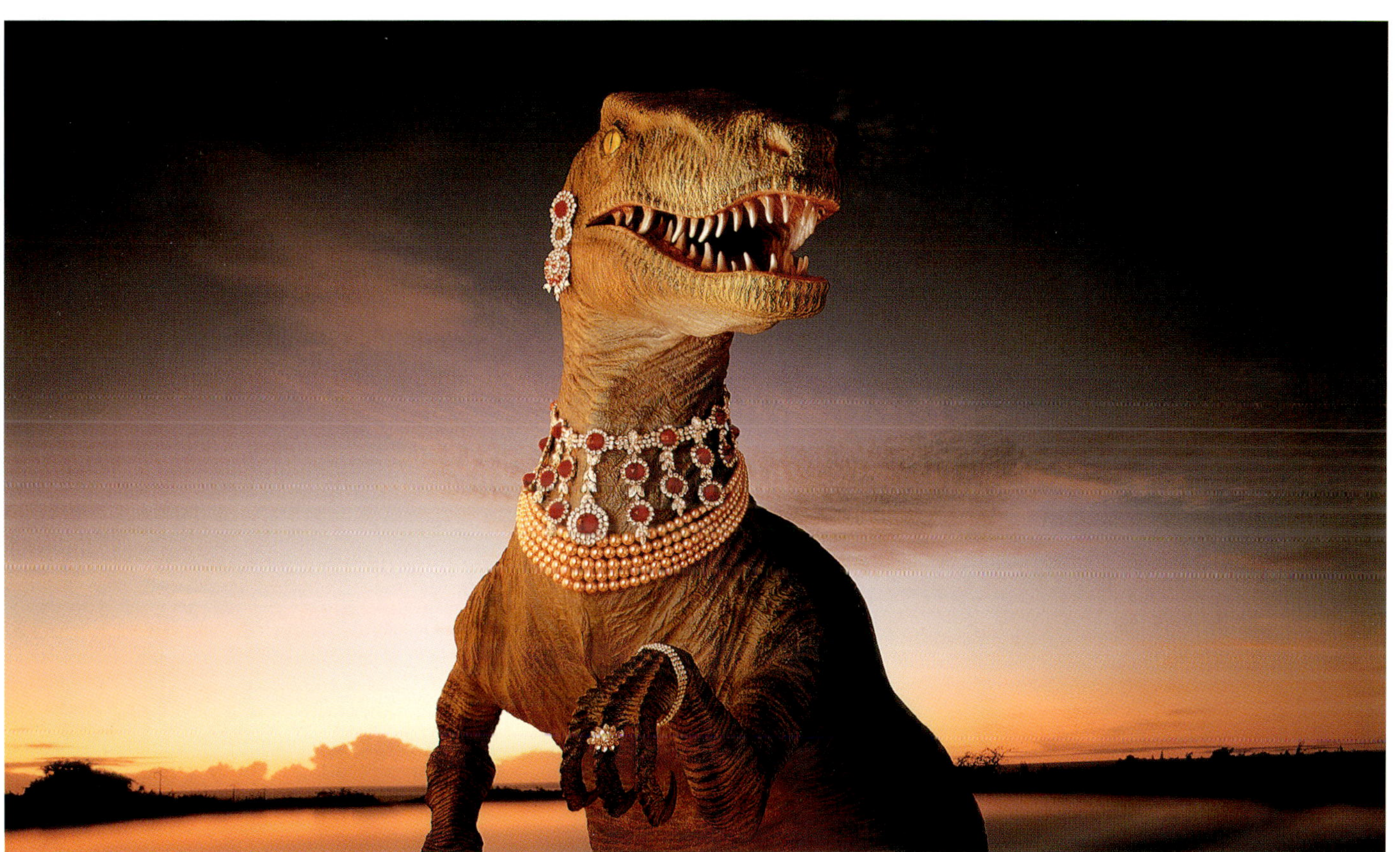

Fernando **Z**uffo

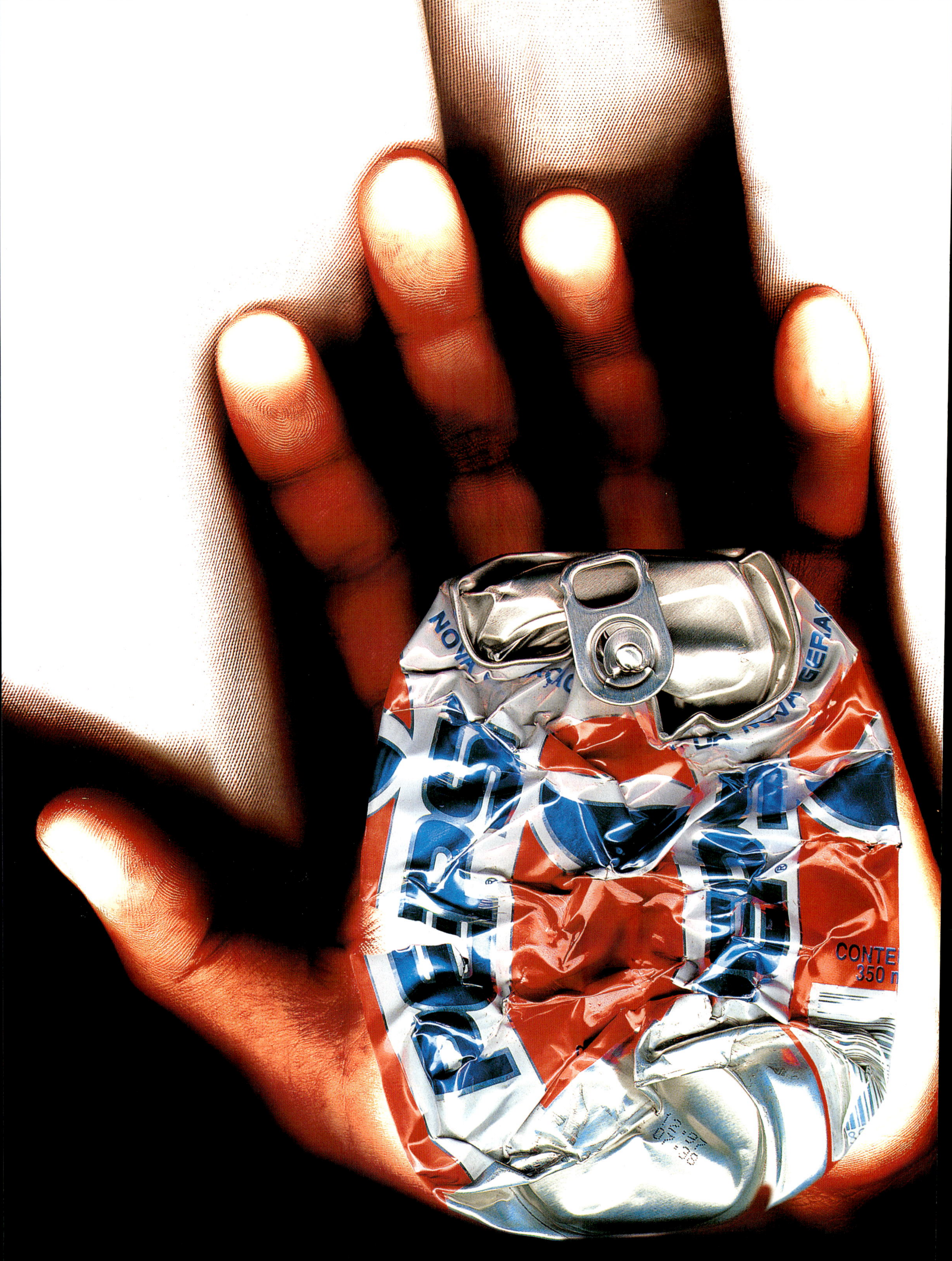
NOVA GERAÇÃO
A NOVA GERAÇÃO
CONTE
350 m

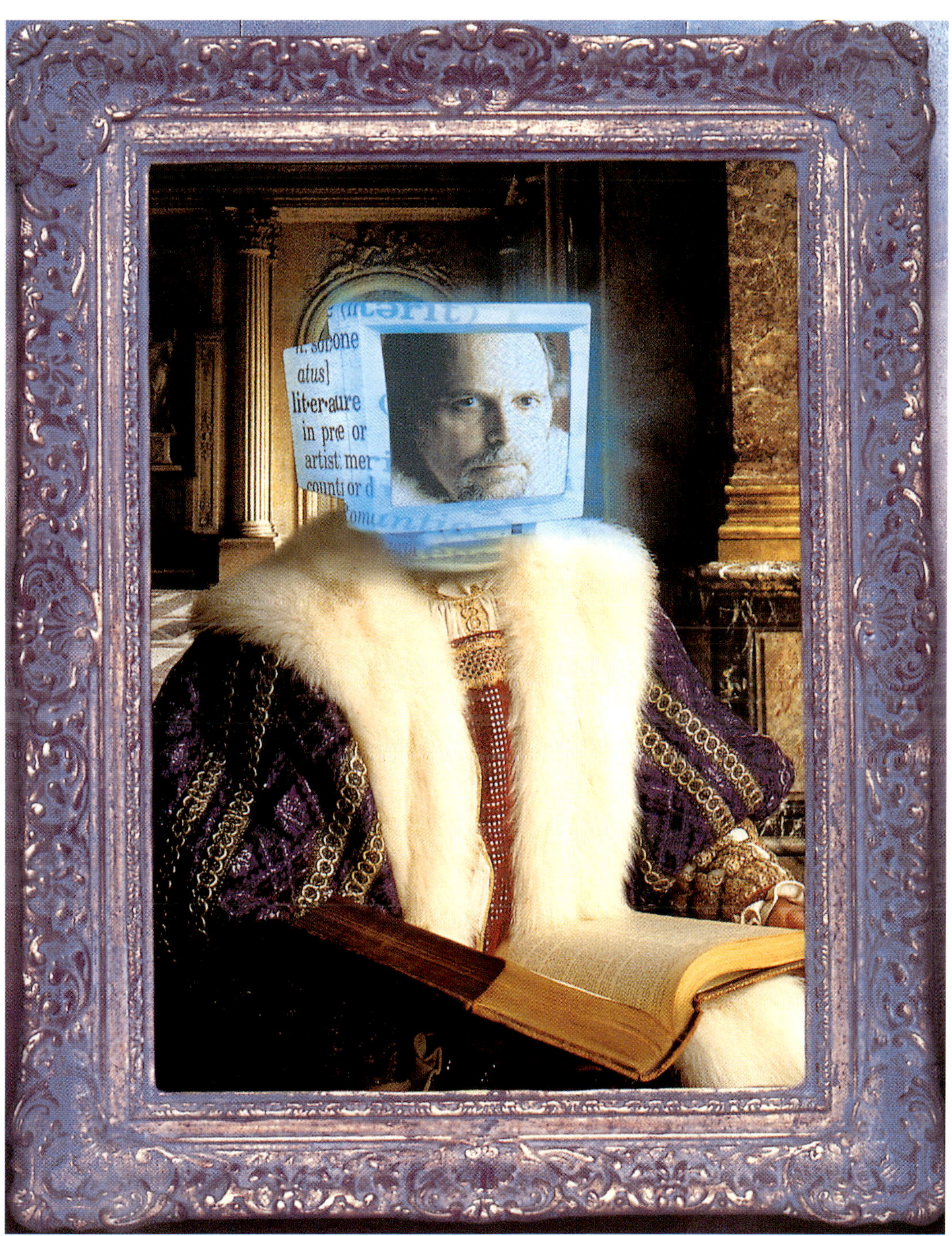

opposite: **F**ernando **Z**uffo this page: **D**an **L**im

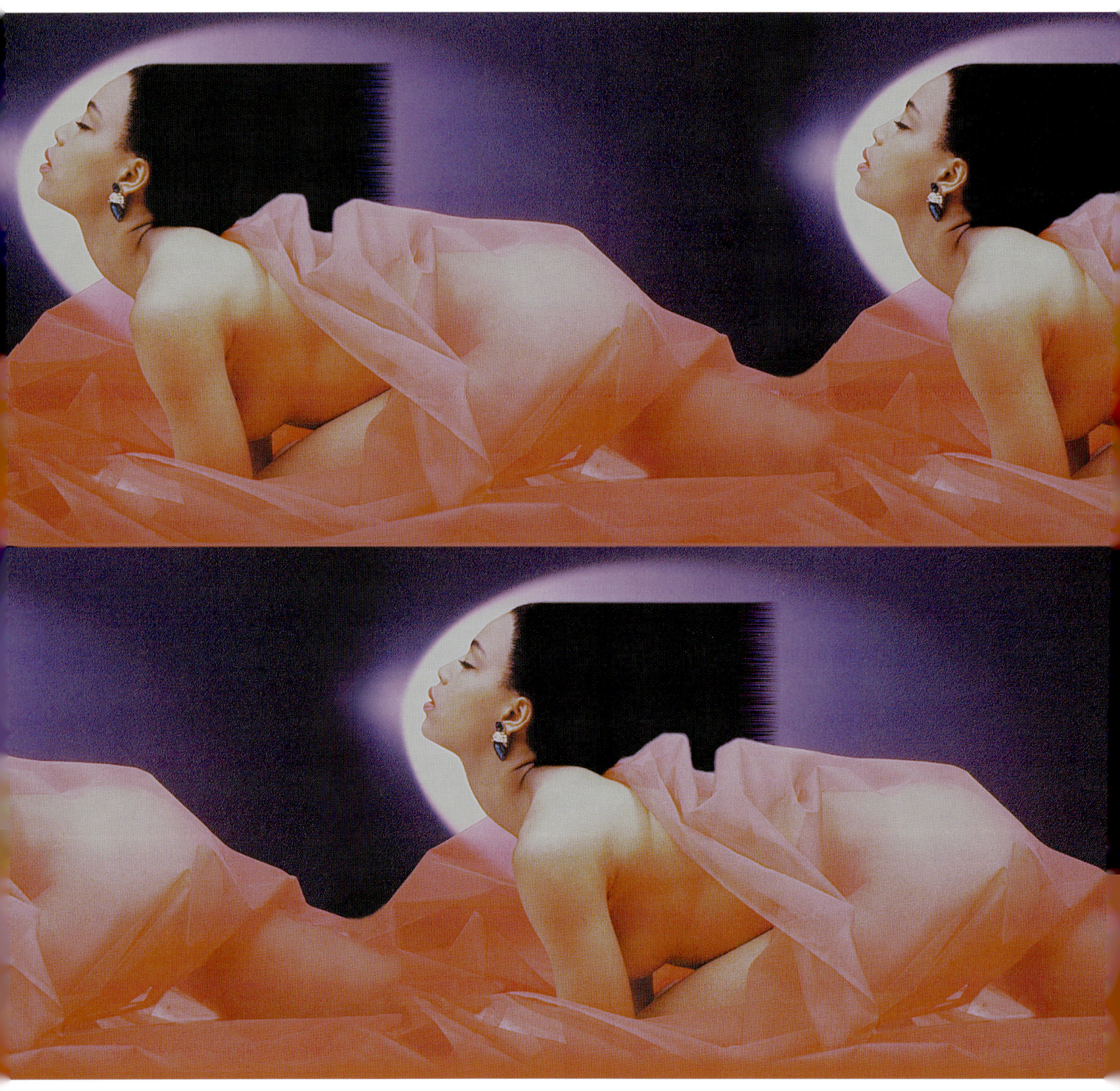

Franco Accornero

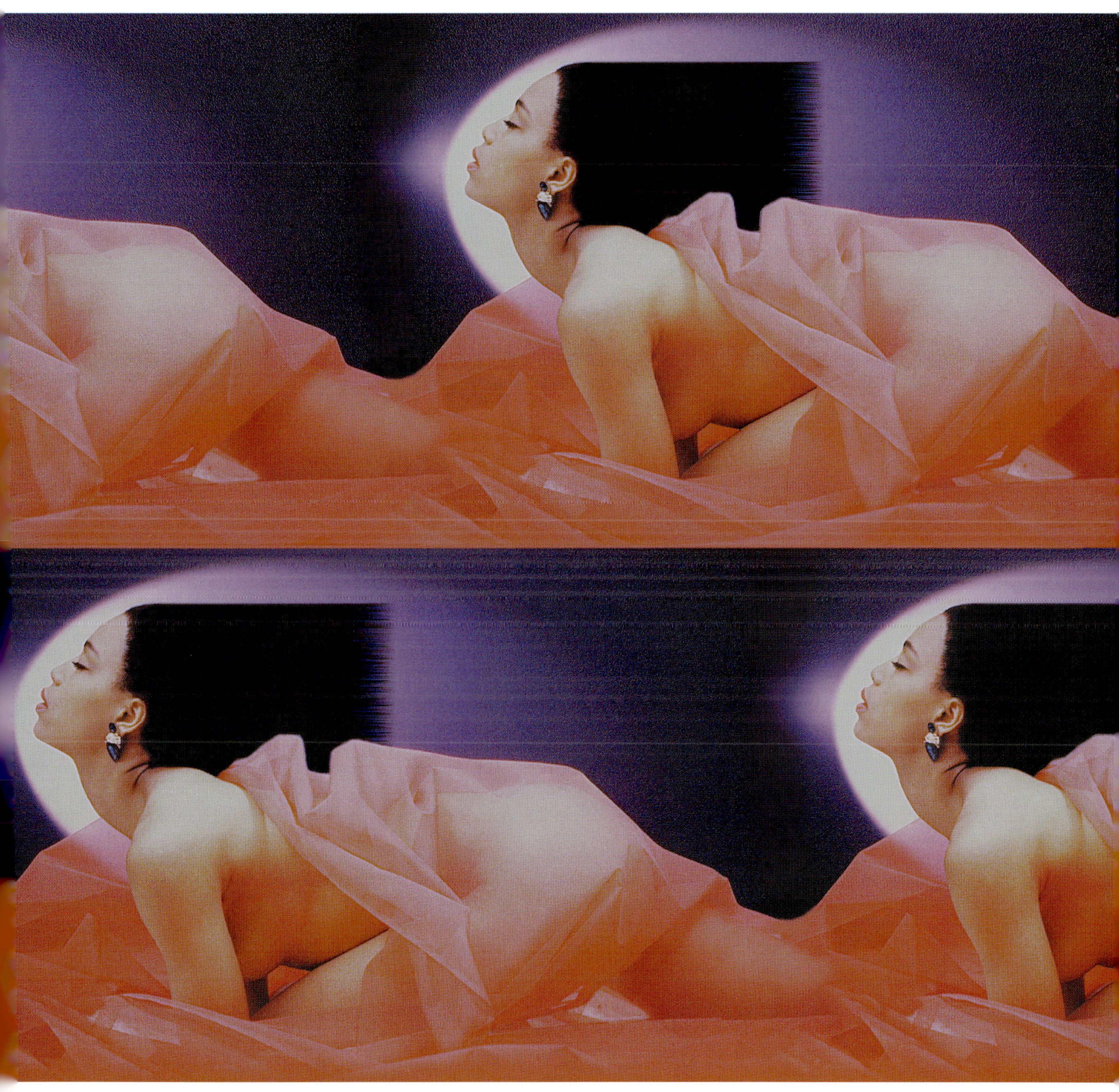

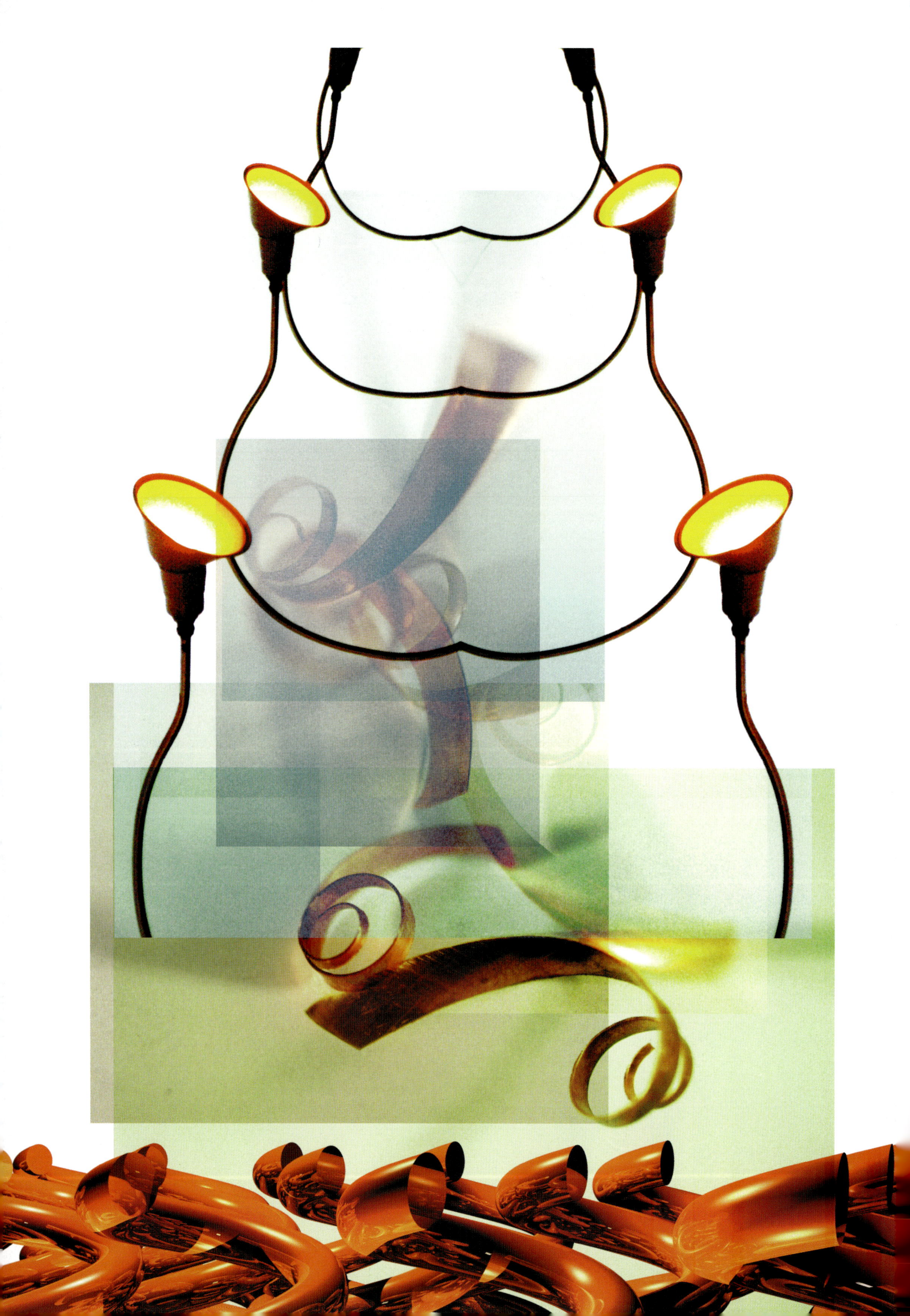

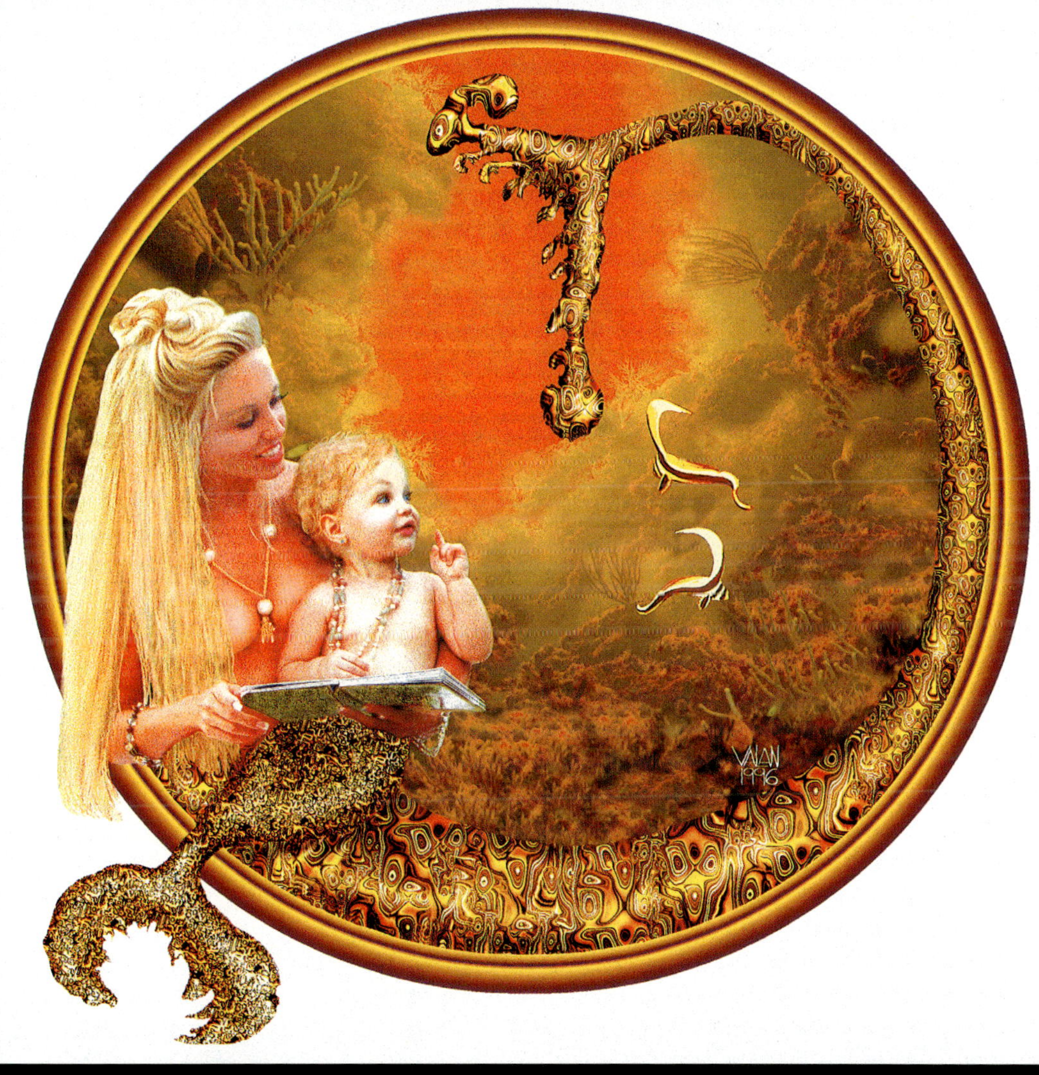

opposite: **C**raig **T**ozzi, **S**teve **T**ozzi this page: **V**alan **E**vers

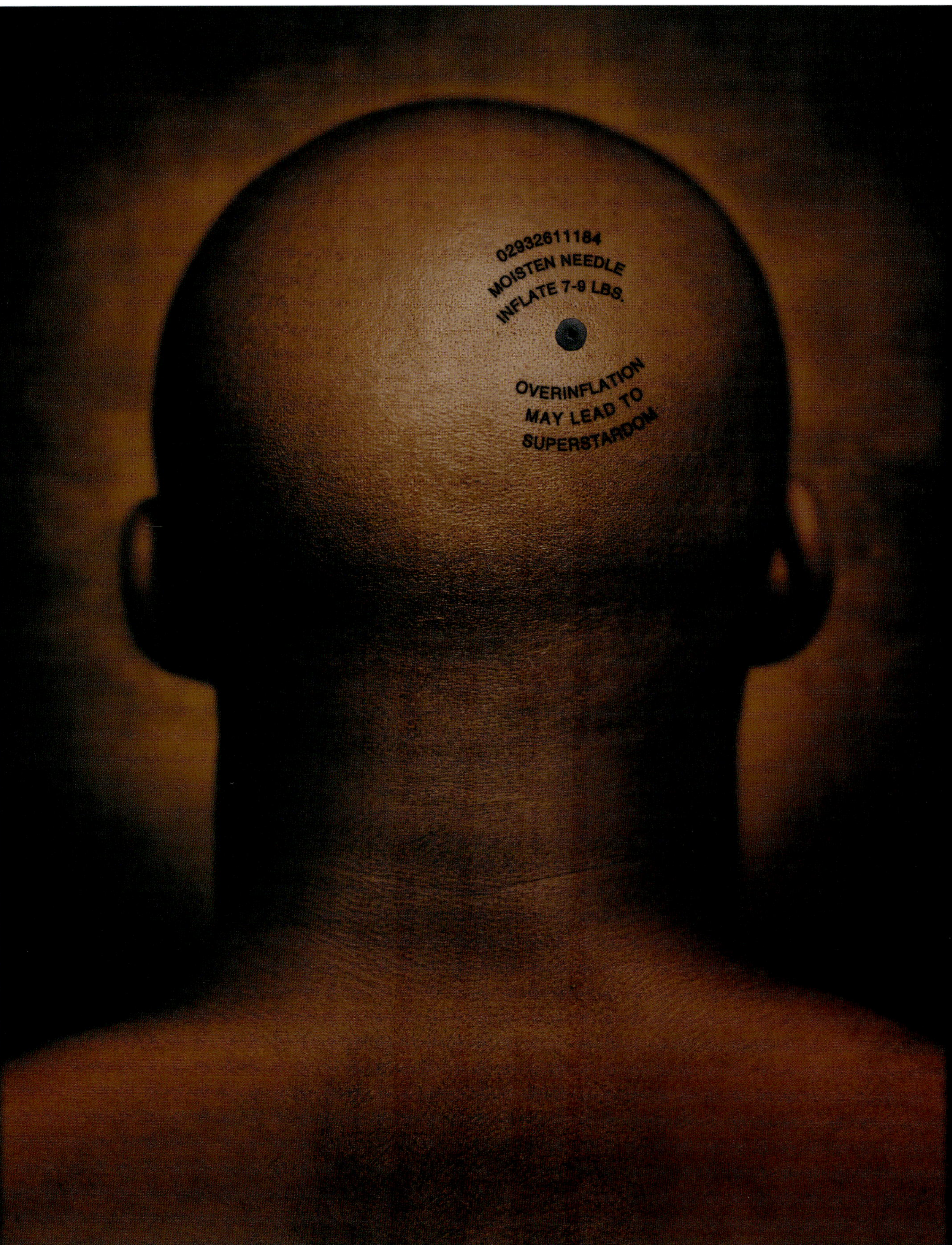

02932611184
MOISTEN NEEDLE
INFLATE 7-9 LBS.
OVERINFLATION
MAY LEAD TO
SUPERSTARDOM

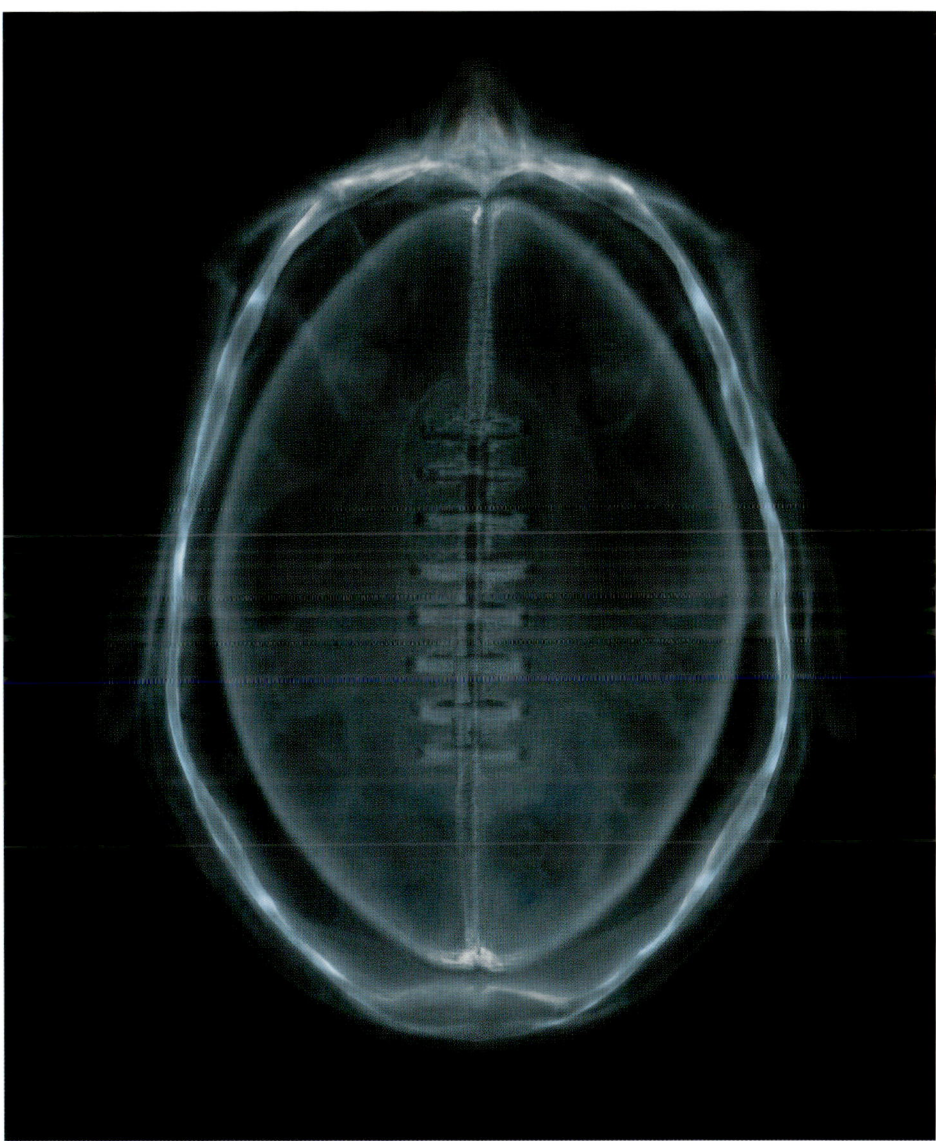

this spread: **S**andro

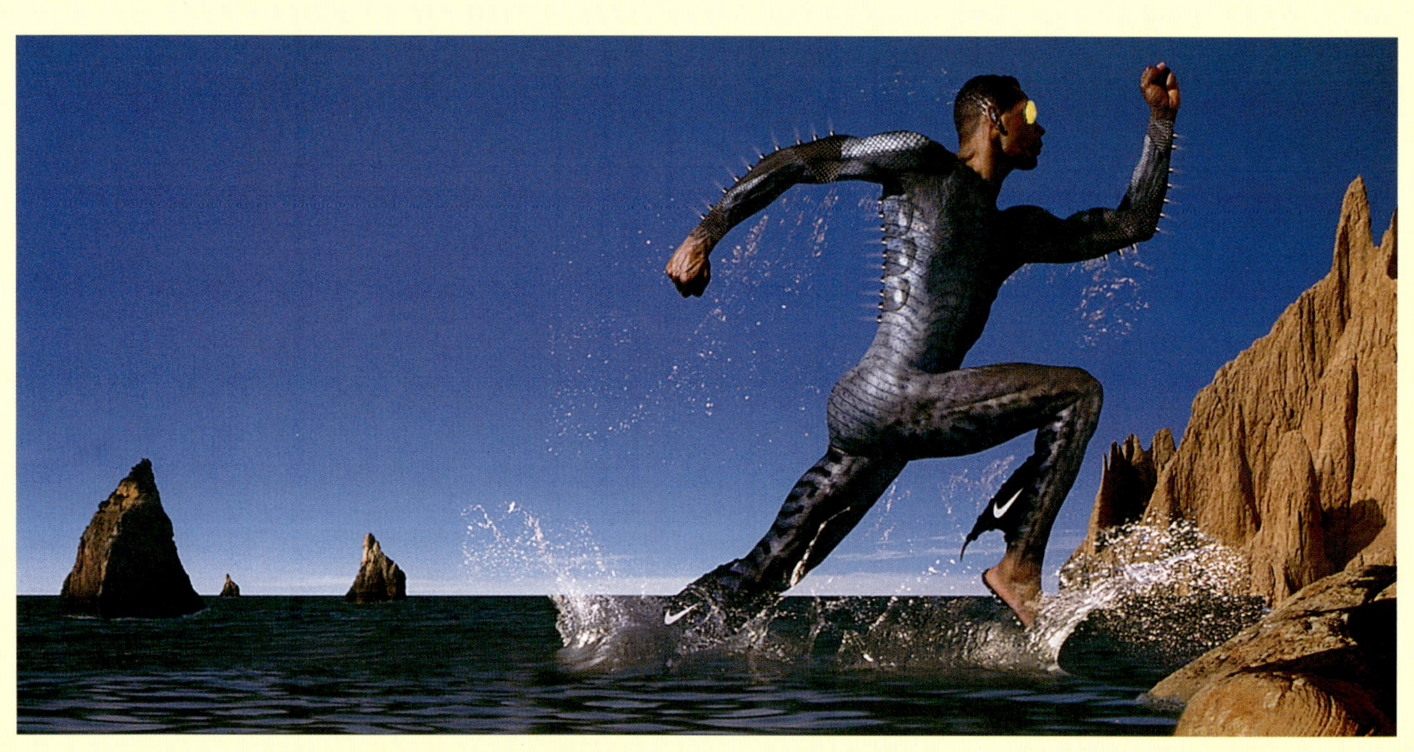

this page: **J**ames **P**orto opposite: **D**an **L**im

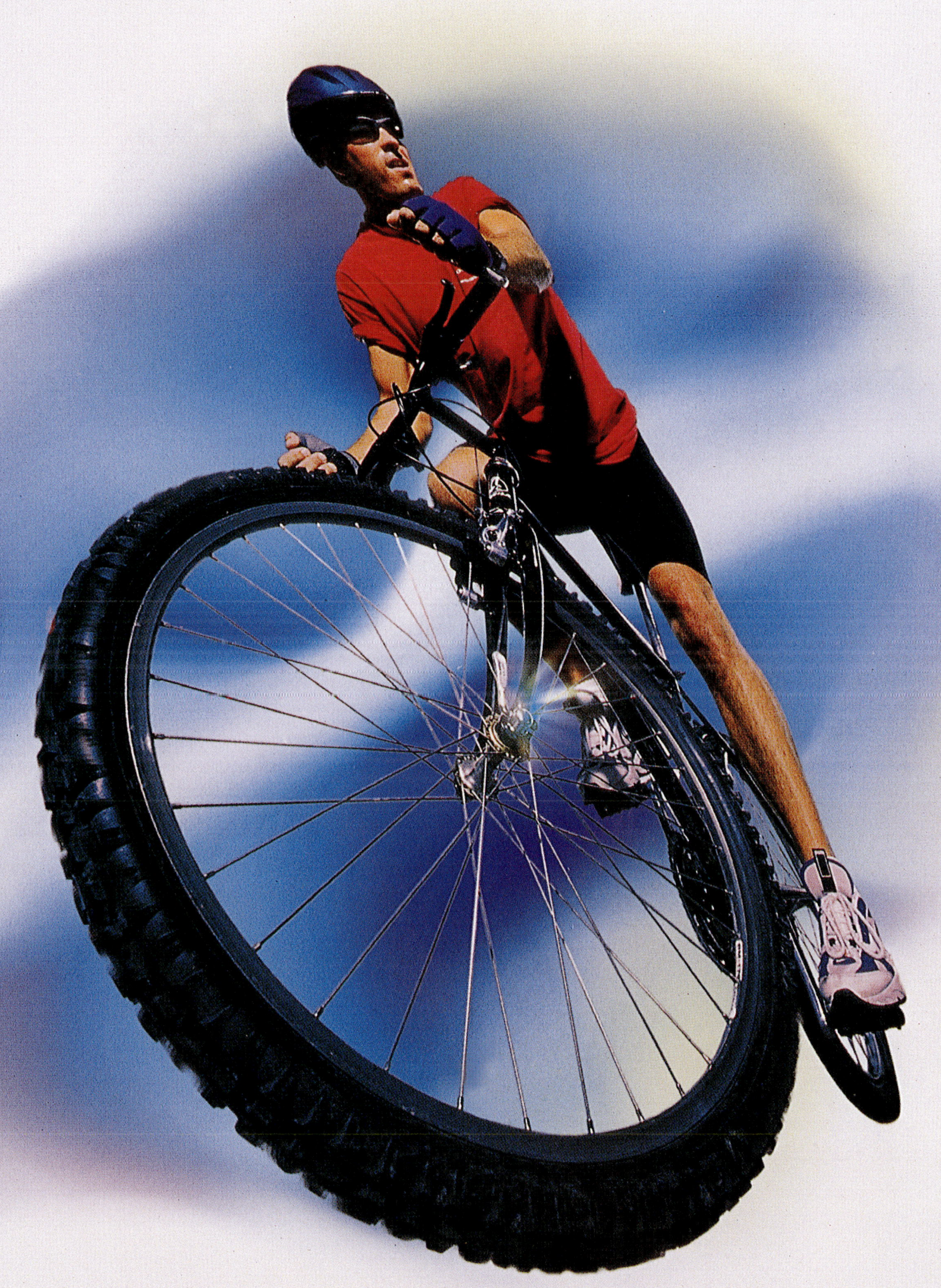

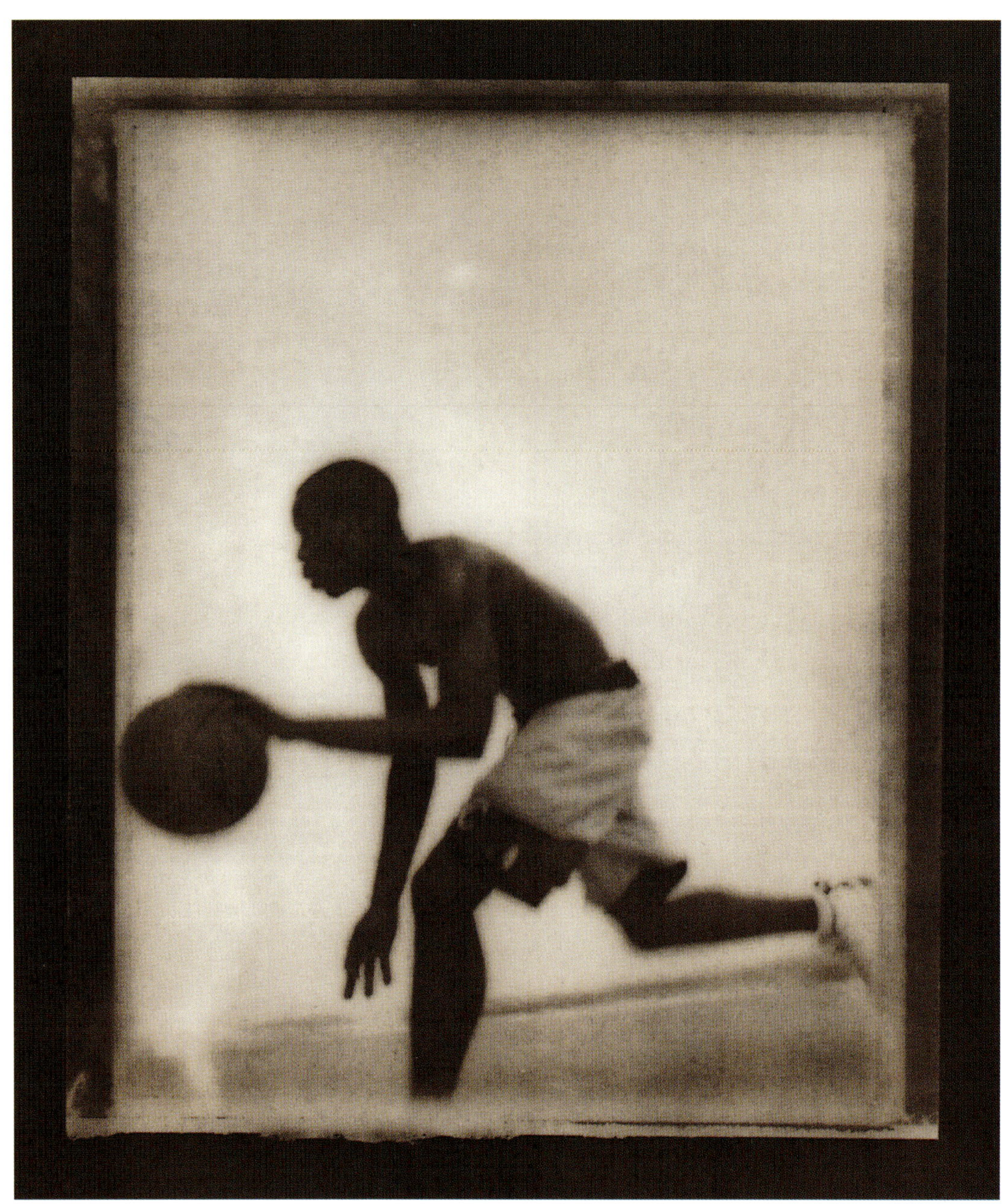

this page: **J**ohn **H**uet opposite: **RJ M**una

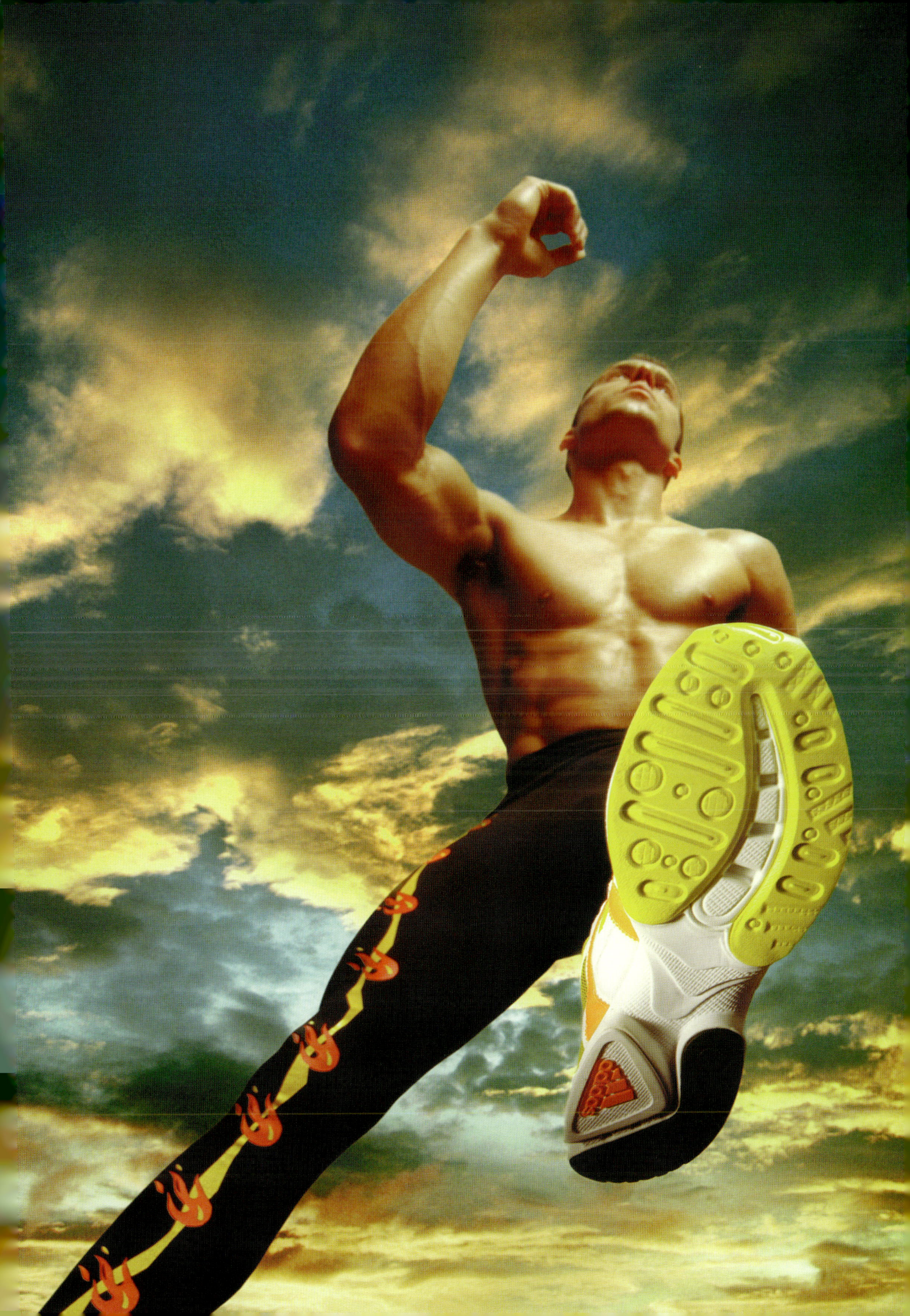

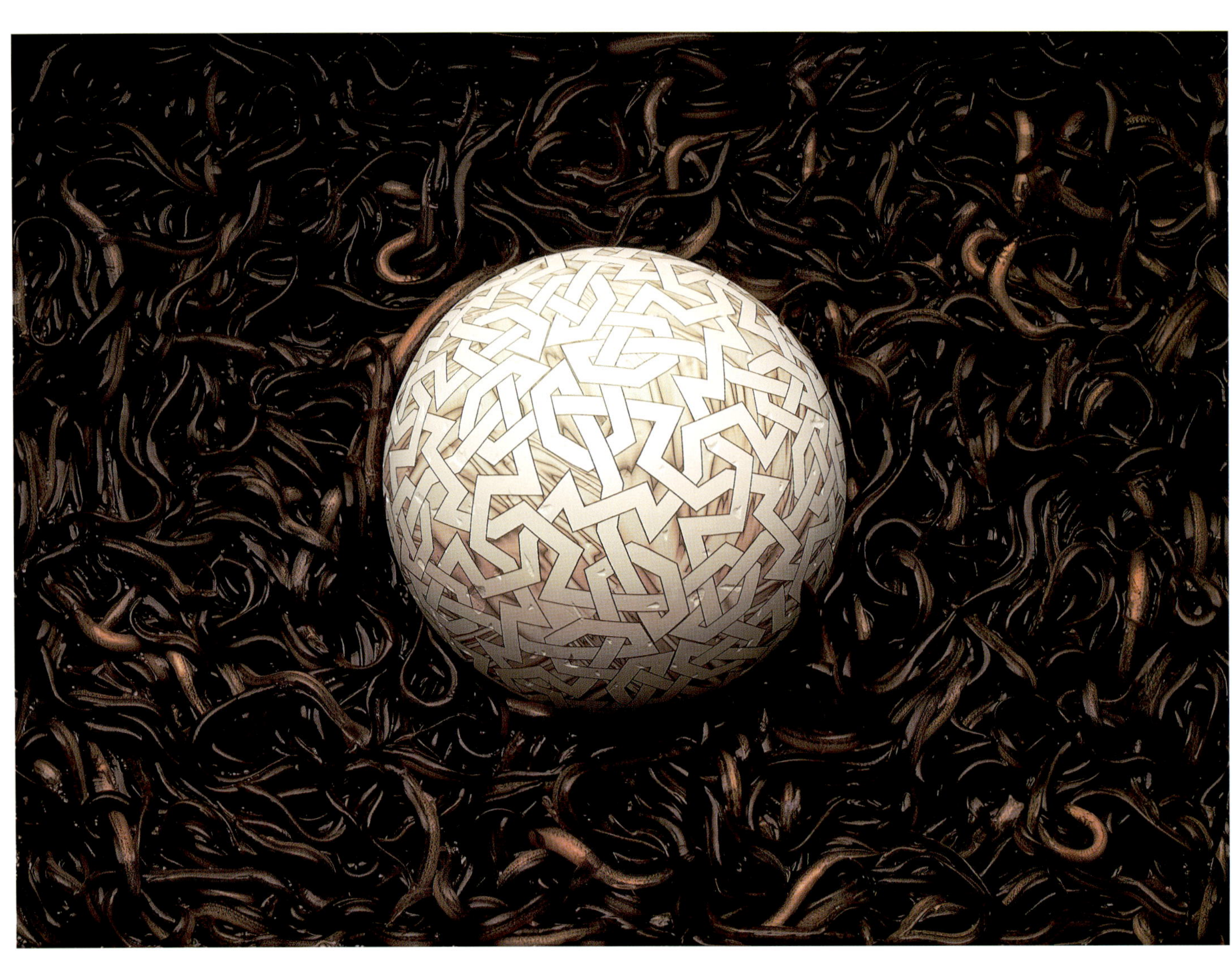

this and following spread: **S**hinichi **H**onda

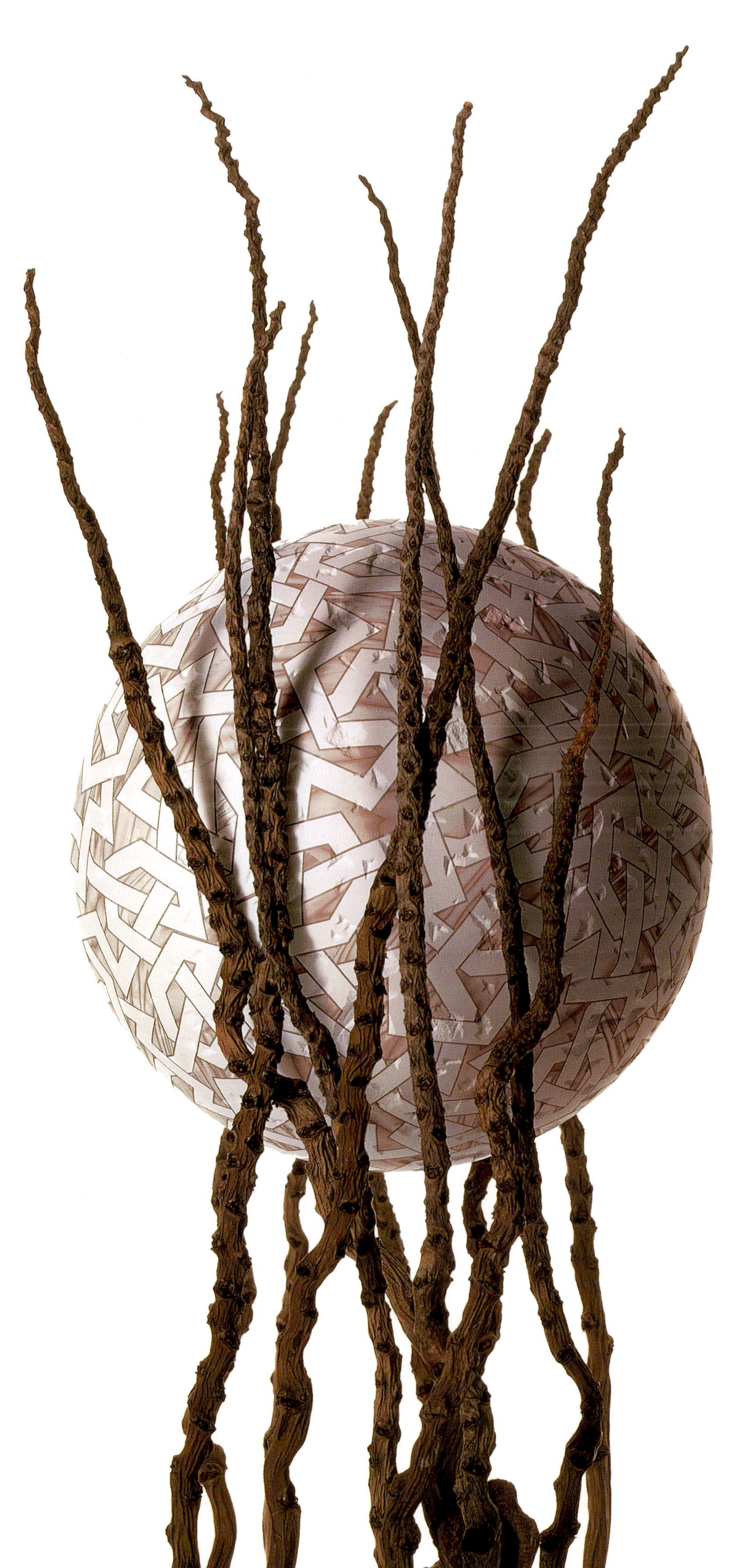

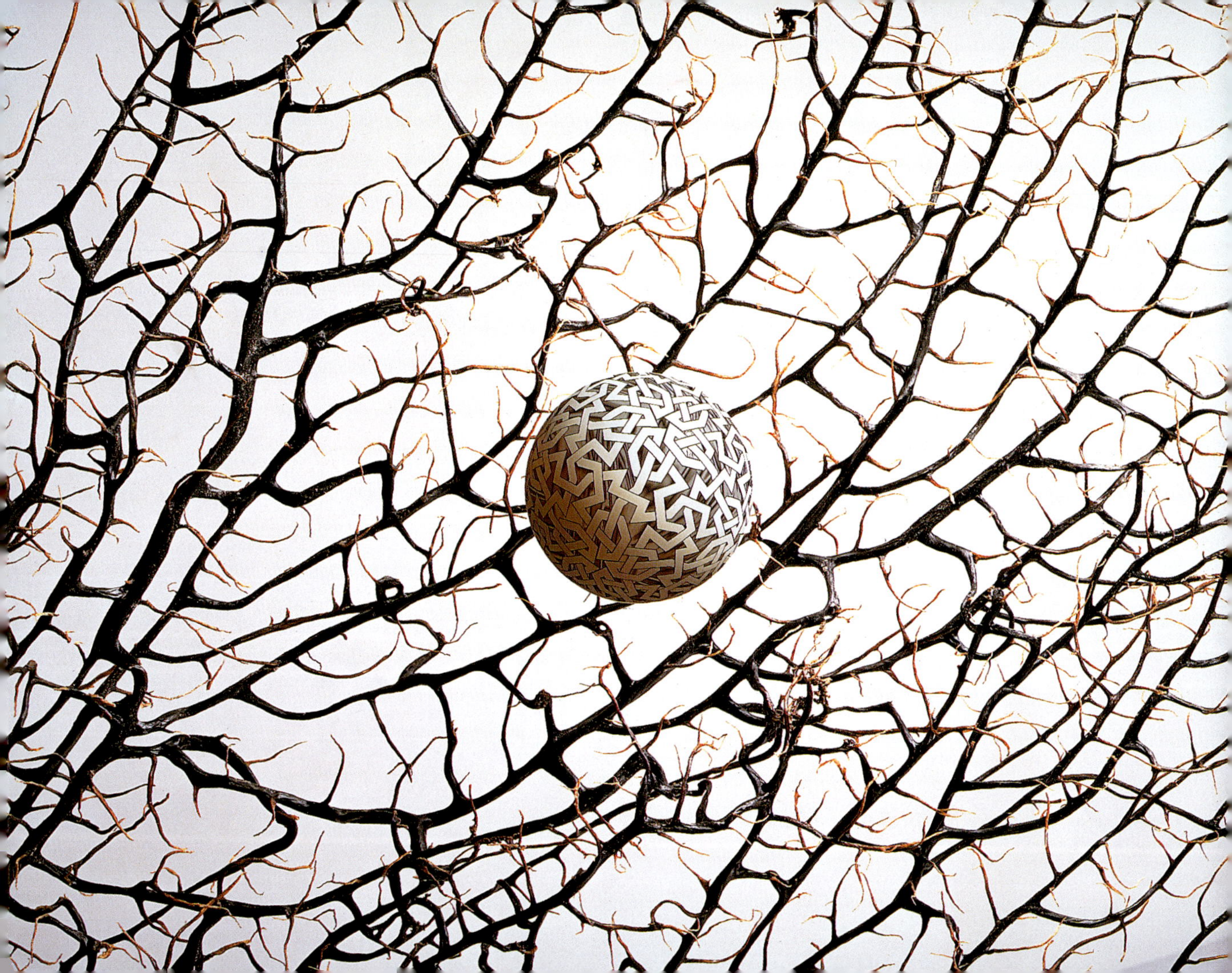

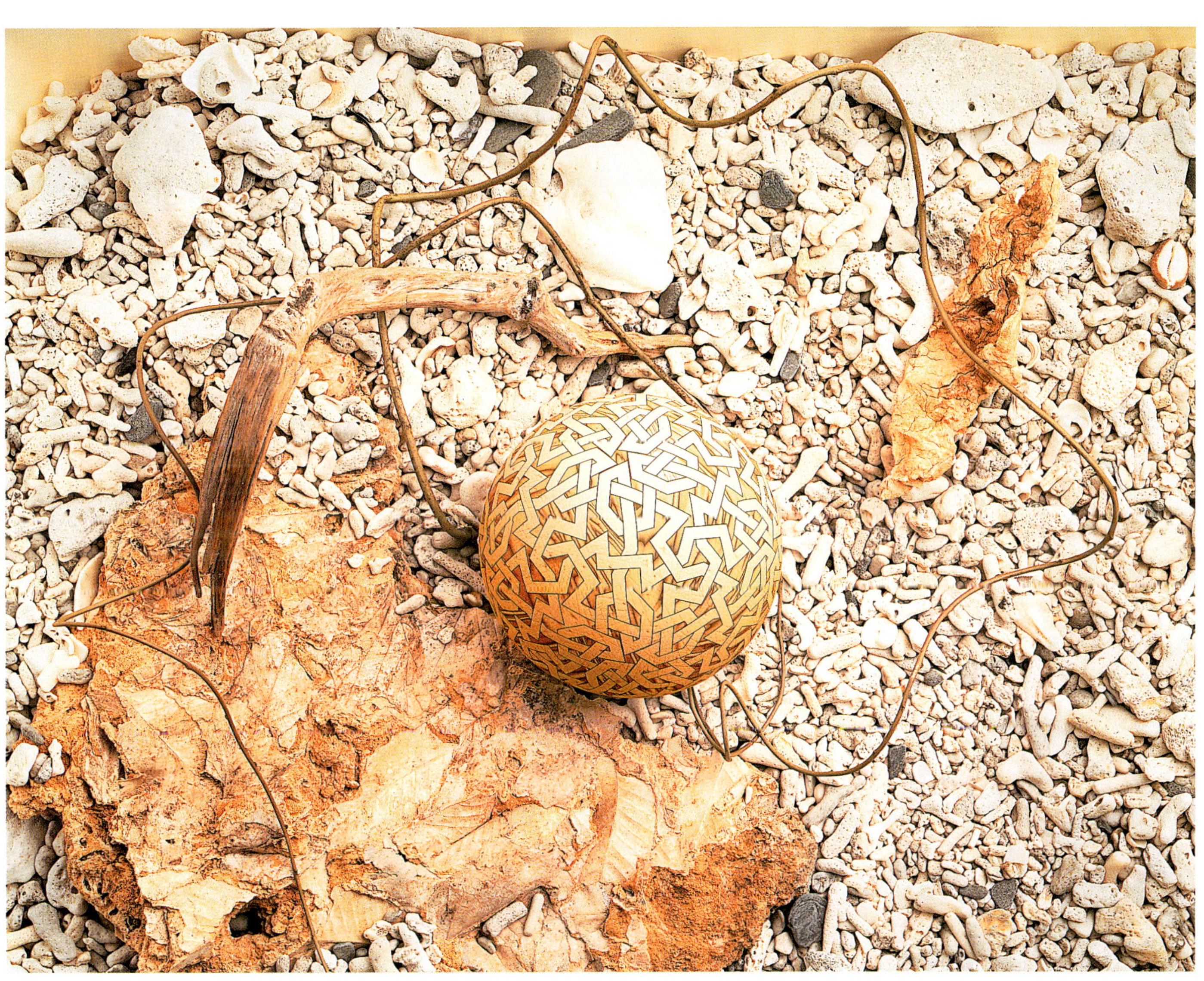

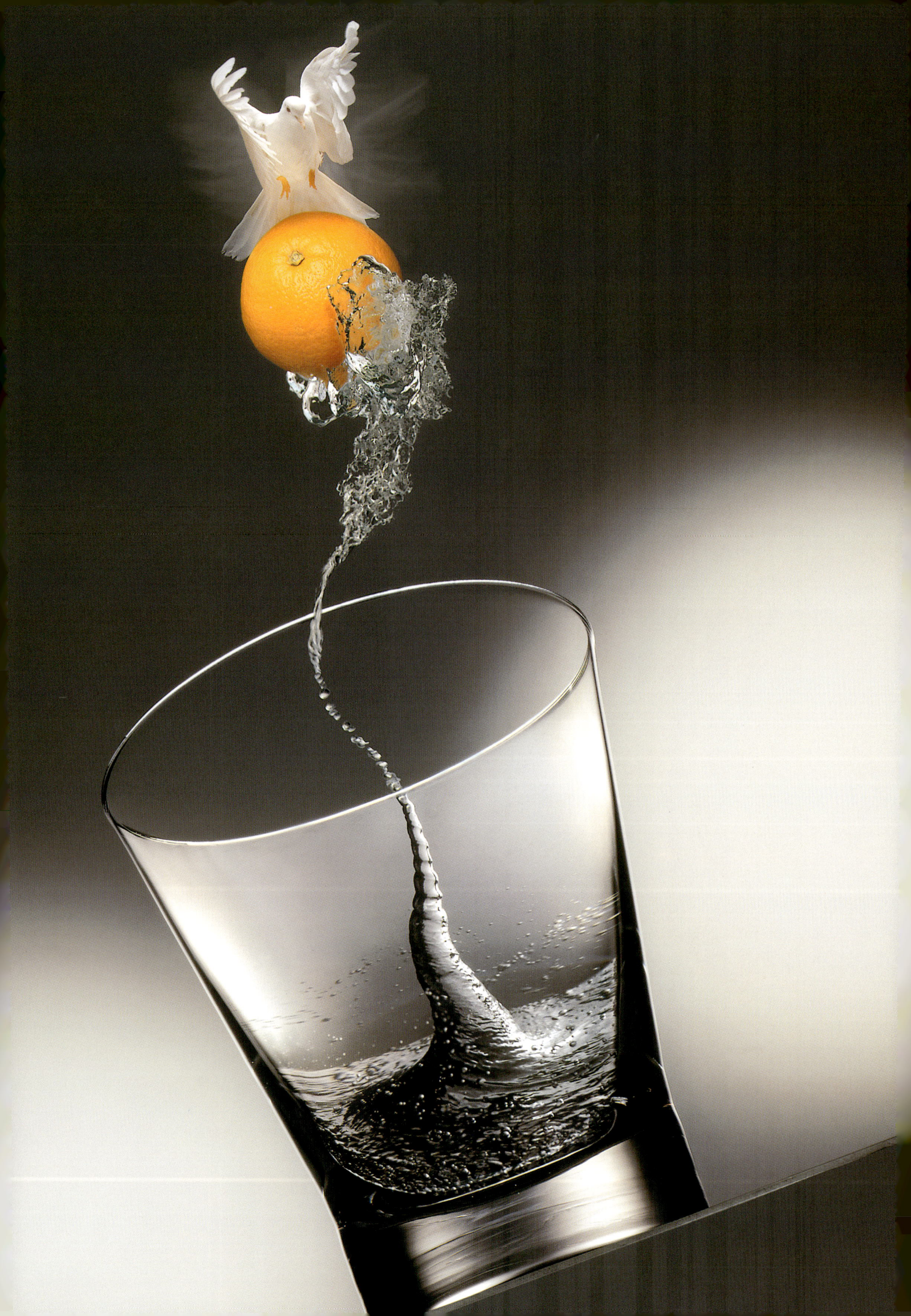

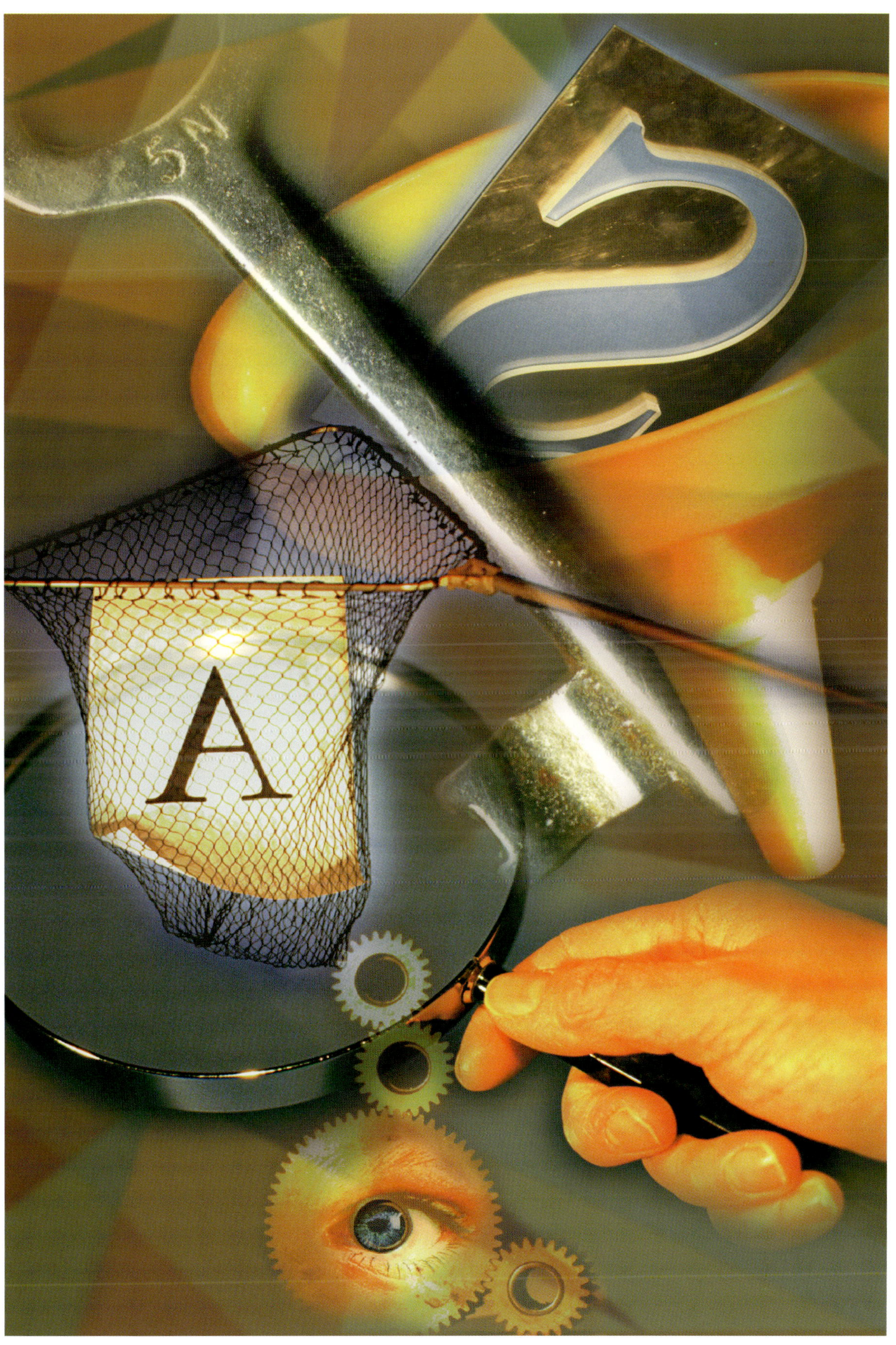

opposite: **R**yszard **H**orowitz this page: **B**ryce **B**ennett

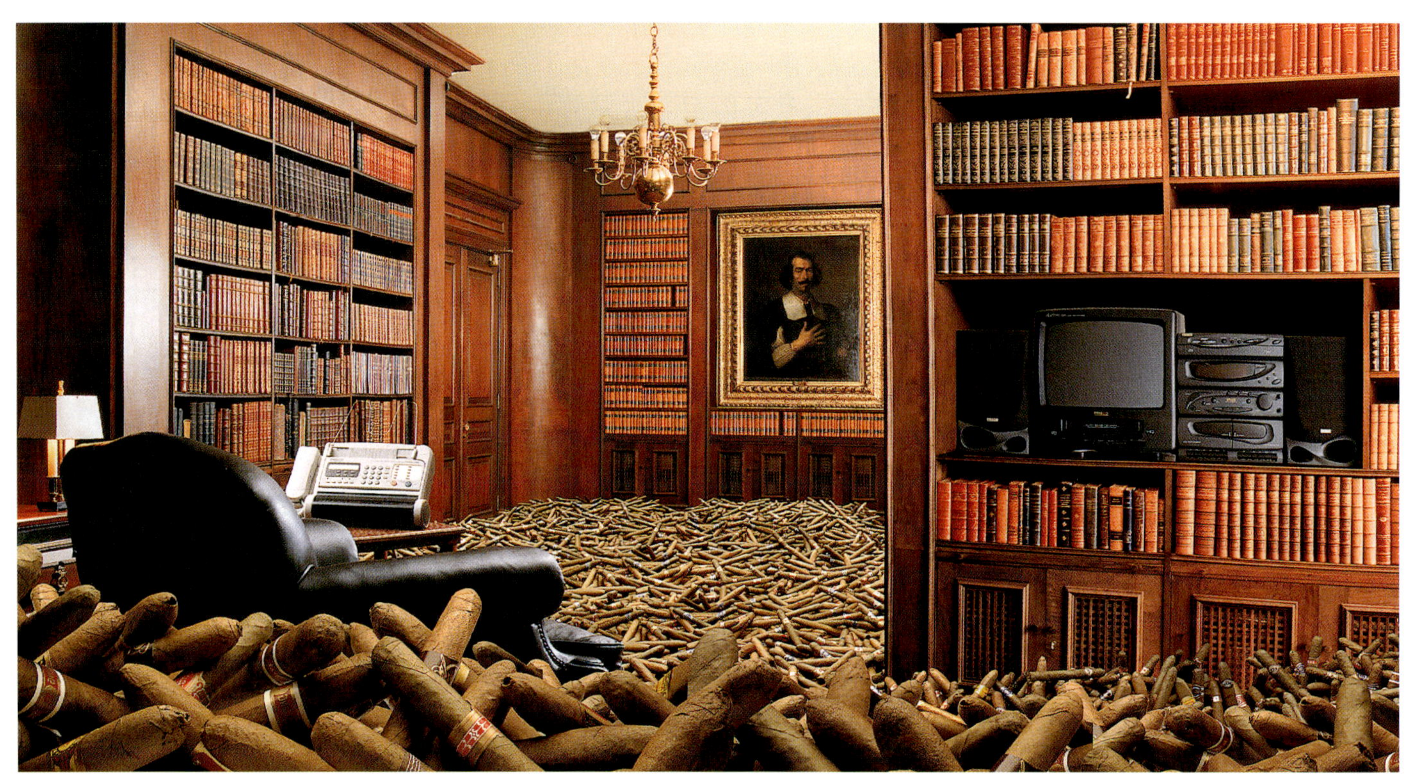

this spread: **F**ernando **Z**uffo

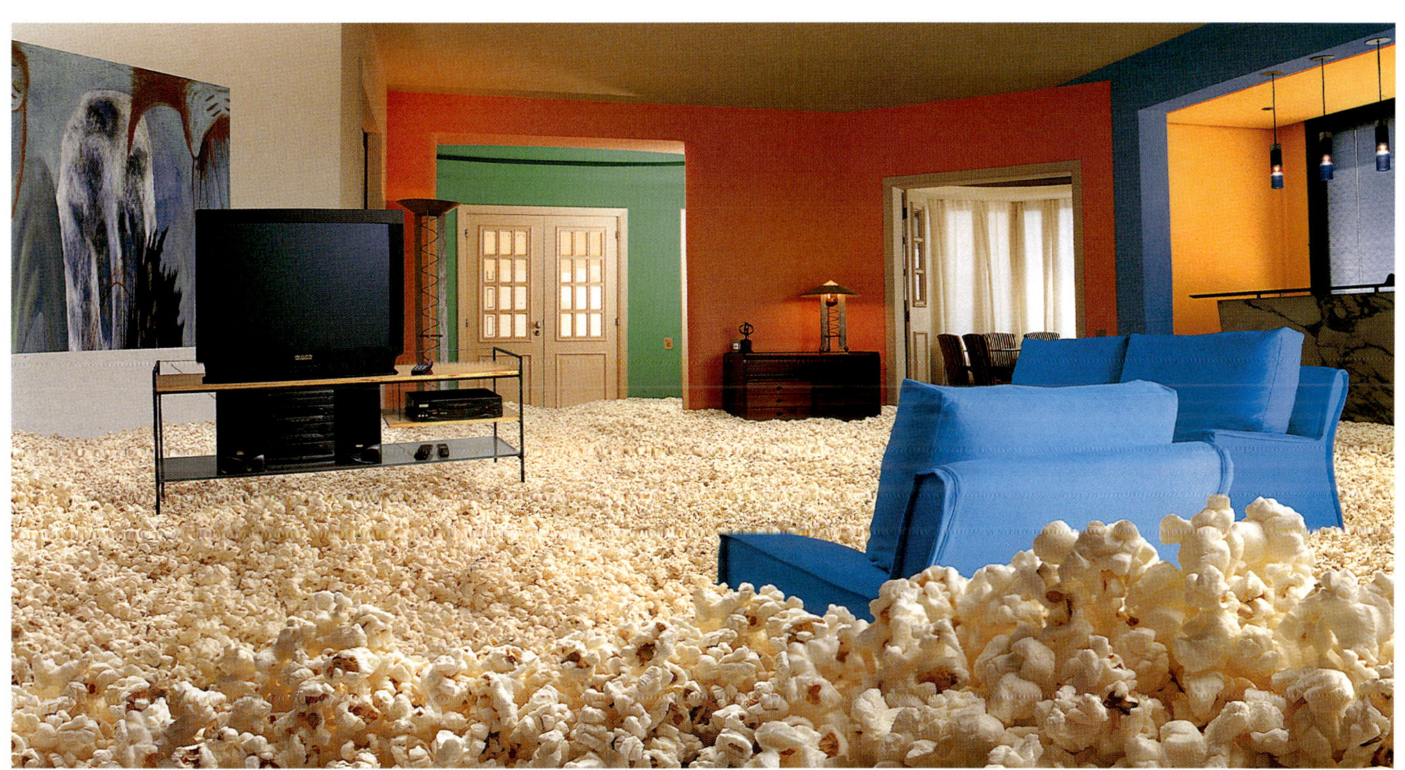

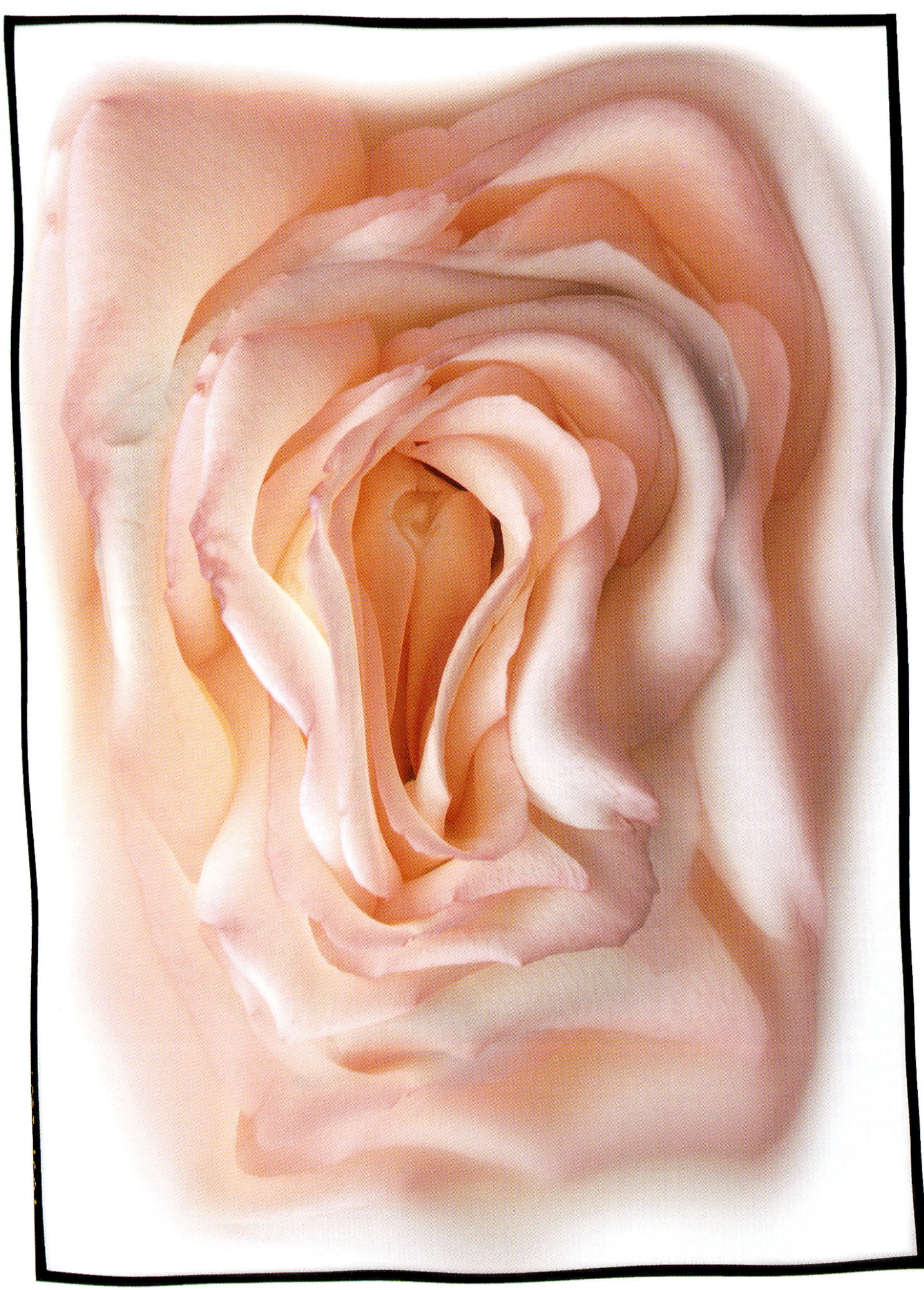

this spread: **G**erald **B**ybee

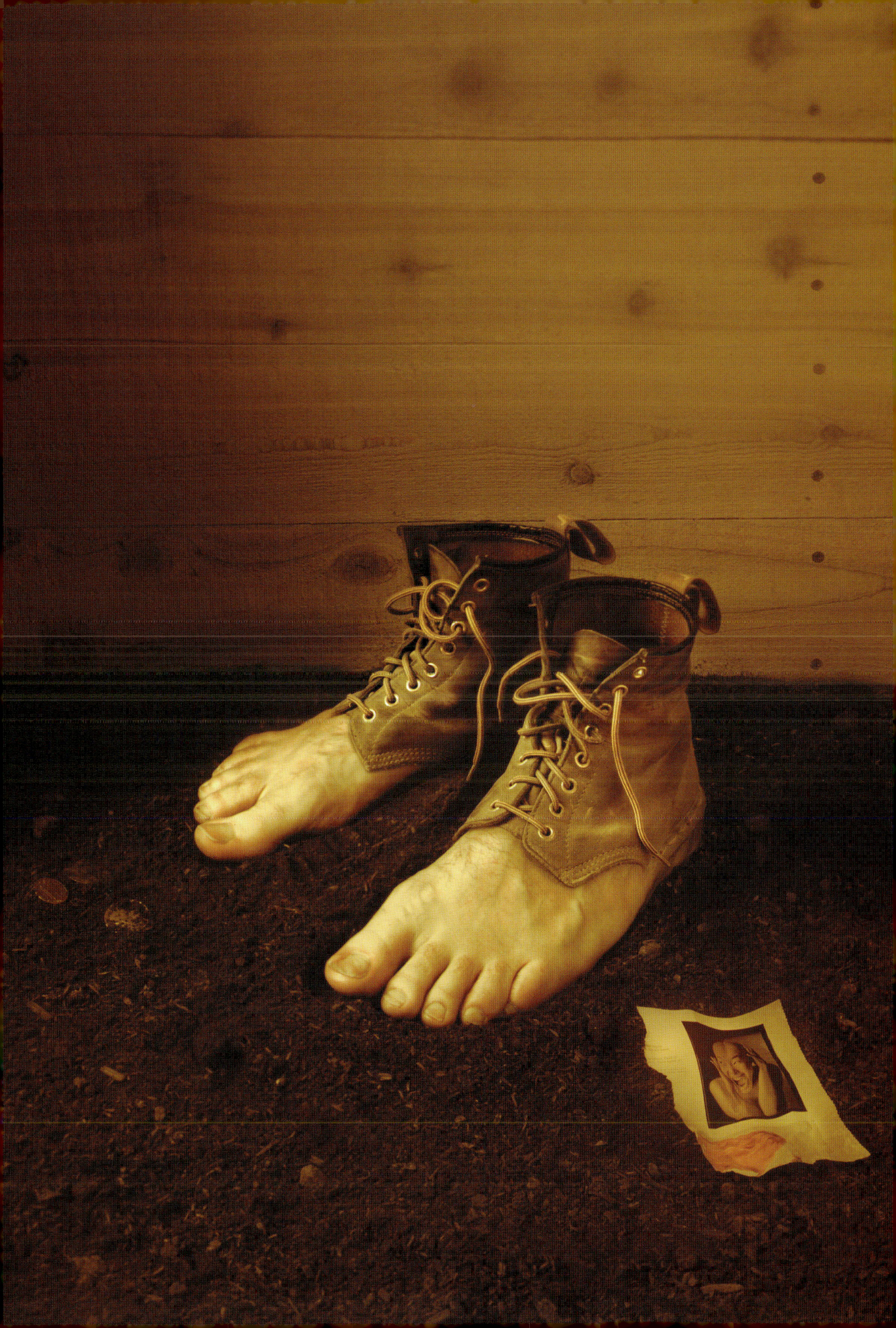

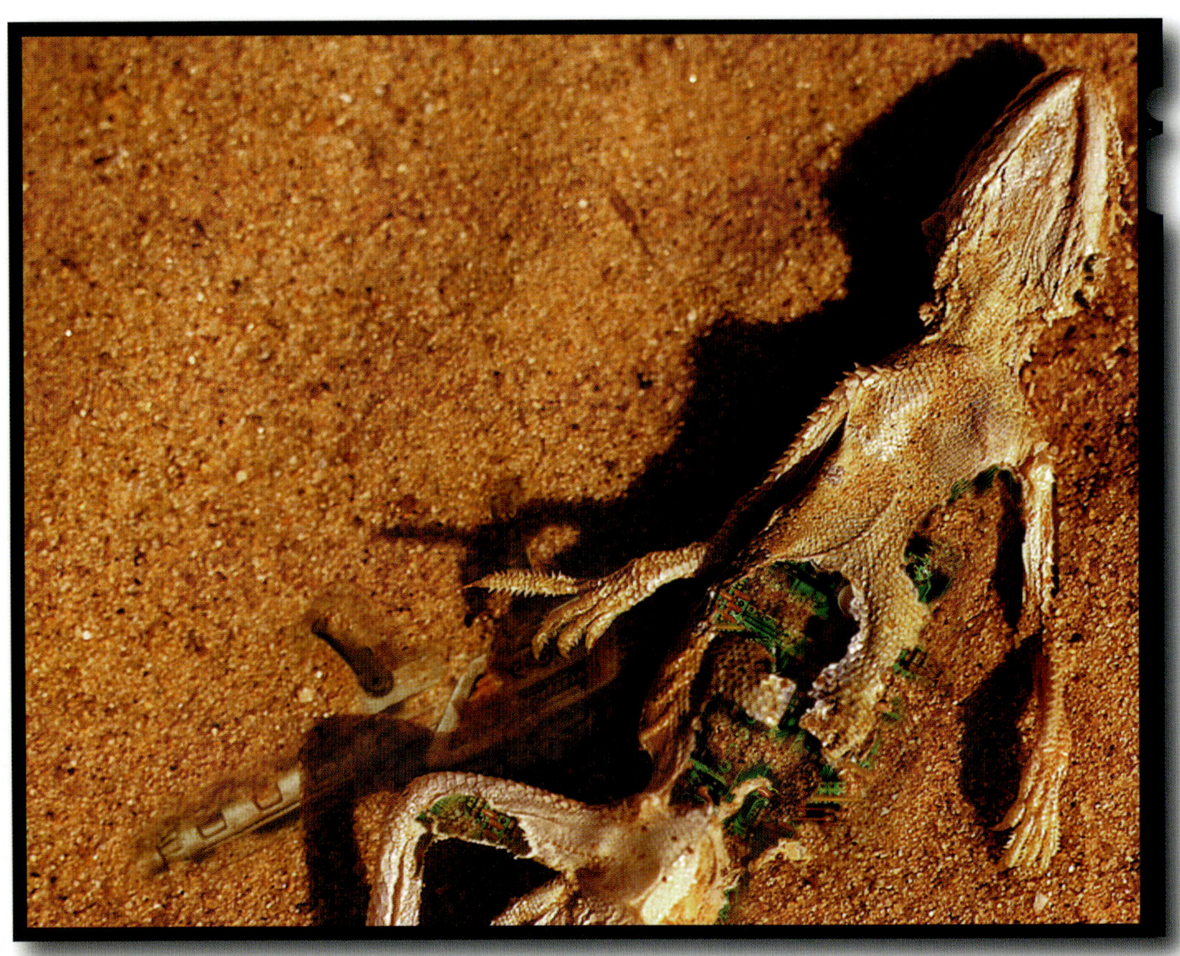

Eric Fairchild

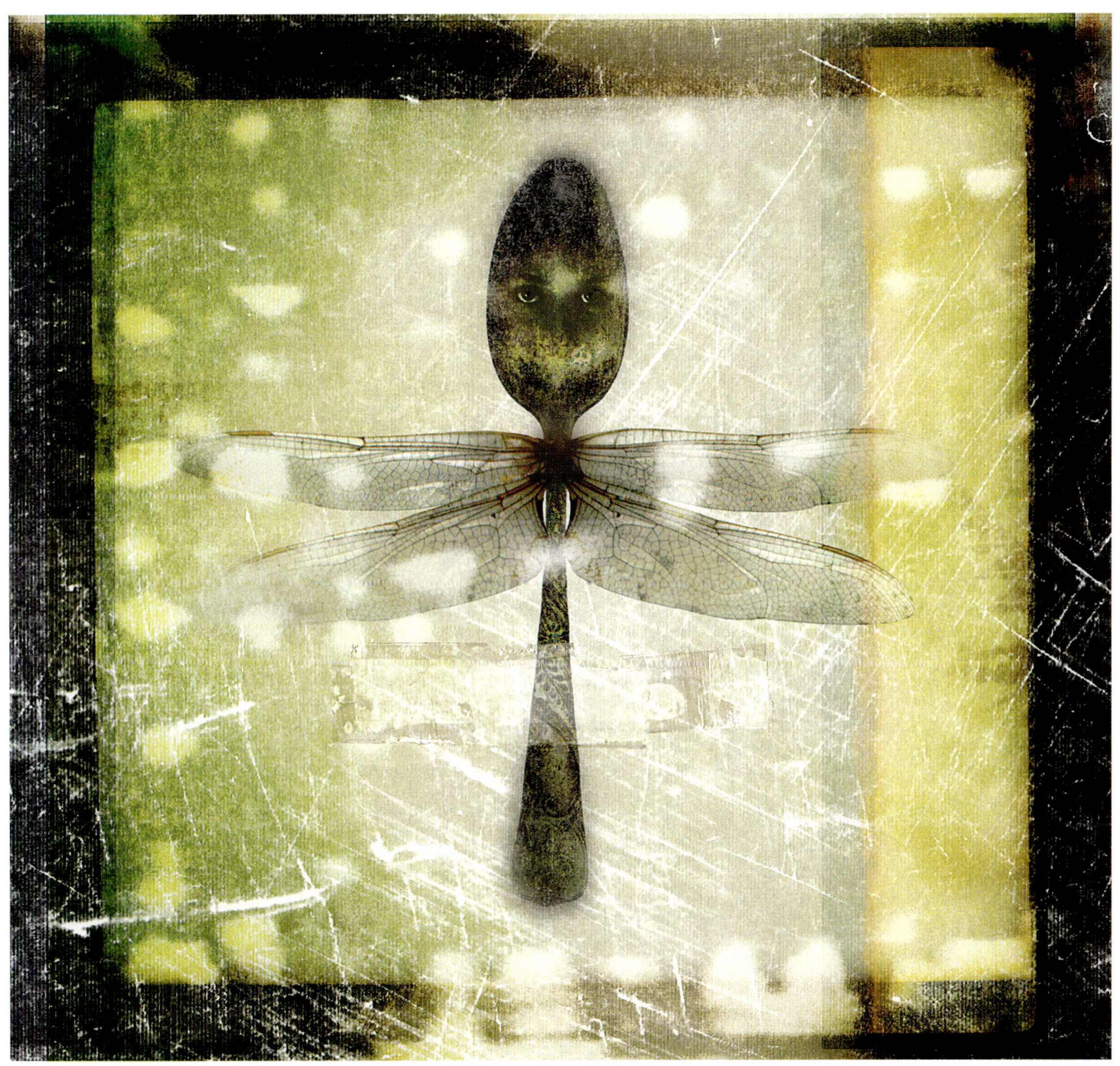

Sean Alatorre, Laura Pizzarelli

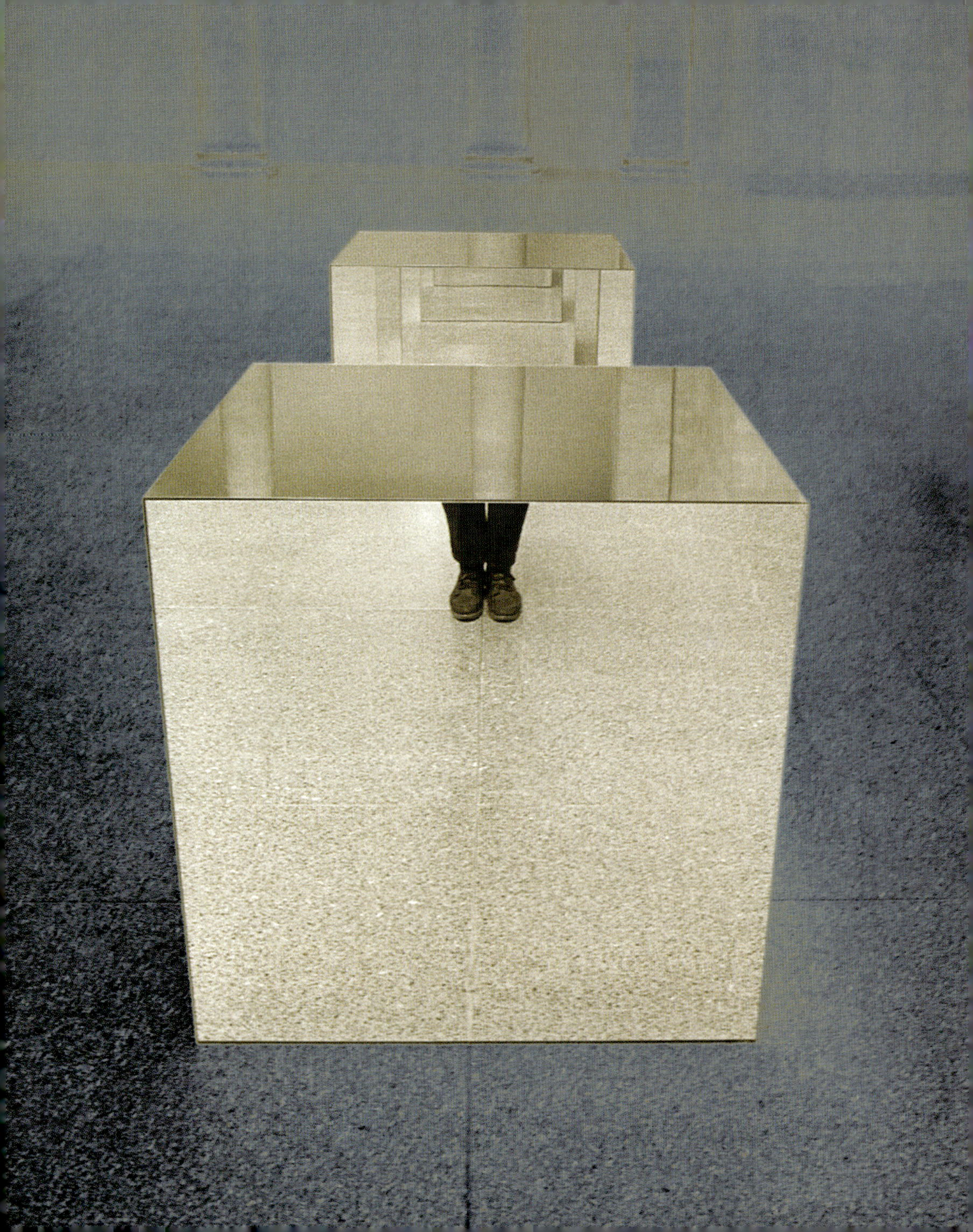

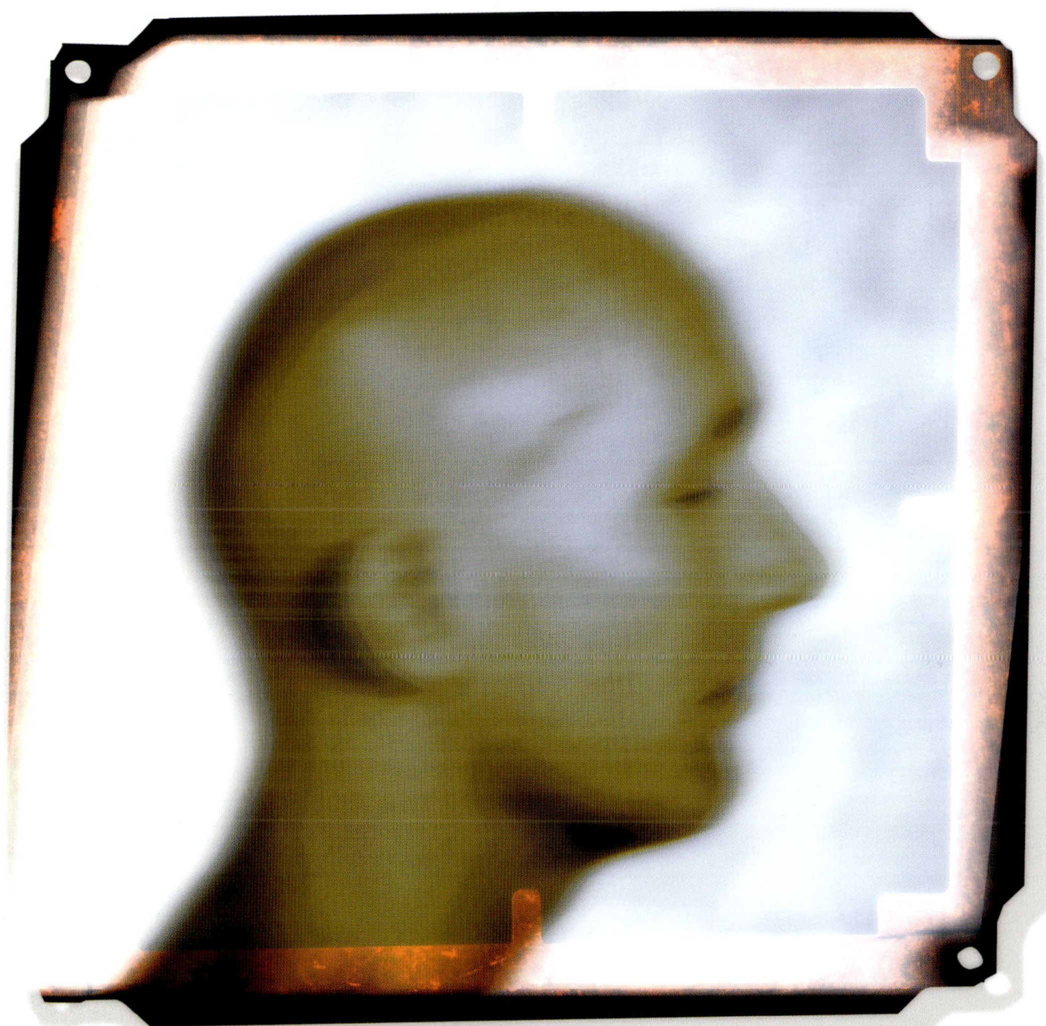

Philip **K**aake

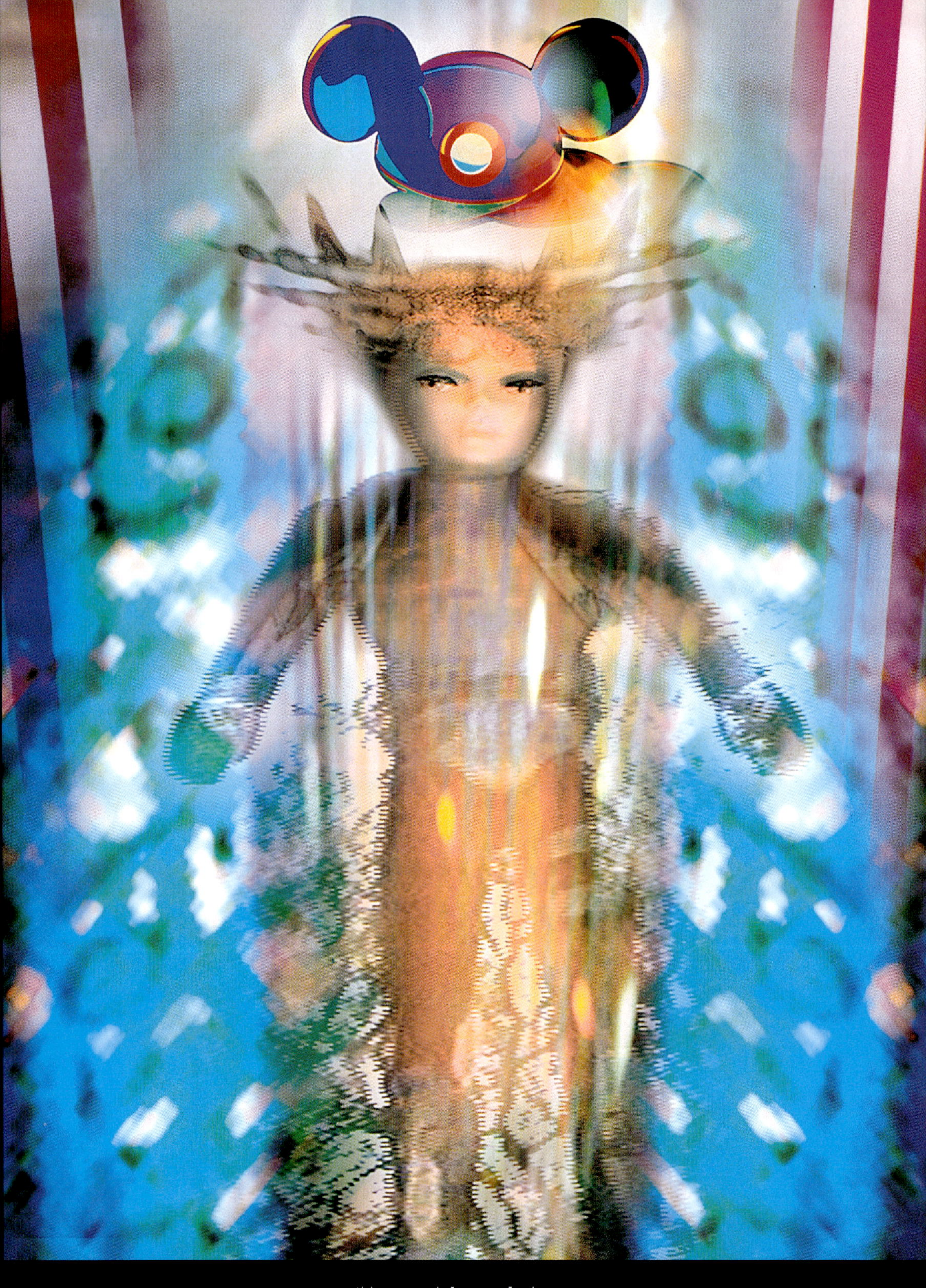

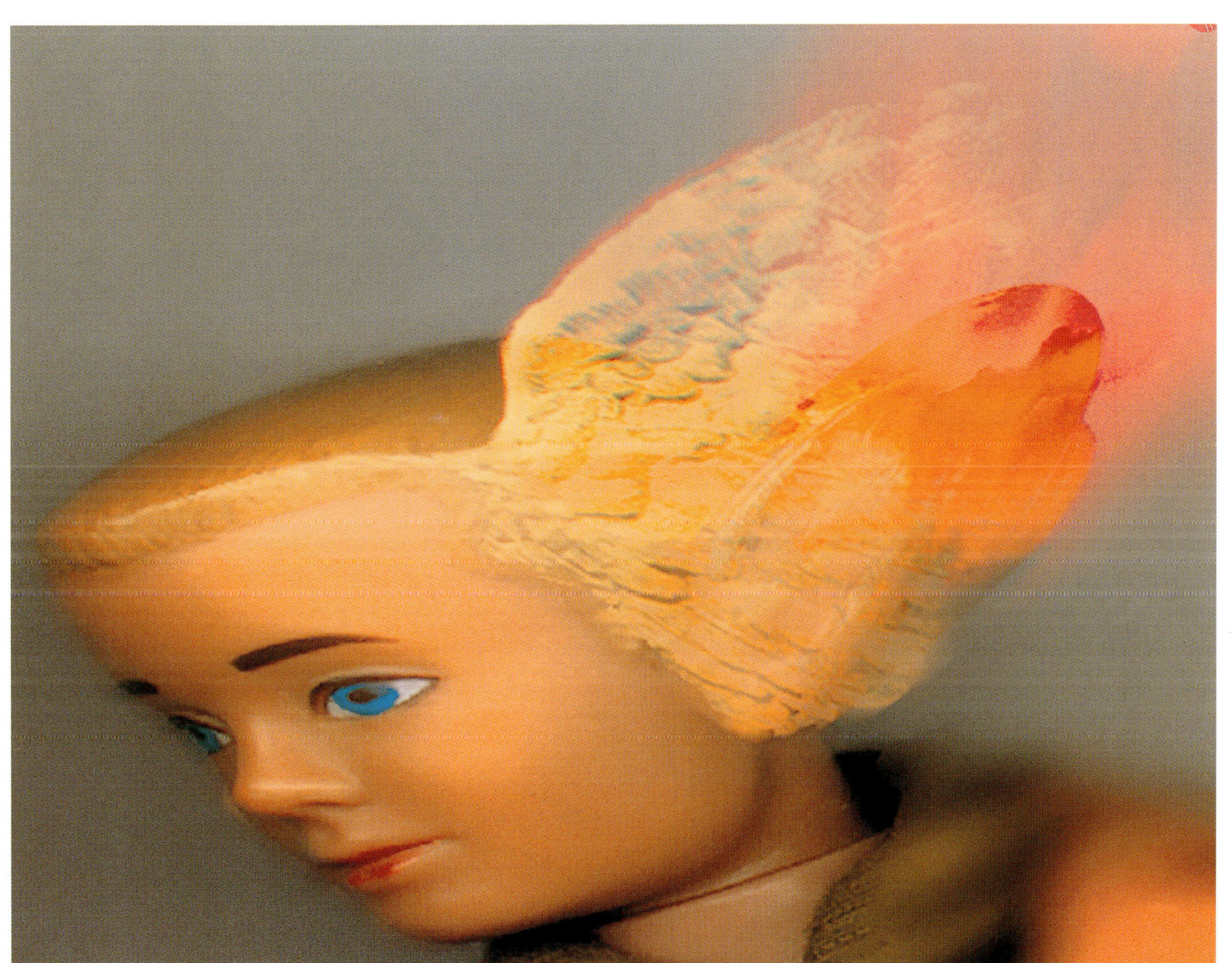

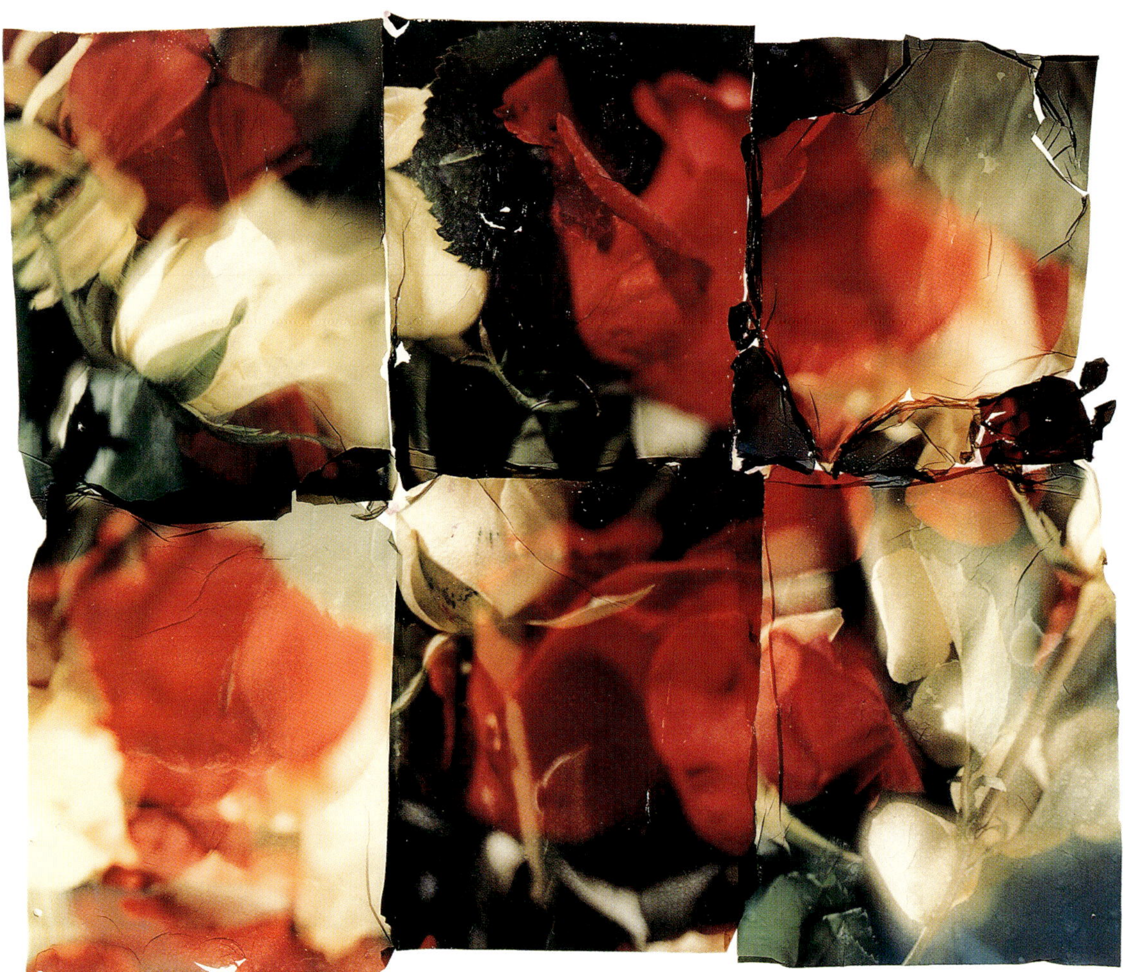

this spread: **S**tefan **L**ongin

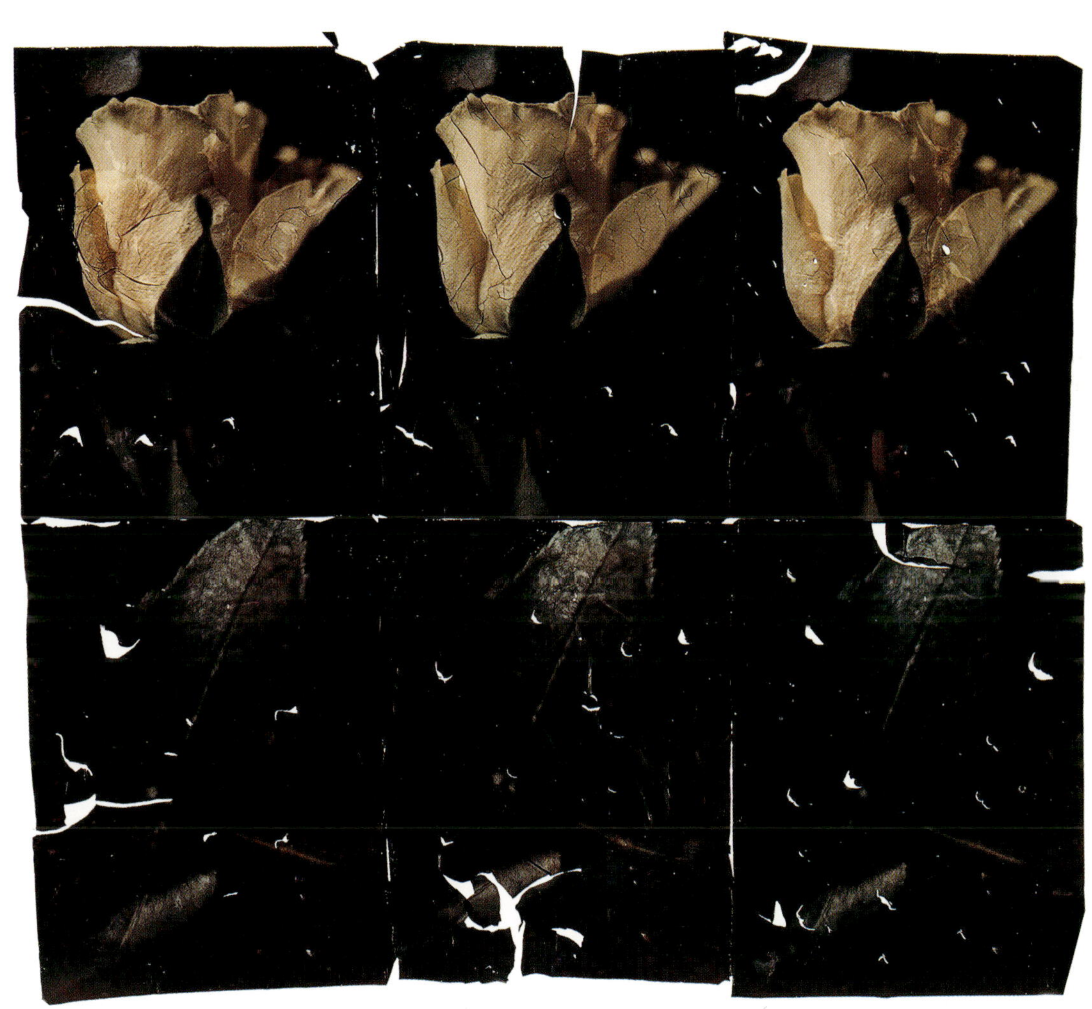

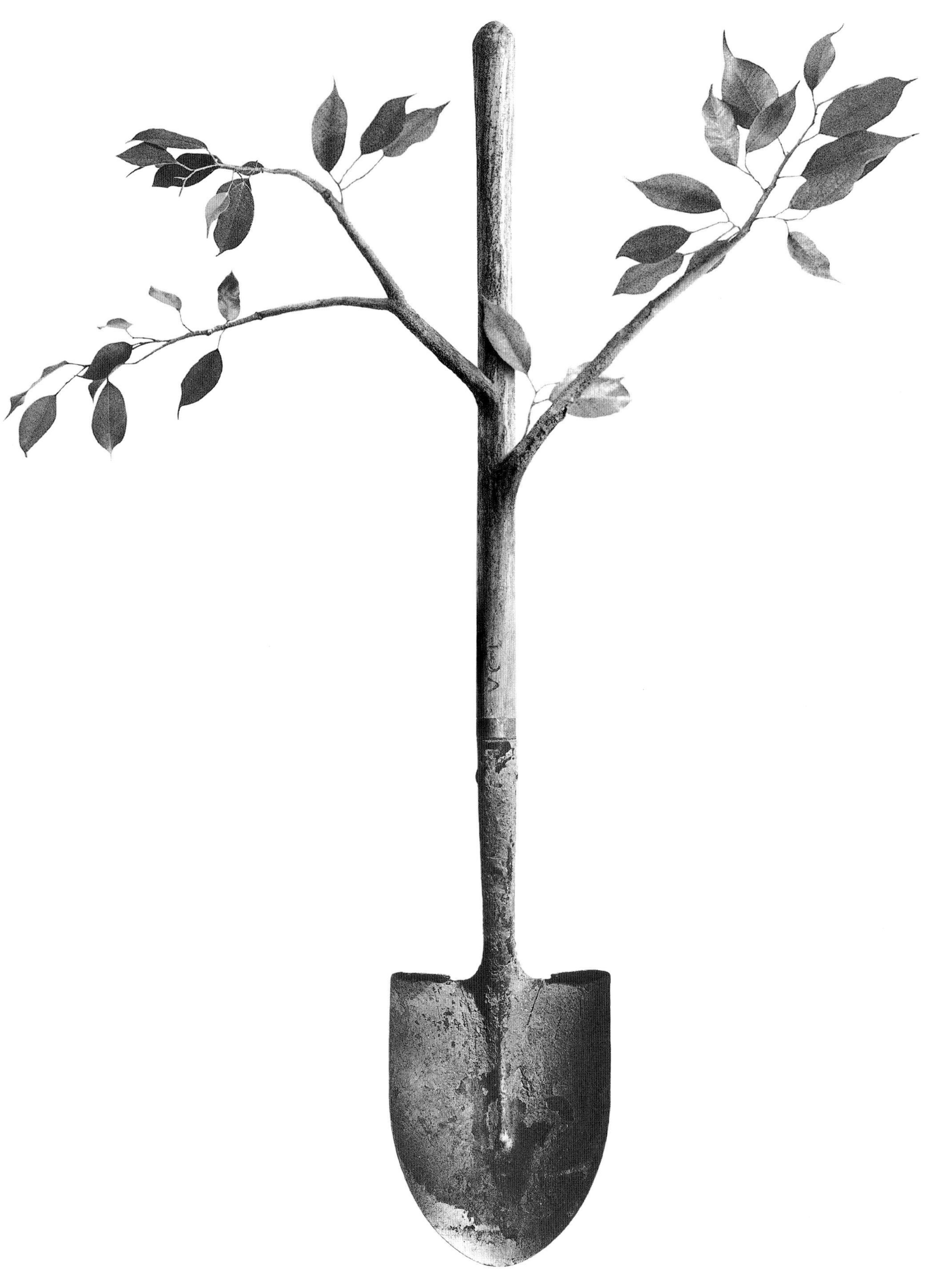

Loren **H**ammer

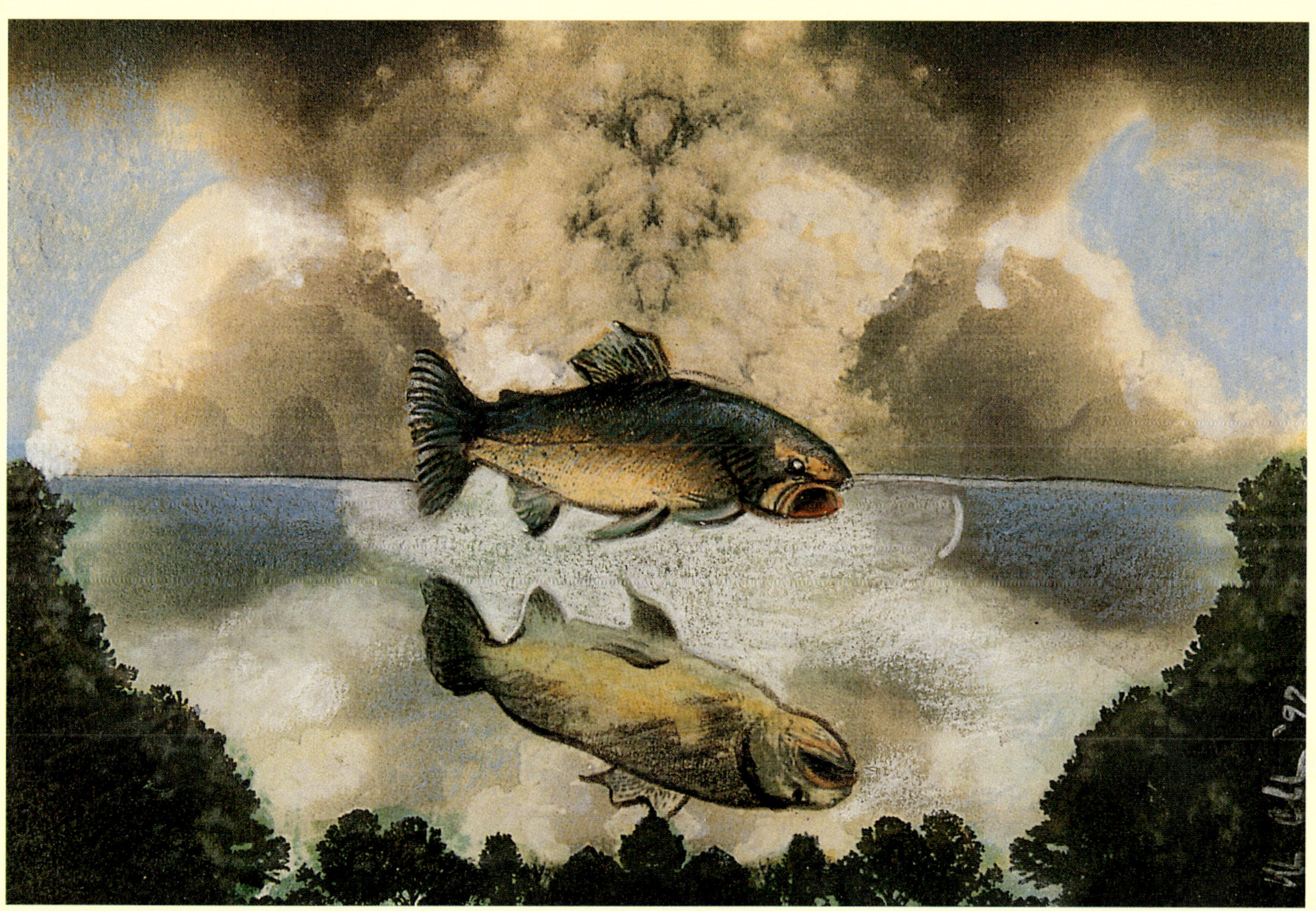

Pete Christman

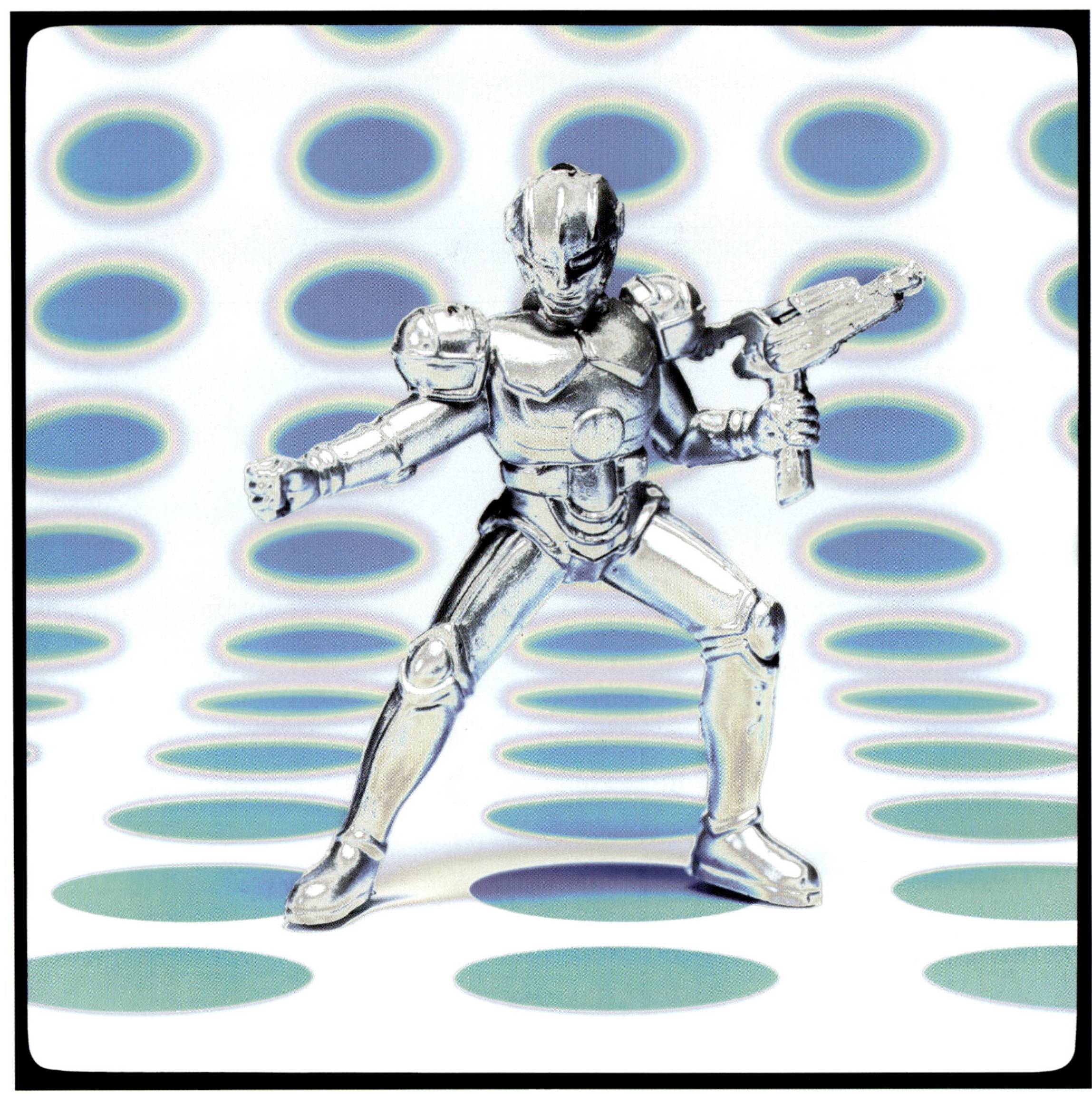

this spread: **E**ric **E**mmings

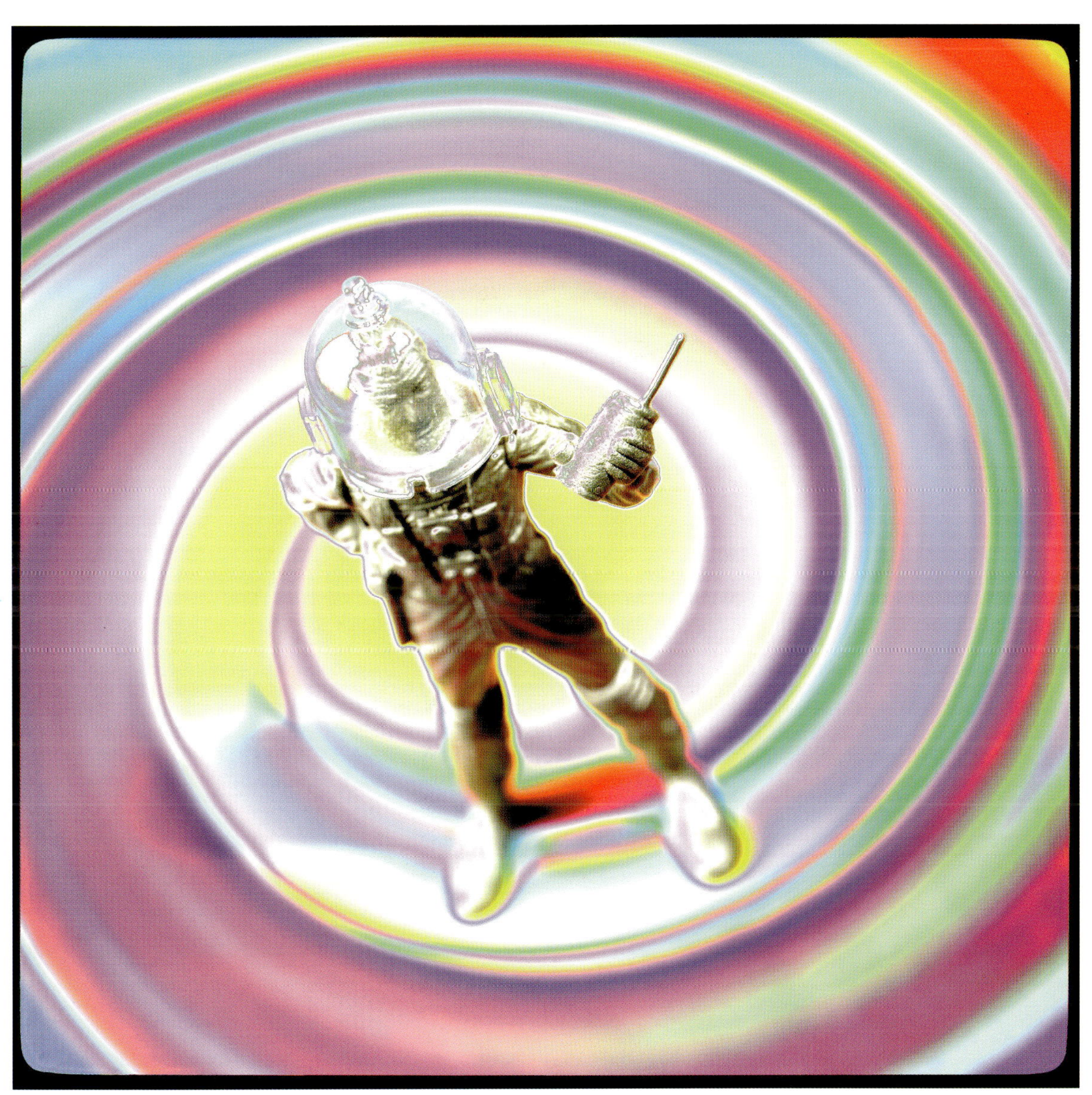

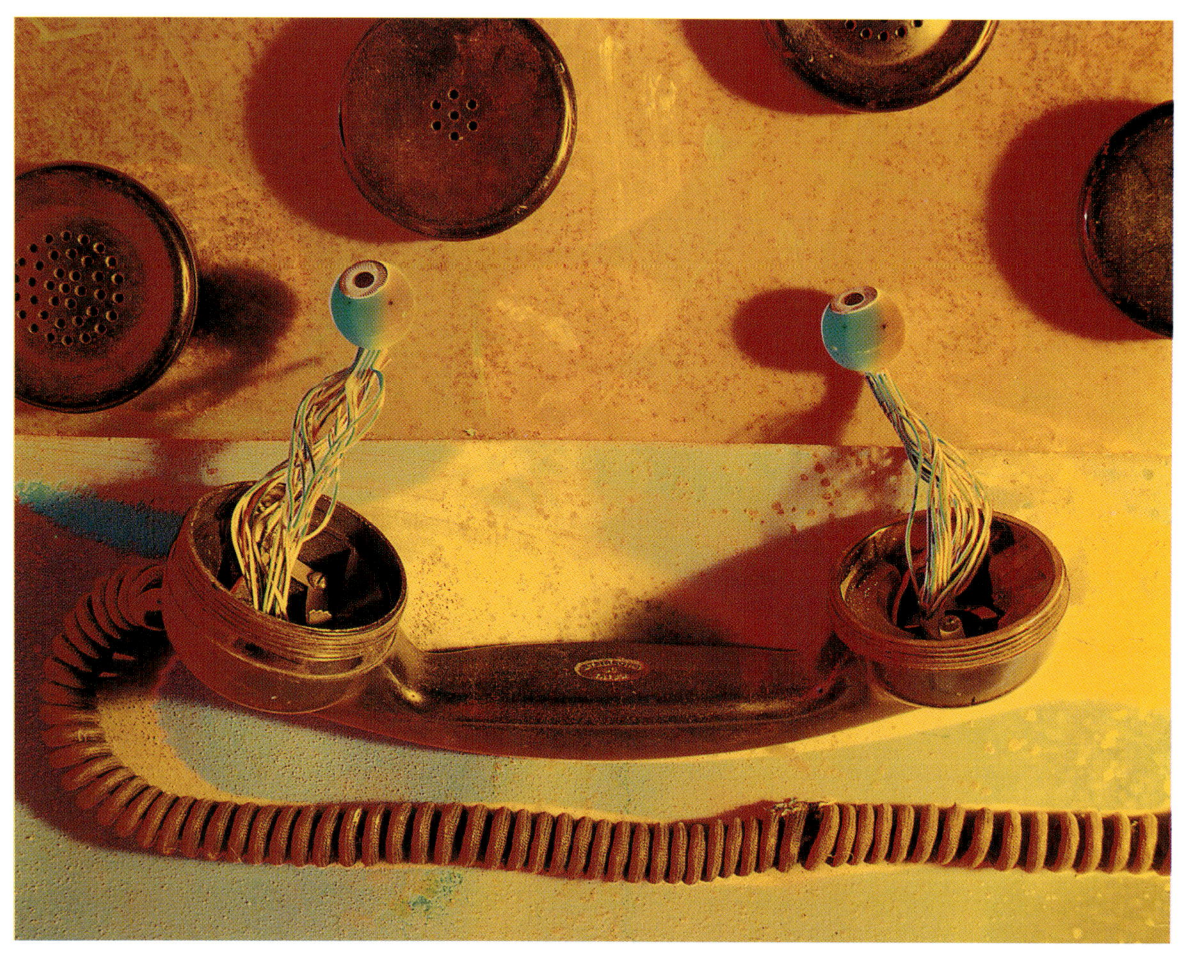

this and following spread: **D**avid **G**az

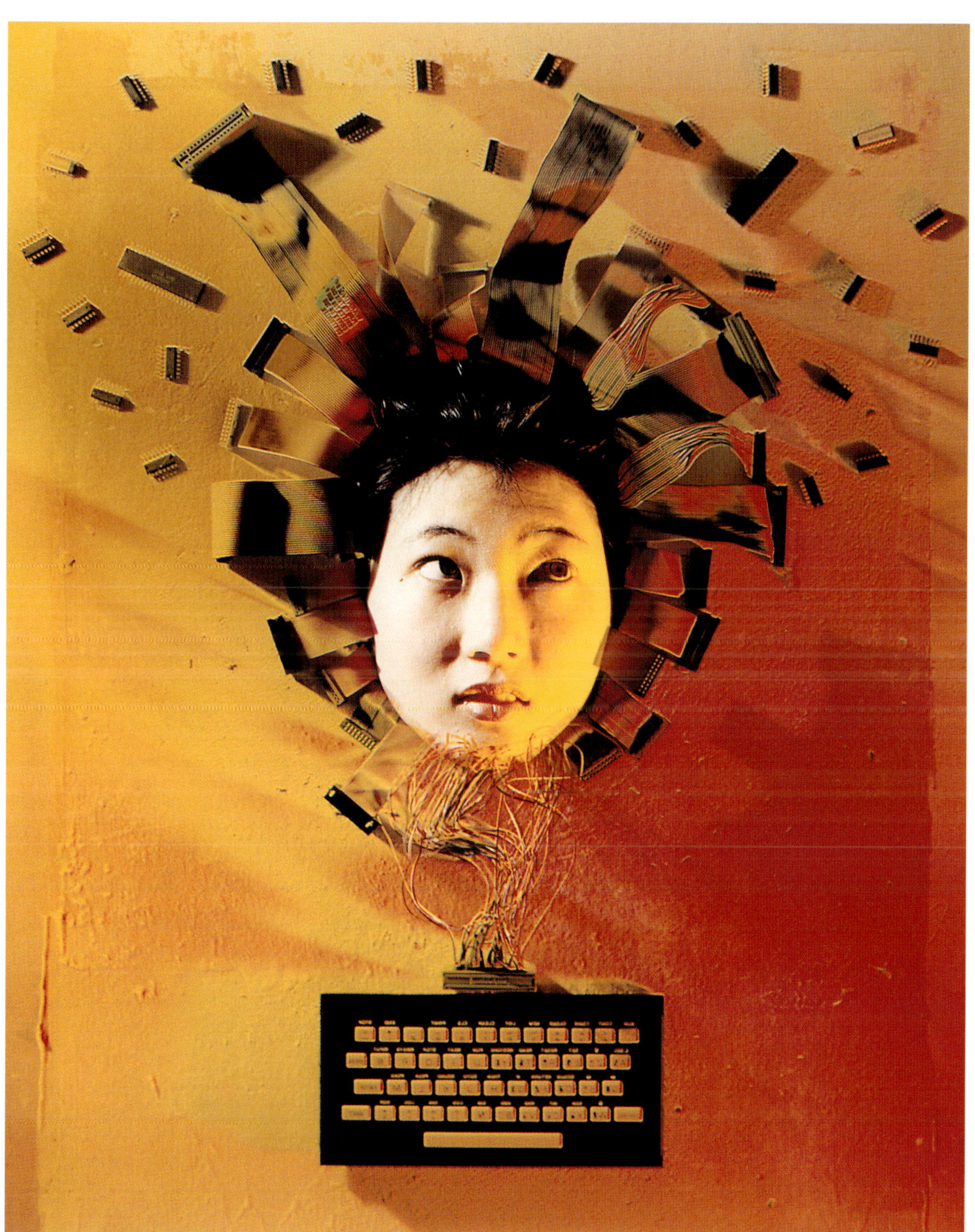

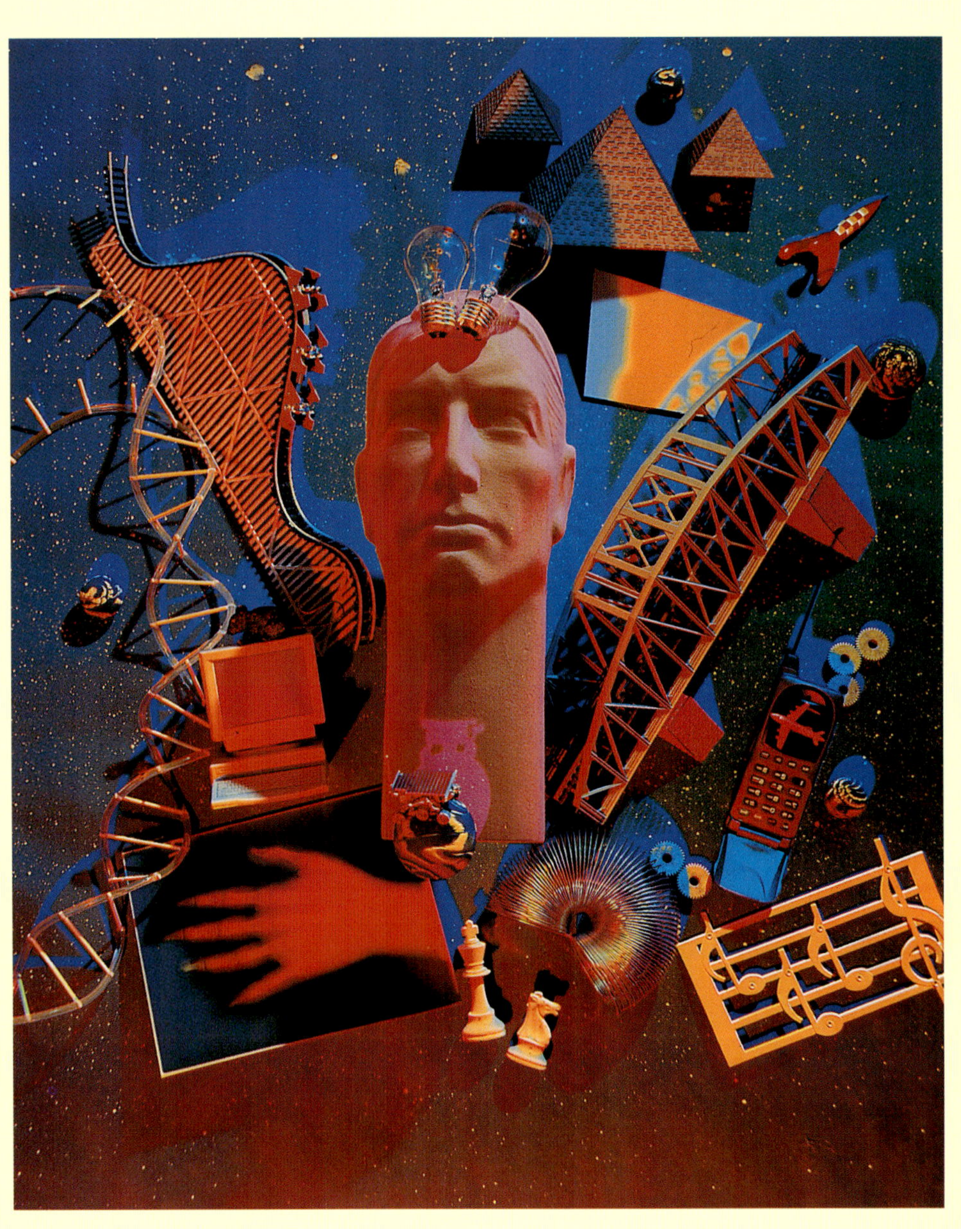

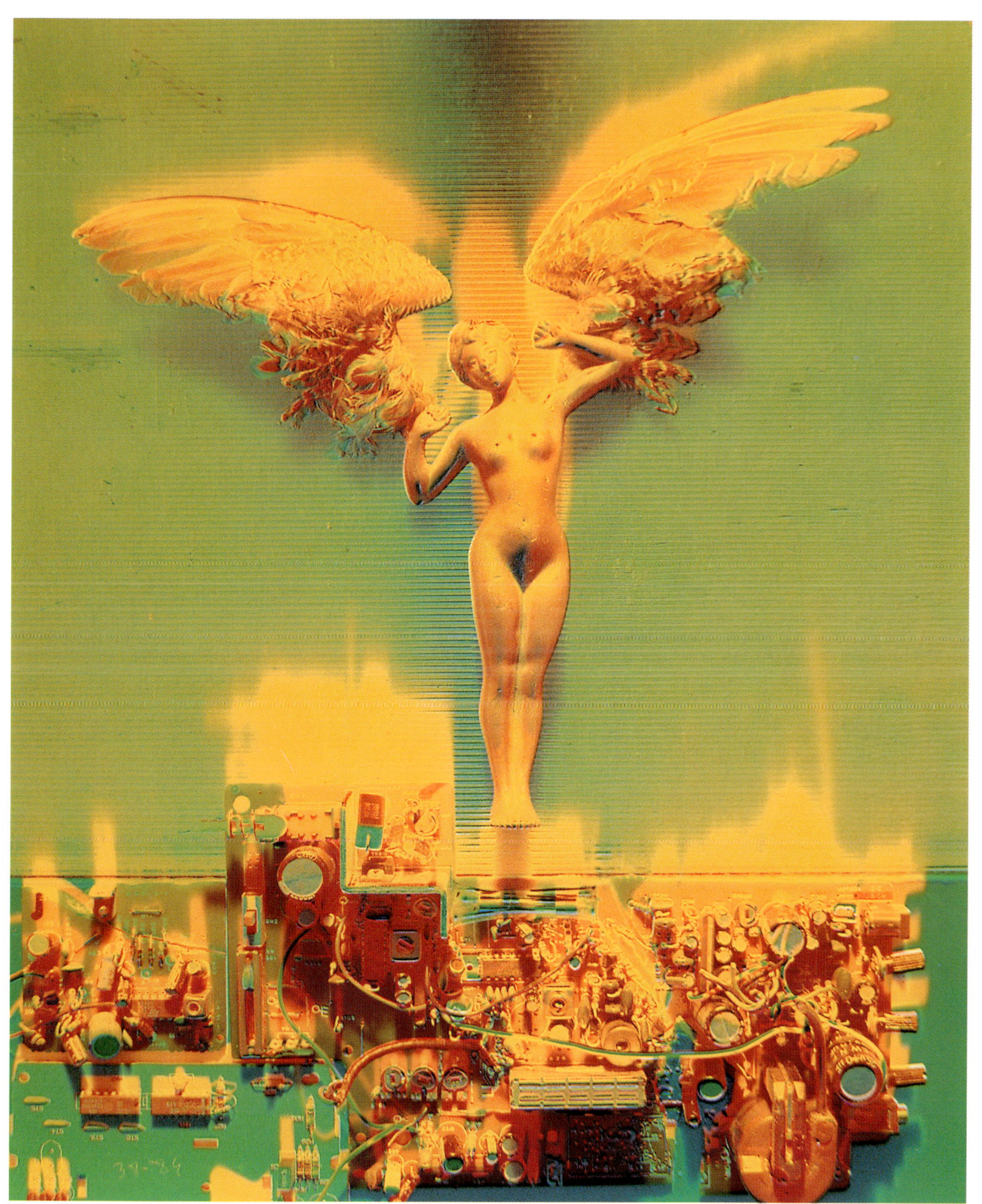

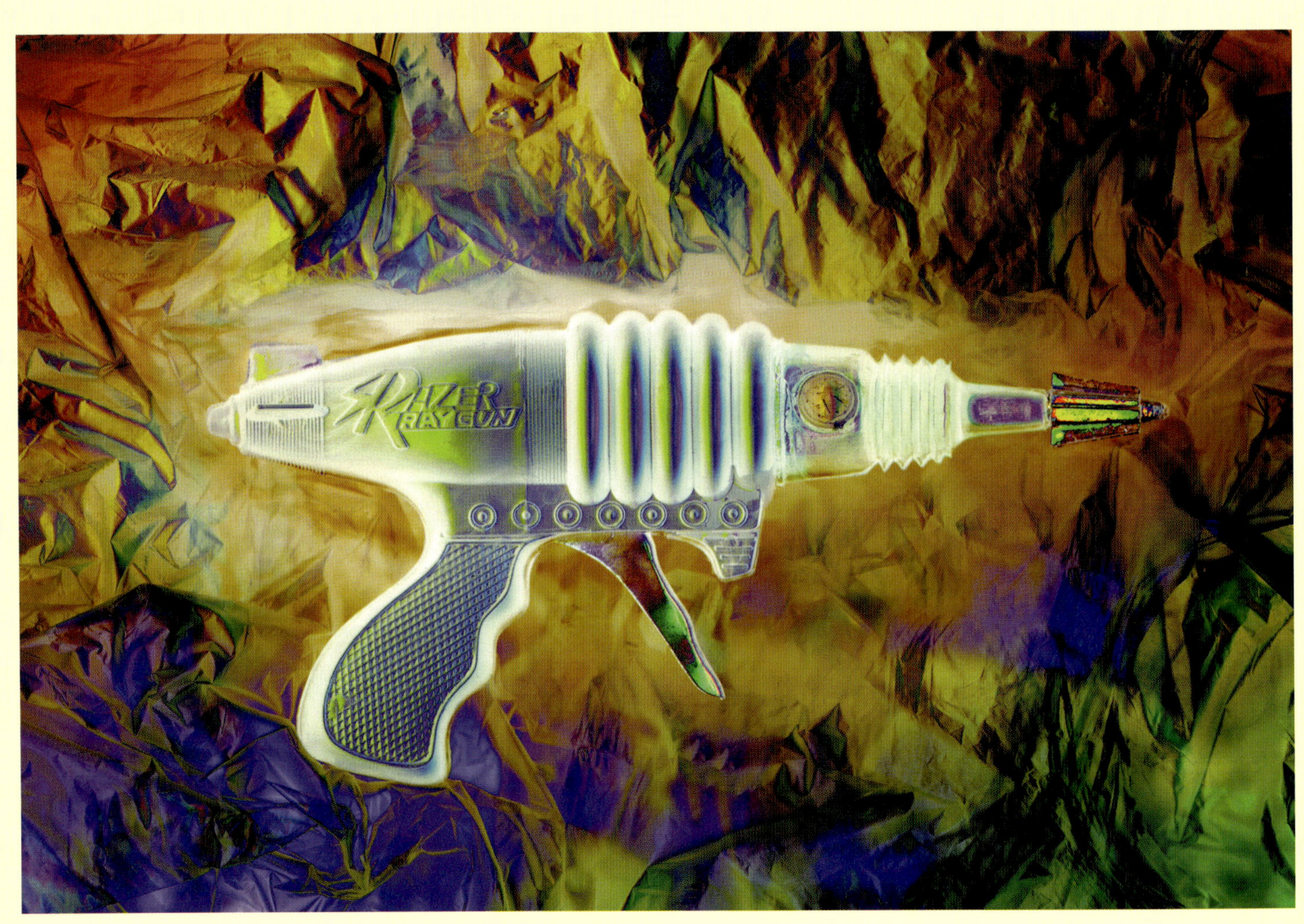

this and following spread: **B**ill **S**osin

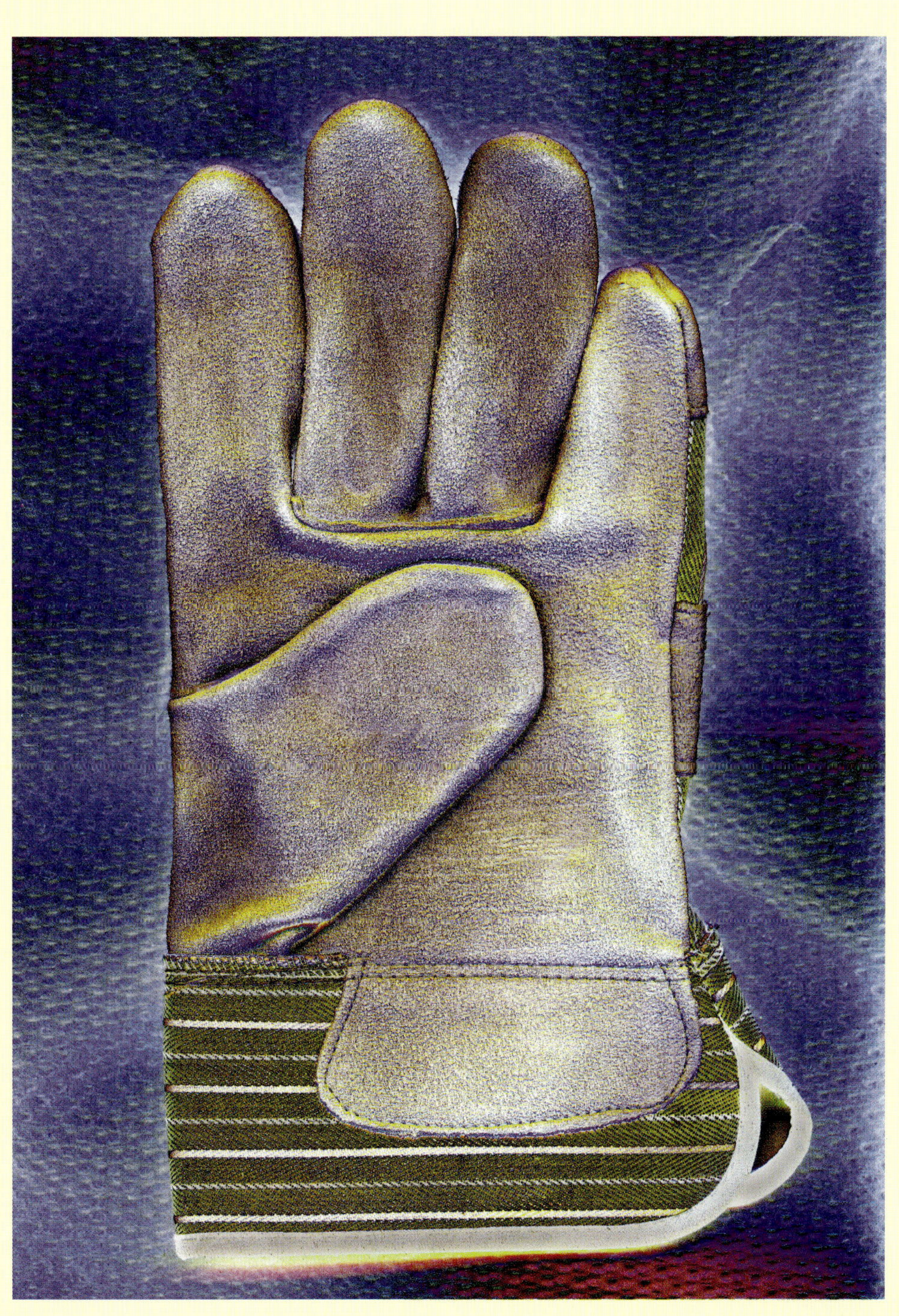

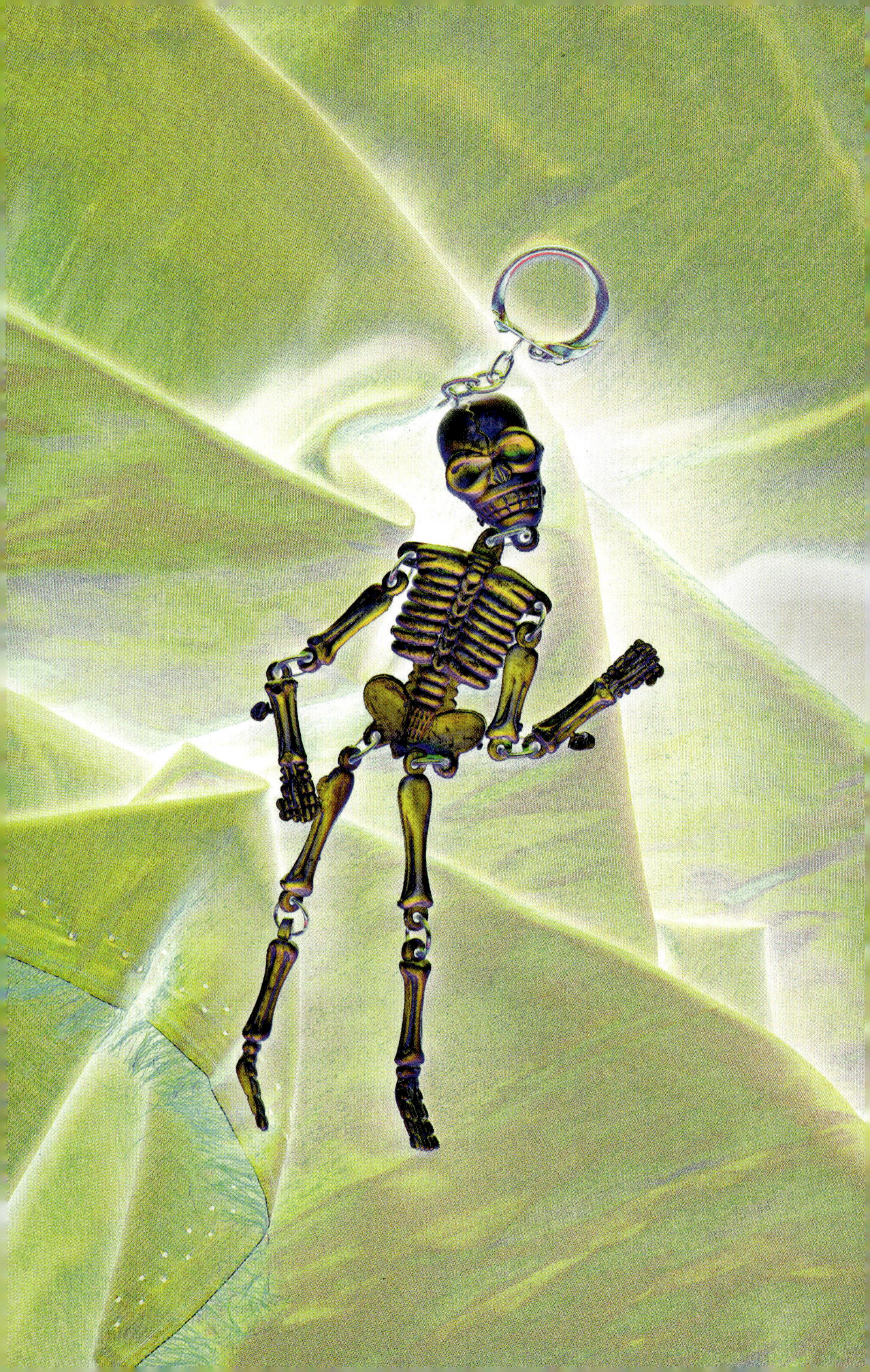

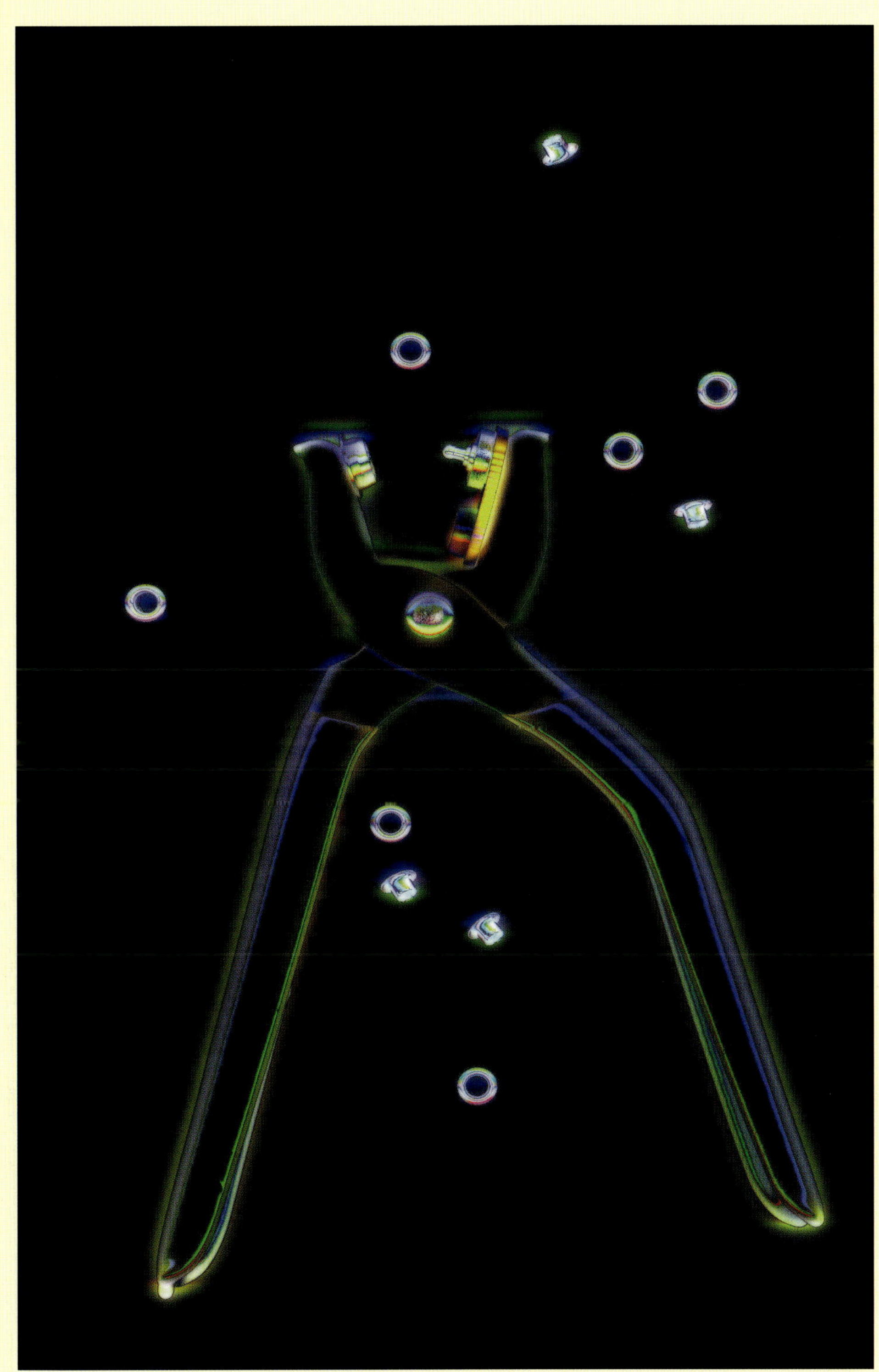

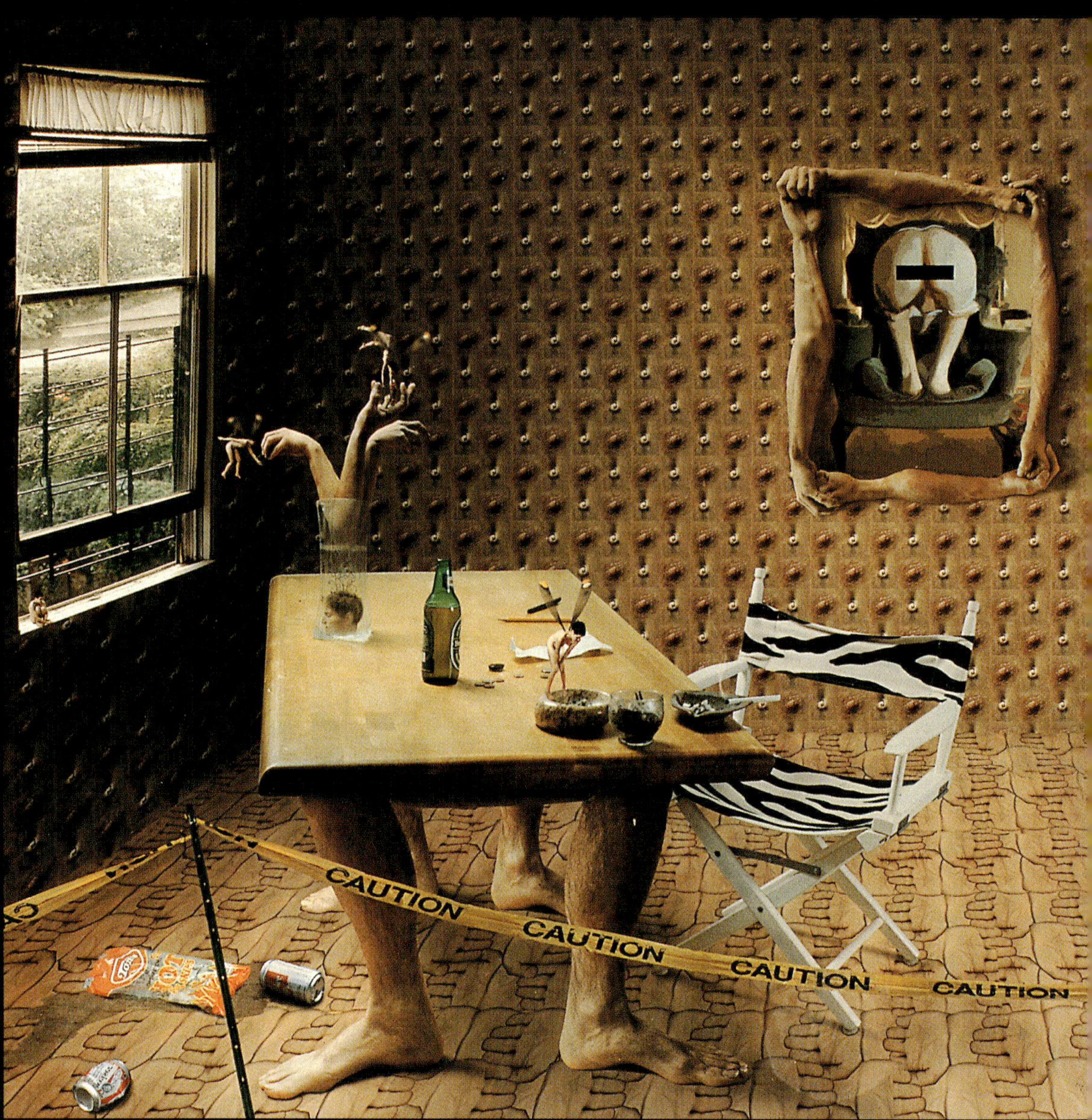

David **F**ischer

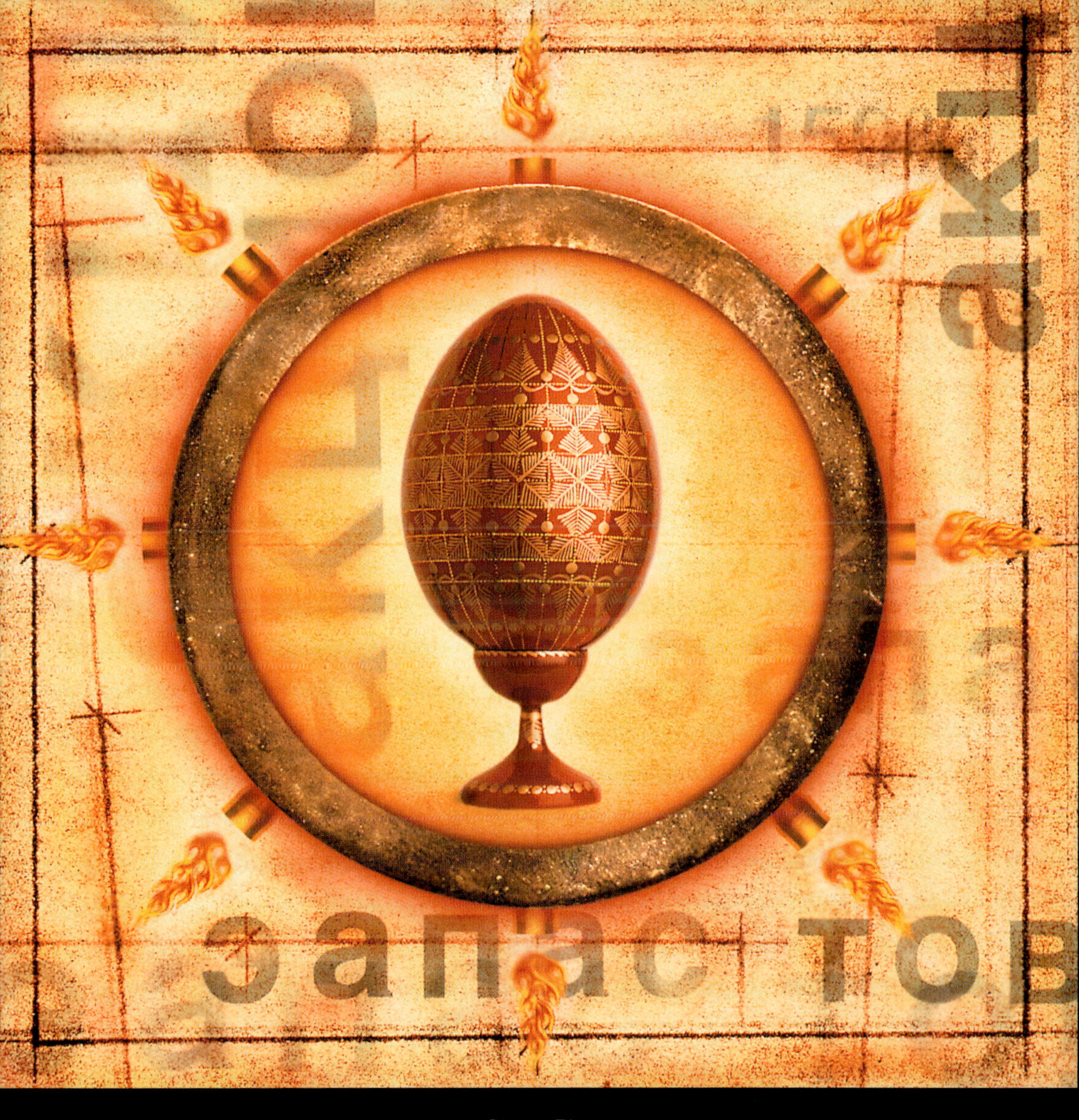

Steven **B**iver

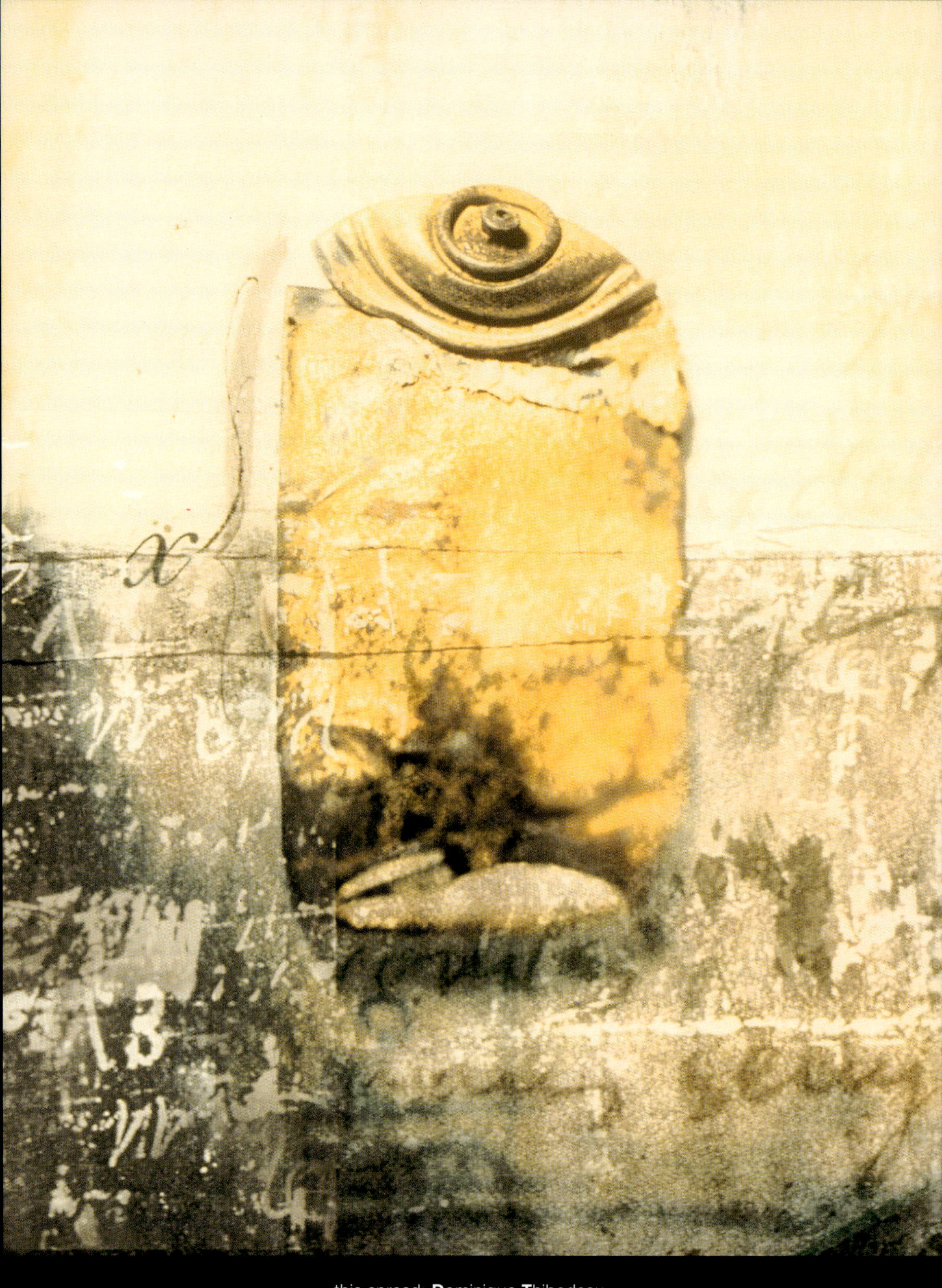

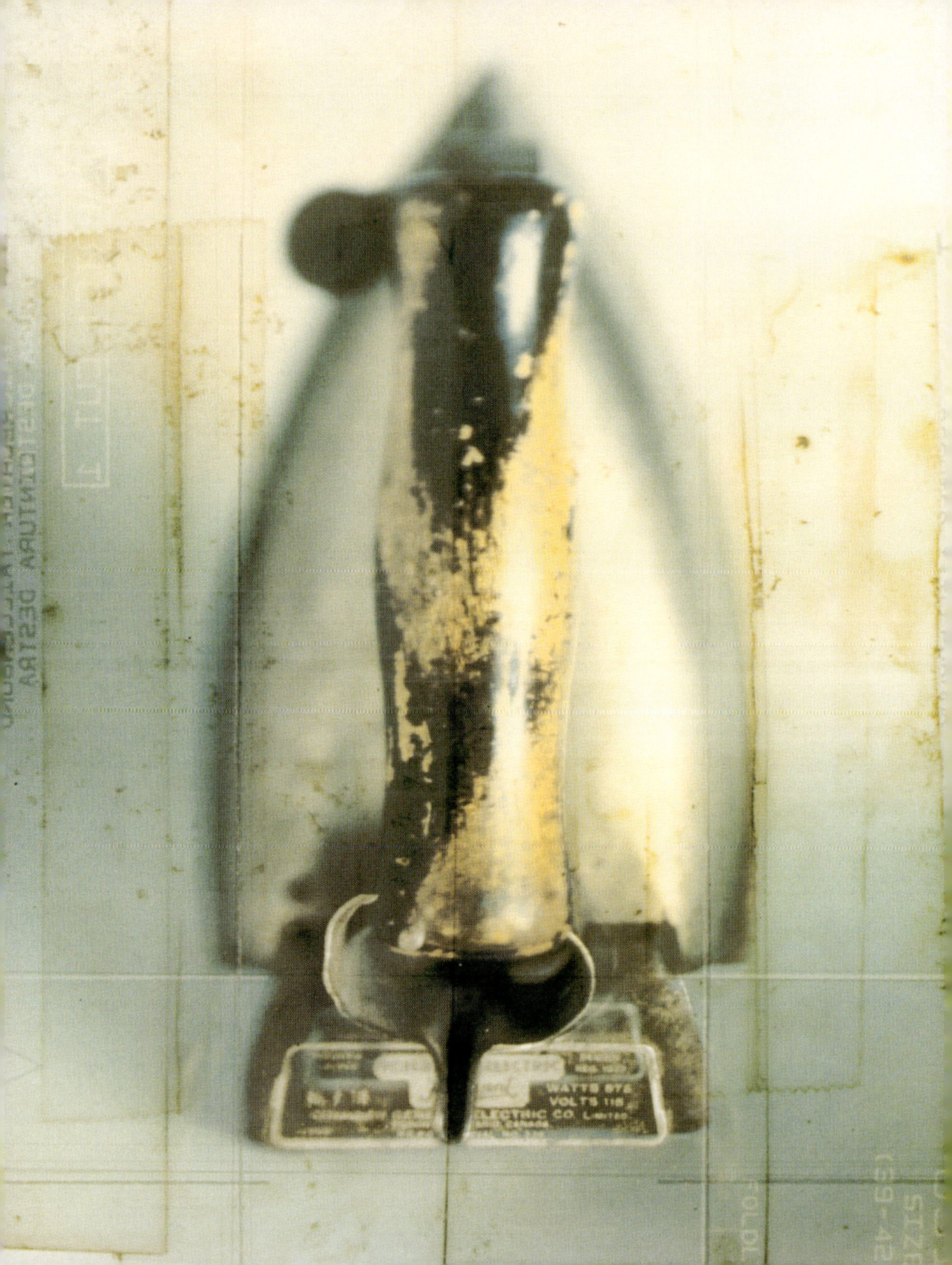

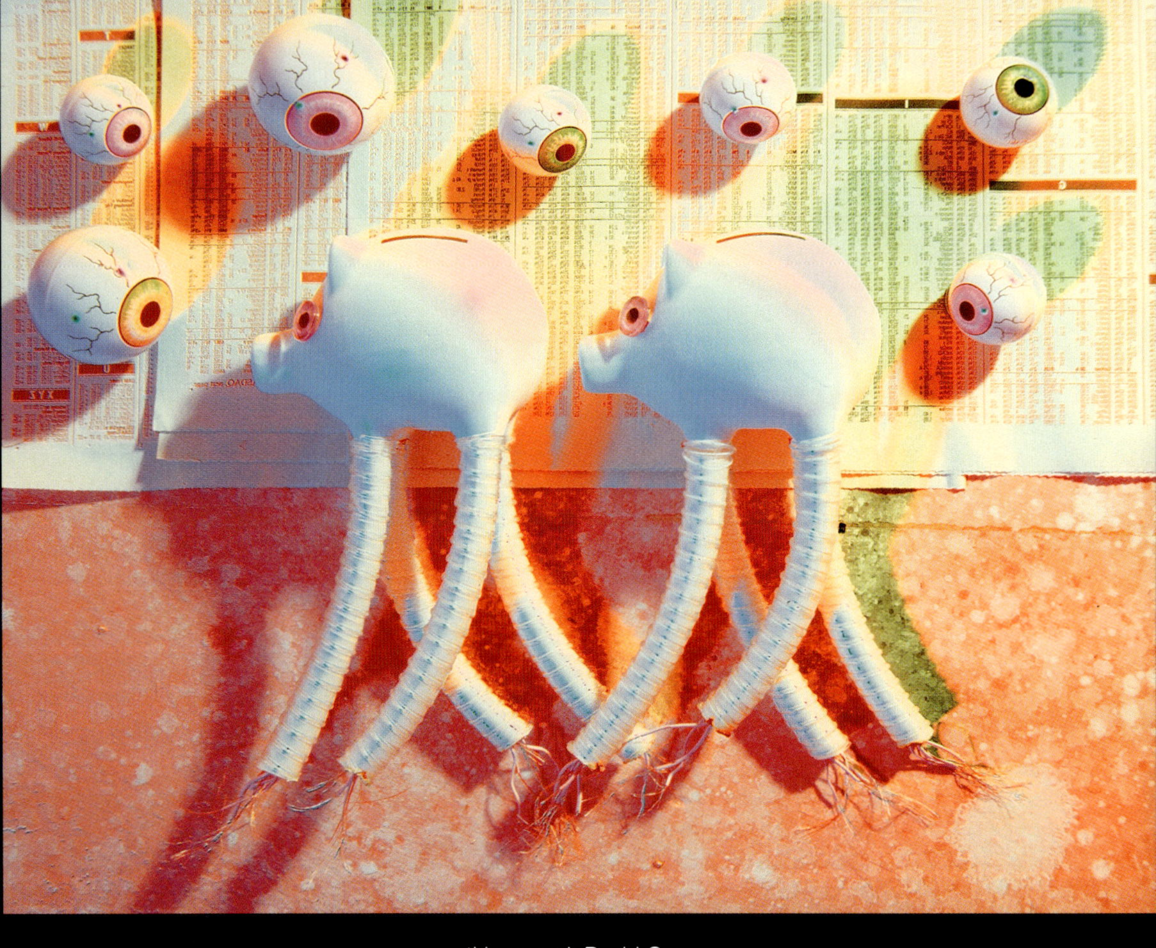

this spread: **D**avid **G**az

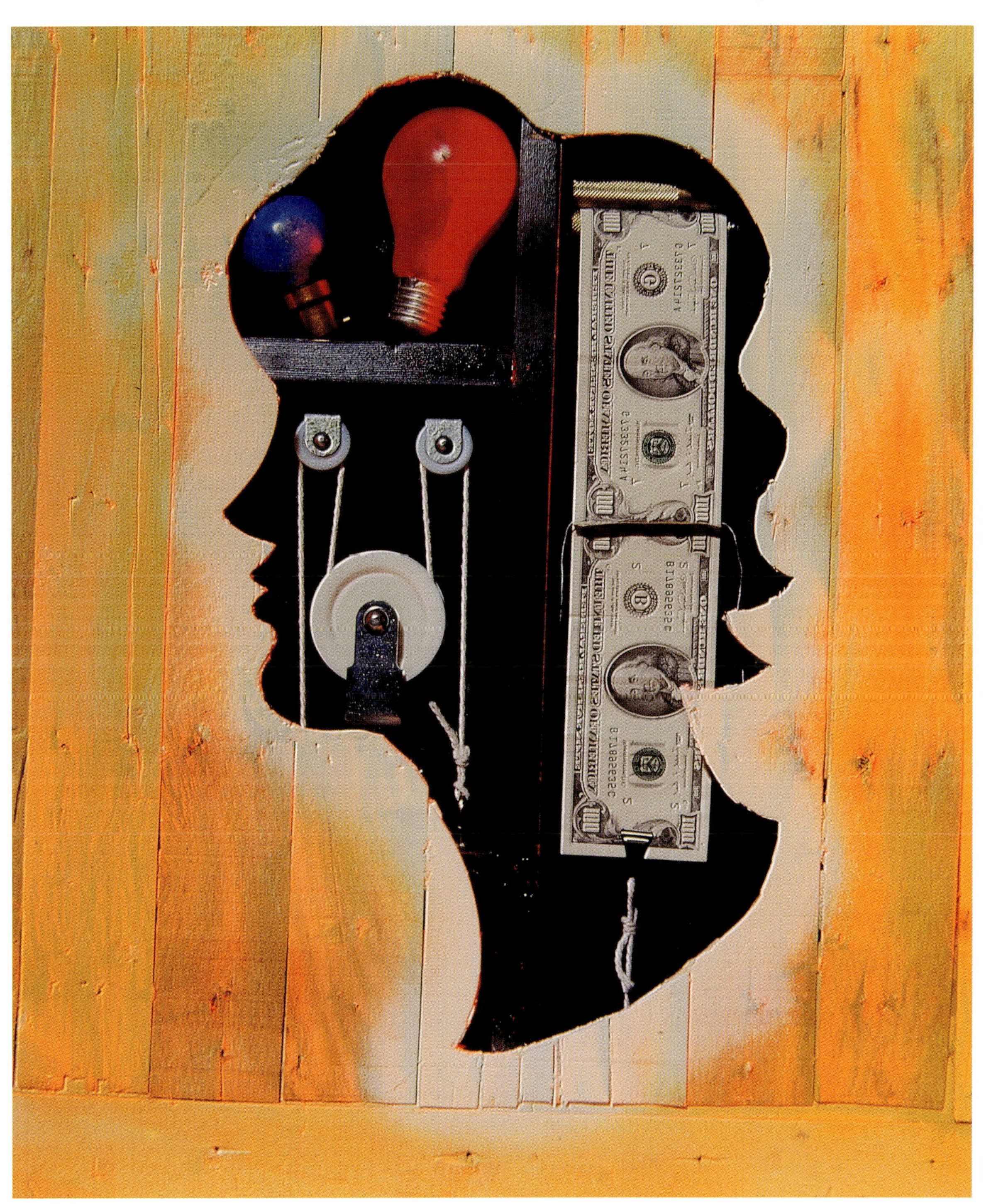

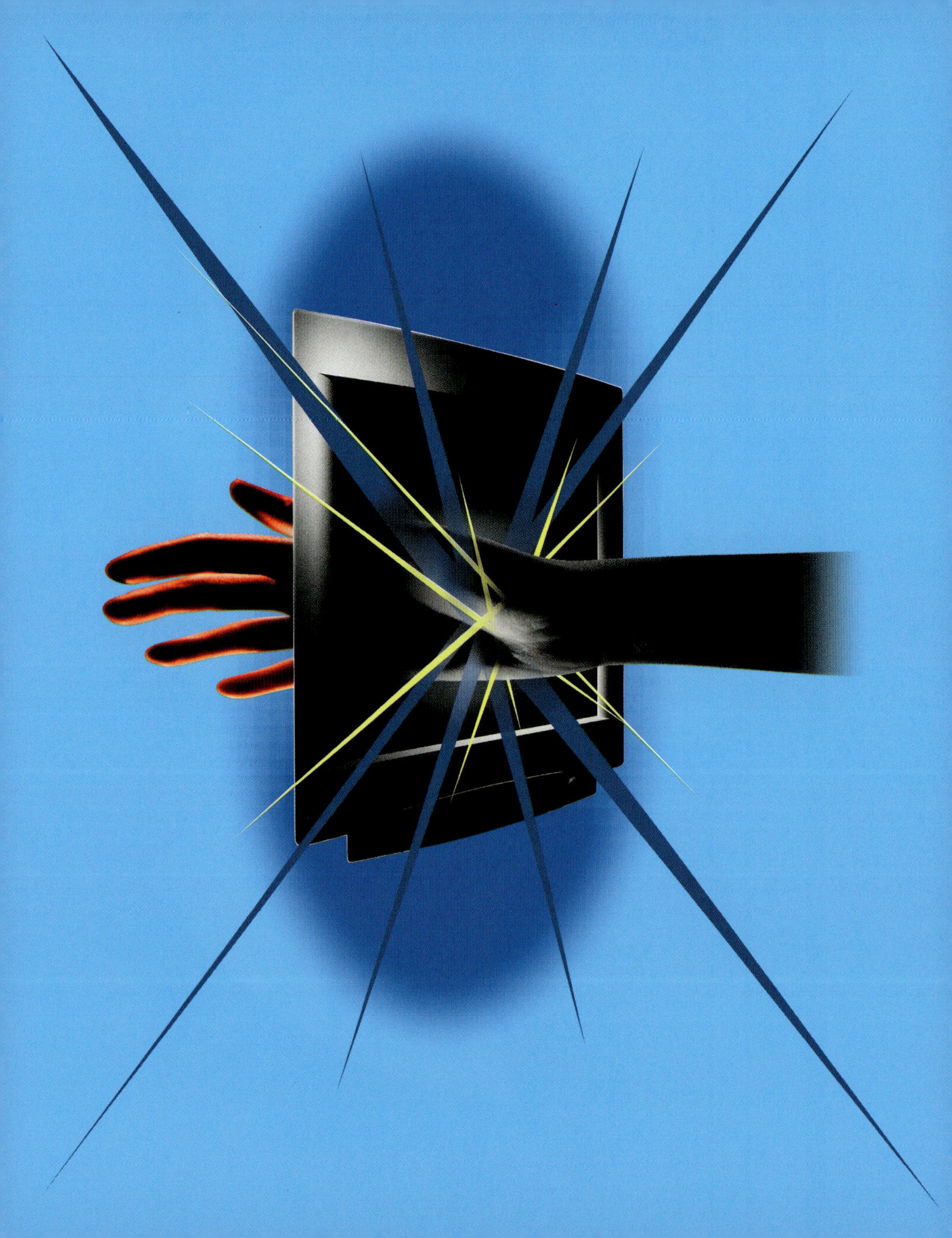

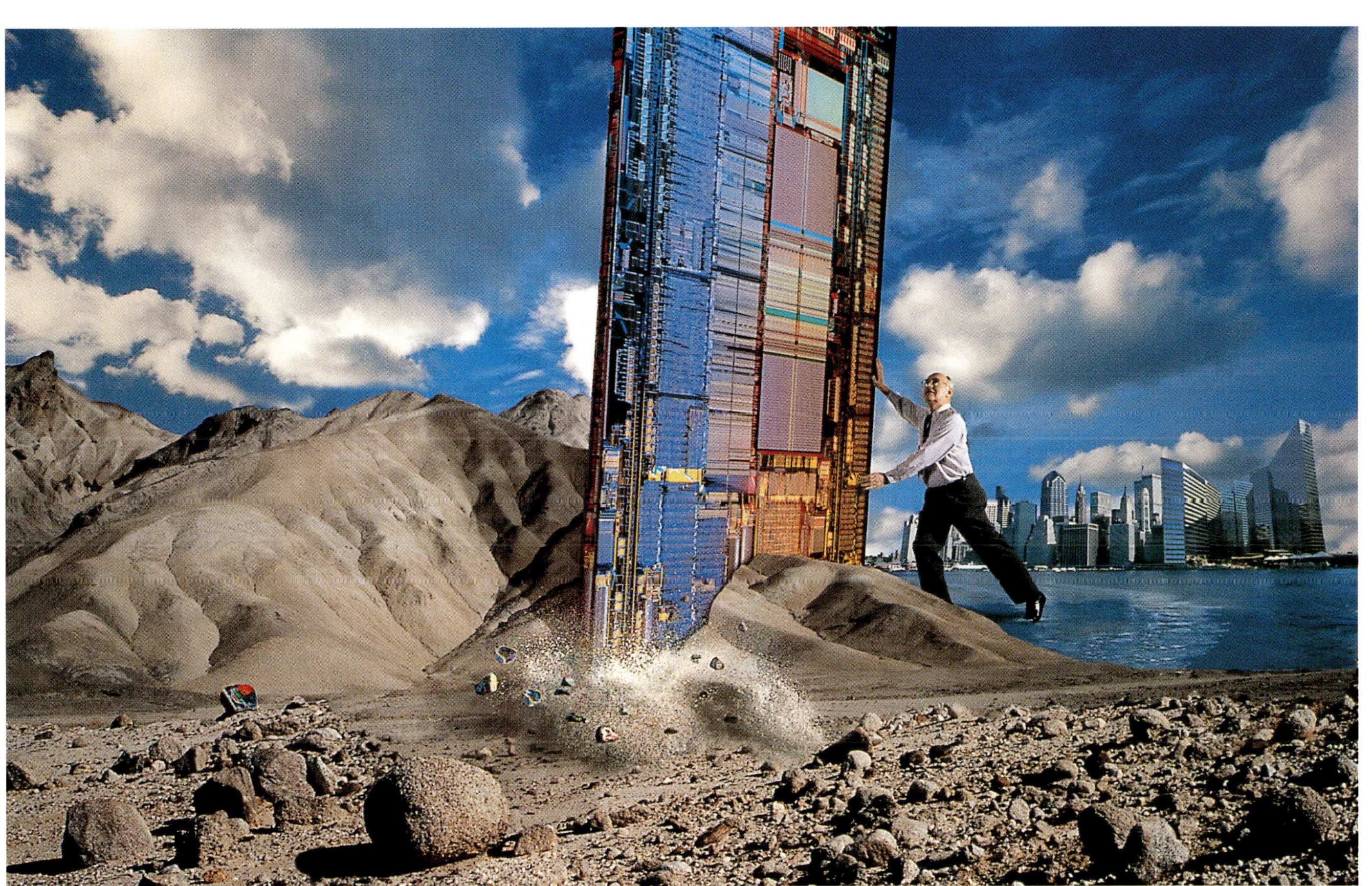

Ryszard **H**orowitz

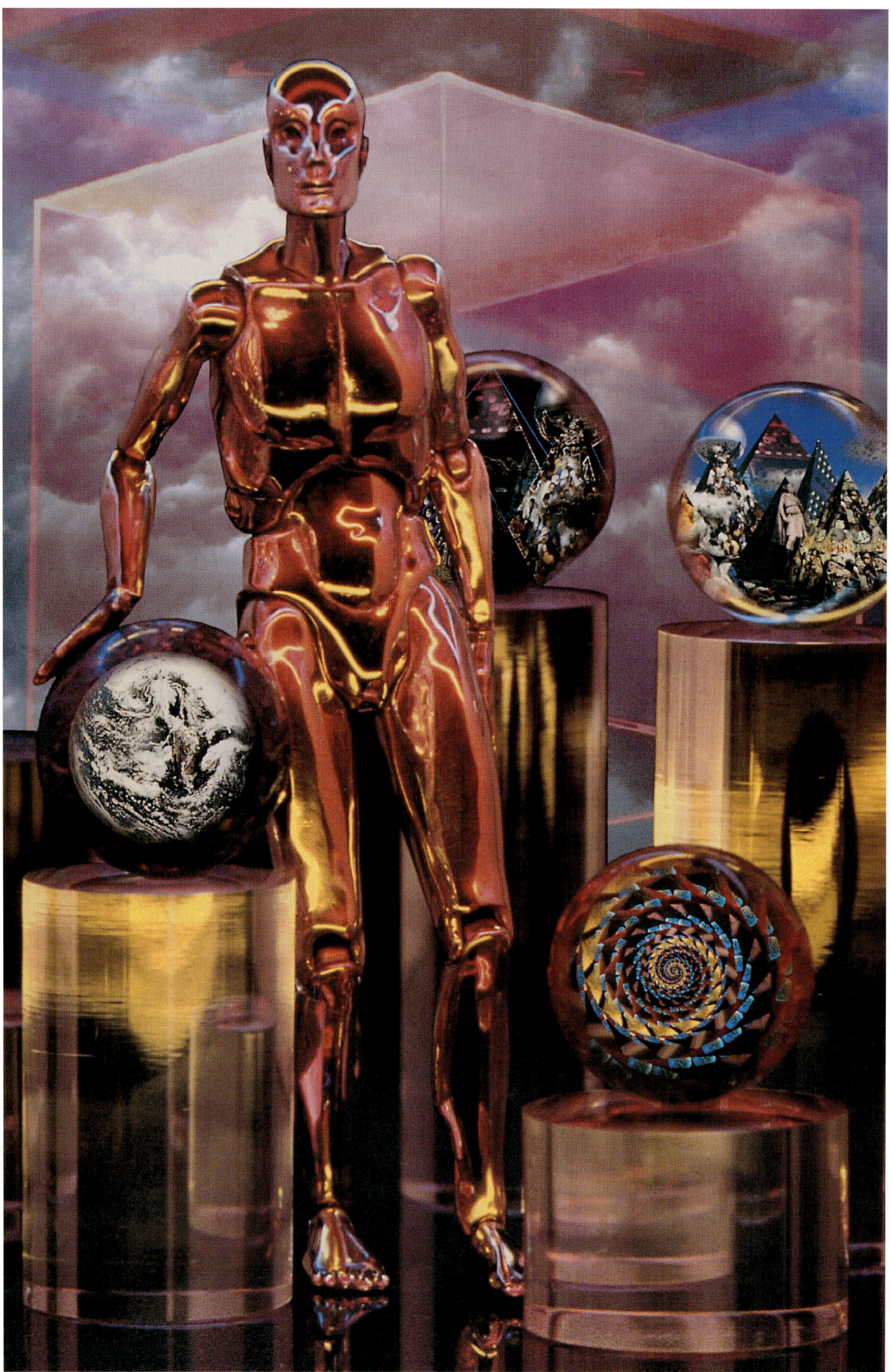

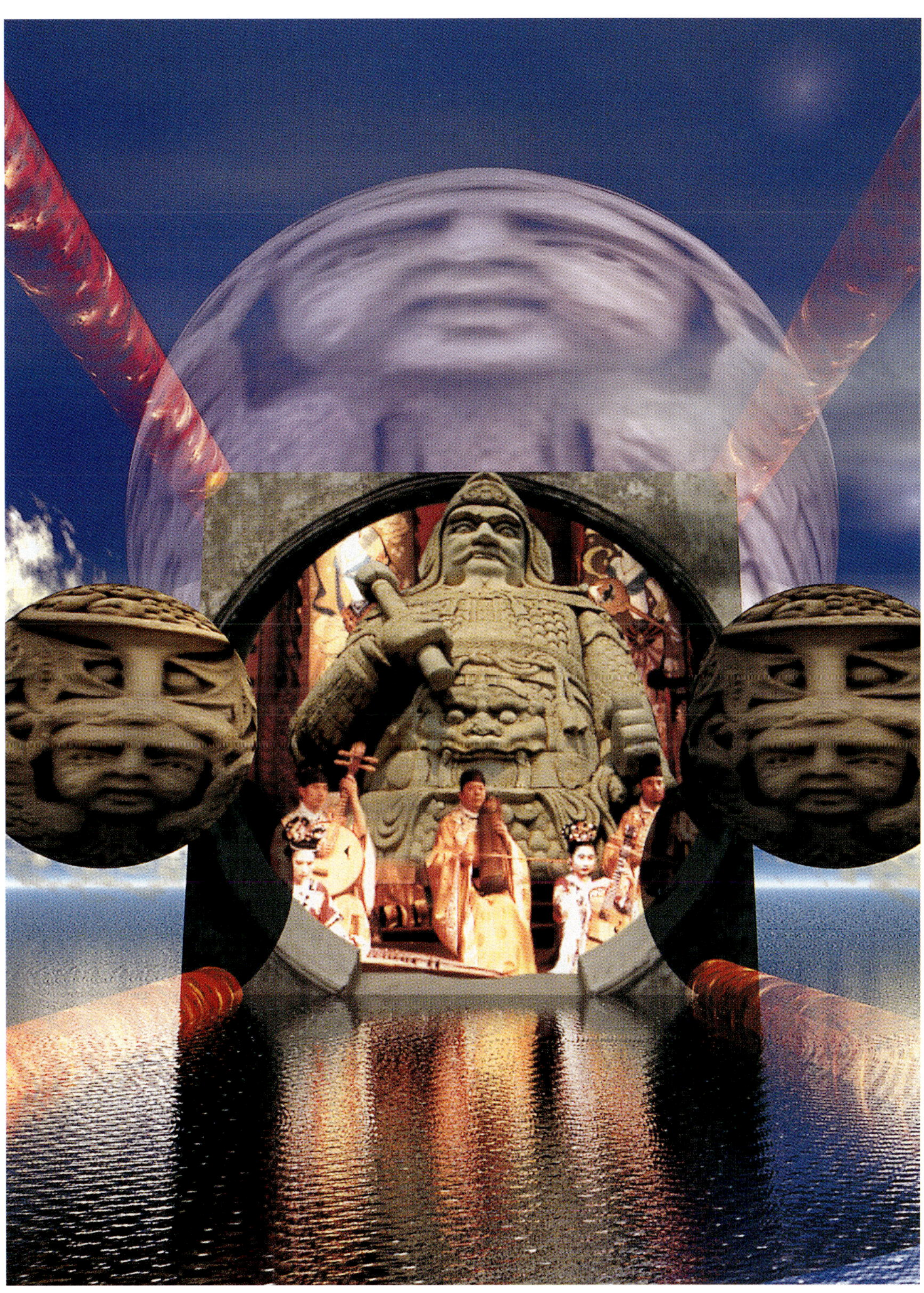

this spread: **L**arry **H**amlll

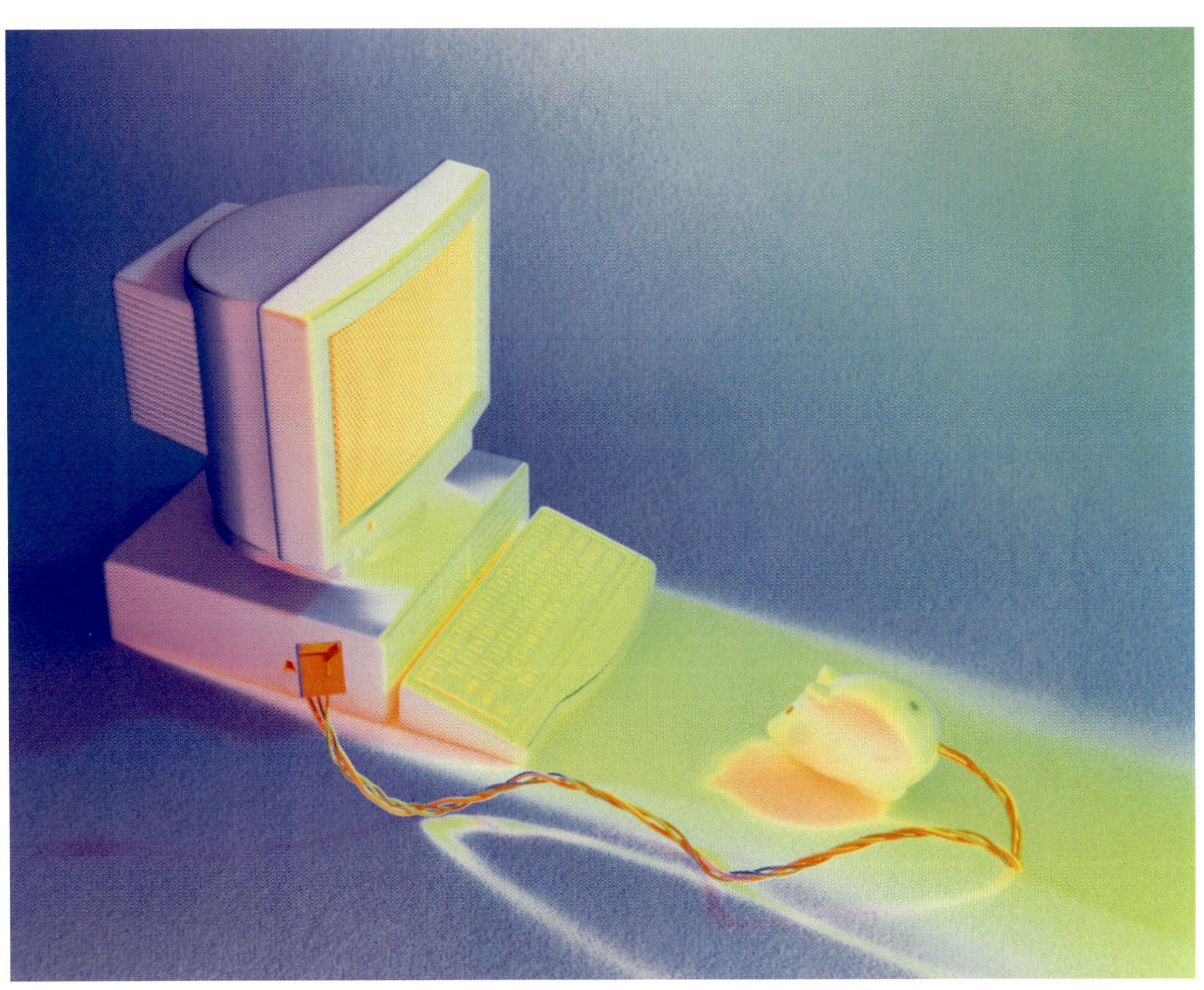

this spread: **D**avid **G**az

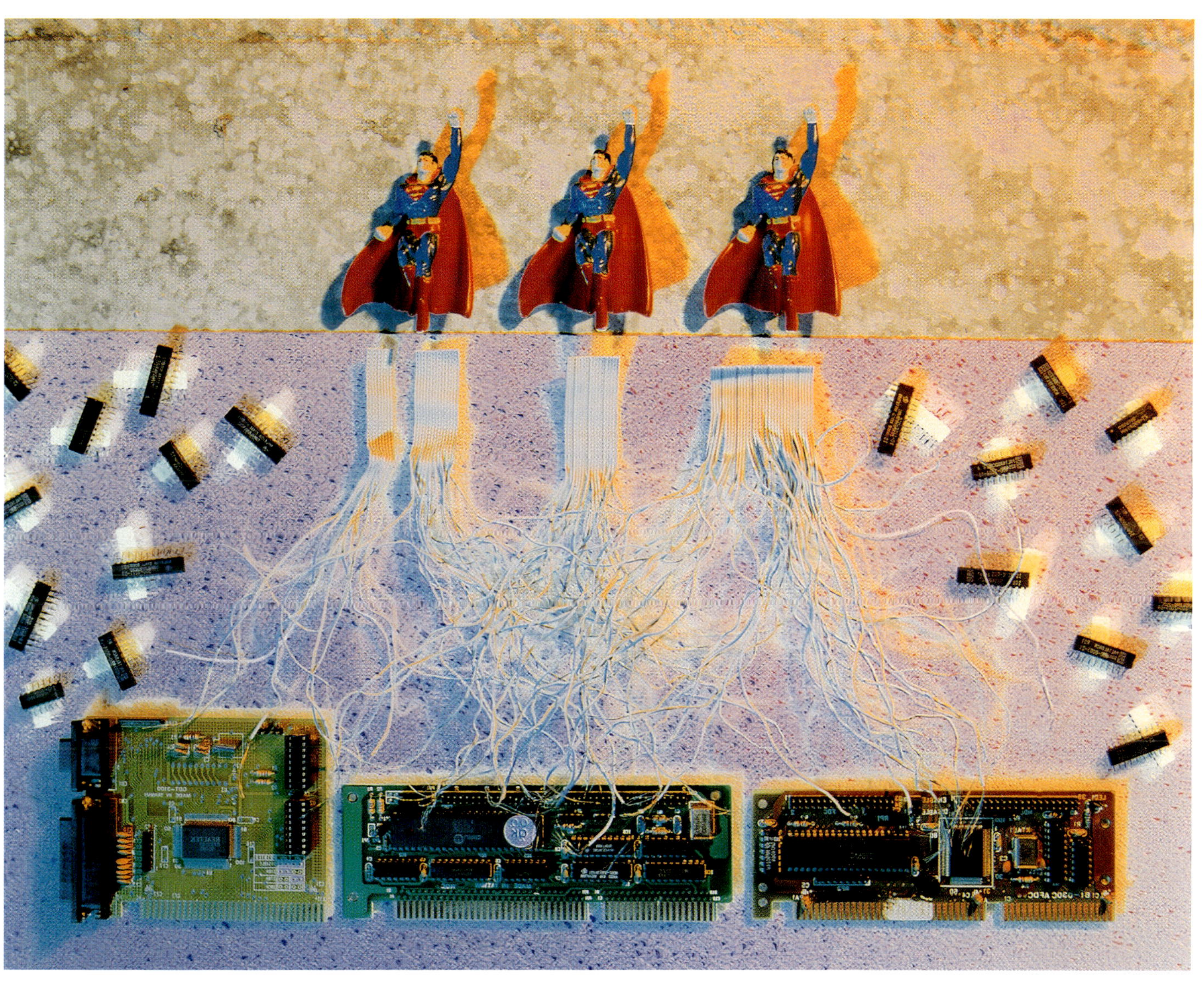

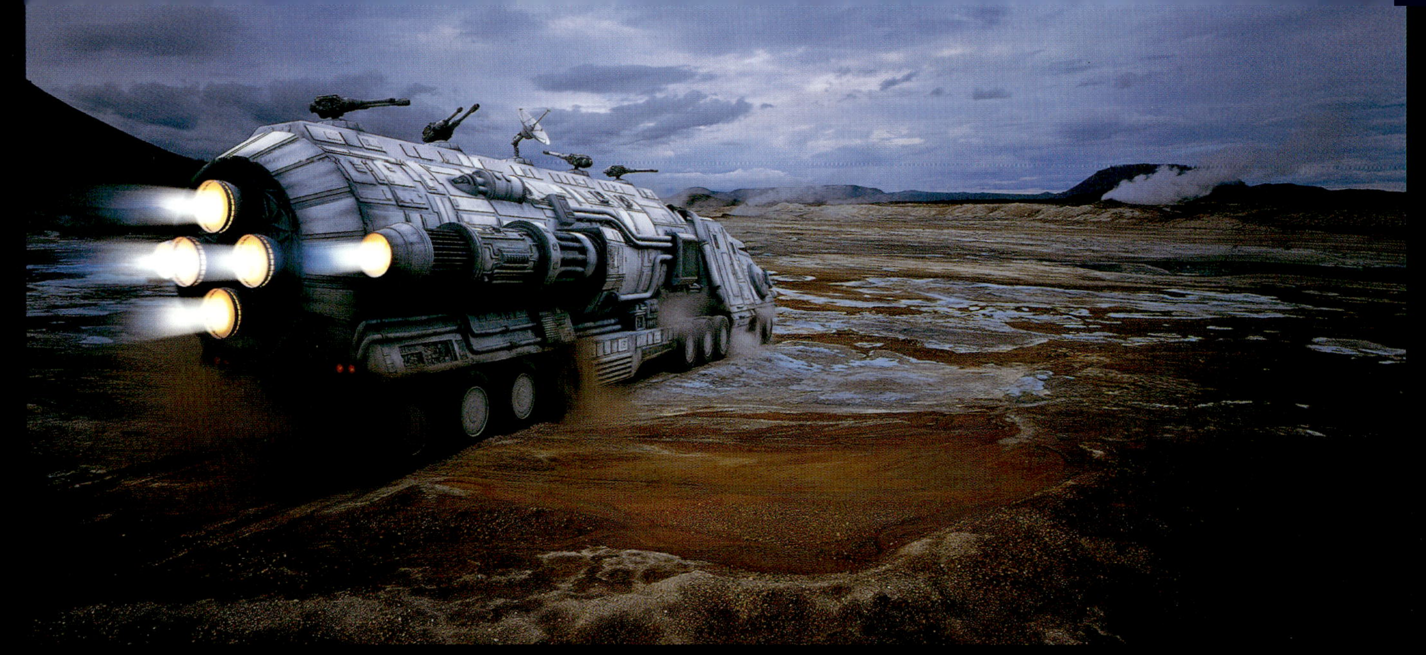

this and following spread: **G**raham **W**estmoreland

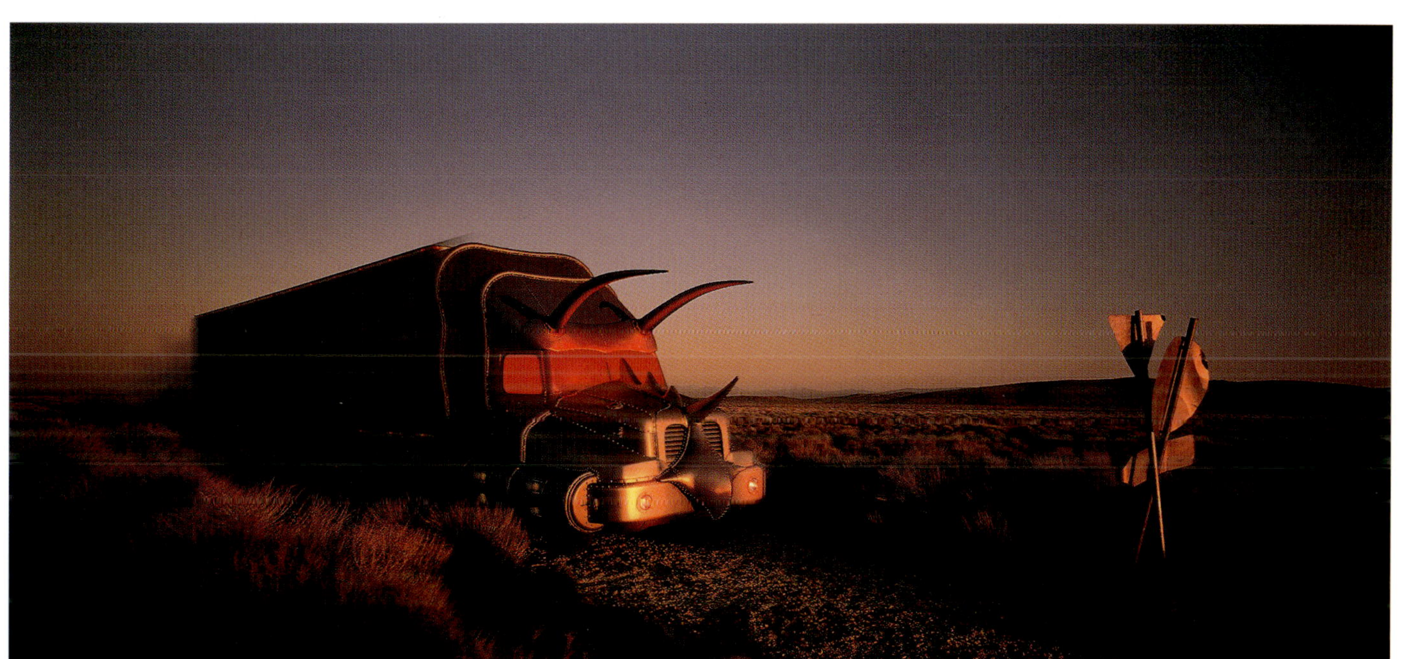

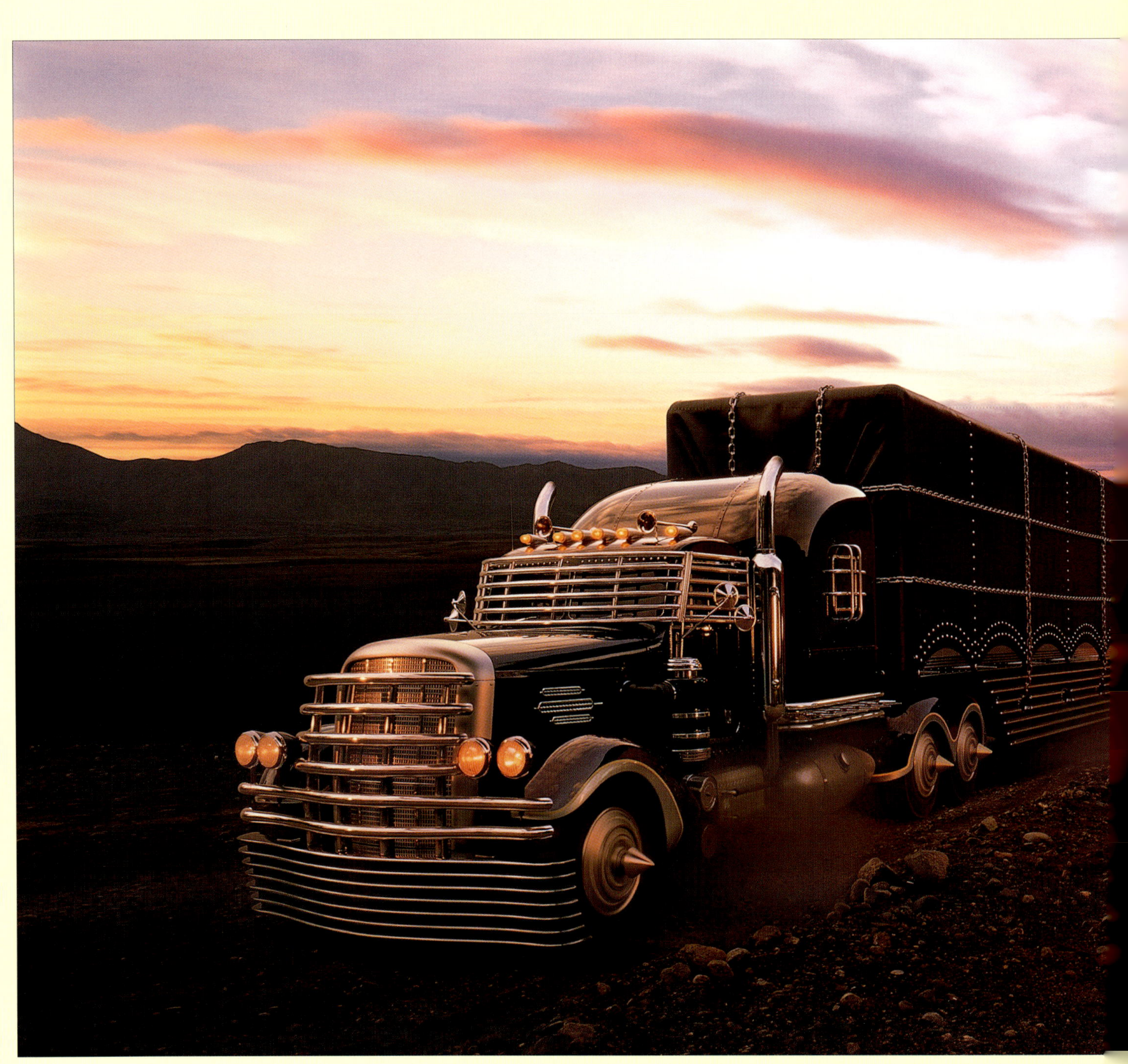

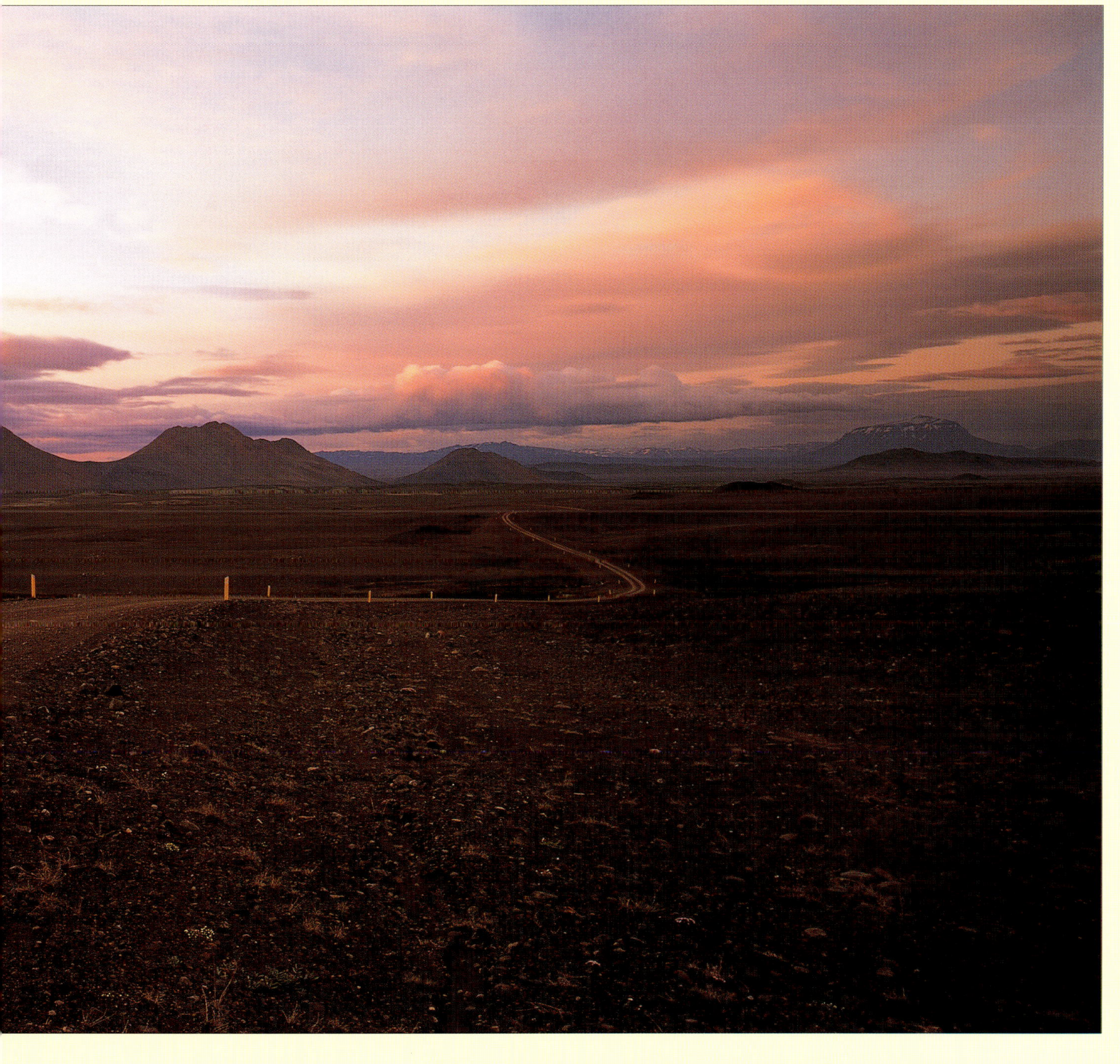

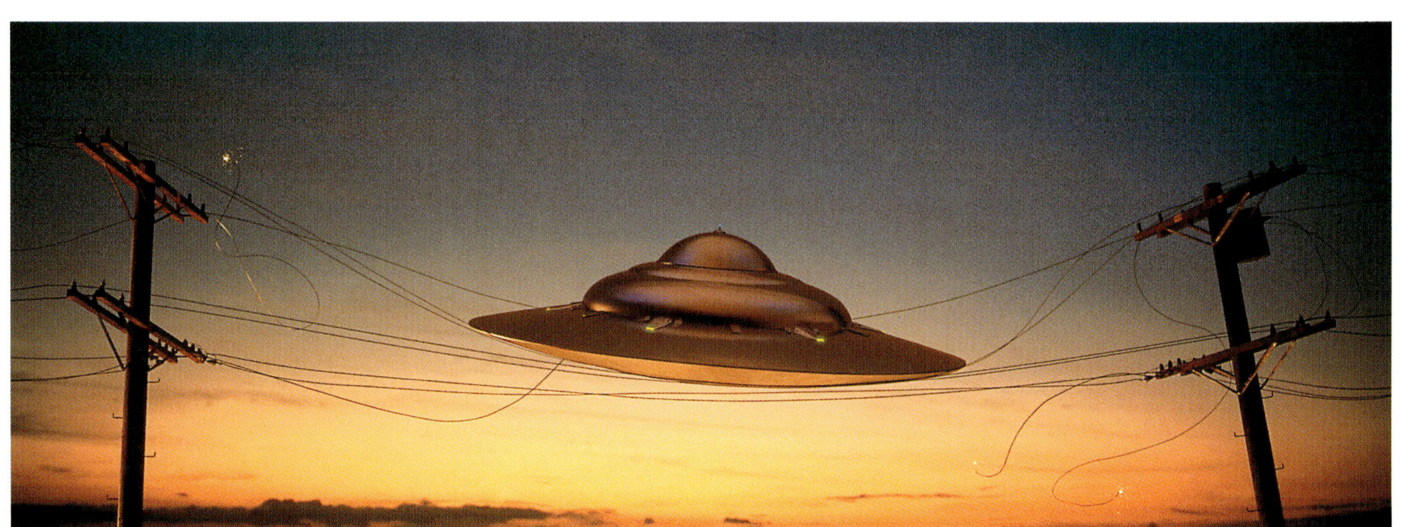

this spread: **G**len **W**exler

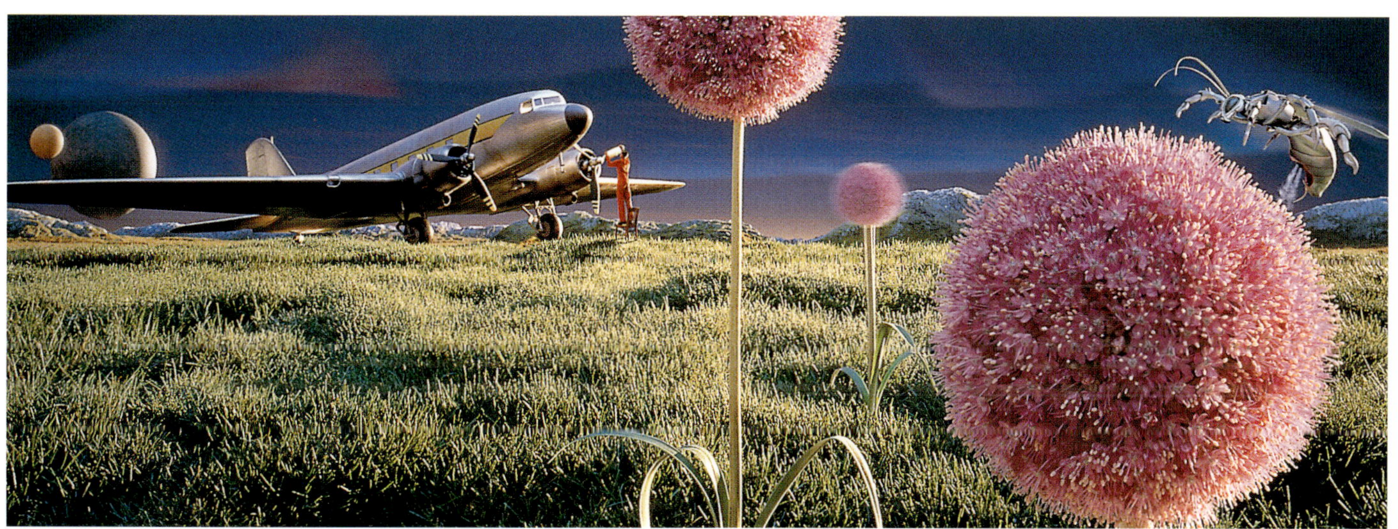

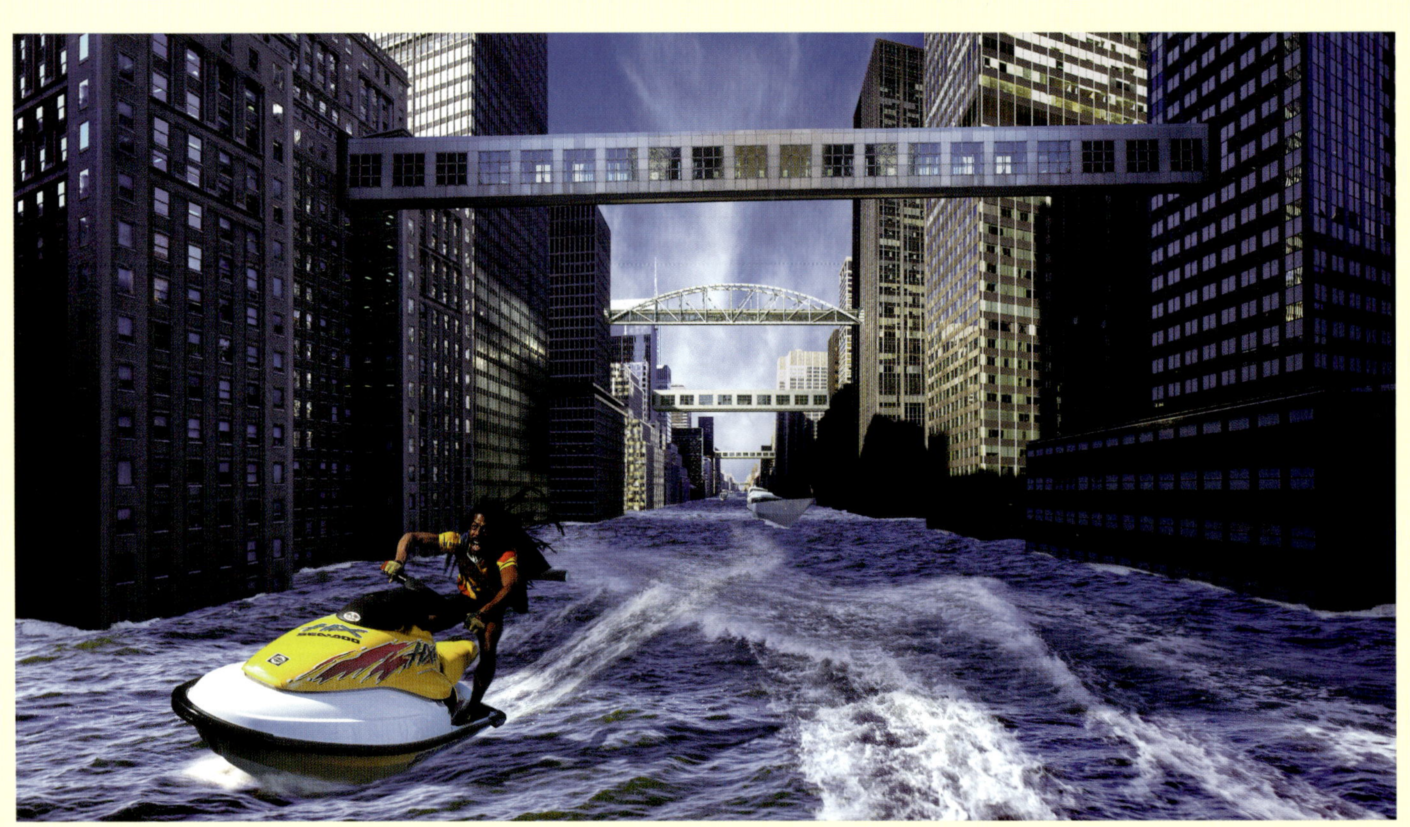

James Porto

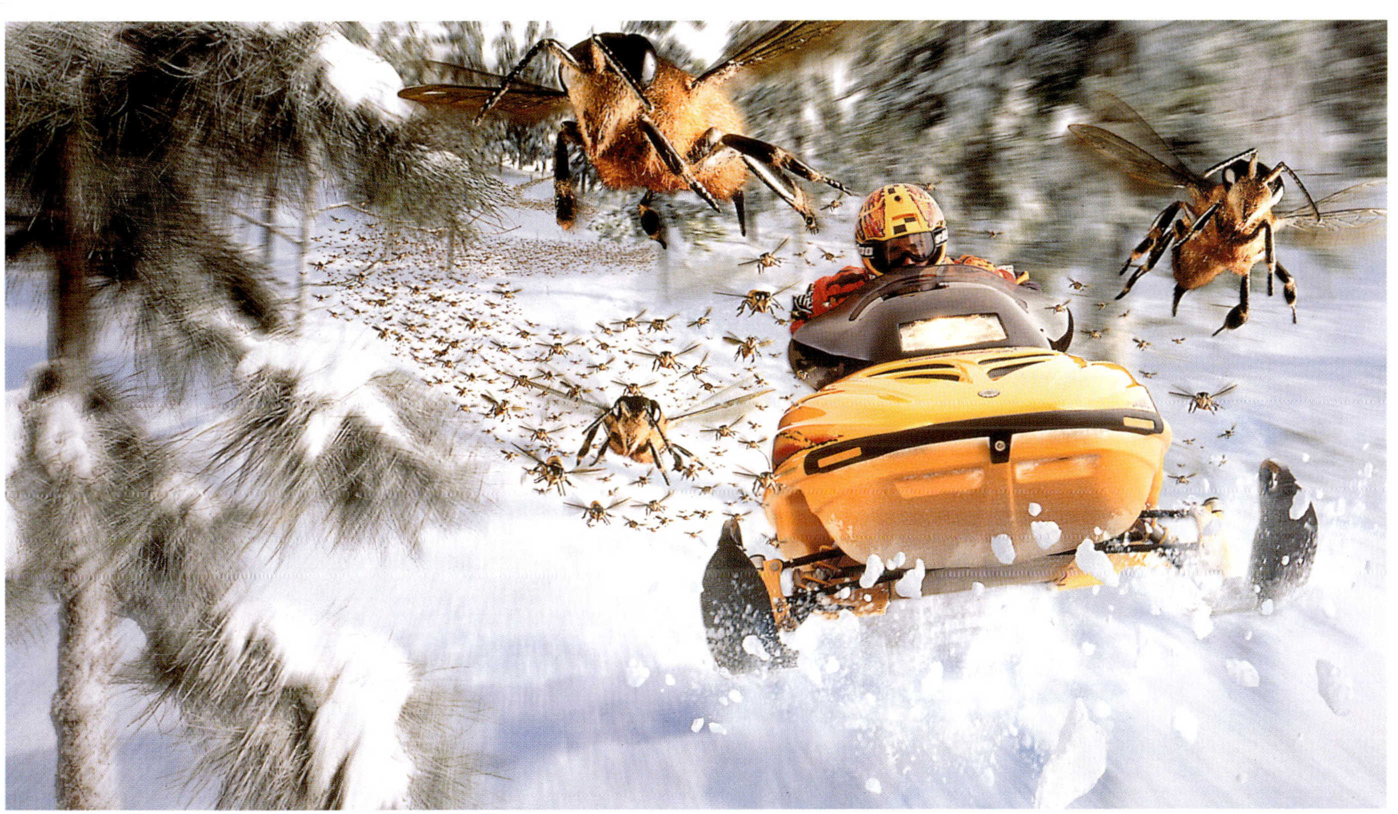

this page, following spread: **G**len **W**exler

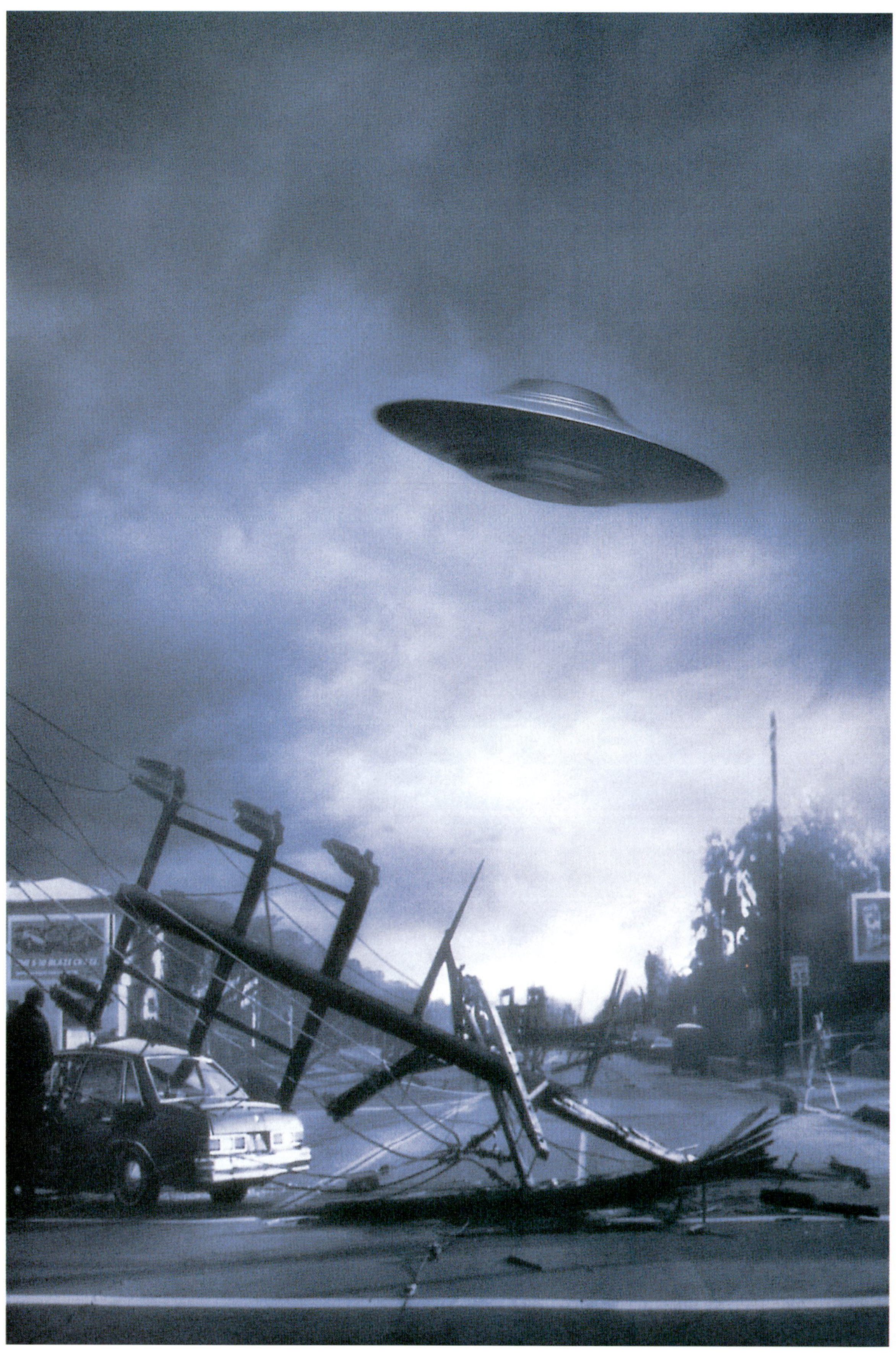

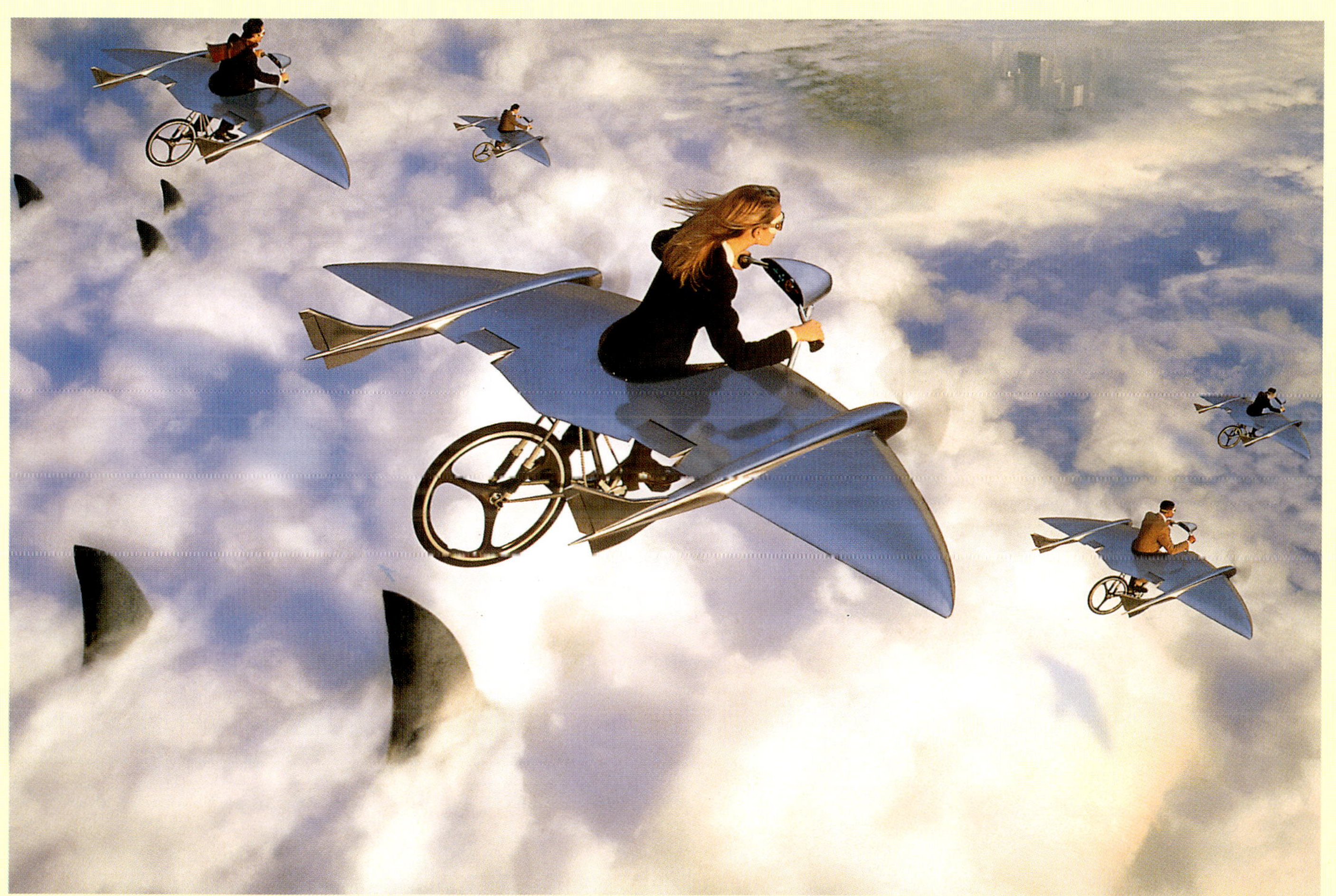

following spread: **D**irk **K**arsten

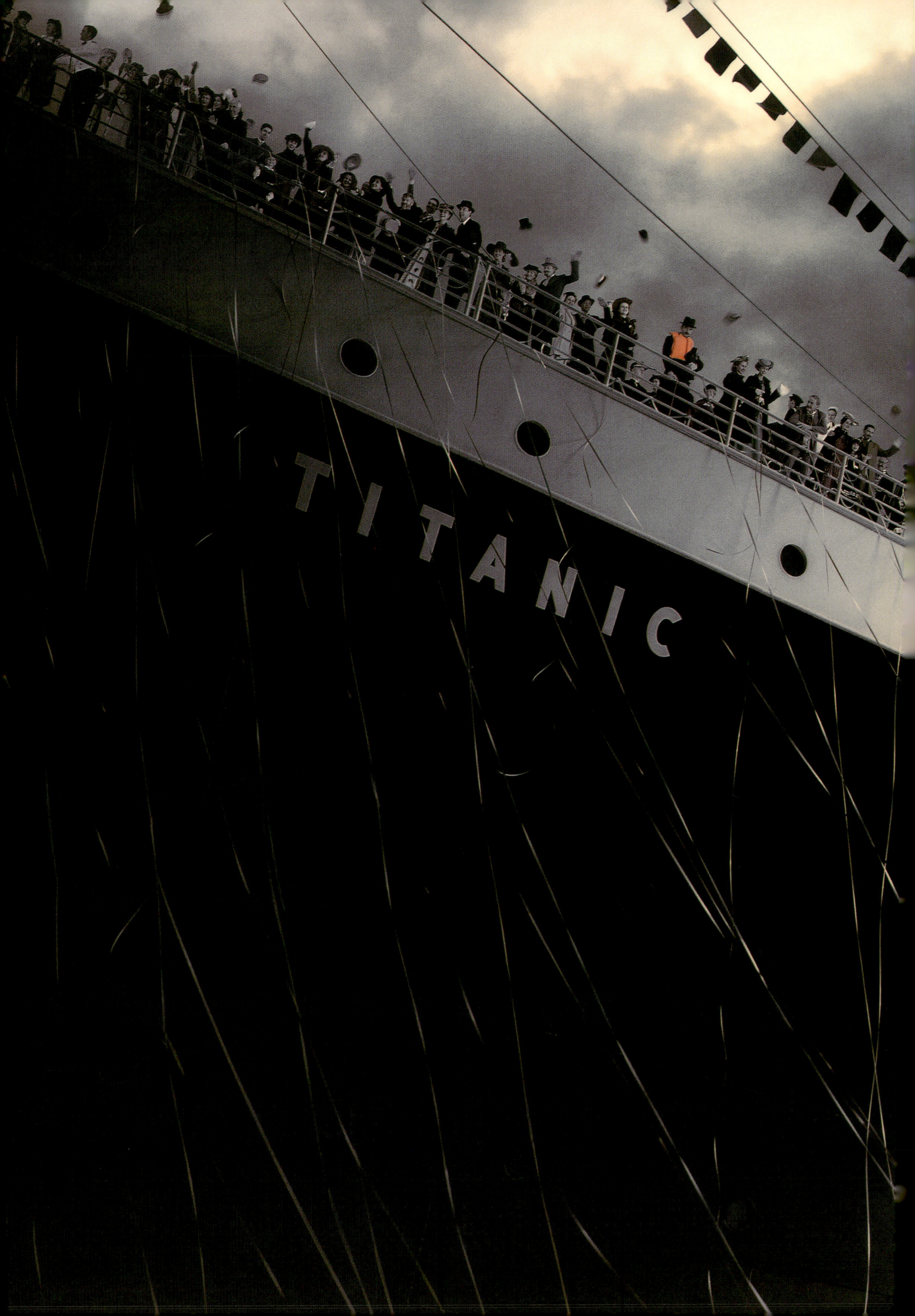
TITANIC

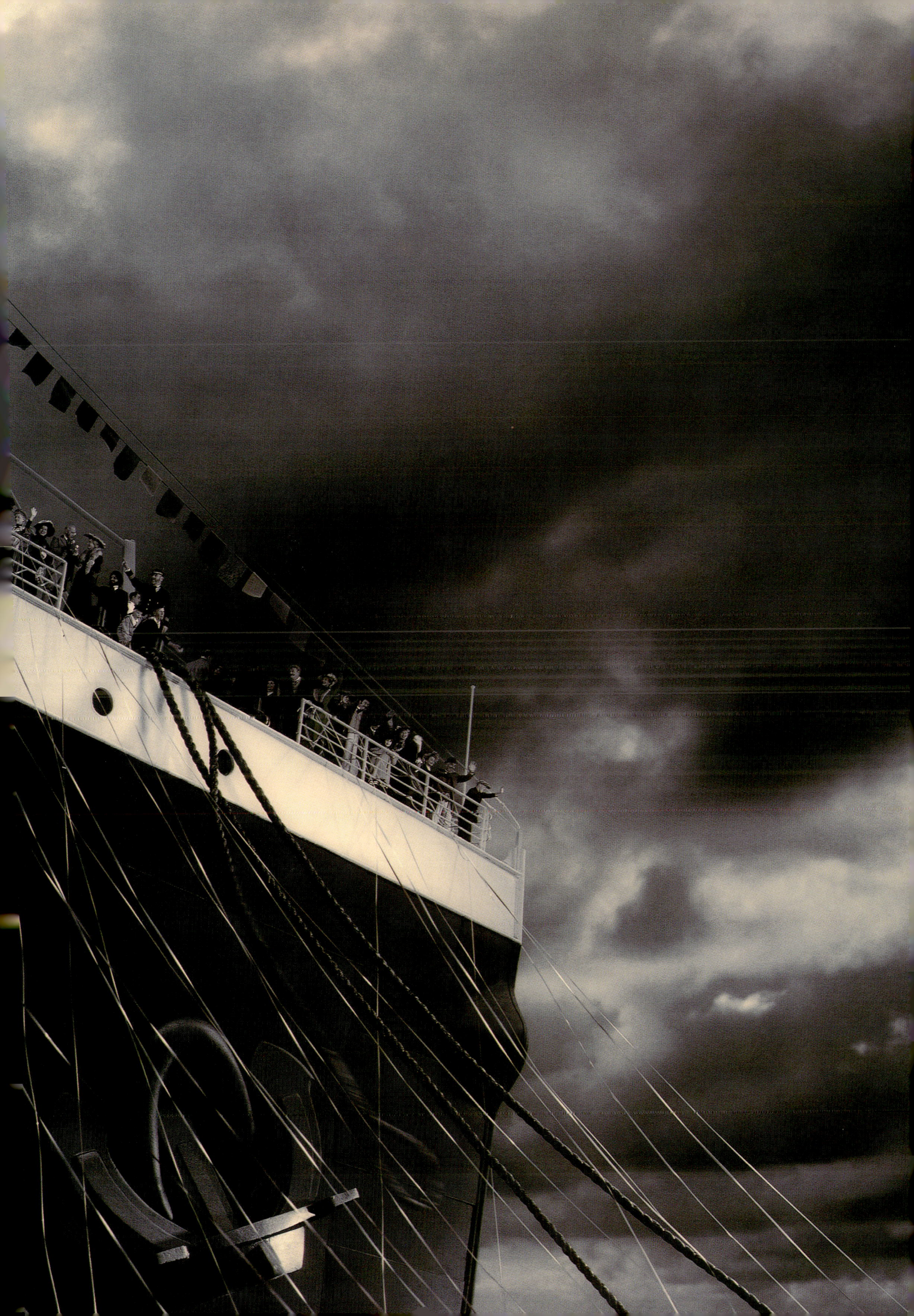

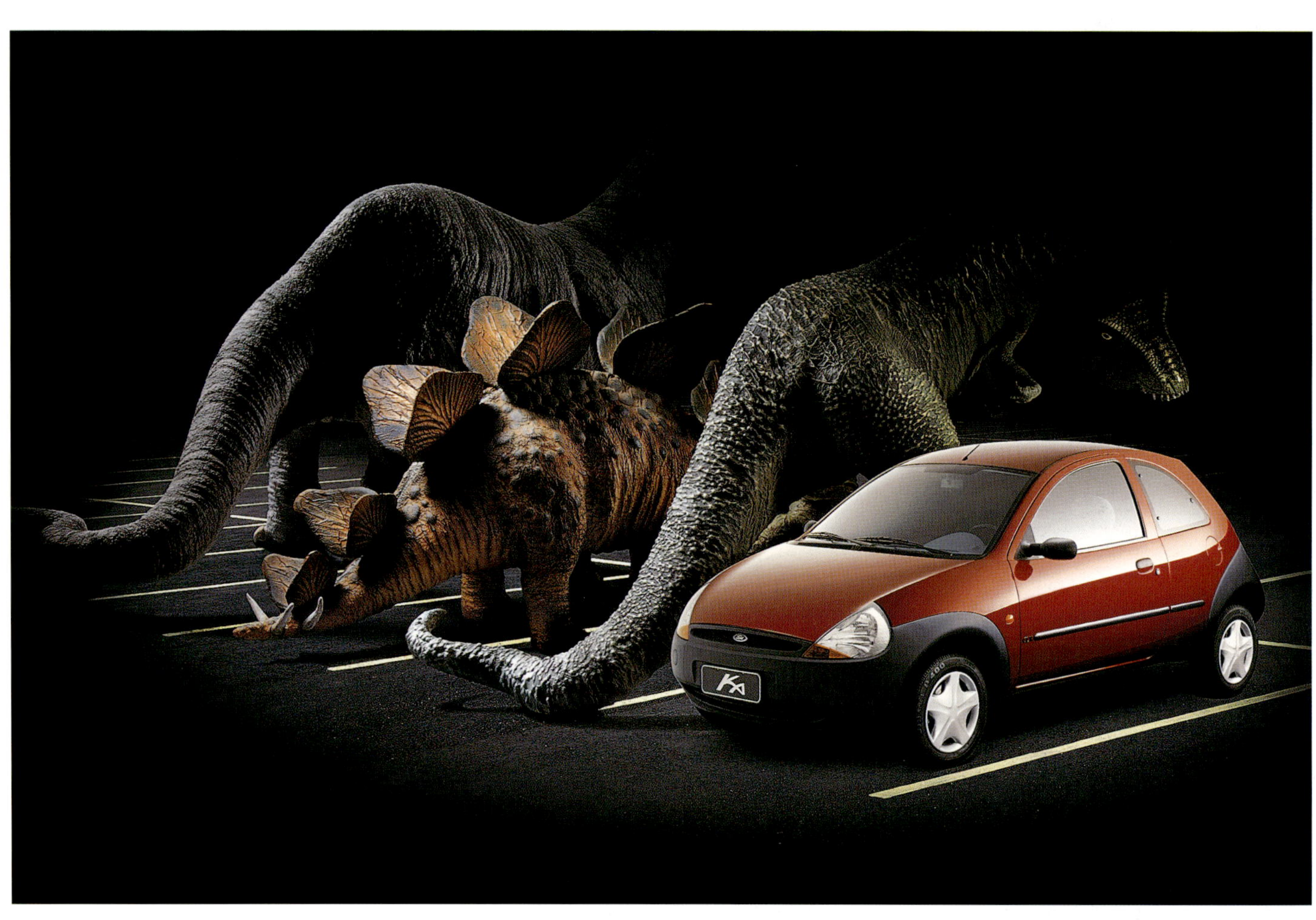

Fernando Zuffo

Page 2
Photographer: Nick Vedros

Page 4
Photographers: Craig Andrews, Tom Balla

Page 6
Photographer: Craig Van der Lende
Representative: Carolyn Potts and Associates

Page 16
Photographer: Hans Neleman
Art Director: Chris De Vito
Agency: Bates USA
Representative: Bernstein & Andriulli
Client: Footlocker

Page 18
Photographer: David McGlynn
Art Director: John Plunkett
Designer: Thomas Schneider
Client: *Wired* magazine / Camera: Nikon N90S
Film: Fujicolor Super-G 200

Page 19
Photographer: Mark Hanauer
Art Director: Peter Nicholson
Digital Manipulation: Peter Nicholson
Agency: Legas Delaney
Camera: Mamiya 645 / Film: Kodak EPP

Page 20
Photographers: Judy Hermann, Michael Starke
Designers: Chris Quinn, Heather Demers
Digital Manipulation:
Judy Herrmann, Michael Starke
Software: Photoshop, Xres, Live Picture
Agency: The Quinn Design Group
Representative: Chris Quinn
Client: Maryland Food Center Authority
Camera: Phase One Photophase

Page 21
Photographer: Frank Herholdt
Art Director: Jill McClabb
Software: Photoshop 4, Dicomed Imaginator
Client: United States Postal Service

Page 22, 23
Photographer: Rick Dublin
Client: Weyerhauser

Page 24
Photographer: Sanjay Kothari
Digital Manipulation: Sanjay Kothari
Software: Photoshop
Camera: Bronica / Film: Kodak Ektachrome 100

Page 25
Photographer: Lynn Sugarman
Art Director: Larry Hyde / Representative:
Imaginary Lines - Chris Brandt / Client: Sherwin
Williams Paint / Camera: 4x5 / Film: Fuji

Page 26
Photographer: Jim Erickson
Art Director: David Curtis
Digital Manipulation: Wes Hardison
Software: Photoshop 4
Studio: Erickson Productions, Inc.
Agency: Richardson, Myers & Donofrio
Client: American Institute of Architecture
Camera: Fuji 680 / Film: Fuji Provia

Page 27
Photographer: Sanjay Kothari
Art Director: Gail Blumberg

Digital Manipulation: Sanjay Kothari
Software: Photoshop / Client: Adobe Systems
Camera: Nikon FM2, Canon EOS A2
Film: Ektachrome, Kodacolor

Page 28
Photographer: Nick Koudis / Art Director:
Jon Trahar / Digital Manipulation:
Nick Koudis / Software: Photoshop 4.0.1
Studio: Nick Koudis Studio, Inc.
Client: Ogilvy & Mather
Camera: Cambro 4x5 / Film: Kodak 64T

Page 29
Photographer: Tim Griffith / Designer: Frank Gehry
Camera: Arca Swiss 6x9, 210 mm Lens
Film: Fuji Velvia

Page 30
Photographer: James Porto / Representative: DLM

Page 31
Photographer: Gerald Bybee
Art Director, Digital Manipulation: Gerald Bybee
Software: Color Quartet, Live Picture,
and Photoshop / Representative: Deb Grisham

Page 32, 33
Photographer, Art Director: Eva Swider

Page 34
Photographer: Paul Maxon

Page 35
Photographer: James Porto / Representative:
DLM

Page 36, 37
Photographer: Don Moravick

Page 38, 39
Photographer: Hans Neleman / Art Director:
Rory Phoenix / Digital Manipulation: Attik
Agency: J. Walter Thompson / Representative:
Bernstein & Andriullik / Client: Nortel

Page 40
Photographer: James Porto / Art Director:
James Porto / Digital Manipulation: James Porto
Software: Photoshop / Representative: DLM
Publisher: *Wired* magazine / Client: Absolut

Page 41
Photographer: Robert Silvers
Art Director: Tom Bentkowski
Designer: Mimi Park
Photo Editor: Bobbi Baker Burrows
Digital Manipulation: Robert Silvers
Software: Photomosaic Software
(proprietary custom-written)
Client: *Life* magazine

Page 42
Photographer: John Swain
Art Director: Michael French
Digital Manipulation: John Swain
Software: Photoshop 4.0 / Agency: Odyssee
Camera: Hasselblad / Film: EPZ & Provia 120

Page 43
Photographer: RJ Muna
Digital Manipulation: RJ Muna
Software: Live Picture Photoshop

Page 44
Photographer: Fernando Zuffo
Digital Manipulation: Fernando Zuffo

Software: Photoshop / Agency: DM9 DDB
Client: Shopping Iguatemi

Page 45
Photographer: David Gaz
Art Director, Designer: Tom Devine
Digital Manipulation: Jeff Raby
Software: Fractal Painter, Photoshop
Studio: Baker Design / Client: Starr Surgical
Camera: Mamiya RB 67 / Film: Kodak EPP 120

Page 46
Photographer: Stuart Block
Art Director: Brien Spanier
Digital Manipulation: Mona Nickell
Software: Photoshop / Studio: Periscope
Client: McFarlane's Beer Of Arizona
Camera: Mamiya 645 / Film: Fuji Velvia

Page 47
Photographer: Fernando Zuffo
Digital Manipulation: Fernando Zuffo
Software: Photoshop / Agency: F. Nazca S&S
Client: Zoomp

Page 48, 49
Photographer: Jeremy Wolff
Representative: Graphistock

Page 50
Photographer: Mirko Ilic
Art Director: Hopkins Baumann
Designer: Angela Esposito
Digital Manipulation: Mirko Ilic
Software: Adobe Photoshop
Studio: Mirko Ilic Corp.
Client: *World Press Review*

Page 51
Photographer: John Eder
Digital Manipulation: John Eder
Software: Adobe Photoshop
Client: Interscope Records

Page 52
Photographer: Russ Widstrand
Art Director, Designer: Russ Widstrand
Digital Manipulation: Russ Widstrand
Software: Photoshop Collage
Agency: Peter Lord, Principal Communications
Client: IBM (Sap Marketing Group)
Camera: Sinar 4x5 / Film: Kodak Ektachrome
100 Plus EPP6105

Page 53
Photographer: Mike McGlothlen
Art Director, Designer: Mike McGlothlen
Digital Manipulation: Mike McGlothlen
Software: Photoshop 4 / Client: Concept 24
Camera: Nikon/Sinar / Film: Kodak

Page 54
Photographer: James Stanley Daugherty
Digital Manipulation:
James Stanley Daugherty
Software: Adobe Photoshop 4.0

Page 55
Photographer: Sergio Spada
Representative: Graphistock

Page 56
Photographer: Jim Erickson
Digital Manipulation: Wes Hardison
Software: Adobe Photoshop 4.0
Studio: Erickson Productions Inc.
Camera: Technika / Film: Fuji Provia

Page 57
Photographer: Fernando Zuffo
Digital Manipulation: Fernando Zuffo
Software: Photoshop / Agency: F. Nazca S&S
Client: Zoomp

Page 58
Photographer: Kenneth Willardt
Editor: Laura Laviada / Digital Manipulation:
Kenneth Willardt / Software: Photoshop 4.0
Agency: Exposure NY / Representative:
Stacy Fischer / Client: *Espanea Bazaar*
Camera: Pentax / Film: Kodak VPS

Page 59
Photographer: John Eder
Art Director: Nancy Duckworth
Photo Editor: Lisa Thackaberry
Digital Manipulation: John Eder
Software: Adobe Photoshop
Client: LA Times *Sunday* magazine

Page 60
Photographer: Sanjay Kothari
Designer: Garland Lyn
Digital Manipulation: Sanjay Kothari
Software: Photoshop
Camera: Bronica / Film: Ektachrome 100

Page 61
Photographer: Barry Seidman
Digital Manipulation: Barry Seidman
Software: Adobe Photoshop

Page 62
Photographers: Judy Hermann, Michael Starke
Designers: Chris Quinn, Heather Demers
Digital Manipulation: Judy Hermann,
Michael Starke
Software: Photoshop Live Pictures XRes
Agency: The Quinn Design Group
Representative: Chris Quinn
Client: Maryland Food Center Authority
Camera: Phase One Photophase

Page 63
Photographer: David Gaz / Digital Manipulation:
Jeff Raby / Software: Fractal Painter, Photoshop
Camera: Mamiya RB 67 / Film: Kodak EPY 120

Page 64
Photographer: Scott Ferguson
Art Director, Designer: Scott Ferguson
Digital Manipulation: Scott Ferguson
Software: Photoshop 4.0
Studio: Ferguson & Katzman

Page 65
Photographer: Lynn Sugarman / Art Director:
Linda Fountain / Digital Manipulation:
Mary Brandt / Software: Kodak Premier
Representative: Chris Brandt, Imaginary Lines
Client: Eastman Kodak
Camera: Toyo 4x5 / Film: Kodak

Page 66, 67
Photographer: Matt Mahurin / Art Director:
Fred Woodward / Photo Editor: Jodi Peckman
Client: *Rolling Stone* magazine

Page 68
Photographers: Alan Abrams,
Francesca Lacagnina
Art Director, Designer: Emily Cain
Software: Adobe Photoshop
Studio: David Carter Design
Client: Color Dynamics

Page 69
Photographer: Charly Franklin
Art Director: Kit Hinrichs
Designers: Anne Culbertson, Karen Berndt
Photo Editor: Charly Franklin
Digital Manipulation: Charly Franklin,
Mick Wiggins / Software: Photoshop
Studio: Pentagram Design Inc.
Client: University of Southern California
Camera: Mamiya 645 / Film: Fuji Velvia

Page 70, 71
Photographers: Alan Abrams, Francesca
Lacagnina / Art Director, Designer: Emily Cain
Software: Adobe Photoshop
Client: ColorDynamics

Page 72
Photographer: Roxann Arwen Mills
Agency: Visages / Representative: Jennifer
Dakoske

Page 73
Photographer: Steven Bliss

Page 74
Photographer: Jules Maclachlan
Digital Manipulation: Jules Maclachlan
Software: Adobe Photoshop 4.0
Representative: Virgina Boggie & Associates
Camera: Hasselblad / Film: Fuji NPS160

Page 75
Photographer: Hans Neleman
Art Director: Rory Phoenix
Agency: J. Walter Thompson
Representative: Bernstein & Andriulli
Client: Nortel

Page 76, 77
Photographer: Amy Guip

Page 78, 79
Photographer: John Weber
Representative: Graphistock

Page 80–83
Photographer: Hugh Kretschmer
Representative: Graphistock

Page 84, 85
Photographer: John Ritter
Representative: Graphistock

Page 86
Photographer: Douglas E. Walker

Page 87
Photographer: Fernando Zuffo
Digital Manipulation: Fernando Zuffo
Software: Photoshop / Agency:
DM9 DDB / Client: Antarctica

Page 88
Photographer: Steve Hix
Art Directors: Tony Halstad, Mike Duval
Digital Manipulation: Judy Rush
Software: Dicomed / Agency: Young & Rubicam
Camera: RZ / Film: Fuji

Page 89
Photographer: Jim Erickson / Art Director:
Bob Ranew / Digital Manipulation: Wes Hardison
Software: Adobe Photoshop 4.0
Studio: Erickson Productions Inc.
Client: Audi / Camera: Fuji 680
Film: Fuji Provia

Page 90
Art Director, Photographer: Glen Wexler
Software: Adobe Photoshop / Client: Glen Wexler
Studio

Page 91
Photographer: Fernando Zuffo
Digital Manipulation: Fernando Zuffo
Software: Photoshop / Agency: F. Nazca S&S
Client: Zoomp

Page 92
Photographer: Charly Franklin
Art Director: Charly Franklin
Digital Manipulation: Charly Franklin
Software: Adobe Photoshop
Studio: Charly Franklin Productions
Client: FPG International
Camera: Mamiya 645 / Film: Various

Page 93
Photographer: Ryszard Horowitz
Art Director: Ilona J. Jones / Client: AT&T

Page 94
Photographer: Ryszard Horowitz
Art Director: Ryszard Horowitz
Client: Rafal Olbinski

Page 95
Photographer: Ryszard Horowitz
Art Director: Ryszard Horowitz
Client: Ryszard Horowitz, Bob Bowen

Page 96, 97
Photographer: Roxann Arwen Mills
Agency: Visages / Representative: Jennifer Dakoske

Page 98
Photographer: Zvia Sadja

Page 99
Photographer: Adrian Van Valen
Camera: Pentax 6x7 / Film: Neopan 100

Page 100
Photographer, Art Director: James Porto
Digital Manipulation: James Porto
Software: Photoshop / Representative: DLM

Page 101
Photographer: Marco Prozzo
Art Director, Designer: Carol Layton
Photo Editor: Mary Shea / Client: Bloomberg LP

Page 102
Photographer: Sanjay Kothari
Art Director: Larry Freemantle
Digital Manipulation: Sanjay Kothari
Software: Photoshop / Studio: Atlantic Records
Client: Atlantic Records
Camera: Bronica / Film: Ektachrome 100

Page 103
Photographer: Roy Volkmann
Designer: Roy Volkmann
Digital Manipulation: Roy Volkmann
Software: Live Picture Photoshop
Representative: L12-L1

Page 104
Photographer: Emy Kat

Page 105, 106
Photographer: James Stanley Daugherty
Digital Manipulation: James Stanley Daugherty
Software: Adobe Photoshop 4.0

Page 107
Photographer: David Fischer
Software: Photoshop 4.0

Page 108
Photographer: Gerald Bybee
Art Director: Gerald Bybee
Software: Color Quartet, Live Picture,
Photoshop / Studio: Bybee Studios
Representative: Deb Grisham

Page 109
Photographer: Matt Mahurin
Art Director, Designer: Carol Layton
Photo Editor: Mary Shea
Client: Bloomberg LP

Page 110
Photographer: Laura Crosta
Art Director, Designer: Brian Tortora
Agency: KMG-365
Client: Adam Paul, "Die Cool"
Camera: Canon / Film: Fuji 100

Page 111
Photographer: James Porto
Art Director: John Plunkett
Digital Manipulation: James Porto
Software: Photoshop
Representative: DLM
Client: *Wired* magazine

Page 112
Photographer: Peter Sorel
Art Director, Designer: Peter Sorel
Software: Photoshop 4.0 / Client: Eastman Kodak
Camera: Fuji 680 9x / Film: Kodak Verichrome Pan

Page 113
Photographer: Sydney Baldwin
Art Director, Designer: Dan Chapman
Digital Manipulation: Dan Chapman, Kerry
Rutz - Metafor Imaging
Software: Photoshop
Agency: Dazu Advertising Inc.
Publisher: Dana Precious
Client: Columbia Pictures

Page 114
Photographer: RJ Muna
Digital Manipulation: RJ Muna
Software: Live Picture Photoshop

Page 115
Photographer: Christiane Scholl
Digital Manipulation: Christiane Scholl
Software: Adobe Photoshop 4.0
Camera: Chinon / Film: Kodak Ektachrome

Page 116
Photographer: Marco Prozzo
Art Director, Designer: Carol Layton
Client: Bloomberg LP

Page 117
Photographer: Scott Ferguson
Art Director, Designer: Catherine Woods
Digital Manipulation: Scott Ferguson
Software: Photoshop 4.0
Studio: Ferguson & Katzman
Client: The 1997 Creative Symposium

Page 118, 119
Photographer: Roxann Arwen Mills
Agency: Visages
Representative: Jennifer Dakoske

Page 120
Photographer: David Waitz
Art Director: Lauren Libent Balsamo
Digital Manipulation: David Waitz
Software: Adobe Photoshop Live Picture
Client: Reed Travel Group
Camera: Pentax 6x7 / Film: Kodak T-MAX

Page 121
Photographer: David Waitz
Digital Manipulation: David Waitz
Software: Adobe Photoshop Livepicture
Camera: Pentax 6x7, Nikon F3
Film: Kodak HIE/T-MAX

Page 122
Photographer: Sanjay Kothari
Art Director, Designer: Tom Kraft
Digital Manipulation: Sanjay Kothari
Software: Photoshop / Client: Monadnock Papers
Camera: Bronica SQ / Film: Ektachrome 100

Page 123
Photographer: Sanjay Kothari
Art Director, Designer: Cynthia Friedman
Digital Manipulation: Sanjay Kothari
Software: Photoshop / Client: Business Week
Camera: Bronica SQ / Film: Ektachrome 100

Page 124
Photographer: Mir Lada / Digital Manipulation:
Mir Lada / Software: Photoshop
Representative: Suzy Johnston

Page 125
Photographer: Mark Seliger
Art Director: Fred Woodward / Photo Editor:
Jodi Peckman / Client: *Rolling Stone* magazine

Page 126
Photographer: Rafael Fuchs
Art Director: Scott Anderson

Page 127
Photographer: Mir Lada
Digital Manipulation: Mir Lada
Software: Photoshop
Representative: Suzy Johnston

Page 128, 129
Photographer: Eric Van Den Brulle
Digital Manipulation: Eric Van Den Brulle
Software: Photoshop 4.0

Page 130
Photographer: Bruce DeBoer
Software: Photoshop / Client: Stone Soup Chicago
Camera: Sinar P2 / Film: Kodak 100 SW

Page 131
Photographer: Fernando Zuffo
Digital Manipulation: Fernando Zuffo
Software: Photoshop / Agency: DM9 DDB
Client: Anuario de Midia

Page 132-134
Photographer: Joe McNally
Art Director: Tom Bentkowski
Designer: Sam Serebin
Photo Editor: Bobbi Baker Burrows
Client: *Life* magazine

Page 135
Photographers: Michale Eibes, Klaus Hagmeier
Designer: Wanja Olten
Digital Manipulation: Michael Eibes,
Klaus Hagmeier / Software: Photoshop
Client: Trust / Camera: Nikon
Film: Polaroid

Page 136
Photographer: Matthew Rolston
Art Director: Fred Woodward
Photo Editor: Jodi Peckman
Client: *Rolling Stone* magazine

Page 137
Photographer: Doug Landreth
Art Director: Ethan May
Digital Manipulation: Doug Landreth
Software: Photoshop
Studio: Landreth Studios
Representative: Kimberly Hoffman
Client: Gravis / Camera: Sinar Leaf

Page 138
Photographer: Greg Zukowski
Digital Manipulation: Greg Zukowski
Software: Photoshop 4.0 / Studio: SJI Associates
Camera: Minolta / Film: 35mm

Page 139
Photographers: Alan Abrams, Francesca
Lacagnina / Photo Editor: Cynthia Currie-
Kiplinger / Software: Adobe Photoshop

Page 140, 141
Photographer: Charles Brackman

Page 142
Photographer: Alan Abrams, Francesca
Lacagnina / Art Director: Carol Layton
Designer: Owen Edwards
Software: Adobe Photoshop
Client: Bloomberg Personal magazine

Page 143
Photographer: Fernando Zuffo
Digital Manipulation: Fernando Zuffo
Software: Photoshop / Agency: DM9 DDB
Client: Shopping Iguatemi

Page 144
Photographer: David Waitz
Art Director: Peter Kobayashi
Digital Manipulation: David Waitz
Software: Live Picture Photoshop
Client: Littleleaf Records
Camera: Pentax 6x7
Film: Kodak EPN, T-MAX

Page 145
Photographer: Dan Lim
Art Directors: Dan Lim, Suzanne Fabien
Designer: Suzanne Fabien
Photo Editor: Karen Viva-Haynes
Digital Manipulation: Dan Lim
Software: Contex Eclipse On Silicon Graphics
Oz Workstation / Representative: Suzy Johnston
Client: Solutions magazine
Camera: Mamiya RZ / Film: E100S

Page 146, 147
Photographer: Hugh Hales-Tooke
Art Director: Tom Bentkowski
Designer: Sam Serebin / Photo Editor: David
Friend
Client: Life magazine

Page 148
Photographer: Rafael Fuchs
Photo Editor: Patrick Baggatte

Page 149
Photographer: Frank Herholdt
Digital Manipulation: Nadege Meriau
Software: Photoshop 4
Camera: Nikon 35mm / Film: Velvia

Page 150
Photographer: Roxann Arwen Mills
Agency: Visage / Representative: Jennifer
Dakoske

Page 151
Photographer: Floyd Dean
Digital Manipulation: Hersh Gutwillig
Software: Unix System
Studio: Dean Digital Imaging, Inc.

Page 152
Photographer: Gerald Bybee
Art Directors: Tony Murillo, Gerald Bybee
Creative Director: Kenny Chan
Software: Color Quartet, Live Picture,
Photoshop / Studio: Bybee Studios
Representative: Deb Grisham

Page 153
Photographer: Gerald Bybee
Art Director: Gerald Bybee
Software: Color Quartet, Live Picture,
Photoshop / Studio: Bybee Studios
Representative: Deb Grisham

Page 154
Art Director, Photographer: Bruce Curtis

Page 155
Photographer: Mir Lada
Art Director: Chris Hoy / Digital Manipulation:
Mir Lada / Software: Photoshop
Representative: Suzy Johnston / Client: Today's
Parent Group, Wellness Guide magazine
Camera: Nikon F4 / Film: Fuji Velvia

Page 156, 157
Photographer: Dirk Karsten / Art Director:
Leon Bouman / Digital Manipulation: Souvere-
in (Jeroen) / Software: Barco
Camera: Cambo / Film: Kodak 100S

Page 158
Photographer: Craig Cutler
Art Director: Scott Bremner / Agency: Team
One Advertising / Client: Lexus
Camera: 8x10 / Film: Tri X

Page 159
Photographer: Ryszard Horowitz
Art Director: Mike Weiner / Client: Stolichnaya

Page 160
Photographer: Hans Neleman
Art Director: Robert Prins / Agency: Team
One Advertising / Representative: Bernstein &
Andriulli / Client: Lexus

Page 161
Photographer: Ryszard Horowitz

Page 162
Photographer: Suzanne Opton
Camera: Hasselblad / Film: Kodak PRN

Page 163
Photographer: C. I. Choi
Art Directors: Ted Kim, H.J. Park, Jeremy
Perrott / Designers: Ted Kim, H.J. Park, J. Perrott
Photo Editor: C.I. Choi

Digital Manipulation: S.K. Kang
Studio: On, Off
Client: IDK Bailey's Irish Cream

Page 164, 165
Photographer: Byron Morris
Art Director: Henry Yoo
Designer: Byron Morris
Digital Manipulation: Byron Morris
Software: Alias / Studio: Pratt Institute
Representative: Henry Yoo

Page 166, 167
Photographer: Jeremy Wolff
Representative: Graphistock

Page 168
Photographer: Ryszard Horowitz
Art Director: Ryszard Horowitz
Client: *Town & Country*

Page 169
Photographer: Fernando Zuffo
Digital Manipulation: Fernando Zuffo
Software: Photoshop / Agency: Almap BBDO
Client: Audi

Page 170
Photographer: Fernando Zuffo
Digital Manipulation: Fernando Zuffo
Software: Photoshop / Studio: Almap BBDO
Client: Pepsi

Page 171
Photographer: Dan Lim
Art Directors: Dan Lim, Chris Hoy
Designer: Chris Hoy
Digital Manipulation: Dan Lim
Software: Contex Eclipse On Silicon Graphics
Oz Workstation / Studio: Dan Lim Photography
Representative: Suzy Johnston
Client: Sympatico/Telemedia
Camera: Mamiya RZ / Film: Kodak E100S

Page 172, 173
Photographer: Franco Accornero
Digital Manipulation: Franco Accornero
Software: Photoshop

Page 174
Photographers: Craig Tozzi, Steve Tozzi
Art Directors/Designers: Craig Tozzi, Steve
Tozzi / Digital Manipulation: Craig Tozzi,
Steve Tozzi / Software: Photoshop 4.0 Infini-D
4.0 Freehand 7 Illustration 7 /Studio: 2000 Strong
Camera: Nikon N50/Film: 100 Kodak Gold

Page 175
Photographer: Valan Evers
Digital Manipulation: Valan Evers
Software: Painter Photoshop
Camera: Nikon 8008 / Film: Reala

Page 176
Photographer: James Porto
Art Director: Katy Tisch
Digital Manipulation: James Porto
Software: Photoshop
Representative: DLM

Page 177
Photographer: Dan Lim / Art Director:
Maureen Bradshaw / Designer: Aymard Angulo
Digital Manipulation: Dan Lim / Software:
Contex Eclipse On Silicon Graphics Oz
Workstation
Studio: Dan Lim Photography

Representative: Suzy Johnston
Client: Domtar Papers
Camera: Nikon F4 / Film: Kodak E100S

Page 178, 179
Photographer: Sandro
Art Director: Art Webb / Studio: Desalvo
Representative: Randi Fiat & Associates
Client: Skybox Trading Cards

Page 180
Photographer: John Huet
Art Director, Designer: Steve Hoffman
Photo Editor: Adam Stoltman
Agency: Redcat Productions
Representative: Marilyn Cadenbach Assoc.
Client: *Sports Illustrated*
Camera: 35 mm / Film: Tri X

Page 181
Photographer: RJ Muna / Art Director: Joey Rigg
Software: Live Picture Photoshop

Page 182-185
Photographer: Shinichi Honda
Art Director, Designer, Photo Editor: Taku
Satoh / Software: Original
Client: Taku Satoh Design Office Inc

Page 186
Photographer: Ryszard Horowitz
Art Director: Ryszard Horowitz / Client: Canon

Page 187
Photographer: Bryce Bennett
Digital Manipulation: Bryce Bennett
Client: Docnet

Page 188, 189
Photographer: Fernando Zuffo
Digital Manipulation: Fernando Zuffo
Software: Photoshop / Agency: F/Nazca S&S
Client: Philco

Page 190
Photographer, Art Director: Gerald Bybee
Software: Color Quartet, Live Picture,
Photoshop / Studio: Bybee Studios
Representative: Deb Grisham

Page 191
Photographer, Art Director: Gerald Bybee
Software: Color Quartet, Live Picture,
Photoshop / Studio: Bybee Studios
Representative: Deb Grisham

Page 192
Photographer: Eric Fairchild
Designer: Carlos Mandelaveiria
Digital Manipulation: Carlos Mandelaveiria
Software: Photoshop 4.0

Page 193
Photographers: Sean Alatorre,
Laura Pizzarelli / Art Directors, Designers:
Sean Alatorre, Laura Pizzarelli
Digital Manipulation:
Sean Alatorre Laura Pizzarelli
Software: Photoshop
Studio: Morbido/Bizarrio
Representative: Angela Paolantonio
Client: Groove House Records

Page 194
Photographer: Beatriz Coll
Digital Manipulation: Beatriz Coll
Software: Photoshop 4.0

Page 195
Photographer: Philip Kaake
Digital Manipulation: Philip Kaake
Software: Photoshop

Page 196
Photographer: Lance Jackson
Studio: Lax Syntax Design
Client: Pacific Paper Works

Page 197
Photographer: Lance Jackson
Studio: Lax Syntax Design
Client: Rave Invitation, Life On The Water

Page 198, 199
Photographer: Stefan Longin
Client: Aids Hilfe Badenvorttenberg
Camera: Toyo / Film: Polaroid

Page 200
Photographer: Loren Hammer
Art Director: Larry Vigon / Designer: Marc Yeh
Digital Manipulation: Todd Reublin
Software: Photoshop / Agency: Vigon,Ellis
Representative: Nancy Costello
Client: Valleycrest
Camera: Pentax 6x7 / Film: Kodak Tri X Film

Page 201
Photographer: Pete Christman
Digital Manipulation: Pete Christman

Page 202, 203
Photographer: Eric Emming
Studio: CSA Archive

Page 204
Photographer: David Gaz
Art Director: Karen Verlander / Designer: Jeff
Mah / Digital Manipulation: Jeff Raby
Software: Pixar / Client: Communications
Week International
Camera: Mamiya RB 67 / Film: Kodak EPY 120

Page 205
Photographer: David Gaz
Art Director, Designer: Josephine Rigg
Digital Manipulation: Jeff Raby
Software: Pixar
Client: *San Francisco Examiner* magazine

Page 206
Photographer: David Gaz
Art Director: Hugh Moore / Designers:
Hugh Moore, Steve Dreyer
Digital Manipulation: Jeff Raby
Software: Fractal Painter, Photoshop
Client: National Engineers Week
Camera: Mamiya RB 67 / Film: Kodak EPY 120

Page 207
Photographer: David Gaz
Digital Manipulation: Jeff Raby

Software: Fractal Painter, Photoshop
Camera: Mamiya RB 67
Film: Kodak EPY 120

Page 208–211
Photographer: Bill Sosin
Digital Manipulation: Bill Sosin
Software: Photoshop 4.0

Page 212
Photographer: David Fischer
Software: Photoshop 4.0

Page 213
Photographer: Steven Biver
Art Director: Carol Layton
Designer: Evelyn Good
Photo Editor: Mary Shea
Client: Bloomberg LP

Page 214, 215
Photographer: Dominique Thibodeau
Art Director: Rene Clement
Digital Manipulation: Dominique Thibodeau
Software: Photoshop 4.0 / Studio: At 47
Client: Quebecor Mil

Page 216
Photographer: David Gaz
Art Director: Carol Macrini
Digital Manipulation: Jeff Raby
Software: Fractal Painter, Photoshop
Client: *Bloomberg* magazine
Camera: Mamiya RB 67
Film: Kodak EPY 120

Page 217
Photographer: David Gaz
Art Director: Caroline Terrier
Digital Manipulation: Jeff Raby
Software: Pixar / Client: Kodak
Camera: Mamiya RB 67
Film: Kodak EPY 120

Page 218
Photographer: Geoff Spear
Art Director: Amy Rosenfield
Photo Editor: Jane Clark
Digital Manipulation: Geoff Spear
Software: Adobe Photoshop
Client: *Smart Money*
Camera: Linhof / Film: Fuji

Page 219
Photographer: Ryszard Horowitz
Art Director: Tom Bentkowski
Designer: Marti Golon / Photo Editor: Bobbi
Baker Burrows / Client: *Life* magazine

Page 220, 221
Photographer: Larry Hamill
Digital Manipulation: Larry Hamill
Software: Bryce Photoshop Mac
Representative: Lori McCargish

Page 222
Photographer: David Gaz
Digital Manipulation: Jeff Raby
Software: Fractal Painter, Photoshop
Camera: Mamiya RB 67 / Film: Kodak EPY 120

Page 223
Photographer: David Gaz
Art Director: Carol Macrini
Digital Manipulation: Jeff Raby
Software: Fractal Painter, Photoshop
Client: *Bloomberg* magazine
Camera: Mamiya RB 67 / Film: Kodak EPY 120

Page 224–227
Photographer: Graham Westmoreland
Art Director: Karen Holland
Agency: Ogilvy & Mather, Houston

Page 228
Photographer: Glen Wexler
Art Director: Jorge Alonso
Software: Adobe Photoshop
Client: Department of Water and Power

Page 229
Photographer: Glen Wexler
Art Directors: George Mimnaugh, Tommy
Steele / Software: Adobe Photoshop
Client: Thanks To Gravity recording group

Page 230
Photographer: James Porto
Art Director: Daniel Carter
Digital Manipulation: James Porto
Software: Photoshop
Representative: DLM

Page 231
Photographer: Glen Wexler
Art Directors: Kevin Heslip, Brian Gorman
Software: Adobe Photoshop
Client: Bombardier Ski Doo Snowmobiles

Page 232
Photographer: Glen Wexler
Art Director: Edward Welch
Software: Adobe Photoshop
Client: Department of Water and Power

Page 233
Photographer: Glen Wexler
Art Director: Paul Zwief / Software: Adobe
Photoshop
Client: M&I Data

Page 234, 235
Photographer: Dirk Karsten
Art Director: Axel Thomsen
Digital Manipulation: Souverein (Jeroen)
Software: Paintbox

Page 236
Photographer: Fernando Zuffo

Art Directors Designers Photo Editors

Clients

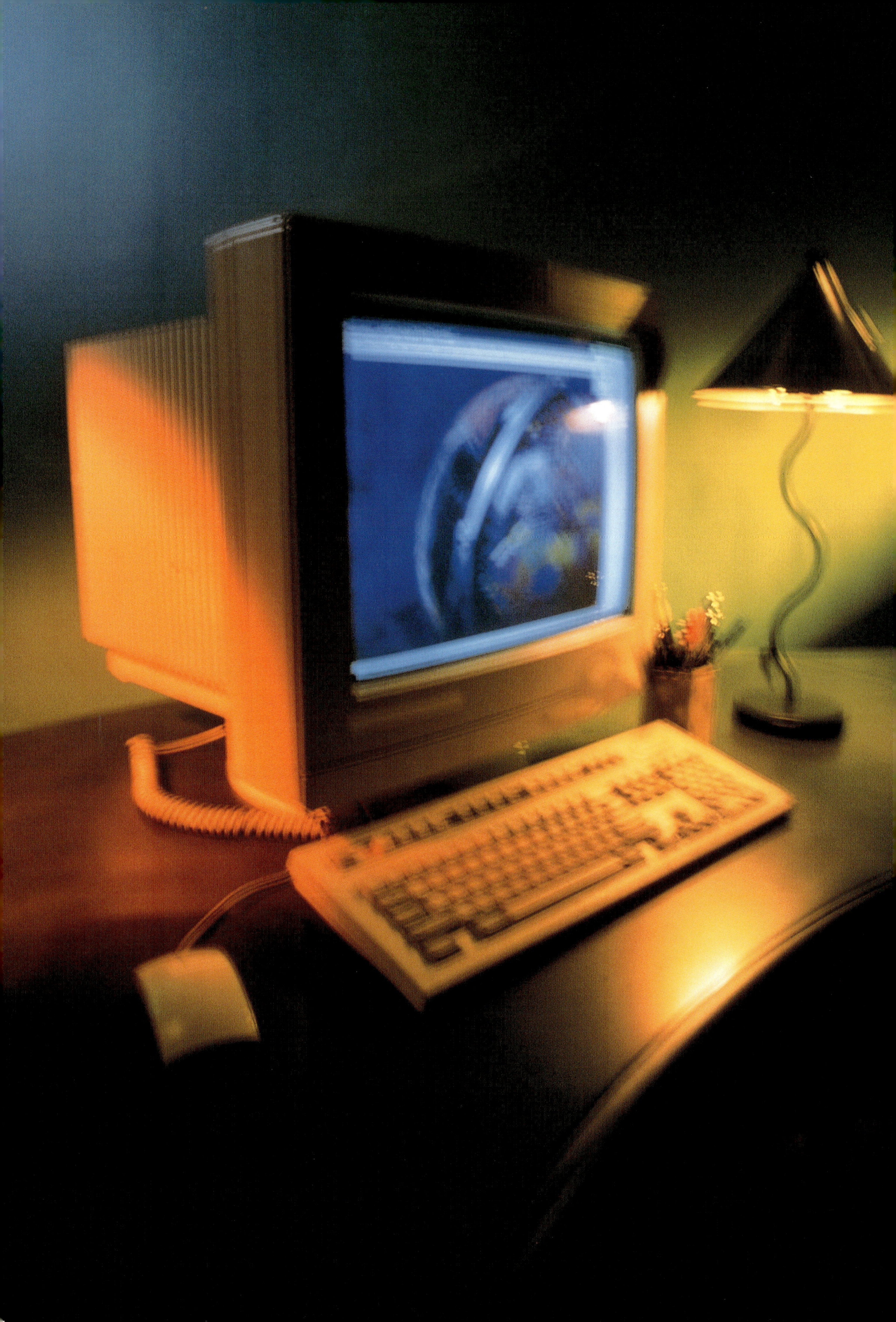

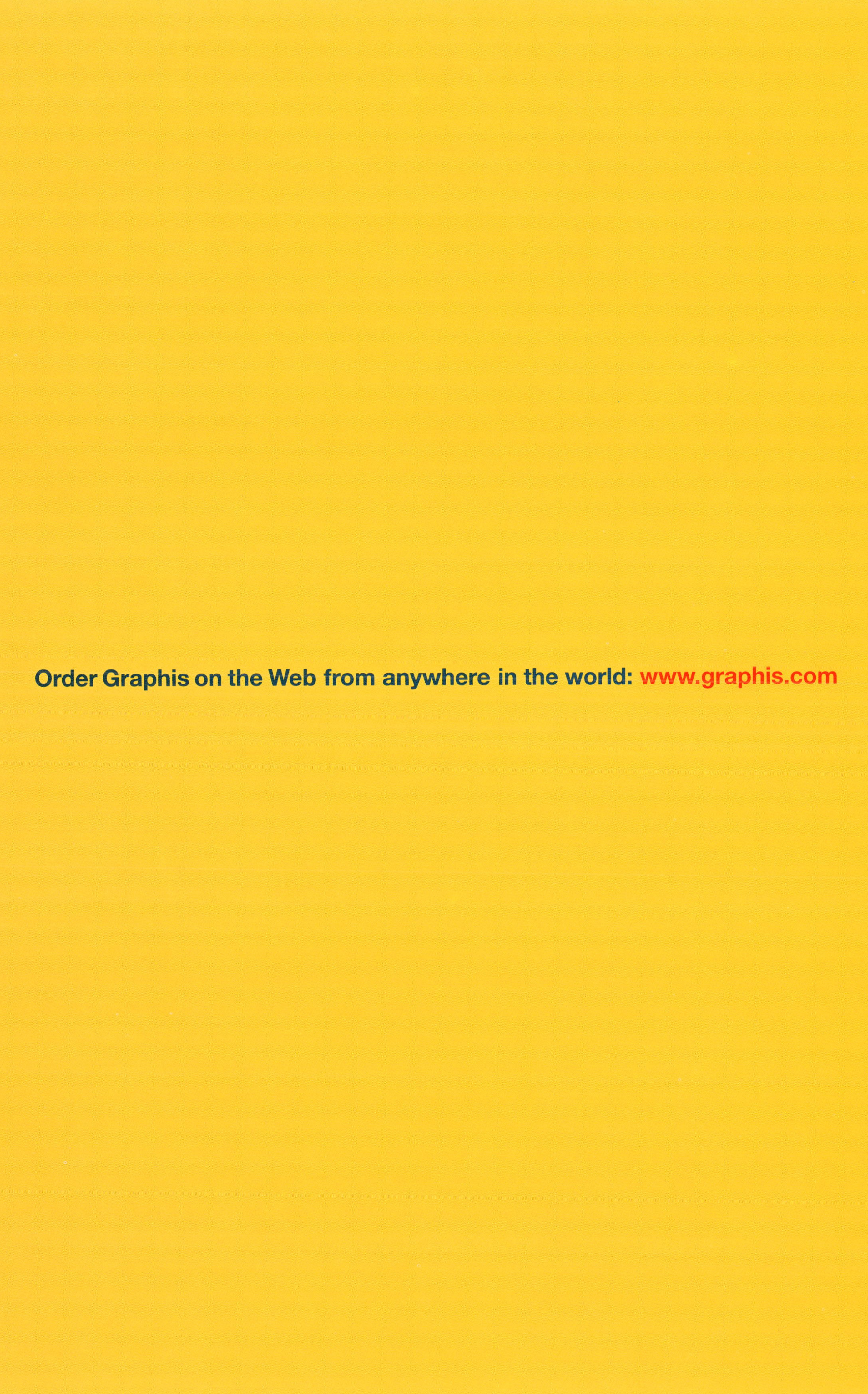

Order Graphis on the Web from anywhere in the world: www.graphis.com

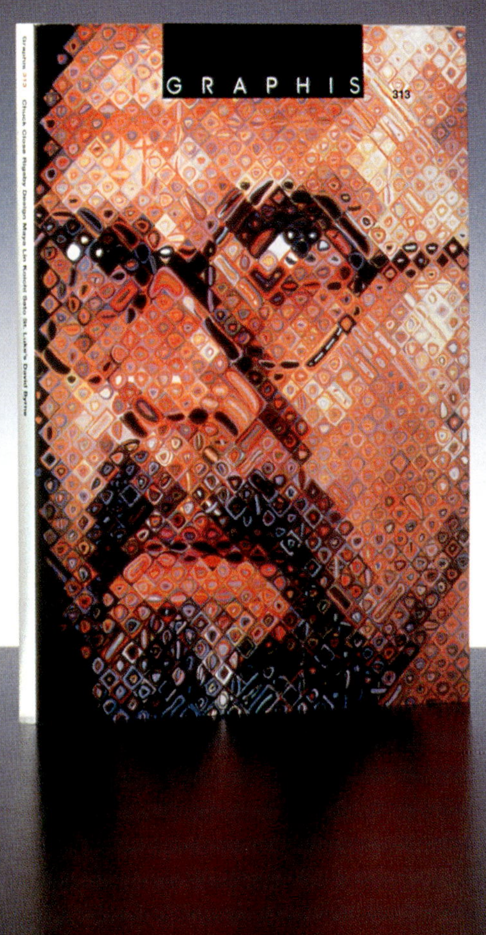
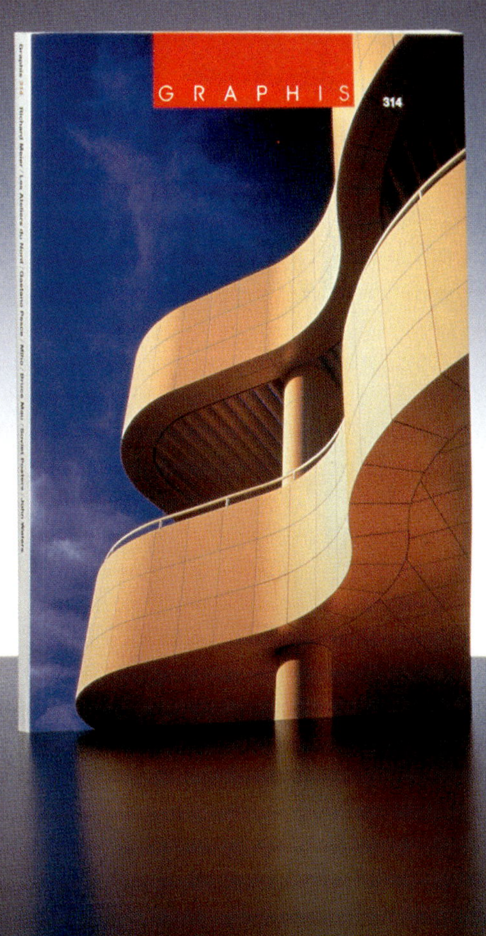
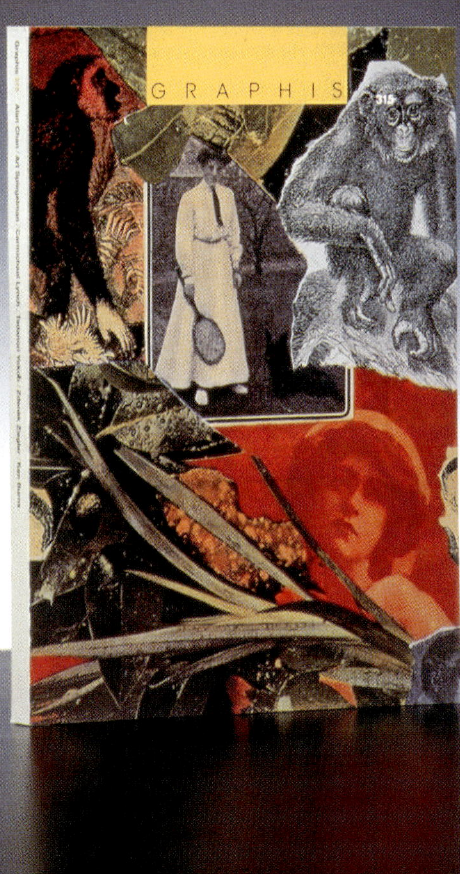
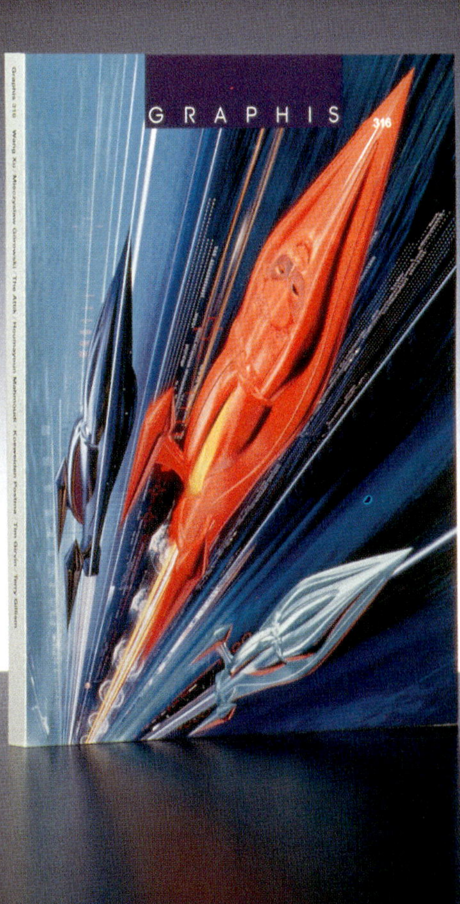

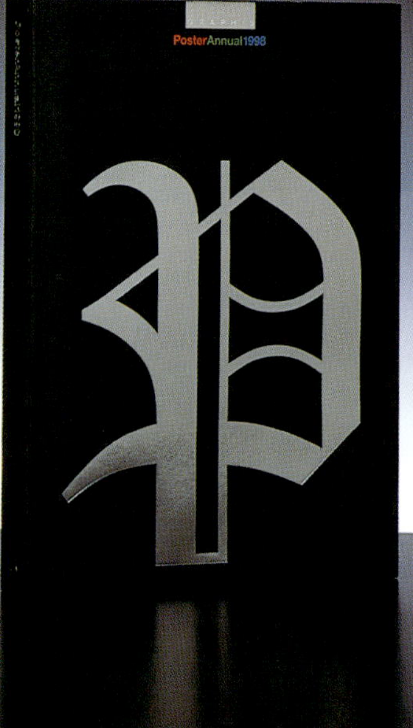
GRAPHIS
PosterAnnual1998
P

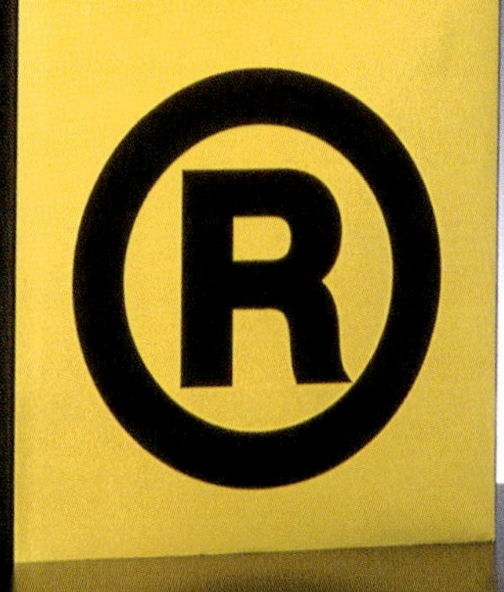
GRAPHIS
Corporate Identity 3
R

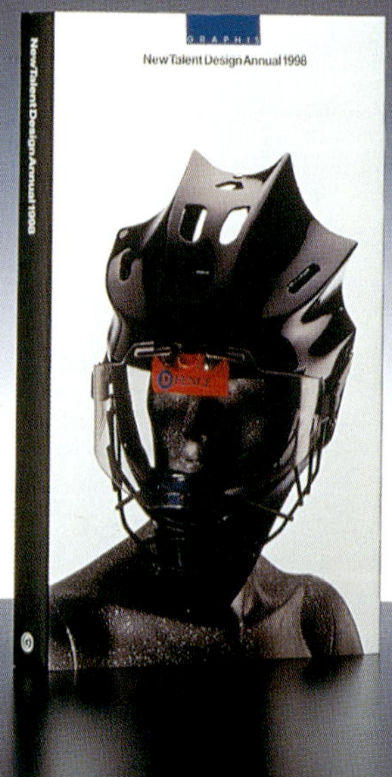
GRAPHIS
New Talent Design Annual 1998

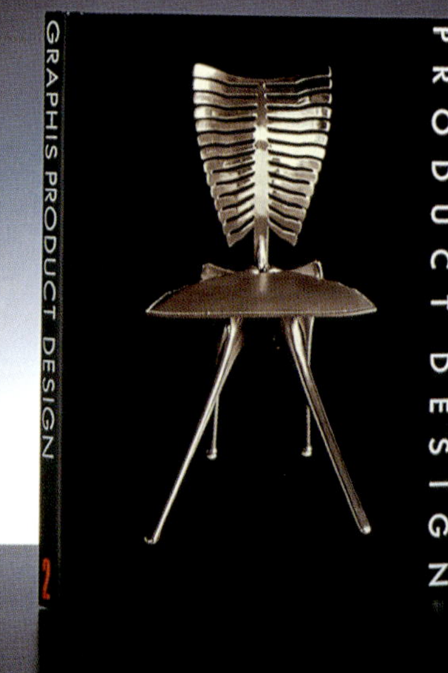
GRAPHIS PRODUCT DESIGN
PRODUCT DESIGN
2

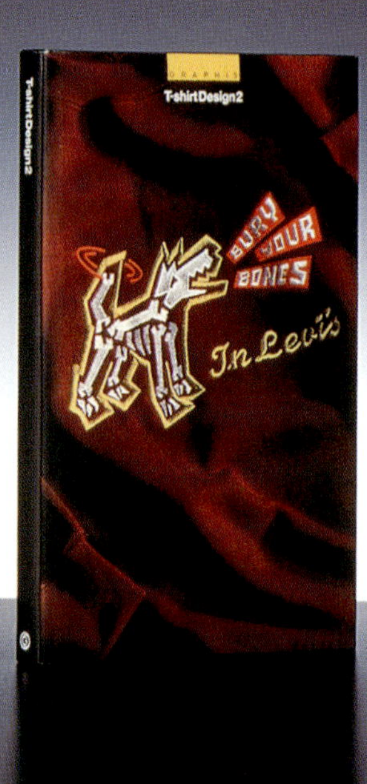
GRAPHIS
T-shirtDesign2
BURY YOUR BONES
In Levi's

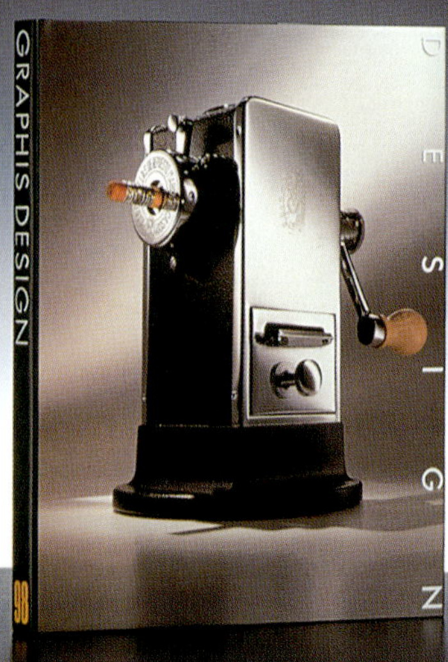
GRAPHIS DESIGN
DESIGN
98

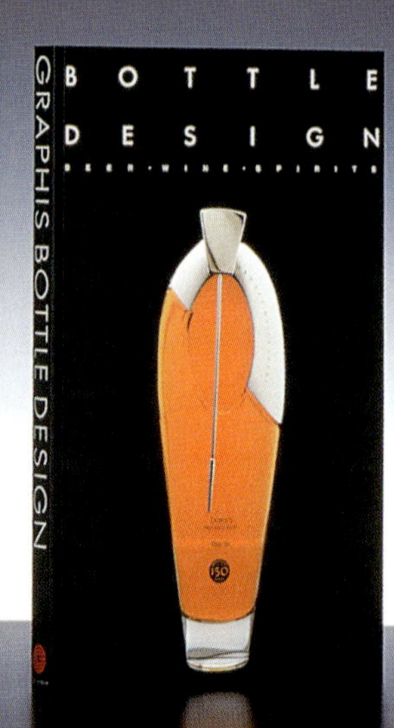
GRAPHIS BOTTLE DESIGN
BOTTLE
DESIGN
BEER·WINE·SPIRITS

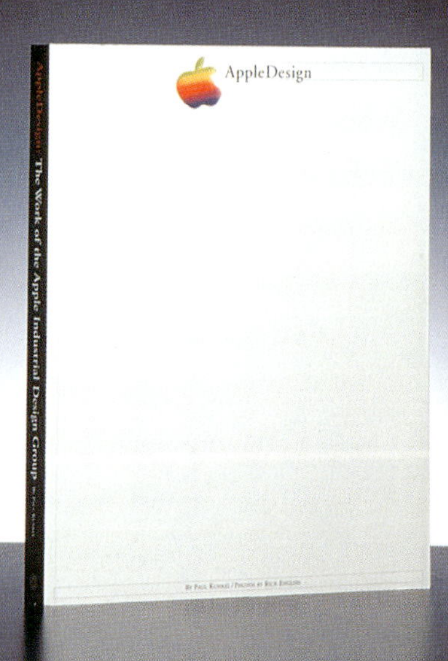
AppleDesign
AppleDesign: The Work of the Apple Industrial Design Group
BY PAUL KUNKEL / PHOTOS BY RICK ENGLISH

Order Form

As a subscriber to the magazine, you automatically qualify for a *40 percent discount* on any of our books. If you place a standing order you will receive a *50 percent discount*. This means any Graphis book you select is sent to you as soon as it comes off press, and you will be billed at half the cover price plus shipping. With a *standing order* Graphis doesn't have to go through the expense of contacting you by mail and can therefore pass the savings directly back to you. Our annuals such as Poster, Photo, Design, and Advertising come out every year. The rest of our books come out every 2-4 years. If you don't wish to receive a particular book automatically when it happens to come out just choose the *40 percent off price*. If you are not a subscriber, then you still receive a *20 percent discount*. For your support we now cover all the communication disciplines and if there is a Graphis book you care to have that is not listed, please call us and we will do everything we can to get it for you. We thank you for your support.

Book Title	Retail	Non Subscriber 20% off	Subscriber 40% off	Standing Order 50% off	Quantity	Totals
Spring Books 1998						
Book Design 2	☐ $70	☐ $56	☐ $42	☐ $35		
Corporate Identity 3	☐ $70	☐ $56	☐ $42	☐ $35		
New Talent 1998	☐ $60	☐ $48	☐ $36	☐ $30		
Poster Annual 1998	☐ $70	☐ $56	☐ $42	☐ $35		
T-Shirt 2	☐ $60	☐ $48	☐ $36	☐ $30		
Fall Books 1998						
Advertising 1999	☐ $70	☐ $56	☐ $42	☐ $35		
Annual Reports 6	☐ $70	☐ $56	☐ $42	☐ $35		
Brochures 3	☐ $70	☐ $56	☐ $42	☐ $35		
Design Annual 1999	☐ $70	☐ $56	☐ $42	☐ $35		
Digital Photo 1	☐ $70	☐ $56	☐ $42	☐ $35		
Letterhead 4	☐ $70	☐ $56	☐ $42	☐ $35		
Logo Design 4	☐ $60	☐ $48	☐ $36	☐ $30		
Photo Annual 1998	☐ $70	☐ $56	☐ $42	☐ $35		

Book Title	Retail	Non Subscriber 20% off	Subscriber 40% off	Standing Order 50% off	Quantity	Totals
General Interest						
Nudes 1	☐ $40	☐ $32	☐ $24	☐ $20		
Nudes 2	☐ $50	☐ $40	☐ $30	☐ $25		
Passion & Line	☐ $50	☐ $40	☐ $30	☐ $25		
Pool Light	☐ $70	☐ $56	☐ $42	☐ $35		
Typography 2	☐ $70	☐ $56	☐ $42	☐ $35		
Walter Iooss	☐ $70	☐ $56	☐ $42	☐ $35		
Design Books						
Apple Design	☐ $45	☐ $36	☐ $27	☐ $23		
Bottle Design	☐ $40	☐ $32	☐ $24	☐ $20		
Magazine Design	☐ $70	☐ $56	☐ $42	☐ $35		
Products by Design 1	☐ $70	☐ $56	☐ $42	☐ $35		
Products by Design 2	☐ $70	☐ $56	☐ $42	☐ $35		
Web Design Now	☐ $70	☐ $56	☐ $42	☐ $35		

Shipping & handling per book, US $ 5.00, Canada $ 10.00, Elsewhere $15.00

New York State shipments add 8.25% tax

☐ I am not a subscriber, but I want to qualify for the 20% off discount.

Graphis Magazine

	USA (shipping included)	Canada (shipping included)	International (shipping included)	International (airmail surcharge included)
One year subscription, 6 Issues	☐ $90	☐ $100	☐ $125	☐ $184
Two year subscription, 12 Issues	☐ $165	☐ $185	☐ $235	☐ $294
Student subscription, 6 Issues	☐ $59	☐ $59	☐ $80	☐ $139

☐ I am presently a Graphis magazine subscriber and therefore, qualify for the 40% discount.

Total

Name	☐ American Express ☐ Visa ☐ Mastercard ☐ Check
Company	
Address	Card #
City State Zip	Expiration
Daytime phone	Card holder's signature

Copy or send this order form and make check payable to Graphis Inc. For even faster turn-around service, or if you have any questions about subscribing call us at the following numbers in the **US (800) 209. 4234, outside the US (212) 532. 9387 ext. 242 or 241, Fax (212) 696. 4242. Graphis 141 Lexington Avenue New York, New York 10016-8193. Order Graphis on the Web from anywhere in the world: www.graphis.com**

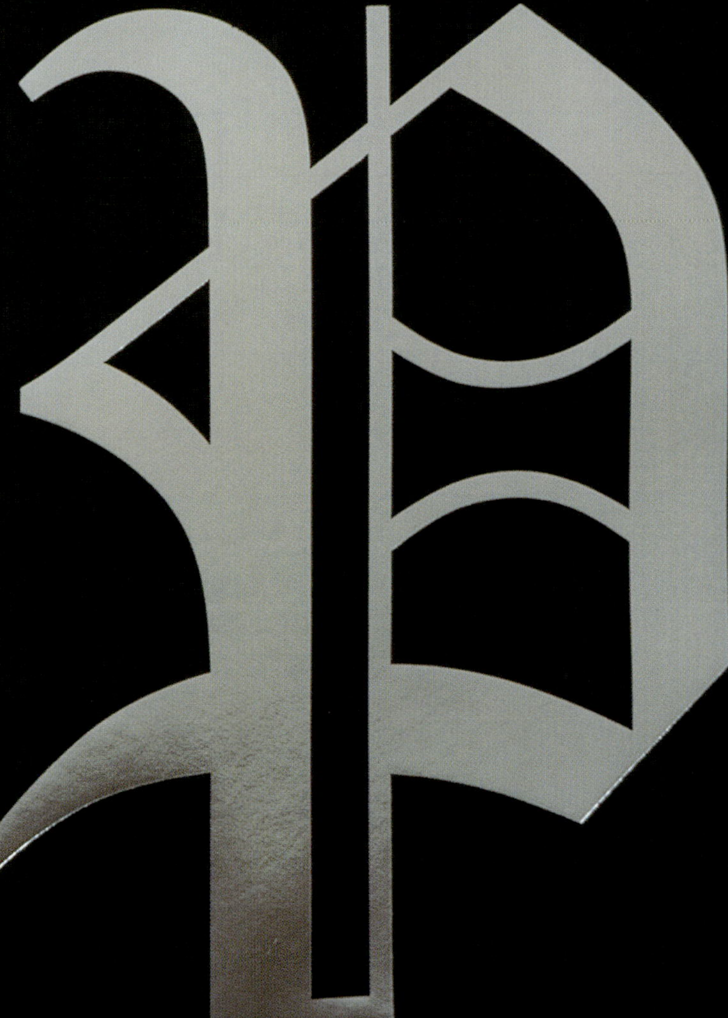

GRAPHIS
PosterAnnual1998

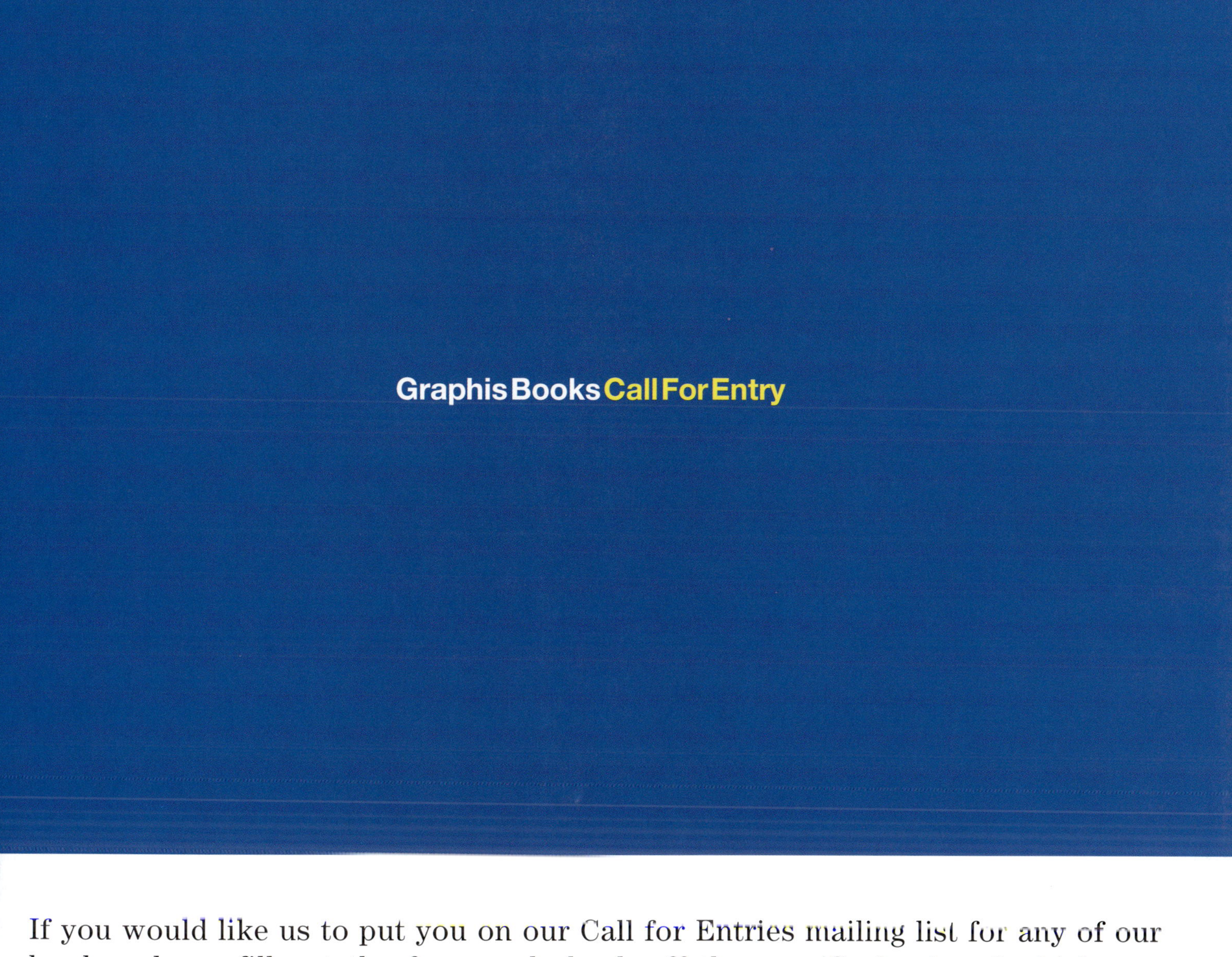

If you would like us to put you on our Call for Entries mailing list for any of our books, please fill out the form and check off the specific books of which you would like to be a part. We now consolidate our mailings twice a year for our spring and fall books. If information is needed on specific deadlines for any of our books, please consult our web site: www.graphis.com.

Graphic Design Books
☐ Advertising Annual
☐ Annual Reports
☐ Book Design
☐ Brochure
☐ Corporate Identity
☐ Design Annual
☐ Digital Fonts
☐ Diagrams

☐ Poster Annual
☐ Products by Design
☐ Letterhead
☐ Logo Design
☐ Music CD
☐ New Media
☐ Packaging
☐ Paper Promotions
☐ Typography

Photography Books
☐ Digital Photo (Professional)
☐ Human Con. (Photojournalism)
☐ New Talent (Amateur)
☐ Nudes (Professional)
☐ Nudes (Fine Art)
☐ Photo Annual (Professional)
☐ Photography (Fine Art)

Student Books
☐ Advertising Annual
☐ Design Annual
☐ Photo Annual (Professional)
☐ Products by Design
☐ **All the Books**
☐ All Design Books only
☐ All Photo Books only
☐ All Student Books only

First Name: ___________________________ Last Name: ___________________________

Company: ____

Telephone: ___________________________ Fax: ___________________________

Mailing Address: ___________________________ City: ___________________________

State, Country: ___________________________ Zip: ___________________________

Copy or mail form to : Graphis, Call for Entries, 141 Lexington Ave., New York, New York 10016-819, USA, or fax to 212. 213 3229